Nora & John
The Russian Love Story

As originally told in the two individual memoirs by

Nora Murray & John Murray

With fascinating new insights into their lives presented in
introductions, prologue and epilogue by Leeroy and Peter Murray

In the Cold War following World War II, two books were published that
revealed the effect on ordinary people of Stalin's Soviet Union. These two
important records – *I Spied For Stalin* and *A Spy Called Swallow* – are now
combined in this special volume commemorating the October Revolution
that changed Russia for all time.

I Spied For Stalin

Times Literary Supplement: The real story is in the simple, graphic and almost entirely persuasive account of her observations as a member of a highly privileged caste in Soviet society.

Oxford Mail: A woman of infinite ingenuity, persistence and great courage. The book would make an admirable film on the lines of "Odette".

Yorkshire Observer: As a work of fiction one would have regarded it as highly exciting and admirably constructed. Yet, astonishingly, every word is true.

Yorkshire Evening Press: How she fell in love and married the man she was forced to spy on is admirably told, but nothing could be more thrilling than her ultimate escape from the secret police.

Yorkshire Post: Told with a simplicity that carries conviction, and with a narrative skill that makes it as absorbing as any novel.

Aberdeen Express: A remarkable story of personal courage. The revelations are grim and often terrifying.

Birmingham Gazette: A curious story, dramatic, moving and always interesting.

Cambridge Daily News: A curious human story.

Good Housekeeper: Told without melodrama or hysterics and indeed with a calmness and sympathy that is surprising. The story is of an immensely courageous woman.

This work is dedicated to our dear elder brother John, who inspired and supported his brothers throughout his life. His early passing in 1998, sadly left behind many writing projects. The reprinting of Nora and John's book was originally initiated by John and finally comes to light one hundred years since the Russian Revolution.

Grateful thanks are also expressed to the families: Emelyanov, Korzhenko and, in particular, Arkady, our brother.

Acknowledgements

Peter and Leeroy owe much to the support of their wives, Wendy and Michelle. It must be said that Wendy above all supported John and the family for many years. And to the tolerance of their respective children for listening to their life story again and again...and again.

The Murray family's life was perhaps always destined to cross with their now lifelong friend Margo Picken. It did so in 1963 when Margo met John junior on a student trip to Moscow. She has kept the 'light shining' over the years for the time when Leeroy and Peter would be ready to write about their rich heritage.

Gratitude is also expressed to George Boughton and Brenda Marsh for their enthusiasm and encouragement in helping bring this project to fruition.

I Spied For Stalin First published by Odhams Press 1950
A Spy Called Swallow First published by W. H. Allen 1978
Published by GB Publishing.org 2017

ISBN: 978-1-912031-67-2 (paperback)
978-1-912031-66-5 (eBook)

These memoirs reflect the authors' personal experiences and knowledge of events
and, while exercised with caution to protect family members who remained in Russia,
there is also the possibility they were written with editorial assistance influenced by
Cold War attitudes. As such, the work is not intended as an accurate historical record
but, rather, a true story with insights into Russian life during one of history's greatest
upheavals.

GB Publishing.org

www.gbpublishing.co.uk

CONTENTS

ILLUSTRATIONS
Page

1

INTRODUCTION by Peter & Leeroy Murray

Republishing *I Spied For Stalin*, gave Leeroy and Peter Murray the opportunity to re-evaluate and reconsider their mother Nora's incredible memoir after her escape from Russia in 1942. Did Nora have any regrets about leaving Russia after marrying an Englishman? Was her escape from Russia permitted in order to allow her to continue spying for Stalin whilst in England? And why did she choose to write about growing up in one of history's most brutal regimes, even to the point of denouncing her father whom she loved?

Notably Nora's life shows that her spirit was never compromised by the tyranny and oppression she faced, or by the new and no doubt intimidating surroundings in which she found herself. Nora's narrative is one shared by millions of people whose lives were – or are – disrupted by historical events which trap them in the jaws of repressive regimes and threaten their survival.

As a foreigner, in England, Nora coped with language, lifestyle and cultural differences. Yet she gained freedom of choice, the ability to walk down the street unafraid and to speak her mind. Publishing her book in 1950 was in itself a mark of such freedom, allowing her to share with the world her account of Stalin's state-controlled regime held together by fear.

Nora's life is linked forever with John's - the man for whom she risked everything and who risked everything for her in return. But it was only towards the end of her life that she really appreciated the unique qualities which made him exceptional. Their story is one of ever-lasting love, set against the backdrop of one of history's greatest events and subsequently the realities and struggles of daily life in post-war Britain.

3

PROLOGUE by Peter & Leeroy Murray

Nora truly possessed an indomitable Russian soul and an insatiable appetite for creative pursuits. In seeking freedom, she longed to experience and explore her passions for dance, music, writing and love. Her rejection of tyranny in all its manifestations was an integral part of her character. She had complete disregard for the politics that sought to repress all people; this embodied her very existence. This die-hard determination and resilience would be a shining light through her darkest hours, whether trudging tired and hungry through the Siberian tundra or aboard a ship in those doomed Arctic convoys.

Nora kept a diary which details the substance and indeed subtext of her life. Within its priceless pages she inscribed her ambitions for herself and her children and kept a meticulous record of the people she met, the books that she read and the influences they had on shaping her thoughts. Peppered throughout would be her personal mantras pertaining to optimism, hope and her love of life.

I Spied For Stalin charts her life up to and during the terrifying time she realised the fuller meaning of Stalin's 'purges.' Her story begins so inauspiciously yet nonetheless dramatically. With both parents fighting in the Bolshevik army, she was born on a troop train destined for Zolotonosha in the Ukraine on 24th February 1919. It concludes in 1942, with an equally extraordinary journey - her escape from Russia which was by then beset by the ravages of war with Nazi Germany. Of course her tale does not end there; this merely sets the stage for the continuation of her remarkable life, this time in London.

4

FOREWORD – I SPIED FOR STALIN

LT.-GEN. SIR NOEL MASON-MACFARLANE, K.C.B., D.S.O., M.C.

It has been my lot to spend a number of years in the police states which came into being in Europe after the First World War. First came four years in the early thirties watching the development of National Socialism in South Germany, Austria and the Sudeten tracts of Czechoslovakia. It was then, too, that I met Fascism for the first time in northern Italy and in unhappy south Tyrol. From 1937 until just before the outbreak of war I was in Germany. In 1941 and 1942 I spent close on a year in the U.S.S.R. as Head of the British Military Mission to Moscow. Both before and after my stay in Russia my work in Gibraltar brought me into contact with the Andalusia of the Spain of Franco and the Falange. In 1943 and 1944 I was in Italy again and was able to see the terrible legacy left by Fascism in a country which had been thrashed into turning its coat.

There was a wide difference between the ideological origins of some of these totalitarian states. But in every case a dictator and a minority party established a police state regime with a ruthless disregard for the liberty and the freedoms of the individual as we in the Christian West understand them. Lenin and Stalin, who followed him, have imposed Communism on backward and vast Slav-Mongol Russia. Hitler and his National Socialists seized power in industrially efficient, militarist and vital Germany by different methods. But in almost every respect there was a remarkable and terrible similarity between the conditions in which individual people in these two dictatorships lived their lives. Such differences as there were could be attributed chiefly to racial characteristics and to the pre-revolutionary degree of industrial development. My experience of conditions in these states has been sufficiently wide to enable me to draw at least one very definite conclusion. The fact that Communism has found supporters in Great Britain, or, indeed, in any democratic Christian country, is largely due to the complete ignorance of conditions in the U.S.S.R. on the part of those who have been influenced by diabolically intensive and equally pernicious propaganda. It is for this reason that this frank book in which the author has set forth her experiences as a child and girl in the U.S.S.R. is so welcome and valuable.

Eight years have elapsed since Nora Korzhenko left Archangel on her voyage with her British husband to the U.K. But there are fellow countrywomen of hers who married members of the British fighting services during the war who have not been so fortunate. Like all of us she has hoped that the Kremlin might, in the end, permit these war brides to leave the U.S.S.R. and rejoin their husbands. While hope remained she had no wish to say or write anything which might prejudice their case. There was, too, the possibility, however remote, that her father, languishing in one of the numerous Soviet labour camps, might be released. Publishing the unvarnished truth about her experiences of life in the U.S.S.R. could not have failed to jeopardize her fathers chances. But the war brides are still held captive behind the Iron Curtain and the Kremlin's attitude remains utterly uncompromising. No news has been received from her father and it is now reasonably certain that nothing will be heard of him again. There is no longer any reason why her tale should not be told. There is every reason why it should. Authentic first-hand information of life on the other side of the Iron Curtain seldom comes to hand and its scarceness increases its value. I can only hope that this book will be widely read, especially by those whose interest in and support of Communist doctrine is based only on what the Kremlin wants them to know.

The author gives such a complete and vivid account of her experiences as a citizen of the U.S.S.R. that adding to the picture from my own knowledge would be superfluous. There are, however, two aspects of police state life which I would like to stress. The first is the ghastly atmosphere of fear and suspicion in which the inhabitants of these states have their being. To those who have not lived in such surroundings it must be almost impossible to imagine the child spying on the parents and every neighbour, acquaintance, friend or even relation a potential informer. The second is the complete control of the Press, radio and all forms of publicity by the government. The public have absolutely no opportunity of obtaining accurate news or facts on which to form their own opinions. They are told only what the government wishes them to know. The facts and comments produced by the newspapers differ only in the way in which government material is dished up. Radio sets tell the same stories while loudspeakers bray them in public places. Communism on paper or on the air is one thing. Communism in practice is another.

The theory of Communism must inevitably prove attractive to individuals indifferently blessed with this world's goods. It obviously makes its greatest appeal in countries in which the standard of life is low. The "have-nots" of this world fall for it. So do a small number of misguided intelligentsia who take it at its face value and who fail to realize that they will probably be among the first to qualify for the Lubyanka or its local equivalent.

But Communist literature and propaganda give a very false idea of the way in which Communism works out in practice. From the share and share alike point of view it is difficult, in theory, to find fault with the constitution of the U.S.S.R. Yet it gives no clue to the conditions in which the peoples of the U.S.S.R. are living. Those in power in the Kremlin know this only too well. And they do everything that lies in their power to prevent foreigners from seeing for themselves what life in the U.S.S.R. is really like. At the same time they make it impossible for their own people to leave their country and to discover how greatly the standard of living in western democracies differs from their own. In effect, no subject of the U.S.S.R. can leave his country except on the Kremlin's business and his mission, while abroad, includes, as often as not, contacting and supporting the local Communist parties in the countries which he visits. With the exception of diplomats, no persons other than carefully selected visitors are allowed to enter the U.S.S.R. Such visitors and the diplomats resident in the country are lucky if they see more than their hosts intend them to see. And the Kremlin ensures that they are shown only a limited number of selected exhibits calculated to leave a good impression.

The aim of Communists throughout the world is to overthrow democracy as we understand it. They attain, or hope to attain, this result by eliminating all except those whom they classify as the proletariat. Much of this elimination has taken place up to date during the revolutionary seizure of power. But in some cases the actual overthrow of the local constitution has been comparatively bloodless, and the elimination process has been, and is being, carried out in the Communist police state.

As a nation and as a civilization we are at last beginning to realize the menace of Communism. But it is difficult to bring this home to an island people with a way of life and standard of living such as ours. The vast majority of us are proud of and thankful for our democratic constitution with its secret universal suffrage, which enables the electorate to choose the government it wants every five years and to turn out a government that displeases the majority pretty well whenever it wishes to do so. We are a Christian country and enjoy absolute religious freedom. We have a deep-rooted admiration and affection for our Sovereign who carries out so splendidly the functions not only of head of our large family in these islands, but also of the Commonwealth countries founded by our forefathers.

7

Do we want to change all this for a police state controlled by a handful of Communist bigots?

Nora Korzhenko's book will help many of us to picture the fate of our country should Communism ever gain control. Such a possibility may, at the moment, appear comparatively remote, but after two world wars our economic problems have become extremely grave, and it is against a background of economic collapse and low standards of living that Communism flourishes. So far in this country we have succeeded, with the help so generously given by the U.S.A. and the Commonwealth countries, in combating our economic difficulties and in maintaining a good general standard of living. But we are still a long way from having attained economic stability in our "Western World"; and we must not forget that the U.S.S.R. and its satellites now form a practically self-contained economic block and are preparing for war as only a dictatorship can.

Here, in the U.K., there is unhappily a small proportion of the population who have been attracted by Communist doctrine and who are either members of the Communist Party, or, to use the current phrase, fellow travellers. The number of these who have visited the U.S.S.R. is minute. And even those who have done so have been carefully shepherded by their hosts and can have little or no idea of the true state of affairs in the country. It is just for this reason that this book of Nora Korzhenko's is of such immense value. The author writes with the unique experience of one born during the fighting in the earliest days of Communism in Russia and brought up by a father who rapidly became a high official of the N.K.V.D. Her story will help to shatter the illusion that the U.S.S.R. is a Utopian classless society. In point of fact the difference in the standard of living between the higher officials of the Soviet state and the millions of the peasantry and workers is far greater than similar differences in the countries of the Christian democratic world. And yet even membership of the ruling classes in the U.S.S.R. brings no security. One of the most striking parts of this book is the description of the sudden and utterly unexpected arrest and deportation of the author's father after years of loyal, if misguided, work as a senior official in the N.K.V.D.

It was my good fortune to meet Nora Korzhenko during her last critical months in Russia which ended in her persuading the Kremlin authorities to allow her to marry a Britisher and to get away from Archangel. As an example of initiative, drive and sheer pluck her adventures and success were truly remarkable. I can well understand her great love for the country of her birth and for its people. I share her hopes for their future, and a little old ikon

8

from Russia looks down on me as I write. But I share also her detestation of those now in power in the Kremlin.

We paid in war for appeasing in peace potential enemies in the shape of the police states of Hitler and Mussolini. Yet in the end we won through. It was through Hitler's attack on the U.S.S.R. that we and our Christian allies found ourselves fortuitously allied with the forces of anti-Christ. We are, all of us, now paying in peace for having appeased in war the police state of the Kremlin. The cold war with Communism has been joined. We must and will win through again. If God so wills it we will do so without shooting. But God helps those that help themselves and we have reason to be very grateful for the assistance which Nora Korzhenko's book will give to the country of her adoption.

CHAPTER I – DAUGHTER OF THE REVOLUTION

The young girl waited in the corridor outside the office of the Chief of Police. In a few moments the door would open and she would be taken before him. She stood there facing the bare wall and felt a sudden tightening in her throat. The walls, like the ceiling, glowed with a strange whiteness reflecting the skyline of snow outside. But the sky itself, like the barred windows of the police station remained grey and leaden. The drab emptiness of the place sent a shiver through her. Deep in the pocket of her fur coat her fingers closed round a folder of stiff cardboard. She gripped it hard, as though to hold it in her hands for ever, but as her fingers tightened, the door opened and a guard stepped forward. The click of his heels made her start.

"Major Dritz will see you now," he said.

The girl entered the office, stood before the seated major and waited. She glanced quickly at him, then at Stalin's wall portrait and only then noticed a plump little man.

"This is a major from the N.K.V.D. who has come from Moscow to see you," said the police officer.

The man from Moscow nodded at the girl. He wore the dull green uniform of the secret police and his eyes were grey and cold like the outside world. He spoke and his words were like a whip; clipped, precise and without expression. At first they only reached the girl through a haze. She heard words, nothing more. And then he stopped, and came very close. His eyes looked into hers and his voice hardened.

"There is one more thing that I must tell you before you leave. Never forget that wherever you are, or whatever you may become outside Russia, you will always remain a Russian.

"You have been technically released from Soviet citizenship but the blood of Russia will still flow in your veins. You must be true to your birthright. You have seen and heard many things which would be of use to our enemies in the capitalist world beyond the boundaries of the Soviet. We rely on you never to divulge these things. We demand your silence."

The man stopped. He was so close now she could smell the garlic as his breath spurted towards her in little white clouds.

"Do you understand, Citizeness? We demand your silence."

From somewhere a woman's voice answered him. The Chief of Police stood up, the interview was over. There were no handshakes and no farewells. Outside in the corridor the girl leant against the rough bricks of the wall.

Then the guard touched her arm and led her out into the snow of Archangel. The crisp air stung her cheeks and she drew from her pocket the thing she had held so long, a British passport. Then, as she crunched her way through the snow she began repeating to herself the same words over and over again: "Now I am free.... now I am free.... now I am free."

It is seven years since I stood before Major Dritz, chief of police in Archangel, and received my release from Soviet citizenship. And even now I find comfort in that blue-backed passport which brought me to England, the wife of an Englishman. From the day I left the Soviet Union I have kept faith with the secret police. I have said nothing of my real life there and nor has my husband. But now my children are growing up. The other day my eldest boy came home from school and asked, "Mother, were you a Communist?"

I told him "No," and then I wondered why he had asked me.

"A boy at school said you were," he answered. "He said all Russians were Communists."

Next they will be asking me to tell of my life there. What shall I say? The truth or lies? Shall I tell them of the glorious Soviet in which Communists believe throughout the world or shall I tell them of the real Russia, that nightmare in which I lived for twenty years?

My answer is in this book for one day my children will be old enough to read it and then, like you, they will be able to judge for themselves both Russia and me.

The Russia that I left is the only one I knew. For I entered life in a troop-train during the revolutionary fighting in the Ukraine in 1919, and my father, Vassily Savvich Korzhenko, was the chief of a ragged partisan band fighting against the Czarist forces. When the Red revolt succeeded, he became one of the heads of the secret police. As his only daughter, I lived a life which was the privilege of few Russians during the twenty years he served as a high official of the N.K.V.D. Through him, I had a grandstand view of the men who rule the Soviet Union, for his last post was that of Director-General of the Soviet Foreign Office under Litvinov.

Then, when Kremlin policy changed and Litvinov was replaced as Commissar for Foreign Affairs by Molotov, my father was purged with hundreds more and sent into exile. I have never seen him since. In the ten years that have passed he may have been shot or he may be working as a ragged nameless slave in a concentration camp. I left Russia for the last time on an Arctic convoy and my last glimpse of my own land was of thousands of slave-workers guarded by sentries with fixed bayonets. Tears blurred their dim shapes as the ship nosed through the ice towards the sea, and freedom. For me, the tragedy of Russia stretched beyond these men and women without hope, for every broken wretch was a grim reminder that somewhere perhaps in Russia was another such slave, my father.

I will never know what has happened to him for that is Stalin's Russia. The men in the Kremlin have no regard for human rights and they have built up a network of terror and sudden arrest which haunts every Soviet citizen. Even though my father was an N.K.V.D. chief, I was not immune, neither was he, from the attentions of the secret police. Secret informers constantly watched us, just as they watch every other Russian. Indeed this web of intrigue, suspicion and terror finally trapped me. Before I left the Soviet Union in 1942 I was forced to spy for Stalin. My final assignment was to inform on every movement of the man I loved and later married. To understand why I, and thousands like me, were made to do such things, we must go back to the beginning and I will tell you my story of Russia since the Revolution.

One of the first things I remember about my childhood was listening to my mother playing Liszt and Chopin in the drawing room of our house in Simferopol, capital of the Crimea. There were cherry trees behind the house and a big garden where I used to play. But I was never allowed to leave it on my own, though I often stood behind its iron gates and wondered about the men and women living in the city beyond. The Crimea is Russia's gateway to the Middle East and Simferopol a clearing house for trade and commerce across the Black Sea. It has a mixed and colourful population and in its crowded sun-drenched streets you see them all; long-robed Persians, hook-nosed Armenians, bearded Tartars, baggy-trousered Turks and Moslem beauties hiding from life behind their yashmaks.

Simferopol had an exotic attraction for a young girl and I was always excited when father or mother took me to see it. For me, it was the Arabian Nights come to life, but our trips were seldom for the Crimea had not yet settled down under its new rulers and beneath the surface there was always the danger of assassination or sudden attack. Our home was a four-roomed flat in Krimgirei Boulevard in a villa which had once been the home of a White Russian nobleman. The parquet floors were brightly polished, the chairs covered with damask and father's study was lined from ceiling to floor with glass-fronted book cases. As a child you naturally accept the surroundings of your own home and it wasn't till years afterwards I realized all our luxurious furniture had been looted from the previous owner. It was in this atmosphere that I used to sit on the traditional *tachta* — a low divan covered with a carpet — and hear from my mother the stories of the Revolution. She was a quiet, homely woman with calm grey eyes and it was strange to hear her gentle voice tell of the bloody battles in which she had fought as a young girl beside my father. He had been head of a partisan detachment, but like all the Communist leaders, he did not use his real name. He called himself Groza, Storm, just as Stalin means Steel and Molotov means Hammer. He was the son of an official of the Czarist State Railway. Youngest of nine, he was sent to St. Petersburg to be educated but at the university he joined the underground movement for which he was arrested and sent to prison.

Vasili Korzhenko student St. Petersburg University circa 1910

The rest of the family remained firm supporters of the Romanovs. Two of his brothers were priests, and although his release made him even more determined to free Russia from the Czars, he was unable to persuade any of them to join him.

On the contrary, when the Revolution began, his eldest sister, Nita, joined the Czar's army as a nursing sister and his brother, Constantin, rejoined his regiment as a commissioned officer. The family were then living in the Poltava region where, like the rest of Russia everything was disorganized and thrown into chaos by the Red revolt. Father at once left home to join the

13

rebels but for months it was uncertain as to which side would win. More often than not he was a man on the run, hiding from the Czar's Cossacks and, like thousands of other Russian families, the civil war found brother and sister fighting on opposite sides. But family life was as strong then as it is now, and when father was captured by the Czar's forces it was his own family which saved him, not his comrades in arms.

His sister Nita happened to be in the local White Russian Staff Headquarters one night when she heard two Czarist officers discussing an execution which had been arranged for the following morning. She had no idea her brother had been caught but when one of the men mentioned that Groza had been captured she realized at once what had happened. Pretending interest in the fate of a "damned rebel" she found out all the details of the execution which had been arranged for dawn the next day. Unsuspecting, the men even told her the time, place and route which the execution cart would take.

It was all she needed and the next morning seven masked men in the uniform of the Czar held up the wagon at pistol-point. Not a word was spoken, the guards were overpowered and the manacled Groza was bundled behind one of the riders who at once dug spurs into the flanks of his horse and took him to safety. The rescue created a sensation in the district and Nita herself had to go into hiding from her own forces. A fearless horsewoman, it was of course she who had led the rescue party and saved her brother's life.

In later years I was introduced to her as one of my aunts and although she never spoke of the Revolution, she would often tell me of her life in Czarist Russia. She was some fifteen years older than father and had travelled over most of Europe. She had also an added attraction for me; she was the first Russian I had ever known who could speak English. Father never forgot her action in saving his life and made her an allowance out of his income till the end.

Father first met my mother when she was a high school student in Poltava. He soon fired her with his ideal of a new Russia and she left home to join his partisan band in guerrilla warfare. They called her Comrade Margarita and for months they roamed the blazing war-torn villages of the Ukraine, where the peasants fed them with black bread. The young revolutionary taught his bride to handle a rifle; she became a crack shot and the band recognized her as equal to any man. Sometimes, when they had returned from a successful sortie against a White Russian encampment the men would chaff her by saying she would soon be as famous as Marusya, the notorious woman bandit who was then terrorizing the Ukraine.

14

This used to anger mother, much to the men's amusement, for Marusya and her men were hated equally by both Reds and Whites. She had joined neither party but had set herself up as an independent bandit chief and took advantage of the general disorder of the revolution to plunder the whole countryside. She would kidnap wealthy farmers, hold them to ransom then shoot them if their families were unable to pay. Another trick was to brand her victims' foreheads with the letter "M" before releasing them and there are still men and women in the Ukraine bearing her mark today. But Groza's men were no terrorists and

Nora's mother, Margarita Emelyanov as a student circa 1916

mother's fighting was inspired, or so she thought, to secure freedom for her country. It was a hard struggle and the winter of 1918-19 found them still warring in the bitter cold of European Russia where they had to wrap blankets and rags round their feet and legs for warmth.

Mother wore a torn sheep-skin lined coat with rags round her feet like the soldiers, and she had little comfort at my birth in a troop-train at Zolotonosha on 24 February, 1919. They had just been attacked by White Russian cavalry and between fighting them off through the slits of the armoured train, rough, bearded Cossacks acted as midwives. Her labour cries were drowned in the rat-tat-tat of machine-gun and rifle fire but in their crude, kindly way the Red Cossacks did everything to help. They must have done a good job because both of us survived.

15

Father's family were of Ukrainian extraction and he was one of the few intellectuals among his band. The result was that when the revolution was over and a slim, fair-haired man moved into the Lubyanka, Moscow, to recruit suitable men for running the new Soviet state, my father's name was one of the first he received. The newcomer was Felix Dzerzhinsky, Commissar of Internal Affairs, and Chairman of the Extra ordinary Commission, or Cheka as the secret police was then called.

Dzerzhinsky was a pole of wealthy parents, but he had been a revolutionary for years. He had spent ten years in prison under Nicholas II, where he contracted tuberculosis, and was one of the first big names among the early Communist leaders. Streets and clubs were named after him and we always had a framed picture of him in our home. He had a clear-cut aesthetic face with a small, pointed beard; a mild-looking little man. But beneath his calm there was a fierceness which became a fanaticism in later years. His job was to take over where the secret police of the Czar, the Okhrana, had left off. And, under him, the whole process went in reverse.

Officer Korzhenko painting circa 1920

Dzerzhinsky must have been impressed with the record of the young Ukrainian, he made him head of the Cheka in Odessa. I was a year old.

By now the Revolution had succeeded, but mopping up operations continued for some time. Bands of terrorists plagued the countryside and it was never safe to travel far alone. One of the most notorious was Mischa Japonchic who had organized a gang of ruffians in the district. He used to lie up in the hills and swoop down on the villages for supplies whenever he thought the Cheka were engaged elsewhere. Often father used to take me, a little girl with pigtails and a muslin dress, on his official visits outside the city. But we never went alone. There was always an armed guard in the lorry with father sitting in front beside the driver. I remember once we were going along a country lane after visiting a farmhouse when suddenly there was a lot of noise and some of the Cheka men around me started falling off the lorry.

"Lie down, Nora," one of them shouted, and the lorry went as fast as it could. We never stopped for the men who had fallen off, and it wasn't till years later when I mentioned the incident to my father that I realized what had happened to them. They had been shot dead by Japonchic's men in an ambush.

But these excursions were not very frequent and I saw little of father. He was a tall man with scholarly features and a shock of brown hair. He was always dressed in the Chekist uniform; a green Russian blouse hanging over his trousers, with black jack-boots, a grey overcoat and a green peaked cap. Sometimes, he would be away all night and return, gun at side, for black coffee at breakfast. Later, mother often told me of those early days; strange times for Russia. Father's duty then as a Cheka chief, was to raise grain for the local population and see that the surrounding farms contributed their fair share. In spite of the Cheka's efforts many people still died in the great famine of 1920. Every day brought another tragic incident. And there was so little food that even the officials could not always help. They did what they could; sometimes with strange results.

One day a woman dragged herself to father's office with the heart-rending plea to save her child who was dying of hunger. Father obtained food for her and sent her away with tears of gratitude. He had forgotten all about the incident when some months later an informer tipped him off that some White Russians were hiding near the Feldman Boulevard by the sea. At this time father used to drive a carriage drawn by a handsome English horse called Nightingale, which had previously been owned by a Russian duke. After midnight he set out with Nightingale to investigate the information. As he walked up to the house in the darkness someone tugged his sleeve. He spun round, gun in hand.

"Don't shoot," said a woman's voice, "I am here to warn you."

She told father she was a White Russian, and that her sister and husband were in a plot to kidnap him and take him that night in a boat to Rumania.

Father asked, "But why are you doing this for me? You are saving my life."

"It is nothing," said the woman. "You once saved my child; you gave her grain during the famine."

Father returned to the Cheka headquarters, collected six men and raided his would-be kidnappers. The woman had not only saved his life, she had betrayed her family out of gratitude.

But my clearest memories are of Simferopol, in the Crimea, where Father was deputy chief of the O.G.P.U., as the secret police was now called. His chief was Stanislav Francevitch Redens, married to Anna, sister of Stalin's second wife, Nadezhda. Our house was opposite the villa where Redens lived.

The Crimea, until 1924, was ruled by three strong men in Simferopol, Stanislav Redens (Stalin's brother-in-law), head of the O.G.P.U., father, his deputy, and Semen Arnoldov, his assistant. These three men had the power of life and death over millions of Russians. Their word was absolute and their first job was the liquidating of all the imperial property along the fashionable Yalta coast. The famous Massandra, imperial wine cellar at Gurzuf, pride of the Czars, found its way into the homes of O.G.P.U. men and selected citizens who were members of the Party.

Father, with the other two Cheka chiefs, had a tough job. The new state had many enemies. But he had moments of wild relaxation. Sometimes I was kept awake for hours at night by the shouts and singing at a drunken orgy of Chekist men and their wives. I would tiptoe from my bed to listen. Outside people were starving. Later, when I was old enough, I learned how to smuggle some of the food to my school friends.

I was too young to understand it all, but to older people Russian life at this time must have seemed as though the whole world was turning upside down. Churches were desecrated, altar cloths and ikons flung out into the street as playthings for children. And every now and then there would be shots in the night and the sound of galloping hoof beats as running battles were fought with the remnants of General Wrangel's White Army. But all these activities were against White Russians, supporters of the old regime. The first portent of how the new Russia was going to develop came when at Simferopol the Bolsheviks staged a purge of one of their own men, an acknowledged revolutionary.

Their first victim was Veli Ibrahimov, local born chairman of the Central Executive Committee of the Soviets of the Tartar Region in the Crimea. This man was the civilian boss of the Crimea, a big post. It was a great shock to the revolutionaries when Redens, head of the secret police, ordered his arrest. I saw him leave the O.G.P.U. headquarters in Krimgirei Boulevard where we lived, a short, portly man in a fez. He was on his way to jail after preliminary questioning and he looked very pale between the Cheka guards in the waiting car. A short trial followed and he was shot as an enemy of the State.

This action — first of thousands — was an inkling of the true nature of the new rulers. It was as though a spark had fired a human trail that was to blaze like gunpowder across the whole of Russia, murdering millions. In the end it even trapped the three strong men of the Crimea who had begun it, the three Chekists Redens, Arnoldov and my own father.

But father was always careful to keep his Chekist life away from me. I remember once going to his study, opening a drawer and finding three revolvers. There were also two other strange objects inside which I learned later were a knuckleduster and a hand grenade. Father found me one day looking at these things. He was very angry and quickly bundled me out of the study while from then on the drawer was kept locked.

Simferopol itself was a city of white-fronted houses, palms and magnolia blooms. One of my greatest thrills as a little girl was to ride with Mama in an *izvoshik*, a horse-drawn windowless tram, where you sat back to back beneath a gay canopy facing the pavement. The driver, Tartar-born and wearing a fez, used to play merry folk tunes on a flute. The days were hot in the summer and shops closed at noon but there were always sweet-meat men with trays ready to assist in persuading a little girl's mother into buying Turkish delight or *halva*, a kind of honey and nut paste. In the winter she would tell me the story of "*Krasnaya Shapochka* and "*Kot V Sapogach.*" Never heard of them? Oh, yes, you have, they're "Red Riding Hood" and "Puss in Boots".

But I'm afraid they will not be known in Russia today; Stalin has forbidden them as "bourgeois nonsense". Each night my mother would kiss me and tuck me up in bed. I was never taught to pray. I knew nothing of God for, like true Communists, my parents were atheists. And there were no ikons in our home. Father would not even allow the common Russian expressions of "*Gospodi*" ("Oh, God!") or "*Bozhe Moi*" ("My God!") to be said in his household. But not because he thought they were irreligious, simply because he denied the existence of any such being. Sunday, of course, has never had

19

any meaning in the Soviet, it has gone from the life of its citizens and I grew up without any knowledge of its significance.

Sometimes father's mother would come and stay with us. She was a very religious old woman and I remember a terrible scene between her and father when he found she had brought an ikon with her to hang in her bedroom. In Czarist days you used to find these ikons of the Greek Orthodox Church, small medallions depicting Christ or a saint, hanging from the walls in every Russian home. Father told her she was a silly, superstitious old woman and flung her treasure on the fire. But by nature he was not a hard man. He was only severe in carrying out Communist doctrine and ideals. In these he remained unshakable, right till the end.

Behind our house we used to keep rabbits and two English pointers. We were very proud of them as they had once belonged to a wealthy White Russian who had given them English names, Daisy and Rex. These names were rather a joke among us and when I first heard them I found it difficult to pronounce them. But they were the only names the dogs understood, so Daisy and Rex they remained. Father used to keep them in kennels and they were seldom allowed in the house, but whenever he could he would take them with him into the country on shooting expeditions and would return loaded with game and sometimes, as a special treat, he would bring us a *drofa*, an ostrich-like bird which was very good to eat. But he had one curious foible about the animals he had shot, he would never eat them though he never minded mother and me enjoying his bag.

Our loot from the counter-revolutionaries did not stop at Rex and Daisy. I also had a number of magnificent toys which could only have been made outside Russia and imported there as playthings for the children of wealthy families. I particularly remember a large china doll which, unlike me, could speak English though her vocabulary was limited to "Mamma." Another of my toys was a large French poodle on wheels that had been made in Paris. Like father, mother was a Ukrainian and by the time I was six years old she had taught me how to jig and bob my way through a number of native folk dances. I also knew by heart some of Shevchenko's Ukrainian songs and at parties I was always expected to do my little piece while mother accompanied me at the piano. Sometimes I would be allowed to play with other little girls who were also the children of Chekist men. It used to be an exciting moment when we were allowed to jump from stone to stone across the dried up river Salgir which runs through Simferopol, and like any other little girl there was always the attraction of half an hour in the park enjoying *skakalki*, skipping.

Another favourite game at Easter-time was called *bitki*. Though this was usually played by grown ups, it was very exciting to watch and very often you would find a whole village surrounding the two players. *Bitki* is played with two eggs and both players face one another sitting at a table. It is rather like English boys playing conkers, the players tap the eggs at the small end one after another until one cracks. Then the process is repeated with the other end and the first egg to be cracked top and bottom is the loser. Country folk spend hours looking for hard-shelled eggs during the winter for the game. Losers forfeit their eggs and a player who is fortunate enough to have one with a sufficiently hard shell can usually win for himself three or four dozen. Some skill is required, of course, for if he breaks his opponent's shell instead of slightly cracking it, even though he is the winner he has lost the chance of adding it to his collection.

In those days no attempt was made to educate young Russians in any Communist theories, but there was an occasion when I brought disgrace on our Chekist family. I had been taken over to father's office in the Chekist Headquarters and somehow, while no one was looking, wandered off on my own down the corridor into the meeting hall. There on the walls were a number of strange looking gentlemen looking down at me. I had never seen them before and something about their appearance must have made it plain to me, even at that early age, that Russia would have been better off without them. At any rate, there was no doubt in my mind the walls would look a lot nicer if they were taken down. So I climbed on a table and ripped down the faces of Marx, Lenin and all the rest. When father came in the Communist leaders lay in shreds on the floor.

"Whatever have you done, Nora?" he cried. "You mustn't do such things. What will people say when they know that the daughter of a Chekist has been so naughty? Don't you know whose pictures they are?"

Of course I had no idea, but looking back, it seems to me this must have been my first personal revolt against Communism!

In the winter of 1924 father was transferred to the Far East and after two weeks travelling across the top of the world by the Trans-Siberian Railway we arrived in Chita near the Mongolian-Manchurian border. Father's main job here was frontier control and the prevention of opium and other contraband smuggling by the Chinese into Soviet Russia. He often used to disappear for weeks in the wild mountains and would return with strange oriental wares and English stockings for mother. During a gun battle on one of these raids he was shot in the head by a Chinese gangster and brought home on a stretcher strapped to the back of a mule. He was in a critical condition but after two months in hospital he recovered.

Vasili Korzhenko convalescing with wife Margarita and Nora circa 1923

Father was always an excellent shot and he loved hunting. He had his own collection of Brownings, Mausers and Colts which hung in a rack in his study, but pride of the collection was an English-made Holland-and-Holland rifle which the Bond Street firm had embossed with the crest of its original purchaser, the Grand Duke Constantine. He used to make his own cartridges and sometimes he would let me help him. He had quite a sense of humour, too, and I remember he once sent a postcard of an English pointer, solemnly addressed to his own dog inside a packet of dog biscuits. On the card he had written: "My dear friend, try to learn to hold your tail still like this good English dog on our next hunting trip."

Once while he was away, a Chinese pedlar came to our house and spread out all his stock; stockings, scarves, perfumes and other smuggled luxuries filled our hallway. Mother was fingering a scarf when he asked her where her husband worked and she said "O.G.P.U." The man asked no more questions. He just turned and fled, leaving his entire collection behind.

Father never returned from his hunting trips empty-handed. He always achieved a good bag as he had done in the Crimea, but this time he was a hunter in earnest for much of our clothing was made from the skins of bears and reindeer he killed. But for me, his most popular bag was when he returned shouting, "Look what Papochka has brought for his little Medvezhonock — two little playmates." And that's just what they were, two little *medvezhonock* or baby bears. He had shot their mother near her lair and finding her offspring unprotected, he had brought them back. I fed them with milk and honey until they grew up and became dangerous, but for a long time we had quite a zoo — dogs, bears, a tame fox, white mice and a Persian cat. Father tried to get the fox to make friends with the cubs but he bit one of them on the nose and we had to keep them apart.

Two others who didn't get on very well together, though they never reached the nose biting stage, were father and the Chinese consul. The latter was a tall, impressive figure in his mandarin silks and long fingernails and I enjoyed visiting him to play with his children, but somehow or other he quarrelled with father and I was no longer allowed to visit him. The consul, who spoke perfect Russian, had given me a complete model Chinese village as a present and some exquisite silks for mother. Father let me keep the village but he returned the silks for fear the gift might be construed as a bribe. But the consul sent them back again saying he would be offended if they were not accepted, so mother was very pleased to be allowed to keep the gifts though she had to promise never again to accept such bourgeois tokens of friendship.

We stayed in the Far East just over a year and in 1925 when we were returning from Vladivostock to Leningrad I had my first practical experience of the underground movement and realized there were plenty of men and women still ready to risk their lives in their fight against the Communist regime. I had often heard father talk about so-called enemies of the State, but now I was to learn how real they were.

We were in a party of Russian officials, travelling in the rear coach. Ahead, in another train, were Zinoviev — author of the famous Zinoviev letter — and Kamenev. They were both members of Lenin's Politburo, the highest men in Soviet Russia. Suddenly, soon after 3 a.m., as we were passing through Baikal, there was a terrible crash. I was flung from the top sleeping bunk to the floor of the carriage. All around me was splintered wood, flames and the screams of dead and dying. My father held me close.

"Don't worry, Nora," he said, "it is just an accident."

I was taken away from the scene and it was not until a relief train had been sent and we were safe again that I heard what had happened. The track had been mined to blow up the train on which Zinoviev and Kamenev were travelling. But someone had mistimed the fuse. Their train passed over the explosives untouched. We were only ten minutes behind. Our train of twelve carriages was blown up instead. Every carriage but one was derailed, hundreds were killed. The only part of the train left standing on the track was the last coach, ours. When father told me the story there was no anger in his voice, only sorrow.

"You see, Obezyanka (little monkey)," he said, "it is still Russian against Russian. Alas, what our country has come to."

The relief train took us on to Leningrad where father had been posted to take up a new appointment with the O.G.P.U. He was made deputy chief of the K.R.O., Counter Revolutionary Department. We were given a flat on the fourth floor of No. 12, Dzerzhinsky Street, named after Felix Dzerzhinsky, founder of the secret police. Our new home was in Leningrad's Whitehall district, almost opposite the five-storied yellow building which was the O.G.P.U. Headquarters.

Shortly after we arrived in the old Czarist capital mother came to me and said,

"You are going to have tea with Mme Stalin."

I did not realize it at the time, of course, but looking back, I regard it as one of the great occasions of my life. Mother combed my long hair, put on my best clothes and we walked hand in hand to No. 19, Gogol Street, the home of Sergei Allilujeva. Like other old revolutionaries Sergei held a unique position in Soviet life. He received a state pension and although he was a known critic of the way Communist theory was being put into practice, he remained unharmed by the secret police. It is Sergei Allilujeva, Stalin's father-in-law, who is credited with coining a well-known Russian joke about the Cheka at that time, "Why is the Soviet like a wheel?" "Because it held together by the Cheka" (for Cheka also means a split pin). There are many

24

such old die-hards in Russian today. Some thirty miles outside Moscow there is a rest home for these old men and women who began as anarchists with the assassination of Alexander II in 1881. Very few of them were Communists; their revolutionary creed is older than Lenin's but they are all members of the Society of Former Political Prisoners. Many of their names are in Soviet history books and the Society used to boast a total of 20,000 years' imprisonment among its members. The Society has also a museum in Moscow recording the underground fight against the Czar, but at the Mikhailovsky Home you can see the real thing.

Allilujeva was, of course, the father of both Mme Stalin and Mme Redens, whom I knew as Auntie Anna from the days when her husband had been head of the secret police and father's chief in the Crimea.

Mme Stalin, who was visiting her father, was sitting in the oak-panelled drawing-room when we arrived to have tea from the samovar. There were bodyguards at the entrance to the flat because already the future dictator of Russia had made himself one of the leading figures in the State, and a few months later, in 1927, he seized complete power for himself.

I remember Mme Stalin, Nadezhda Sergeevna, sitting drinking her tea and saying very little. To a child like me, she seemed a strange, aloof creature, but very beautiful with her pale, classical features and her light brown hair drawn tight across her forehead into a Grecian bun at the nape of her neck. Yet there was an air of sadness about her, almost as though she felt a great sorrow that the new Russia was not the land of freedom for which she and her father had worked. She talked with my mother while I was given toys to play with. But just before I left she said, with a sudden sweet smile: "What a pretty little girl you are; one day you must come to Moscow."

I said I hoped I would, little knowing what the capital and her husband had waiting for me. She was Stalin's second wife and I heard later both she and her father were frequent critics of the dictator's mass terror policy. They were married in 1919, the year I was born, and they had two children, Vassily, now a Red Air-Force General, and a daughter, Svietlana.

She died in 1932 and her death was hushed up by Soviet officials with the result all kinds of wild rumours circulated. The story most widely told at the time was that she had died through drinking a glass of poisoned wine intended for Stalin, but the truth has never been revealed. Obviously Stalin was very much in love with her because after her death he did a strange thing for the dictator of an atheist state. He granted her dying wish to be buried in consecrated ground, and her body lies in the monastery of Novo Diewitchy, outside Moscow.

Stalin, maybe remembering his days as a divinity student in Tiflis, ordered a Christian memorial to be erected above the grave. It includes a life-like marble head of Nadezhda, his dead wife. Her death was obviously a great personal blow to Stalin.

I was only a small girl, but somehow I felt an indefinable sense of sadness at that tea-party. It was almost as though I had a premonition that both the women, Mme Stalin and my mother, who sat drinking tea were destined for tragedy. Mother's sad end was not far away. It happened like this. Father had been assigned to interrogate suspects of the German colony. One man, a wealthy insurance magnate, Adolf Mitcherling, confessed to being an enemy of the State. Everything he owned was confiscated. He was sent to Siberia. My father also interrogated his wife, Frau Ursula Mitcherling, a beautiful young woman of twenty-eight. It was within his power to send her to follow her husband to Siberia. Instead he offered her a job as my governess. No one thought anything of it at the time as he had been anxious for some months about my education.

For two and a half years Frau Mitcherling taught me German, how to play the piano and deportment. Later, I went to the German School in Leningrad.

On the 22 March, 1928, my father's birthday, Semen Arnoldov (father's assistant in the O.G.P.U. in the Crimea), came to see us. He was my father's best friend. I loved him and called him "Uncle Arnold".

That day he walked past me as if he did not recognize me. "Where is your mother, Norochka?" he asked. Mother appeared and they went into a room together shutting the door so that I could not hear. A few minutes later my father came home, white and trembling. He joined Mother and Uncle Arnold behind the closed door. When they came out I heard mother say with a sob in her voice, "Dear Vassily, I will not stop you from taking this step. I will set you free and I wish you every happiness."

I could not imagine what had happened between my parents, but a few days later I came home and found Mother unconscious on the floor of the drawing-room; a small, empty bottle lay beside her.

"Mamochka," I cried, "get up, get up." But she did not answer me.

Just then Uncle Arnold and Father arrived in a great hurry. As soon as he saw my mother Uncle Arnold screamed like a madman at Father, "You killed her, Vassily, you killed her."

She was then taken to hospital. Two days later I went to see Mamochka. I carried a little posy of flowers for her. But when I saw her dear, white face, I could not speak.

She lifted herself from the pillow slightly and murmured, "Remember me when you are a big girl, won't you, dear?"

I stood for a long time at the door looking at her and then walked away ... a lonely, tearful little girl of nine years old. I never saw her again. I was sent to stay with relations in the city. One day a kind old charwoman who used to do odd jobs met me on the staircase and said, "Poor darling, if there is anything I can do now your mother has gone, let me know. Whoever would have thought he'd have married that foreign woman."

I rushed home through the streets of Leningrad. Father opened the door. He came forward to embrace me. But he could see by my eyes that I knew. He looked older and his hair had turned grey.

"So, Norochka, you know she is gone," he said.

He led me across the room to meet my governess, Frau Mitcherling. I curtsied.

"This is your new mother," he said, "you must be a good girl and she will look after you."

I faced her in silence, then left in tears for my room. That night I cried myself to sleep. They had married a week after Mother's death.

From then my life was changed. My stepmother reorganized our home in the German way. Everything had to be done at the correct time and she made a lot of restrictions and regulations. Father had taken a big risk in protecting her for he had to stand surety for her behaviour. As my governess she had joined the Communist party and renounced her Lutheran religion to become an atheist. During the two and a half years she had taught me a friendship must have sprung up between her and Father; Mother suspected nothing and it wasn't until the very end she realized what had been going on. Uncle Arnold was a pall-bearer at Mother's funeral and she was buried next to Sergei Garin, the writer, in an unmarked grave in the Alexandro Nevskaya Lavra cemetery. Father, a member of the League of the Godless, attached no importance to the human remains of the dead; to him, death was the end of everything.

Two years after the marriage Adolf Mitcherling was released from Siberia and returned to Leningrad. During his five years exile Ursula had written and sent food parcels but she never told her husband she had divorced him and married again. When he arrived home he found his wife gone and her mother in sole possession.

"She has married Vassily Korzhenko, the O.G.P.U. officer," she told him.

Herr Mitcherling came to see us at once. He stood in the doorway when I opened the door, blinking nervously from behind his spectacles.

27

"I would like to see Ursula Georgievna," he said.

I took his hat and was about to run and fetch my stepmother when father appeared.

"Ah, Herr Mitcherling," he said, "I thought you might be coming to see us — let's go into my study."

No one seemed to bother about me so I followed them in. Father kept talking.

"Many things happen which ought not to happen, but who can say what is right and what is wrong? Ursula tells me you are a good chess player. So am I. Sit down and let's have a game. She will belong to the winner."

The two men settled back in their chairs and arranged the chess board while I went out quietly. Some time later I heard the front door slam; Herr Mitcherling had left the house, leaving his wife behind. I honestly believe that if Father had lost the game he would have insisted on the man taking his wife with him. Father, in his turn, would have merely had to go to Z.A.G.S. the marriage registry, fill up a form and automatically divorce himself. Under Soviet law the presence of a second or third party is quite unnecessary. After the chess game Ursula collapsed and was in bed for two days. Even when she was well enough to get up there were frequent bouts of tears. Sometimes Ursula used to send me round to her former husband's flat to take things to her mother. Herr Mitcherling was always very kind and polite to me and he soon found himself another wife.

Ursula now controlled my life but there was always a barrier between us; a barrier that was only broken years later when I said good-bye to her in a Moscow prison before she went into exile.

CHAPTER II – THE SECRET INFORMERS CAME AT MIDNIGHT

By the late 'twenties, St. Petersburg, capital of the Czars, had settled down peacefully under its new name of Leningrad. The great city with its fine boulevards and tall buildings remained unchanged except for the Communist aristocracy ruling it. One of these was father, whose flat was one of the best in Leningrad, near the Admiralty building and the Nevsky Prospect.

Our home was one of several in a terraced building with a courtyard in the rear. Once a beautiful mansion, it had now fallen into neglect and refuse was thrown into a huge communal tank in the courtyard to be emptied only once a month. In the summer the stench was unbearable and you could never pass through without a handkerchief over your mouth.

My room had been a nursery, for its white walls were already adorned with animal pictures when we arrived. The kitchen was a big room overlooking the courtyard and painted in brown and cream. The built-in stove had water tanks giving us the luxury of a hot water supply, and after her day's work the maid would turn the kitchen into a bedroom for herself. This was really a privilege for her because most servants used to sleep in corridors, on top of baths or any other place they could find.

Father had a fine collection of books, many of them were translations from English classics, and some were covered with the skins of wolves he had shot. These wolf hunts were always a great event for father. They were organized with two sleighs; the first sleigh was drawn by two horses and carried the hunters and the second was towed along behind. On this the only passengers were a pig and a pig-sticker, a young lad whose sole job was to keep the pig squealing by poking it in the ribs with a pointed stick. In this fashion the hunt used to set off and as the sleighs ran over the thick snow the only noise heard would be the pig's squeals. The hungry wolves came out to look for the pig and as soon as they appeared the hunters picked them off with their rifles.

Father enjoyed these expeditions and used to write stories and articles about them. He had, in fact, always wanted to be a writer himself and spent as much time as he could among the revolutionary writers and poets who had by now settled down in the city where Lenin had plotted to overthrow the Czars. Cafés and restaurants had become a meeting place for Bohemians whom the new regime could not reform. In an atmosphere of tobacco smoke and vodka fumes, they met each night to talk over old times.

One of the most outstanding of the Leningrad *salon* was Sergei Yessenin, the famous young poet whose work is still among the finest examples of the gay, lyrical type of Russian poetry. Father enjoyed his company and a favourite meeting-place was in the apartment of Sergei Garin. Garin had known us in Odessa. He was now chairman of the Rabis (workers of art), the trade union for writers, artists and poets in Leningrad. His saga of Russian seamen is famous in my own country and he lived in a luxurious block of flats named after Count Tolstoy. Sometimes I used to go to see the Garins and I was always awed by the magnificent carpets and Japanese furniture which they had received from the State.

Yessenin lived in the Hôtel d'Angleterre which was just around the corner from our house. His story was a sad one. Blue-eyed, still in his twenties, he had been in love with the American Isadora Duncan, whose barefoot dancing had conquered the theatrical world of St. Petersburg in the days of the Romanovs. The young Russian's love for a woman nearly old enough to be his mother became the talk of the city. The position wasn't improved when Yessenin took her to stay as guest of Maxim Gorki in his villa at Sorrento in Italy. Gorki is said to have told Yessenin the truth. He put it bluntly.

"Young man," he said, "she is too old for you."

Russian ballet circles still talk about the dancing of Isadora. It was unique of its kind and quite different from the tradition of Diaghilev which she called "a false and artificial art."

But Yessenin never recovered from their parting. He became morose and took to drink. His poems and songs which had made him the idol of Russian youth were banned by the Soviet as romantic, sentimental corruption.

Then, one day the maid came rushing in to us and said, "Something terrible has happened in the hotel, the poet Yessenin is dead."

Mother rushed to the Garins taking me with her. Mme Garin was crying bitterly and huge tears fell down her dark, swarthy cheeks.

"Sergei phoned us at three this morning," she cried. "He wanted to come round and see us. He sounded drunk as usual and I told him to go to bed and not worry people so late at night. This morning we heard they'd found him hanging in his room.

Yessenin had first cut a vein and written a suicide note in his own blood. His body was taken to Moscow where there was a big funeral. The streets were lined with weeping women and a young woman shot herself at his graveside. Such is Russia! Admirers still keep candles burning on his grave.

At the time one of his close friends and colleagues, Vladimir Mayakovsky, criticized his suicide in the Soviet press by pointing out that it was a simple enough matter to die, living was much more difficult. A few years later Mayakovsky himself was to find out the truth of his obituary notice for he followed Yessenin to the suicide's grave, having become another disillusioned citizen of the Soviet Union.

Mayakovsky's writings supported the Revolution and I never liked them. Later at Stalingrad, I was failed in a poetry examination because I could not learn his celebrated "Passport" poem which says:

"I spit at that blue British passport and its two lions' heads, Give me the simple red passport of the glorious Soviet Union."

My childhood in Leningrad remains a vivid memory. There were so many exciting things to do, so much to see. In winter I would walk hand in hand with Father, crunching the snow underfoot on our way to the Alexandrovsky Gardens. I had a little woollen snow-cap in white and blue, knitted black leggings, skirt and jumper. In the gardens we would ski together and sometimes Father would take me for a ride in a reindeer-sleigh which slit-eyed little Eskimos used to bring to Leningrad every winter and we would drive round the park to the merry tinkling of the bells. On other occasions we would go to the public gardens and the zoo. Here they had an amusement park where the giant switchback was called the "American Mountain". Father used to love this and none of the crowd watching would guess that the tall, carefree man in his fur-collared coat, laughing like a happy schoolboy was a chief of the dreaded O.G.P.U.

Opposite the Khazan Cathedral, there was an open-air skating-rink, with a band and buffet. You put your skates on in a little wooden hut where there was a big warm stove and a bust of Karl Marx. Here too you could hire Finnish chairs, a simple wooden chair mounted on two thin strips of iron for pushing on the ice from behind. But my biggest thrill of the winter was when we went ice-sailing on the frozen Neva. Here the O.G.P.U. had their own sports club or Dynamo. It was a huge place with a swimming-pool, tennis courts, boats and sail-planes fitted with skis and a sail for racing down the frozen river.

Then, in summer, there was always the attraction of the Zarskoje Selo, former summer residence of the Imperial Russian family. Here the O.G.P.U. had taken over part of the Alexander Palace as a rest home for its staff, and father was able to take us there as guests of the State. Alexander Pushkin was

31

educated here at the Imperial Lyceum, formerly Russia's Eton College where the nobility used to send their sons. Rasputin is said to be buried nearby.

In the suburbs there used to be a gypsy market where the sellers sat on the damp black earth beaten flat by thousands of feet. In front of them lay their stock, anything from empty beer-bottles to balalaikas. Gypsy markets attract crowds of people all over Russia and any one can set up a stall. In the old days they were reserved for the gypsies, but now they are open to everyone and there you find anything too small for the government commission shops (where second-hand goods are sold on commission).

In World War II the prices rose to phenomenal heights. People were asking £240 for a bicycle and £100 for a goat. Two cups, saucers and a small teapot would fetch £10. Newspapers, too, sold for two and three roubles, six times their normal price, but wartime Russia used them for cigarette paper and smoked home-grown tobacco. There has always been a big sale of foreign fashion books such as *Vogue*, and *Harper's Bazaar*. They are rare in Russia and fetched a thousand roubles (£20) during the war. Soviet dressmakers, catering for the wives of well-to-do Soviet officials, were quite willing to pay this price in order to get news from the fashion world.

Father knew Leningrad well as he used to live here with his own family before the Revolution. It was here that we saw a great deal of his elder brother, Constantin, despite the fact that he had fought as a captain in the Imperial Guards and also under General Wrangel's command during the Revolution. Uncle Constantin was an engineer by profession, an expert on diesel engines and aeronautics on which he lectured at Leningrad University. He stayed on in Russia after the defeat of the White Army but his record always haunted him. He became an outcast in the new regime and workless. It was only father's influence that kept him from being arrested, yet despite this, he always entered into heated arguments with his younger brother whenever he came to see us. He regarded father's atheism and Communism with horror and he remained a firm Royalist and devout Christian right till the end.

Every year father used to get six weeks' holiday. We always went in an official chauffeur-driven car, and one summer we returned to the Crimea. At the Black Sea resort of Eupatoria I had been sent to bed early and my crying attracted the attention of the one of the guests in the next room. She came in to see me, asked where I came from and when I told her she said she lived in the same street. She was returning the next day and she promised to write to me, and in a few days' time I felt very important to receive a postcard all to myself. It was the first time anyone had written to me and it brought an invitation to call on the lady when I returned to Leningrad.

She had also written to my father and it was arranged for me to accept. That first visit to Mme B. was the first of many. She was the wife of a doctor. Mme B. was the mother of two daughters but they were both married and she treated me as her own little girl. I used to visit her very often for tea after the first visit and her husband used to help me with my arithmetic. After knowing her for two years Mme B. drew me aside as I was about to leave.

"I'm going to trust you, Nora, with a great secret."

She took me into her bedroom, unlocked a drawer, and brought out a long linen envelope.

Inside were a number of thick pieces of paper in various colours and with strange writing on them.

"Do you know what this is?"

"It looks like money."

"Yes, but it's not Russian money, it's *valuta*."

I knew at once what Mme B. meant. At this time it was a capital offence in the Soviet Union to possess foreign currency, in Russian *valuta*. The O.G.P.U. were combing the whole of the Soviet Union to hunt out valuta owners in a desperate attempt to obtain as much foreign currency as they could. Even as a child I knew of the tortures of the Parilka, the Russian "Black Hole of Calcutta" where men and women were kept standing upright, wedged together in a sweating mass in an attempt to prise from them the secret of their hidden hoards.

I looked at Mme B. and there were tears in her eyes.

"You must help me, Nora," she said. "I believe someone has told your father that we have this money; if we burnt it they still have proof of how we obtained it.

"We wanted to send one of my daughters abroad but now it is impossible. Our only hope is to confess everything and offer the money to the State. Will you do that for us, Nora?"

"Do what?" I asked, not understanding.

"There's £25,000 here; take it to your father."

Mme B. wrote a note and sealed the envelope. She put it in my hand and kissed me.

"Our lives are in your hands," she said.

That night I went straight to father when he came in.

"Papochka," I said, "will you promise me something?"

"That depends," he answered. "What is it?"

"Promise me if I give you something no harm will come to the B.s?"

Father took the envelope, opened it and went very pale. He left the room and I ran after him clutching his arm.

"Don't hurt them," I pleaded, "Please don't hurt them."

Father grabbed his coat and went off into the night. He never spoke about the incident again but the next time I saw Mme B. she gave me a copy of *David Copperfield*.

"This is for you, Nora," she said, "I will always be grateful to you."

And then she told me my father had reported the incident to Moscow and persuaded them not to take any further action. He did more than that, he arranged for her to be paid a reward of three thousand roubles for her patriotism.

Father's main job, as deputy head of the counter-espionage, was to obtain information of any unrest or plots being hatched against the new regime. To do this, he built up a spy network of all nationalities, working in all countries. Some of his chief informers were themselves White Russians ready to betray their comrades for a handful of Red roubles. He also had a Buddhist priest on his payroll. These people were called *seksots*, secret informers. They came to see my father at all hours of the day and night and often I used to open the door to them. The important ones called after midnight when I was in bed and I used to lie awake listening to the murmur of voices in the next room. Sometimes it was dawn before I heard the door shut and I heard Father walk slowly to his room.

Among Father's visitors was Mrs. W. an Englishwoman, married to a Russian who was employed to give secret information to my father. Mrs. W.'s activities did not stop in Russia. As one of Father's agents she often visited her own country and I recall opening the door to her once when she brought a sheaf of English newspapers with her. She had to translate them for Father, but when I heard him talking about her visit later it was quite clear that she had brought him London newspaper accounts of the British police raid on Arcos in May 1927. Arcos, of course, had originally been established as a Soviet trading agency in London, but the fact that my father, deputy chief of counter-espionage, had dealings with them is sufficient proof that the British were justified in closing it down for subversive activities. It would appear that Father's O.G.P.U. agents used Arcos to cover their movements while they were in England.

I have proof of this for I remember two more of his informants very well. One was Captain X, skipper of an Arcos cargo-ship travelling between

Leningrad and London docks. He used to take both cargo and passengers for Arcos to handle and as the latter's trips were fixed by Father, there was no doubt they were more than the ordinary trading officials which their passports said they were. The captain would come every six weeks to report. He always brought me a tin of English cocoa or some chocolate.

The other secret agent was a very different person from the rough, genial sea-captain. She was tall with high cheek-bones and long blonde hair, a traditional Russian beauty. She came every fortnight normally, but often she was away for long periods. When she came back she was reporting from abroad. I knew this because she used to bring me albums filled with foreign post-cards, many of them English, decorated with silk and velvet. I had never seen anything like them in my life and used to keep them by my bedside.

Soviet citizens would not have been allowed to associate with a person like the princess, who, by reason of her aristocratic background, would be considered an enemy of the people. Obviously, the O.G.P.U. had some hold over her. In return for her reports, father protected her from the fate which had overtaken so many White Russians. Father was such a trusted member of the Party that he was allowed to associate with international spies of her calibre without being in any fear of being tainted by the capitalist ideology. He had other privileges, too, forbidden the ordinary people of Russia. Our flat had a radio and a grand piano, all confiscated property, and father used to bring home banned records by the White Russians, Peter Leschenko and Alexandre Wertinsky. These singers made records of Russian sentimental songs which had been banned in the new Russia because of their sentiment and romance. The traditional Russian nostalgia of Czarist days had no place under the Soviets, they regarded it as useless frivolity.

Father also had access to forbidden anti-Communist propaganda. One day in his study drawer, next to the one where he kept his revolvers, I found a newspaper which frightened me. It was called *Sevodnya* (Today) printed in Riga by the White Russians. The contents were violently anti-Soviet. I became so afraid when I read it that I put it back and never told my father. A few days later I saw him burning some papers in the grate. Curling up in the flames was the copy of the dangerous *Sevodnya*.

In spite of the official sternness of the Soviet officials, life was not always drab for the privileged few. Sometimes members of Father's staff used to come to parties in our flat and the O.G.P.U. had first claim on everything. Father took advantage of few of these privileges. At heart he was an ascetic Communist, and refused to exploit his position. I was always the worst-dressed girl at school because he felt that an O.G.P.U. chief was one of the hard core of men who should set an example to the rest of Russia. He refused to allow his daughter to be better dressed than any other Soviet citizen. When he had to entertain on an official level, it was different. It was expected of my parents they should entertain elaborately in accordance with father's rank; and the O.G.P.U. paid.

On party nights waiters came from the Hotel Astoria carrying hampers of caviar, smoked salmon, chicken and other delicacies. There were crates of vodka and champagne, all served on china, glass and silverware still bearing the crest of the Romanovs. The parties were very Russian, everyone talking, drinking and singing till dawn. Many of the Czar's glasses were broken as people threw them over their shoulders in a real Russian frenzy.

If the party ever looked like becoming slow everyone would pile into black O.G.P.U. cars and tear through the streets firing their revolvers into the air or shooting at stray cats. One of the most frequent party-goers was my father's chief, Philip Demjanovich Medved, the Bear, head of the Leningrad O.G.P.U. Often when the party was starting my father would say, "Go and open the door to Comrade Medved." This always frightened me as Medved was like an ape, stubby fingers covered with long red hairs, a shock of red hair and beard to match. He always wore a long, brown leather coat with a Mauser in his belt. I used to shudder when he put his hairy arms around me and said in a deep voice, "Hullo, Norochka."

He was the life and soul of the parties. I often tip-toed out of bed to hear his great roar of laughter resounding through the rooms. Sometimes I would hear people clapping with delight when Medved, very drunk, took off his black jack-boots and drank champagne out of them. Medved was the real ruler of Leningrad. With my father as his assistant he had to protect the leaders of the Communist Party in the city. Chief of these was Sergei Kirov, Secretary of the Leningrad Party Committee, a member of the Politburo and a great friend of Stalin. He was far too big a man to come to our parties but I met him several times on official occasions and when father took me to his office.

He was a man as stiff as a ramrod, with greying hair brushed back. He wore a black, three-quarter length coat with a peaked cap. It was the uniform of a typical revolutionary.

The danger to these people, even years after the Revolution, was very real. One winter's night conspirators planted a bomb in the Communist club of the Moika. It was timed to explode when Kirov and other leaders would be present, but they were late and escaped. Even so, many leading Leningrad Communists were killed and twelve suspects were arrested. One of the interrogators of these men was my father. I was present when they were brought up for trial in the Leningrad court, twelve men, pale and almost uninterested who listened to a long list of their confessions read out by the Public Prosecutor.

But at that time I had no idea of the methods used by secret police interrogators to obtain these public admissions of guilt. Russian court procedure is very different from the Western system. In the Soviet, no one appears before a judge until he has been interrogated and found guilty by the police. The court appearance is a pure formality for punishment. The drunken O.G.P.U. parties still continued in Leningrad. But some years later they resulted in a tragedy which nearly involved my father.

On the evening of 1st December, 1934, after we had moved to Stalingrad, father came home with tears in his eyes. I had never seen him so moved. It was some moments before he could speak. Then he said, "Kirov has been shot. I knew it would happen if that drunken Medved was allowed to remain looking after him. He was far too careless."

Father went to his study and shut the door. He did not come out until the next day when the morning papers were full of the assassination. At breakfast all he said was "Someone will pay for this."

None of us at that time had any idea what was to follow the murder. Kirov had been shot by a young Communist, Nicolayev. The next day a special train left the Kremlin for Leningrad. It contained Stalin and Voroshilov. They went immediately to the Chekist Headquarters where Nicolayev was being held for questioning. Stalin's anger — terrible as it was — was not directed so much against the assassin as against the O.G.P.U. men who had allowed the murder to take place. Many of them were shot on Stalin's order. Father would have been executed with them if he had not, by a fortunate chance, been posted from Medved's command. By some miracle, Medved escaped with his life. He was sent into exile in Siberia where he became commandant of a camp for slave-workers.

All the guests at our parties were either shot or exiled. Stalin personally attended the interrogation of Nicolayev. Later, he used the assassination as an excuse for one of the most terrible purges ever carried out in the Soviet Union. Every day we read names of people we had known in Leningrad published in the newspapers. They, and hundreds more, were banished or shot for their alleged share in Kirov's murder. The purge engulfed the whole of Russia. Thousands of innocent people were punished ruthlessly — only a small percentage could have been anti-Stalin. There was no doubt Kirov's death was a great personal blow to Stalin. They had been comrades and friends since the earliest days of the Revolution. Stalin himself marched in procession through the streets of Leningrad beside the coffin.

After the funeral, Stalin ordered that the name of the Opera House in Leningrad should be changed to the Kirov Opera House, and the biggest factory in the city was renamed Kirov Works.

CHAPTER III – LADY ASTOR'S BOLSHEVIK

It was in Leningrad that my schooldays began. On 1 September, 1928, father took me to school 57, opposite St. Isaacs' Cathedral. I took with me a brown leather satchel, pencil-box and exercise books and I felt very superior as I should really have been at school a year earlier, but Father's position had enabled him to engage governesses and this qualified me for the second class.

In Russia, children up to the age of eight attend kindergarten and junior school. And Communism enters their lives with the alphabet; each letter standing for a principle of the Communist State and in English the equivalent would be — "A" stands for the assassination of Alexander II, "B" for Bolshevik, "C" for Communist, "D" for December Revolution and so on. In the next stage words employing all the vowels and consonants are brought into the lessons and written on the blackboard by the teacher. Each word is a subtle step forward in Soviet propaganda... We are all equal," "Everyone works for the State," "No one is poor."

And every Russian child soon knows the dates of the birth of Lenin, Stalin, the October Revolution and other landmarks in Soviet history... not because he is taught them direct but because the system of education is to teach numbers and dates by interesting the children in actual numbers and dates relating to the Communist State. As soon as the child is old enough he is given short talks on the principles of Sovietization, the collectivization of the farm lands and the growth of Communism throughout the world. But education proper begins at eight years old and each child has ten years' education, spending a year in each class.

At eighteen, pupils matriculate and are ready to pass on to universities. But this depends on your ability to pass all of the yearly examinations and it is considered a terrible disgrace to fail, for this means spending another year in the same class.

School 57 was a former Czarist ministry with big windows like a palace. It was a very nervous little girl who trotted beside her father on that dull autumn morning, past the two stone lions at the entrance and on to the second floor. Huge pictures of Marx and Lenin frowned down on us and then suddenly I found we had stopped. A tall, friendly woman in a blue smock with a neat white collar was talking to father.

"Good morning, Citizeness," he said, "I have brought my daughter."

The teacher smiled and turned to me.

"And what is your name, young lady?"

"Nora."

"That's an uncommon name for a little Russian girl."

"Yes, I was named after a play."

"And a very good play, too," said the teacher.

It seemed that she shared father's admiration for Ibsen.

The teacher took my hand and opened the door into the classroom. We were friends at once and I didn't even notice father's departure. Inside there were thirty-five other boys and girls of my own age sitting two to a desk. I was placed beside Irene Eleesiev. Her father had been a wealthy china-merchant with a chain of shops in the old city. Irene was very anxious not to talk about her background for the Russian Revolution had written off such men as her father as bourgeois renegades. It was indeed a tremendous handicap for a child to be born of even middle-class parents. Everyone except the wage-earners and peasants were lumped together as undesirables; only exceptions were writers, musicians and artists of the ballet. Irene's background haunted her and in later life she took the step so many Russian children have taken. She renounced her parents.

It used to be quite common to read in the official Soviet newspapers a formal notice similar to that of a husband refusing to pay his wife's debts. Only in this case it would be a teen-age child telling the world it was renouncing its parents. In any people's court or factory enquiry into the political beliefs of any Soviet citizen, one of the first points made by the accusers is an attack on the parental background of the accused. And to be denounced as the child of a capitalist means instant banishment from the Party with little hope of employment in the state. Irene's anxiety therefore was quite understandable.

Every morning, when our teacher entered we would all get up and chorus, "Good-morning, Antonina Ivanovna," and back would come her response, "Good-morning, children of the Soviet Union."

I was taught to sing the *Internationale*, the *Marseillaise* and other revolutionary songs. We had organized games and Swedish exercises in the gymnasium. Political education took the form of subtle references in our school-books to the wonders of the Soviet Union and the outmoded capitalism of the rest of the world. But as the first generation of the Revolution, the Communist education authorities had not yet made up their minds how best to instil the Marxist doctrine. They were always trying out and discarding new systems, among them the Dalton system from Britain which called for communal work and communal answers from small groups of students as opposed to the system of individual initiative.

Irene's parents had fled to Paris and she was living with her grandparents. Through her I began to know something of Czarist Russia for the first time. For Irene loaned me books her mother had given her. Of course, the books were banned in Soviet Russia but that did not stop my enjoyment of the writings of Lydia Charskaya, a popular writer for children of the Czarist era. Her girls' books told of life in the finishing schools of the Institutes of Noble Maidens, where every girl had to be approved by the Empress before being allowed to enter.

One night father caught me reading one of her stories "Nina — Princess Dzhavacha of Caucasia," the very title was enough to make him angry.

"What can I do with a daughter reading such rubbish?" he raved. "Give it to me at once."

And he threw it on the fire. He then made me promise I would never read any other books that hadn't the approval of the new Russia. I told him I would do as he wished but I still found the stories of old Russia much more romantic to a young girl than the grim, factual anecdotes approved by the Soviet Union. Even so, the world of the Institutes of Noble Maidens remained very remote.

Soviet children are expected to join the Communist youth organizations as soon as they can read and write. These are the Octoberites, Pioneers and Komsomol from which teen-agers graduate to the Party itself. Every factory, office and state department has its youth club branch of one of these organizations. I used to get taken to the Octoberites club run by the O.G.P.U. in Leningrad where as a little girl I would be taught to play games through all of which ran a strong theme of Communist ideology. After going to school I joined the Pioneers but not with much enthusiasm. But at school membership of the Pioneers automatically placed you above your schoolfellows. Each Pioneer takes an oath not to disclose what takes place at their meetings and after taking this oath I received my red tie. We had our own club house — the dilapidated mansion of a former nobleman — decorated with red banner slogans and portraits of party leaders. Every meeting began with a trumpet call at which boys and girls would parade like toy soldiers. Then the leader would enter and shout, "Be ready, Pioneers."

He gave the clenched fist salute of the Communist Party and then we all used to do the same, shouting back, "Always ready."

The meetings were dull stuff. They had none of the instruction or interest found in the Girl Guides or the Boy Scouts Organization in Western Europe. They remained what they set out to be, a form of political instruction for Soviet Youth and on which Hitler was later to base his own Youth Party.

41

Another of my school-friends was Alica, the daughter of a factory worker. Alica had no fear of renouncing her parents for they were true members of the proletariat. They shared a communal kitchen and her mother had to work as a seamstress to make up the family income. Food was still scarce at this time but we were in a privileged position as we were able to buy from the O.G.P.U. store. This was stocked with all the staple foods while its shelves were also lined with all the seized contraband goods handed in by the customs men and I soon found out how to help Alica and her family. Whenever I was sent to the store on my own I had only to show father's card to the sentry on duty and I was then allowed to buy anything I wanted. So I asked Alica to give me some money from her mother and I was able to buy the family as much food as they could afford. I used to go to most of the entertainments in Leningrad with my parents or the servants. The N.K.V.D. were the censors of all films and plays and, of course, we always had the best seats. At the Kirov State Opera House, formerly the Marinsky Imperial Opera House, I had my first introduction to fine music, ballet and the opera. At the Tuz — Theatre for Young Spectators — I saw the *Adventures of Tom Sawyer*, *Huckleberry Finn, Don Quixote* and *Robinson Crusoe*.

It was in Leningrad, too, that I saw the first Russian talkie, "Ticket in Life," a heart-rending account of the ordeals of the children during the Revolution. Naturally, there was a fitting moral showing how the new regime had turned them into useful citizens, but the novelty of this first Russian talking picture gave Leningrad something to talk about for months. In those days it was still possible to see foreign films, for the Kremlin had not yet imposed its iron censorship and Russian audiences enjoyed Douglas Fairbanks, Mary Pickford, Dietrich, Harold Lloyd, Chaplin and other stars of the silent screen. Among the films I saw were "Bluebird", "Earth in Captivity", and "Kirpichiki" which was later banned. We also had a good selection of dance records at home including such hits of the twenties as "Ramona", "Valencia" and the inevitable "Charleston" which we played at our parties. Father was a great dancer and it was always my honour to have the first dance with him. But there was one song never heard in our home and that was "Bublichki", a song of the White Russians. It was a strident, attractive tune and although it was banned, you would often hear snatches of its refrain whistled or hummed unconsciously by passers-by in the street.

As the daughter of a good Communist I had never been inside a church, though many of the museums I visited had been places of worship prior to the Revolution. I had vaguely heard of God and his son Jesus Christ and once, greatly daring, I asked father who they were.

42

"Just characters from capitalistic fairy tales," he told me. "People who believe in them are called Christians, but the only Christians left in your country now, Norochka, are silly old fools who will never know any better."

At that time I accepted everything father told me without question, but I noticed Olga, our maid, always wore a little cross beneath her blouse. She was a plump and jolly peasant girl who had been with us for ten years and one day I asked her what it was. The girl blushed and at once tried to hide it, saying "Oh, just a cross, Nora; my mother gave it to me when I left home."

I danced around teasing and holding out my hand.

"Come along," I cried, "let me see it or I shall tell Father."

To keep me quiet she finally slipped the cross and chain over her head for me to look at.

"We village folk treasure little trinkets like this," she said. "But promise me you won't tell your father I have shown it to you?"

"But what is it, Olga?" I asked. "What does it mean?"

Olga refused to talk about it any more but when we were walking along the Nevsky Prospect later in the week she asked me if I would like to go with her to the Khazan Cathedral — one of the few churches the Communists had allowed to remain open.

It was a great adventure for me when we went inside for Russian and Greek Orthodox churches have no pews and the nave of the cathedral was packed. The congregation were of all types but most of them elderly. Shawled women stood shoulder to shoulder with fur-collared men. They stared straight ahead with moistened lips and bright eyes. Their quiet hush awed me. I had never seen such beauty and colour before and standing on tiptoe I was able to see the floodlit altar at the far end. The officiating *batushka* was Father Nicholai, a benevolent, bearded figure in multi-colour vestments with a kind, understanding face; not at all the type of person I had been brought up to expect in the priesthood. The cathedral was heavy with incense. The congregation then began to join in the responses and from time to time, I noticed the men and women around me bow their foreheads and cross themselves during the mass.

"*Gospodi Pomilui... Gospodi Pomilui*," intoned the bearded *batushka*, "Lord have mercy on us."

Then suddenly Olga and the rest of the congregation dropped to their knees. But I remained standing, alone and uncomfortable, not knowing what to do. I began to get frightened and to wonder what would happen to me if Father found out. It was late and I knew I would have to explain my absence. When the service was over Olga begged me not to tell him she had taken me

43

to church; she was terrified he would dismiss her. I promised to say nothing, we separated and each of us made our own way home.

Father was waiting for me and I told him I had been learning a lesson with a school-friend. This was, of course, a part-truth though I had in reality learned a much bigger lesson than I realized at the time. My first visit to church did not make me a Christian, but it left a deep impression and the next time my grandmother brought out her ikon, hiding it so that father wouldn't throw it on the fire again, I felt I was sharing her Secret.

But she would never dream of discussing Christianity with me; she had tried once but father had discovered her and made her promise never to tell me religious stories again. The Christian festivals of Christmas or Easter were never celebrated in our home, only the New Year. But once father accepted a Christmas Party invitation to join some neighbours.

The Petrovs were a very hospitable couple and their party was very Russian. It went on for two days and three nights and the feasting rivalled an imperial banquet. There was a Christmas tree with coloured lights and the Star of Bethlehem above, and even the atheist Communists joined in the shouts of *"S Rozhdestvom Christovim…* Christ is born… Merry Christmas."

Our host was an artist and somehow he had managed to accumulate a wonderful collection of food and drink, roast sucking-pig, jars of caviar, eels, smoked salmon and *Sauerkraut*. Most of the time I was asleep in an armchair but father's energy never wilted. He was always the hit of any party. Midway through Mme Petrov collapsed and mother, who drank little, took over the duties of hostess.

But parties were dangerous things in Soviet Russia. You never knew when some indiscreet remark might not be reported back to the secret police. The story of Vera Michalova, accountant to the Leningrad Port and former wife of a Soviet consul in China, illustrates this. Vera had struck up an acquaintance with our maid Olga and when Olga called one evening at Vera's house she found an hilarious party in progress in which she joined. Two weeks later Olga was summoned to the N.K.V.D. Headquarters where she was closely questioned about her friend. Vera was by then under arrest for it appeared a disappointed suitor had told the N.K.V.D. that she had proposed a toast to the banished Trotsky at the party Olga attended.

Olga could neither read nor write and had never heard of Trotsky, but she had to report weekly for ten months to be interrogated. Finally, no action was taken against her, but Vera served two years in Leningrad's Kresti prison. Then she was released and the N.K.V.D. apologized for their mistake— a rare thing for the secret police. She returned to her old post a broken and embittered woman, her beauty drained from her in a prison cell. Such is the power of an informer in the Soviet Union.

In the autumn of 1926 — Leningrad buzzed with excitement. An English family had arrived to live as Soviet citizens. They were James Morton, a steel worker from Bootle, in Lancashire, his wife Rose and his two children, Mary and Alan.

The Mortons were Communists and they had accepted an offer from Lady Astor to pay their fares to Russia, provided they lived as ordinary working-class people and stayed among us for two years. Lady Astor had made this offer as a result of a dispute at a political meeting when Morton had alleged that people lived better in Russia than they did in England. The British Press called James Morton "Lady Astor's Bolshevik". He had agreed that if at the end of two years he wanted to return home he would bring his family back at his own expense.

Alan was placed next to me at school. He was a strange, quiet little fellow at first, until he picked up the language. Then he was a terror! He used to tease me and pull my pigtails, but I didn't mind that. For in return he told me tales of the England they had left behind. He told me of good homes, clothes and food, a life free of O.G.P.U. spies. These stories to a little Russian girl like me were like a fairy tale. He was old enough to understand what had happened and he told me that his father, an active Communist, had heckled Lady Astor so persistently at a public meeting in Liverpool that she had replied: "Why don't you go to Russia? I'll pay your fare." His father had accepted her offer on the spot.

When James Morton came to Leningrad he was thirty-eight and was given a job in the great Putilov steel works as a moulder. On arrival he was interviewed by the official Soviet press and articles appeared under big headlines in which he paid tribute to Communist Russia, saying that it was a much better place to live in than England. Later, even his two children, Mary and Alan, were enlisted for propaganda purposes.

Articles appeared under their names in the Soviet newspapers. In one of these Alan said how much better Russian schools were than English ones. Although he was only twelve at the time he paid tribute to Russia in the article, saying that he was learning music and German — which he had never learned in England — and the food and standard of living was much higher than in his own country. He also added in the article that he liked Russian schools because in England they caned him when he came to school late. They never did this in Russia.

45

I was puzzled by these articles, as I sat at the next desk to Alan in school and the account he had given me of England was very different from the one which appeared in print. When I showed him the newspaper and explained it to him he was amazed — it was the first he knew of it.

The English family were accommodated in the Hotel Astoria at the expense of the Soviet Government while a home was found for them. Mary and Alan, when they first arrived, were the best-dressed children in the whole of Leningrad. People used to point to them in the street saying: "Look, there are the English children — see how well-dressed they are. Things can't be so bad in capitalist Britain."

Their father was very enthusiastic about the Soviet Union and made his two children join the Octoberites (the infants' political movement). And later on they became members of the Young Communist League.

Before their father's two-year stay in Russia was up a tragedy overtook the family. James Morton died of an incurable disease. The Soviet Government even viewed this with suspicion. They took great trouble to announce in the newspapers that his illness was in no way caused by his life in Communist Russia. Copies of his death certificate appeared in the press, saying that he had been ill for years before leaving England. Copies of the death certificate, signed by Soviet doctors, were also sent to the Foreign Office in London.

The last time I saw the Mortons was in May 1941, shortly before I left Russia. They were still living in Leningrad but they were very different people from the happy family which arrived from Liverpool on that September day fifteen years before.

Alan, now aged twenty-two, had not benefited very much by the "improved" education which he was once supposed to have boosted in the Soviet press. The only job he could obtain upon leaving school was as a guide-interpreter for the Russian Intourist Organization, catering for official foreign visitors. Alan was still living with his mother and Mary, two years older, was teaching English at Leningrad University on a small salary. She was married, with a son, and her husband, a Russian officer was, I heard later, killed during the defence of Leningrad against the Germans.

It was shortly after this that I met Alan, who hailed me from a car in a Leningrad Street. At first I did not recognize this young man who addressed me in Russian.

"It's me, it's Alan Morton," he said. How are you, Norochka? Do come and see my mother. It will cheer her up."

I went with him to the four-roomed flat at No. 4, Dzerzhinsky Street where they had lived ever since they left the Astoria Hotel. I had remembered the comfortable, well-furnished home they had, but now it was bare and unfurnished. There were empty shelves and blank spaces on the walls where pictures had once hung. They must have been selling their valuables to live.

Mrs. Morton burst into tears when she saw me. Although she was only fifty, she was ill and drawn, an old woman before her time.

She gestured towards the bare walls and sobbed: "Look what they have done to me. I have been dismissed from the Party. My job has been taken from me and everything is lost. No one comes near me any more. No one will speak to me — I have no friends." Then dabbing her eyes, she told me her story.

After her husband's death she had been given a job in the steel plant, receiving in addition to her earnings a pension of £2 10s.0d. a week.

The regular purges in the factory by the N.K.V.D. on their usual mission to hunt out enemies of the state had passed her by. She had been a good timekeeper and had given no trouble to the foreman. For timekeeping is an important factor in Soviet factory life. When a worker is ten minutes late through his own fault, he gets reprimanded by a factory official and his name is posted all over the factory by way of punishment. If he is late again within a month he is given a similar punishment and the third time he must appear before a people's court. Unless he has a good excuse he is automatically sentenced to have his wages cut by as much as thirty per cent. Every day a check is made on absentees in Soviet factories and the unions send someone to their homes immediately. This strict time keeping produces few late comers in Soviet factories and Mrs. Morton made a special point of saying, "I was never late."

"Ah, then," I said "perhaps your production figures were down?"

For I knew enough of the Soviet factory system to know their speed-up methods which rely on workers having to equal or surpass picked men and women specially chosen for their speed on the job. This campaign for increased productivity runs through the whole of Soviet industry. It is called Stakhanovism, a system of production efficiency introduced and named after a miner who had broken all records by digging over one hundred tons of coal in one shift. The slogan, "Anything he can do, you can do too" was at once adopted in every branch of Soviet industry and picked Stakhanovites were placed in every tool shop, mine and production chain.

"No," she said, "It was nothing like that."

"What has happened then? Tell me," I cried.

47

Mrs. Morton smiled, looked across at a picture of her husband in the clothes of a Russian workman which stood on the mantelpiece.

"You remember, Jim, my husband? You know why we came here? Can you believe that I, his widow, should want to go around spying in Russia and reporting back to the British Intelligence?"

"You — a spy! What nonsense! But how could they believe such a thing?"

Mrs. Morton shook her head sadly. "I just don't know, Nora. I just don't know... but it's happened. One day I got a summons to appear before a people's court at the factory and there I found three of my workmates waiting to testify that I was a traitor.

"I ask you — do I look like a spy? I haven't spoken to more than half a dozen English people since I came to Russia."

"But they must have had details, surely they had some evidence, some proof?"

"Proof! What is that?" she answered. "It was a pack of nonsense from start to finish — no facts, no details... just wild accusations. When they saw they were making fools of themselves they changed their tune and satisfied themselves by saying I was anti-Communist and an enemy of the people — whatever that might mean.

"I could find no one to speak for me and finally, after three hours' talk, they found me guilty and asked for my membership card of the party. That meant, of course, that I lost my job. I've nothing left but my pension."

When she finished this broken-hearted recital I tried to cheer her up by saying that perhaps she would be reinstated one day, but she knew, as I did, they were just empty words. As she led me to the door, she put her hand on my shoulder and said: "You see in me, Nora, a broken woman. If Lady Astor could see us now she would know that she had had the last laugh. At least she was right about Russia.

"I wish with all my heart that we had never come — Oh, how I wish we were back in Bootle! "

I never saw the Mortons again in Russia, but I heard news of them from time to time. Alan joined the Red Army and fought bravely under Marshal Timoshenko on the Moscow front, where he was killed. Mrs. Morton, her daughter and grandson, were captured by the Germans in the Leningrad suburbs during the twenty-nine months' siege of the city. They were sent, with hundreds of other Russian civilians, to a slave camp behind the Nazi lines. Towards the end of the war the Americans freed them and they asked to be repatriated to England.

CHAPTER IV – THE O.G.P.U. WAS MY FATHER

It was not until we left, in the summer of 1932, for Smolensk — the capital of the Western Region of Soviet Russia — that I realized the full power of the O.G.P.U. And the man who held it was my father.

Before then I had accepted everything with a child's lack of curiosity but an incident happened shortly after our arrival in Smolensk which made me realize the sinister import of my father's work. Father was transferred from Leningrad to be chief of a special department of the O.G.P.U. in Smolensk. Here for the first time I had a practical experience of the spy mania, and terrorism which riddles Soviet Russia. I realized that my father was one of the men who had built it up. And it had gripped him too.

I mentioned to a girl-friend and her brother, Yasha, about the forbidden records of the White Russians, Peter Leschenko and Alexandre Wertinsky. They were very excited and asked me if I would let them hear them. The three of us went to our house when everyone was out, locked ourselves in a room, and for half an hour played the banned gramophone records.

Some weeks later my girl-friend came to see me. She was in tears and said: "They've taken Yasha."

I did not understand when she said he had been arrested by the secret police and sent to a concentration camp. My father never welcomed any enquiries about his O.G.P.U. activities' work from his family, but I was determined to ask him about Yasha.

When I did, he thumped the table and shouted: "You silly little girl, you don't understand!

"I am an O.G.P.U. official and no one must enter this house without my permission. Anything might have happened when you brought this fellow here. He might have been in a plot to kill me.

"I have definite proof that he is an enemy of the State and only came here to pretend to listen to the gramophone. If I had come home he would have shot me. You will never hear from him again."

I was so frightened by father's rage that I never dared mention Yasha again. Yet I am still convinced that Yasha was as innocent as I was, and that his imprisonment was a result of the hysterical spy mania which gripped all the high officials of Russia. Father's position made him suspect everyone. All our servants were carefully screened by the secret police before they worked for us. He never went to bed without searching the whole house, gun in hand. For these nightly manhunts, in his own home, he was never alone.

At his side there was always our Alsatian police-dog, Admiral. One night I woke up to hear shouting in the hall and the noise of shots. I rushed from my room terrified to find father standing at the top of the cellar steps with a gun in his hand. Beside him stood men with their hands up and a third had tumbled down the cellar steps, shot. Father kept the men covered and called me to ring the O.G.P.U. Headquarters. The men stood there cowed and silent and after the guards had come and taken them away father told me he had found them hiding in the cellar. The O.G.P.U. investigation that followed disclosed that our cook had joined in a plot to kill her employer and had secretly let the men into the house and hidden them in the cellar during the daytime. She joined the two conspirators in front of the firing squad.

I was thirteen years of age when I arrived in Smolensk and we stayed there two years. I passed through classes 6 and 7 at school and it was here that I noticed for the first time how cleverly Communist propaganda was being introduced into our school lessons.

All our school books carried the same theme: Russia was the only free country in the world and everywhere else was slavery.

There was nothing very light-hearted about our text-books. Arithmetic lessons would deal with problems based on the running of the Communist state. If Ivan could make three tractor parts in two weeks working eight hours a day, how long will it take Yura to complete the same tractor parts if he is sick and can only work six hours a day?

And even the simplest stories in Soviet text-books centre around war, spies and communist doctrines. Here is the story of "a brave girl" taken from an official book on English:

"Lena lives in Belgrade. Her father is a communist, and the police watch him strictly. Once Lena was returning home from school. It was about twelve o'clock. Suddenly she saw her father on the other side of the street. A stranger was following him. Lena understood at once that the man was a spy. "How could she tell her father about the spy? Maybe her father had some secret documents on him. Lena crossed the road and said loudly:

"'Daddy, give me some money for the tram,' and quite softly she added 'Father, be careful, a spy is after you.'

"Lena's father gave her some money, and quickly disappeared round the corner.

"Very often party meetings take place in the house of Lena's father. The police try to find out where the workers have their meetings. When the workers have such meetings, Lena has to stay in the street and tell the workers when the police come. The girl sits on the steps pretending to play.

"Whenever she sees a stranger who may be a spy, she runs to the house and tells the workers about the danger.

"In the evening Lena and her friends go about Belgrade with communist leaflets and try to put them up in places where everybody can see and read them."

A more advanced lesson has this to say to the children of the Soviet Union: "In our country the right to work is ensured by the Stalin constitution and the worker has no fear of the morrow. The young people who have grown up since the Revolution know only from books what a factory owner, a banker or a *police official* is! (the italics are mine). The U.S.S.R. is the land with the shortest working day in the world."

The same book prints this poem by V. Lebedev-Kumach beneath a sky filled with 'planes:

> "If tomorrow is war,
> If tomorrow we fight,
> If the enemy dares an offensive,
> All the Land of Soviets
> As one man will arise,
> Swift and merciless on the defensive."

Great stuff for nine-year-olds!

Other story titles are "Marusya Captures a Spy" and "The Heroine from Oviedo".

The Soviet's attitude to English and American authors whose work they reproduce in official books for State schools may be of interest.

A government school-book containing selections from English and American literature says this of Oscar Wilde — "though an aesthetic, Oscar Wilde sometimes introduces social motives in his work. Thus we have the problem of social inequality in all of the above tales (i.e. "The Happy Prince", "The Nightingale and the Rose" and "The Devoted Friend"). Of the latter, the Soviet says Wilde shows the exploitation of the poor by the rich who pretend to be doing things for others while they have nothing but their own interest in view — "this tale is a satire on bourgeois life, the greedy, hypocritical, selfish miller being a typical representative of the parasitical class." I wonder what Wilde would have to say about that!

Nor does America escape and whenever the Soviet education authorities can, their English lessons include stories of racial Disturbances.

But of course they have no faults to find with Shelley, "a representative of revolutionary romanticism in England ... a Utopian socialist... his revolutionism bears a somewhat abstract character in his earlier poems."

The Soviet teaches that Shelley's poetry protests against tyranny and oppression, "he rebels against social injustice and expresses his militant love of humanity that he likes to represent as regenerated, free and happy, with socialism in place of capitalist slavery."

I'm sure this version will be a surprise to many of Shelley's admirers!

H. G. Wells, always called Herbert Wells in the Soviet, which he visited and there saw Stalin, is referred to as pessimistic, "like the work of so many other capitalist writers".

Sheridan's *School for Scandal*, often produced in Russia, is distinguished in Soviet eyes as an exposure of the "mercantile basis of bourgeois marriage".

And here are some biographical notes published about Dickens, a great favourite in the Soviet Union.

"Dickens came of a petty bourgeois family. His father was ruined when Charles was a little boy. He had to go through many hardships while his father was in a debtors' prison and learned at an early age what capitalist exploitation was like. His early life was one of want and poverty.

"Though an original observer, Dickens does not offer a very wide range of social portraits, ignoring the army, the fleet, parliament and the industrial world except in his *Hard Times* where he does not give us a typical representative of the proletarian class in Stephen.

"His attitude is negative, not only towards the bourgeoisie but towards the landed aristocracy as well. Dickens is a philanthropist. His art sometimes reveals a criticism of the capitalist system more far-reaching than he had originally intended.

"Among the portrait gallery of his capitalists we have the unforgettable Mr. Pecksniff, Mr. Bounderby and Mr. Dombey.

"His humour has definite social functions, that of smoothing down class contradictions and removing or softening his bitter criticism of the cruelty and hypocrisy of bourgeois society."

Such are the things taught to Soviet children about the writers of the Western world.

In recent years Soviet education has become a very strict and serious business. The People's Commissar for Education has laid down official rules of conduct and these are now strictly observed. The order says the first duty of school children is to obey commands by their head teacher, assistant teachers and parents and they must also show respect towards them. They must not use bad language and there must be no lateness. If a Soviet pupil arrives late, he can only take part in the day's lessons with the teacher's permission and this is only given in exceptional circumstances. If he misses school entirely without a reasonable excuse, the child must do all the home work given to his classmates in his absence. For breaches of discipline the head teacher has the right to reduce the pupil's conduct marks and, as a last resort, expel him. Boxing and physical sport are now compulsory.

In Smolensk I attended School No. 3, and although I did not enjoy it so much as in Leningrad I welcomed the chance of getting away from life at home. Neither Ursula nor Father seemed to have any time for me. My stepmother was working at Voks, the organization for cultural relations with foreign countries and her attitude towards me remained cold and aloof. Both she and Father used to bring work home at night so that they always had other things to bother about apart from me.

The year before, in May 1931, three years after Mother's death, Ursula had given birth to a son. Father was overjoyed and the flat was filled with flowers. He threw a big party when my stepmother was well enough to return home. The baby was called Felix and for the first time I met all my new German relatives; half the German colony seemed to be there. One of Ursula's relatives, Aunt Katherina, became his nurse and as he grew up Ursula kept her son away from me as much as she could. She planned out a great future for Felix, a university career and then a high post in the glorious Soviet. But as she drank champagne to celebrate her motherhood, fate had already decided her son's future, instead he was to live the life of a ragged youth in exile.

The arrival of Felix made no difference to Ursula's employment. She used to do much of her translation work at home and Father would sometimes stay up all night with her, fortified by black coffee and puffing away at his beloved Russian cigarettes — half paper and half tobacco. He wrote a number of film scripts during our stay here and also some poetry. One of these poems "Dance of the Skaters" was set to music by Richter and became a popular fox-trot.

But I seldom knew what my father and stepmother were doing, I was never in their confidence. The whole household ignored me, and although Olga was still with us, her main job was to look after Felix. At weekends they often went to the "Red Boar", a luxurious hotel for state officials on the river outside the city — but I never joined them. In his position as chief of the special division of both the civilian and army O.G.P.U. of the western region of Russia, Father also had to attend military manoeuvres and used to pay flying visits to Minsk and Vitebsk on tours of inspection. Sometimes he took his wife with him but it would have been better if he had left her behind for later the N.K.V.D. grilled her for days about these visits.

I became a sad, lonely little girl in Smolensk; Ursula seemed to monopolize most of Father's time and we very seldom spent more than a few moments together alone. She insisted that I should have few clothes for she was determined to stamp out any "bourgeois pride" in my appearance. There were many quarrels and I had no friends, because Ursula persuaded my father that any form of social life would distract me from my schooling. At night I often cried myself to sleep because I knew Father was completely in her power and the only escape I had were secret visits to the family of our cook. My stepmother became a tyrant and I grew to hate her. But Father seemed quite oblivious of my unhappiness. I began to hate Smolensk so much that when he came home and told us he was to be transferred again to Stalingrad I was at once excited.

Stalingrad, formerly called Zaritsyn, had been renamed in recognition of the way Stalin had led the Red Army men to victory in this sector. He had been in command of the Revolution troops with Voroshilov and although his initial attacks on the city had been thrown back by General Wrangel he was joined by fresh troops under Sergei Kirov and General Wrangel's White Russians were routed. The new Stalingrad became a show city for the Communists. Foreign engineers were engaged from England, America and Germany and the old city was gradually turned into a great industrial centre. In the summer of 1930, supervised by American production experts from Detroit, the Stalingrad tractor factory had produced its first vehicle and by the time Father's posting arrived a number of other industries had been set up in the Stalingrad region.

Every child in the Soviet Union knew the story of Stalingrad for it was told in every school and Father recognized the great honour he had received in being picked for such an important post. It was a fine modern city and a much more interesting place in which to live than Smolensk.

Father had already left to take up his post as deputy chief of the Stalingrad O.G.P.U. when the phone rang and I ran to answer it. It was a call from Moscow and Uncle Arnold was on the line. Father's transfer was news to him and when he heard I would soon be leaving with my stepmother he suggested she should let me spend a few days with him on the way. Ursula was only too pleased to get me out of the way and at 11 o'clock I arrived at Moscow's Belorusski Station. Uncle Arnold was on the platform waiting for me. He wore the uniform of a senior N.K.V.D. officer and he flung his arms around me as though he were greeting a lost daughter.

"My, what a bonny girl you've grown into!" he laughed.

It was three years since I had seen him and I was so excited I could hardly speak. But I tucked my arm into his and he picked up my heavy portmanteau.

"Come along Norochka," he cried, "Aunt Liza is waiting for you with the samovar all ready."

I trotted beside him to the black limousine where his chauffeur had the door open. Arnold was now chief of the third department of the O.G.P.U. of the U.S.S.R. and the O.G.P.U. pennant on the bonnet of his vehicle cleared the way through the Moscow streets. As we went along he pointed out the sights to me and soon we had arrived at his home — a fine flat in the diplomatic quarter of Lubyanka. A bed had been made up for me in Uncle's study and the next ten days passed like a dream. He took me to the Bolshoi Thearte to see Tchaikovsky's *Eugene Onegin*. We sat in the N.K.V.D. boxes, once only used by Russian royalty. Quite by chance Uncle Redens and his wife, Auntie Anna (sister of Stalin's second wife) sat in the next box. They at once asked how father was and then Redens asked me the one question I dreaded to answer.

"Well, Nora," he said, "are you finally a Komsomolka?"

I stammered awkwardly and told him that I wasn't.

"I'm joining as soon as I get settled down in Stalingrad."

Redens nodded approvingly and we all settled back to enjoy the opera. Aunt Liza herself was childless and because of her inability to have children, her husband had deliberately carried on a clandestine affair with another woman. When she presented him with a baby daughter he called her Nadezhda, brought her home to his wife and she looked after her as though the baby was her own. Nadezhda had just begun going to school when I arrived to stay with Uncle Arnold in Moscow and she had already attracted the attention of Stalin. Arnold's home was full of pictures of Stalin and Nadezhda for, like Hitler, the Russian dictator likes to be seen and shown with photographs of children to show his paternal instinct.

I used to get on very well with her and the next morning, as a special treat, Aunt Liza took us both to the famous toytown of Russia. This is Zagorsk, some fifty miles outside the capital, and I don't suppose there's another place like it in the world.

Zagorsk is a child's paradise, for it is here that the toys of the Soviet children are modelled by hand and later mass-produced by toy factories throughout the Soviet Union. We went by electric train and we arrived soon after mid-day. Jumping down on to the muddy platform the town looked as though it had stepped straight out of "Snow White and the Seven Dwarfs". Above us, perched on a hill, was the old monastery with its onion domes and walls checkered with green and red tiles. A great cobbled square lay in front of us and a little winding hill formed the main street.

It was market day and peasants stood along the kerb selling salt cucumbers, tomatoes, apples and sunflower seeds which Russian country folk always seem to be chewing and spitting out the husks. We found the factory half-way up the hill but first we were taken round the toy museum. The things I saw amazed me. I had never seen their like before.

There was a musical chair in beaten brass which played a tune when you sat on it; a rocking-horse which Catherine the Great had given her son, the infant Czar Paul I, with the Romanov crest on the saddle; a French-made toy of a man playing tunes on a guitar; singing birds in cages; a French doll which blew kisses while looking at herself in a hand mirror; a rabbit playing a drum and a man who smoked if you gave him a cigarette.

There was also a German-made speaking book which Aunt Liza told me was the only one of its kind in the world. It looked like any other picture book but it had this big difference, the pictures spoke. If you pressed a button under a picture of a cow, it mooed, the dog barked, the pig snored and the lion roared. In one picture a whole group of children chattered and laughed. I could have stayed there all day playing with it.

But I suppose the most ingenious toy of all was a working picture of a scene in Austria and there must have been immense time and patience spent in making it. Even today I cannot help wondering about it, for this is what it did: a woman waved from the window of a chalet; outside twittering birds flew from tree to tree, tiny couples danced and a man played a horn, but not all the time, sometimes he rested. Inside the tiny window of the house four people were at dinner, moving knives and forks up and down on their plates. Not one of them was more than an inch high.

Then there were the dolls — dolls which had their own dolls, a doll which said not only "Mamma" but "Dadda", centuries-old dolls from China,

56

miniature dolls, walking ones as big as me. ... It was a toy-shop I could have stayed in for ever and I talked about the visit to Zagorsk for months afterwards.

On the way back to the station we passed a funeral moving along the high street. Russians funerals have none of the pomp found in other countries; the proceedings are always stark and simple. On this occasion, four men carried the open coffin and lying inside passers-by could see the body of a fifteen-year-old girl, pale and serene. The coffin was decorated with red, white and blue artificial flowers. Behind followed her parents, the mother weeping and the father carrying the coffin lid. This is the normal funeral procession in Soviet Russia and only Jews use a hearse and closed coffins. Once in the suburbs of Moscow I saw a young couple walking alone to the burial ground. They walked along the street staring stolidly ahead without turning to left or right. Under one arm the man carried a small open coffin and his wife held the lid. Inside was the body of their four-year-old child.

The Redens also had a villa outside the capital where we spent a weekend and on our way back to Moscow in the O.G.P.U. car, Uncle dropped off at the Butirki prison to interrogate some political prisoners. I never thought that one day I should be going there myself to visit my imprisoned stepmother.

The ten days I spent in Moscow were the happiest I had known for a long time. Uncle Arnold had always been very fond of me and after Mother's suicide he had asked if he could adopt me, but Father would not agree. Though he always said, "Whatever happens, Nora, you will always have your Uncle Arnold." But one morning I opened the door to find an O.G.P.U. officer outside in uniform.

He saluted, clicked his heels and said, "Nora Vassilevna? I am your father's adjutant and carry orders from him to escort you to Stalingrad."

Arnold came into the hall and invited the young officer to coffee. The next morning I left Moscow with him and on a crisp autumn night we arrived in Stalingrad. Father was waiting at the station, a white-haired figure in a grey, military overcoat. His greeting had not the warmth of Uncle Arnold's.

During our two years in Smolensk, where father had been chief of the special division of both the civilian and army O.G.P.U. of the western region of Russia, he had become very friendly with his commanding officer, General Uborevich and while we were there he had rewarded father with a gold watch.

Inside was an inscription acknowledging his services to the Soviet Army. Father was very proud of this watch which he kept in the left-hand pocket of his uniform. He showed it to everyone to prove how friendly he was with his commander.

But in Stalingrad the watch became an embarrassment to him. After we had been there for three years, Marshal Tukhachevsky, one of the three leading generals of the Soviet Union, with seven other high generals, was sentenced to death for espionage. One of the generals accused with Tukhachevsky was my father's friend Uborevich. As soon as my father heard of his arrest he became very agitated. He took the watch out of his pocket and tore off the casing with the inscription on it. He continued to use the watch, but I noticed he was not so eager to show it around.

The accused generals were tried *in camera*. No details of the trial were ever revealed, but it was well known in O.G.P.U. circles that Tukhachevsky was accused of selling plans of the Russian armaments to Hitler. The trial caused a great sensation in Russia because Marshal Tukhachevsky was very popular. With the Commissar for Foreign Affairs, Litvinov, he had represented the Soviet at King George V's funeral. It had been announced that he would return to England for the Coronation. Instead, he was shot. Another victim was General Vitovta Putna, who, two weeks before his arrest, had been Military Attaché at the Soviet Embassy in London. He was recalled to Moscow without any explanation, leaving his wife and fourteen-year-old daughter, Valovja, in the London Embassy.

It was not difficult for the O.G.P.U. terrorists to get Mme Putna back to Moscow. They sent her a telegram saying her husband was ill. She caught the next train back. When she arrived in Moscow she found her husband in a prison cell. Shortly afterwards he was shot. At the same time as the arrests, *Pravda* announced that Russians could no longer talk to foreigners.

Said the official Kremlin announcement: "All intercourse with foreign subjects, even to the extent of ordinary conversation, can only be considered as being dangerously near the realm of high treason."

Foreign tourists were no longer wanted in the Soviet Union. Soviet Embassies abroad stopped granting visas for people to visit Russia. It was the start of the Iron Curtain.

While this was going on I was living with my father and stepmother at 47 Krasnozavodskaya Street — Red Factory Street — the headquarters of the O.G.P.U. While we were there the name of the O.G.P.U. was officially changed to the name by which it is now generally known today — the N.K.V.D. Father, as one of the chiefs of the N.K.V.D., was one of this new Russian aristocracy. They all knew each other and they controlled the destinies of millions of Russians. They were a freemasonry of terrorists.

Father, shortly after he arrived in Stalingrad, was given a brand-new Zis car — the Russian Rolls-Royce — made in Moscow. I began to see the part Father was playing in the new order and what he had to do to earn his car and his luxurious apartment, and what Communists of his type had brought to the Russian people. I wasn't very proud when I learnt the facts.

We were staying at the Stalingrad Intourist Hotel waiting to move into our new home. Living in a suite of rooms in the same corridor were six engineers from Tbilisi, capital of Georgia in the Caucasus. They had come to work in the Stalingrad Tractor plant, and one of them, Niko, was very kind to me. He and his friend, Sholo, gave me books and sweets. Six months later, when we had moved into our new home, I found I could look down into the yard of the O.G.P.U. prison from my window. Prisoners came into the yard for exercise and, by peeping behind the curtains, I could watch them. Sometimes they would wave to me but mostly they walked round with bowed heads with their hands behind their backs.

One day, when I was looking from behind the heavy curtains, I watched two men trudging round dejectedly, watched by armed guards. They were my friends Niko and Sholo. I was very upset but I had seen so many strange things by this time that I no longer had the courage to speak about what I had seen. I never dared ask my father why these two young engineers had been imprisoned.

The commandant of the N.K.V.D., a short, stout little middle-aged man called Sokolov, saw me one day peeping through the window and told father. Again father was very angry. He told me it was bad for the prisoners' morale to see me gazing at them and he ordered me never to do it again. I promised him I would not, but I could not resist it. All the time I was in Stalingrad I continued to peep occasionally into the yard.

Sokolov realized I was still doing it because, shortly after he had reported me, heavy metal shields appeared on the prison windows. The only light which could filter into the cells after these shields were fitted was a glimmer at the top. The prison was a four-storey building surrounded by a high brick wall. At each corner there were soldiers armed with machine guns and on the top of the wall was electrified wire.

Living in this atmosphere, it was not surprising that something of the sinister terror which grips Russia began to affect me, although I was still only in my teens. I noticed these things and remembered them, but I never spoke about them.

One incident I particularly remember concerned a girl-friend of mine called Rita. We shared the same desk at school. She was very pretty, tall, blonde, with blue eyes, who used to love to play the piano and sing. At this time the Soviet Union had sold their Chinese Eastern Railway to China and a number of employees of the railway came from the Far East to Stalingrad. Rita became friendly with one of these men who told her all kinds of exciting stories about life in the East. They used to go dancing together and he taught her the fox-trot, which he had learned from the Americans in Harbin.

Harmless enough, you say? But the N.K.V.D. thought differently. They feared these Russians who had lived in the world outside the Iron Curtain.

One morning, when I went to school, Rita's desk was empty. No one knew why she had not arrived. Worried, I phoned her home in the lunch-hour. When her mother heard my voice she just sobbed and hung up the telephone. She could not bring herself to speak to me. Later, I understood why Rita's mother did not wish to speak to a daughter of an N.K.V.D. official. A few days later I met one of Father's officers in the street who said: "A friend of yours was asking after you. We have her in prison. Her name is Rita. She sings to me at night."

I was terrified. She was my best friend and when her mother, overcoming her fear of the N.K.V.D., telephoned me a few nights later and pleaded with me to intercede for Rita, I decided to speak to Father. When I raised the subject after dinner, he said very coldly: "I can do nothing for her. She has become too friendly with the enemies of the State."

I never saw Rita again. For all I know she may still be in prison or in Siberia, all because she was a feather-brained young girl who wanted to learn the fox-trot.

The block of flats in which we lived had only just been finished before we moved in. It stood on the side of the Volga and I used to spend hours on the balcony watching the boats glide beneath me as the boatmen sang to their concertinas.

I was now finishing my education at Lenin School No. 9 in Lenin Street. At this stage the Soviet education system gets into top gear in an effort to cram as much Communist doctrine as the young minds and bodies can stand. We had to know *The History of the Bolsheviks* and *The Constitution of the Soviet Union* backwards. Most of the class could recite whole passages by heart. These two books are the bibles of Communist youth; they represent the Old and New Testament of the Christian world. Father had first editions of both books and though I mastered them sufficiently to pass my history examination, they had no thrill for me. My favourite subjects remained literature and languages, never politics. Military training was compulsory. Our instructor was an emaciated ex-Army officer who still wore his uniform, though it remained badgeless and I think he only wore it because clothing was expensive and hard to find. Boys and girls alike spent two hours a week on parades, shooting, sniping, map reading, strategy and other military topics. We had no uniforms but we paraded on a big square in front of the school.

Our first parade seemed so funny that a bunch of girls — including me — couldn't help laughing.

"It's no laughing matter, Korzhenko," shouted the instructor. "If there's war tomorrow, you'll be only too glad to know how to defend yourself against the armies of capitalist Europe."

Sometimes it was my turn to be platoon commander, but whenever I shouted any orders the boys in the squad used to laugh outright and had to be called to order by an instructor.

Although I had told Uncle Redens I would join the Komsomol in Stalingrad I always remained outside its ranks. This was quite an achievement, because Father's position naturally drew attention to me, and nearly every week one or other of my schoolmates used to come up and try and persuade me to join the movement.

The final stages of our schooling were all centred on the one theme, a burning hatred of the capitalist world. Our school director, a member of the Communist Party, did his utmost to produce the rising intelligentsia urgently needed by the State. The glory of Stalin and the Soviet Empire came first in everything. For a boy or girl to wish to marry one day, set up a home and rear a family was of no consequence. Home life and marriage were taught to be old-fashioned bourgeoisie customs. There were no domestic schools for girls — you were trained to be a factory worker, a farm hand or an intellectual. No one taught me cooking, sewing or mothercraft. The theory was that if I became an intellectual I would be employed at a high salary by the State and this would enable me to have my own servants. We received sex instruction but it was soon explained to us that there was no stigma or shame in any unmarried woman bearing children. The State would take them into a creche and assume full responsibility for their further upbringing and education.

It was everyone's ambition to be labelled as an "intellectual" for in post-war Russia they are in a class of their own. They receive high salaries from the State and are the only people exempt from the incentive method of payment, that is, piece work. Father remained in the high income group all his life but although he later held one of the highest paid jobs in the Foreign Office he had little chance to save any money.

Income tax, similar to the P.A.Y.E. system used in Britain, was deducted from source, and there were further levies of three per cent to the Communist

61

Party and five per cent to the Ministry responsible for cultural education such as the building of schools, museums and similar institutions.

To encourage the birthrate, Russian citizens also have to pay a special tax if they are unmarried. They must also pay an additional levy if on marriage they remain childless. They are not asked to rear or educate their children, for most Russian women work as well as their husbands and there are always State creches to take care of the children while both parents are at work. In theory Russian women have complete equality with their menfolk. There are women barbers and women dentists, and women are to be found in industry, government positions and artistic posts everywhere. But in practice very few have made the grade and joined the élite rulers of the Soviet. About one-third of all the workers in industry are women and half the doctors, but there isn't one woman member of the Politburo.

The women of Russia are a tough lot. Although I was by now nearly eighteen, cosmetics were unknown to me. Ursula, my stepmother, would not even allow me powder though she sometimes gave me a dab of perfume for my handkerchief. The more masculine a girl looks the better the Soviet Union likes it. Short hair cuts and Eton crops have always been the vogue. Ursula, my stepmother, took full advantage of the situation. She was horrified when I asked if I could have daintier underwear. She forced me to wear dresses looking like corn-sacks, ribbed black stockings and coarse underclothes that chafed my skin. I had no gloves for the winter and was such a scarecrow I was ashamed to go out.

The only time I managed to break away from her surveillance in the matter of clothes was when the school staged a masked ball. I knew Ursula would give me no help in making a fancy dress so I decided to try and borrow one from the Gorki Drama Theatre which was just across the square opposite our school.

One afternoon I went to see the director of the theatre and when I told him who Father was, he readily agreed to loan me a costume. He took me along to see the wardrobe mistress and after trying on several period costumes we finally decided on a Nell Gwynne outfit — just the thing with which to win a prize in Soviet Russia!

I put it on and she helped me tie the black laced bodice. A voluminous white blouse and enormous skirt went with the outfit and as a final touch she lent me a red wig! I didn't tell anyone at home about the ball and when the evening came I arranged with the wardrobe mistress to change at the theatre. I arrived at the school with my mask in place, no one knew who I was and when I had won first prize of a box of chocolates and removed my mask the whole school was amazed. They had never seen me in such finery before.

On another visit to the Gorki Theatre, as a member of the audience, Father introduced me to Alexei Rykov, a member of the Politburo who was on a tour of inspection in the Stalingrad region. Father told him the story of my winning first prize with one of the dresses and Rykov congratulated me on my initiative. He had been Lenin's successor as Chairman of the Council of People's Commissars. He was a thin, bearded man and was later sentenced to death in the great treason trial of March 1938.

It was while I was in Stalingrad that Russia heard of the death of Maxim Gorki. Attracted by a huge crowd in the Square of the Fallen Fighters, I went there to hear the news over the loudspeakers. Gorki had a tremendous following in the Soviet republic and I read all his books. He was my favourite Russian author and his death was like losing a friend. I stood in the huge square and wept unashamedly. All around me men and women stood with heads bowed in sorrow, a grief which later became fury when the true story of Gorki's murder was disclosed in the trial of N.K.V.D. chief, Henry Yagoda, in Moscow.

By this time Ursula's German mother, Frau Heine, was living with us. She was a cold woman with a big nose and thin lips. She had money of her own but she was very mean. She did the housekeeping and kept the place as neat as a chemist's shop, and I was always terrified in case I had left foot-marks on the polished parquet flooring. She carried a bunch of keys on her skirt and if the cook wanted anything she could not get it without Grandmother's permission. The old lady weighed all the food in case the N.K.V.D. had given short measure, and the servants were as terrified of her as I was.

She joined her daughter in her hatred of me. When my father and stepmother were away, I used to be left in her care and when she heard them coming she used to feign a collapse, proof of how great the strain had been. She was an extremely fit old lady and it used to fascinate me to watch her slip to the floor with the ease of a gymnast while I sat still and watched the inevitable pantomime that followed. I knew the routine backwards, but what could I do?

Ursula would come rushing in, and rush out again to fetch a glass of water and smelling salts. Once, when she took too long, the old lady opened one eye and when she saw me looking at her it closed in a flash. The quarrels were never of my choosing and very often they existed only in my grandmother's imagination, but it was useless to protest my innocence.

One day Father said, "I will give you your last chance, Nora, if you don't do what Ursula and her mother want you to do I shall send you away. And as you know there are a lot of places where I could send you."

On another occasion he said that I had a good home, plenty of food and clothes and he could not understand why I was not happy. "What more can I give you?" he asked.

I could have mentioned love and understanding but Father did not expect to return home and find a daughter waiting to tell him all her worries, so I kept quiet and said nothing. Every month the gulf between us widened and I longed for the day of my graduation when I planned to go to Moscow University and live with Uncle Arnold. As the time approached for the final exam Ursula kept saying that I would fail, but — as though to spite her — I matriculated. That was my revenge against my stepmother.

CHAPTER V – LOVE ON THE VOLGA — BUT NOT FOR ME!

While we were still in Stalingrad, in August 1936, the Soviet was shaken by the news that Henry Yagoda, chief of the N.K.V.D. and Father's boss, had rounded up more than a dozen of the highest placed men in Moscow. They were known throughout the Soviet Union for their loyalty and devotion to the Revolution. Some of them, in fact, had been the General Staff of the Revolution working under Lenin to overthrow the Czarist regime. Stalin had ordered their arrest as enemies of the State, and they were charged with plotting to kill him. It was said they had entered into a pact with the exiled Trotsky. Gradually their names leaked out.

Chief accused were Zinoviev and Kamenev, both original members of the Politburo. These men — both in their fifties — were known to have been under suspicion for some time. Both had been expelled from the Communist Party twice and reinstated. Zinoviev was the reputed author of the famous "Red Letter" exposed in 1924 as a Soviet plot to excite the British Navy and Army to revolt. The disclosure of the letter swept Britain's first Socialist Government from power. It was later denounced by the Soviet Government as a forgery. When Zinoviev, Kamenev and fourteen others were placed on trial in Moscow everyone followed the proceedings with tremendous Interest.

The hearing was in public and Vishinsky, then Public Prosecutor, conducted the State's case. The trial was broadcast, filmed and reported fully in the Russian Press. This in itself was unusual. But it was a definite move by Stalin to show the world that the men involved had made free admissions of their guilt. This trial, the greatest State trial since the French Revolution, also named Tomsky, head of the State publishing house, Bukharin, one of Lenin's closest friends, Rykov, a former Soviet premier and at that time a transport chief, Piatakov, an intimate friend of Trotsky, Uglanov, former head of the Moscow Party Organization, Serebryakov, a party leader, and Gregori Sokolnikov, former Ambassador to London.

All these had been implicated by Zinoviev and Kamenev, two of the co-founders of the Soviet State and members of the original Bolshevist Old Guard. With Rykov, they were the last survivors, apart from Stalin and Trotsky, of the original political bureau of the Bolshevist Party. Trotsky was, of course, later assassinated in Mexico. Stalin alone is alive today.

Sokolnikov's case was interesting because his wife, well known as a London diplomatic hostess giving parties at the Soviet Embassy at No. 13 Kensington Palace Gardens, had been a great friend of Mme Stalin. The

Sokolnikovs were recalled to Moscow from London after Mme Stalin's death in 1932. He had been under suspicion before for being a Trotskyist sympathizer. It was only Mme Stalin who saved him and got him the job in London. Even though he had been dismissed from his post in the Finance Ministry, he had been given the job as Ambassador.

Then the N.K.V.D. found incriminating letters at the Russian Embassy in London. Sokolnikov was recalled. Only his reputation saved him; he joined Litvinov's staff and then the Timber Control. But, named at the trial as a wrecker, he was later arrested and sentenced to ten years.

The final scenes of the Zinoviev trial, which were very moving, were described fully in the Russian newspapers. Men and women covered their faces and wept as Kamenev, Zinoviev's brother-in- law, stood up and said "I ask no mercy."

Zinoviev himself admitted that he was chief organizer of the terrorist plot.

He drew himself to his full height, faced the court and said "I ask to be shot. I am not worthy to remain alive. The death sentence will be a just one. I am not afraid."

At dawn on Tuesday, 26 August, 1936, the sixteen men were shot in Moscow's Lubyanka Prison. I heard afterwards that Zinoviev, organizer of the Cheka in which my father had served, had collapsed on his way to the firing squad. He had to be lashed to hooks in the quadrangle wall. Kamenev walked to his fate unaided. Their fourteen fellow victims looked on. Then, when their turn came, they died shrieking curses at the N.K.V.D. men who had promised them their lives if they confessed.

Attorney-General Vishinsky had himself visited the jail and told the men there would be no reprieve.

Judge Ulrich, who had sentenced them, was present. Twelve picked N.K.V.D. men were the firing squad. The victims were blindfolded. They were all dead in less than twenty minutes. Afterwards the bodies were taken to Khodinka, a Moscow suburb, and buried in a common grave in "The Cemetery of the Executed". No grave is marked, there are no tombstones. The sixteen men had died thirty hours after sentence.

The next day *Pravda* carried reports of resolutions passed in all parts of Russia at factories, collective farms, etc., approving of Stalin's action. The paper added a warning that "all the nests of the enemies are not yet destroyed".

For some days the Press was full of reports of the discoveries of Trotskyists, the new name for "enemies of the State". Father was kept busy hunting for them.

Zinoviev's execution was perhaps retribution for the thousands he had killed. He organized the Cheka and ran the Red Terror in Leningrad when the rest of the Bolshevik leaders left for Moscow. Great round-ups of Trotskyists followed throughout the country. Father worked day and night, and suspects arrived by the van-load in Black Ravens, Russia's police wagons. The next few weeks were a nightmare. Thousands were rounded up to be shot or exiled.

A great wave of fear engulfed the men in the Kremlin. They saw plots everywhere. All Russian journalists, writers and intellectuals who had visited foreign countries in the last two years were clapped in jail by the N.K.V.D. in case they had become anti-Stalin.

For a long time afterwards a brooding terror hung over Stalingrad like a storm cloud. Father's fanatical preoccupation with the enemies of the State was not entirely unfounded, as often there were mysterious fires and explosions which were never explained.

One night a State granary caught fire and burnt for several days. The day after the fire started the N.K.V.D. men questioned every member of the staff of the granary. Then they had their usual round-up and many families lost their men. Purges were also frequent in the gigantic Stalingrad Tractor Plant. The N.K.V.D. kept a special detachment there all the time to maintain party discipline and prevent so-called sabotage. No one ever talked of these things, because you never knew who you were talking to. If you entered into a casual conversation in a tram or a train you might find that you had been talking to an N.K.V.D. agent. At midnight there would come the dreaded knock on your door and you would be taken off to prison, all for a casual comment.

As the daughter of the N.K.V.D. Chief I was watched as if I were some sort of dangerous animal. After the episode of Rita I never dared make a friend unless I told my father first. I would give him the name of any girl at school with whom I had struck up a friendship and he would send one of his agents to check on her family and background. After a week or so he would call me in and say: "It is all right for you to associate with Natasha (or Olga). My agents report that her family is quite correct, and not one of them is an enemy of the people."

Even my holidays were supervised. Once I went to stay with the family of Alexandrov the N.K.V.D. Chief at Astrakhan. One afternoon we went up the river in a launch. It was a lovely day and I was enjoying myself. We glided peacefully over the water. Then Alexandrov suddenly pointed to the bank and shouted: "*Ostanovis*! (stop)".

The man at the helm swung the launch round.

67

"There's a fugitive," shouted Alexandrov. A poor wretch was standing in the water up to his neck. He was crouching under the branches of the trees which hung down on to the water, trying to escape our attention as we cruised up the narrow river.

A look of utter despair passed across his face when the launch swung towards him and two N.K.V.D. men jumped into the water and dragged him aboard.

"Don't shoot me," he cried, "Don't shoot."

He was in rags and had escaped from the Astrakhan concentration camp. guards hit him across the head with their clenched fists and dragged him below screaming.

Alexandrov, now the grim-faced N.K.V.D. official, harshly ordered the launch to put about and return to the city. As we sailed back in the sunshine I could hear the prisoner moaning in the cabin below. No one spoke and I gazed at the sparkling water feeling unhappy. I decided that this was the last time I would come for a cruise on an N.K.V.D. launch. This sort of grim little episode happened so often that after a time I became almost used to it.

The spy mania which gripped Russia sometimes led to ludicrous incidents. I remember one day when I was in my class, we had just finished the physics lesson, when the director of our model co-educational school came in and told a young boy called Sasha to come with him to his study. Sasha raised his eyebrows at me quizzically and walked out. After ten minutes the director came back and said to me: "Will you come too, please."

When I followed him into his study there was Sasha looking very pale. One of Father's N.K.V.D. men was standing near him.

"Both of you come with me for questioning," he said. He led us to the N.K.V.D. car outside and we drove to headquarters. In a locked room one of my father's adjutants started to question Sasha. He held out a little note. I recognized it at once. It was a note that Sasha had written to me and I had left it on my dressing table at home.

"Did you write this?" barked the adjutant.

"Yes," replied Sasha looking very frightened.

"This has been found by the head of the N.K.V.D. and we demand an explanation," the adjutant said.

"But there is none," Sasha answered.

"Do you realize what you have written?"

"Certainly," said Sasha. "It says 'Can you obtain the bullets to shoot Tregor?' "

"You asked this girl to get you bullets? How did you expect her to get them?"

"From her father's gun."

"How do you know he's got a gun?"

"All Chekists have guns — you've got one too, haven't you?"

"Silence! Don't be impertinent or it will be the worse for you. Why did you want to shoot Tregor?"

Sasha paused for a moment and looked puzzled. Then he said slowly: "But he deserves to die — he is old and useless. It would be a kindness."

"A kindness!" shouted the adjutant. "You intended to shoot him yourself?"

"Of course, he's just an old dog."

"You call him an old dog, you little whippersnapper. How dare you!"

The adjutant gazed for a few seconds at Sasha. Then he threw his hands in the air, turned and whispered to one of the men standing by. The man clicked his heels and left the room.

He returned with Father. All the N.K.V.D. men stood up and saluted. Father looked very stern and walked past without looking at me.

The adjutant turned to him apologetically and said: "It's no good, Chief. I am sorry to tell you the boy has confessed to everything. What is worse he is still determined to kill the man.

"Man!" cried Sasha. "What do you mean? I'm not talking about any man — am I Nora?"

"No." I replied. "Don't you understand? Tregor is Sasha's dog."

For a moment the grim-faced N.K.V.D. men looked furious and then they started to laugh. For the first time my father looked at me and smiled. He said: "I'm sorry about this, but you understand we have to check everything very thoroughly. And one of the heads of the tractor plant is a German, he is a specialist from Berlin."

"What has that got to do with us?" demanded Sasha angrily.

"Well you see," explained my father with a wintry smile, "we cannot be too careful. The German's name is Karl Tregor. We thought we had discovered a plot to kill him in which you were involved, my boy."

Sasha did not give an answering smile, and when we returned to the classroom he muttered: "That's what comes of being friendly with the daughter of an N.K.V.D. official."

And he never spoke to me again.

That sort of incident played a large part in my life. When a man learned that I was the daughter of a secret police chief he often refused to have anything to do with me, or I was afraid to continue my friendship with him in case he turned out to be an enemy of the people.

Father had a red book which gave us free entry to every theatre and cinema in Stalingrad. I used to go as often as I could and it was at a Stalingrad cinema that I saw René Clair's *Sous les toils de Paris* with Russian sub-titles. Shakespeare was also popular in Russia, particularly *Othello* and *Lady Macbeth*. But my favourite was Windsor Beauties — known to you as *The Merry Wives of Windsor*. There were opera companies, too, with Italian and German singers and Hagenbeck's Circus used to send acts to appear in the State circus in Stalingrad. Whenever we went to one of these entertainments we sat in a specially reserved box for high officials. It was, of course, the best place in the house.

One day, at a performance of *Carmen* given by artistes from the Moscow State Opera House, I strayed away from my family into another part of the auditorium and sat down alone. A young man beside me spoke to me in German. At this time there were German, French, American and English engineers at the Stalingrad Tractor Plant, mostly experts who advised on production. Because of my German stepmother I spoke good German and we talked together.

He told me he was a German engineer working in the plant and asked if he could see me again. He was the first foreigner I had ever met and I was quite fascinated by him. I told him to write to me but I gave him the address of a girl friend because I knew that my father would not let me receive any letters from foreigners. Several letters came for me, but I never answered them. I was too frightened.

Shortly after this, however, I did have my first flirtation, although it ended disastrously as a result of the intervention of the secret police. One day a young commissar came from Moscow to visit my father. I will call him Tovarich X as I happen to know that he is still holding a high post in Moscow under Lavrenty Beria, present head of the N.K.V.D., who also controls Russia's atom bomb experiments.

Tovarich X came to dinner at our flat several times. He was one of the coming young men of the Moscow secret police, but that did not interest me very much. What did interest me was that he was young and handsome and kept me enthralled with stories of his life in Moscow. One evening he asked my father if he could take me to Gorki's Drama Theatre to see *Othello*. I thought my father would refuse but instead he agreed at once. He told me later that it was a great honour for me to be seen in the company of such an important young man.

It was a lovely spring evening when we came out of the theatre so we decided to walk home slowly along the gardens beside the Volga. We walked hand in hand, talking of the things that young people do on such occasions. The Volga flowed past — the most romantic river in Russia — and beside me was the most romantic young man I had ever met. I felt that I was in heaven…

Until, out of the comer of my eye, I noticed two men shadowing us. If we stopped to gaze at the beauty of the river, they stopped and stood in the shadow of the trees. As my companion did not seem to notice anything, I did not mention the two men I had seen. We came to a seat on the bank of the river and the young commissar suggested that we sat down for a moment. He put his arms round me and I closed my eyes. Then I felt a movement, turned round, and there standing on each side were the two men who had been following us. I jumped up alarmed.

"How dare you," I cried. "Why can't you leave us alone? You are nothing but Peeping Toms. Have you nothing better to do?"

The men looked uncomfortable and Tovarich X coughed with embarrassment.

"I'm sorry, Nora," he said, "I should have told you that these men were with me."

"With you?" I said in surprise. "Do you always bring your boy friends with you when you take a girl out?"

"They are not my boy friends," he replied. "They are my bodyguard. You see I am a commissar and I can't be too careful."

I looked at the young man — a commissar of the Soviet Union. He was blushing with embarrassment. Miserably I suggested that he had better take me home at once. And without a word we walked along the river bank together, dogged by the two shadows, a melancholy quartet.

I was a Russian girl in my teens and like every Russian I loved the Volga. But the Volga on a summer's night was no place for me, I was the daughter of an N.K.V.D. chief, and my friend had to bring his bodyguard. Often I used to watch young couples walking hand in hand along the banks of the Volga. I envied them, knowing that I would never be allowed to walk there as they did, alone with my lover.

CHAPTER VI - LIFE AT STALIN'S COURT

Soon after my eighteenth birthday, in February 1937, Father was called to Moscow to report to the chief of the N.K.V.D., Nikolai Yezhov. I was completing my passing out examination at school for Moscow University. The night before the results of the examination were known, the telephone rang. It was father on the line and he sounded quite excited when he said: "Pack up everything as soon as you can and come to Moscow. The Politburo have appointed me to the Foreign Office."

I just had time to attend the graduation. It was an evening that every young girl would remember, with dancing, caviar and wine. A banner hung from the wall saying in red letters: "Happy road in life".

All those who were going away, as I was, to study at universities made a solemn pledge to return to Stalingrad at the end of five years. None of us could look into the future and know that in five years' time the Soviet Union would be at war with Germany and the reunion we planned would never materialize. Most of the young students who stayed behind gave their lives in the bitter battle of Stalingrad. But they knew nothing of this as they stood with N.K.V.D. officials and waved us a cheerful good-bye at Stalingrad, and we began our thirty-six hour journey to Moscow.

As the train rattled across the flat plains I realized that I was saying good-bye to life as the daughter of a Chekist official. It had been a strange secluded life for a young girl. Apart from school friends, whose antecedents had all been investigated by my father, I knew no one except N.K.V.D. officials. I had never done any shopping or housework, it was all done for us. Even the hairdresser came to our home. So did the shoemaker, the dressmaker and Father's tailor.

It was important that Father should be well-dressed as he had so often to speak on official occasions, like the anniversary of the Revolution. He wore well-cut uniforms with badges for five and fifteen years' service. In his collar was the insignia of his rank, four diamond studs, and he was an impressive figure when he took the salute at the May Day Parade.

As the train drew into Kazhan Station in Moscow, we hardly recognized the man in the smart lounge suit who met us. It was father, without his uniform. After he left Stalingrad he never wore uniform again because he had joined the diplomatic service. A shiny Cadillac from the Foreign Office whisked us through Moscow to the Chekist Hotel, the Select, at Stretenka near the Foreign Office. Within a few days we moved to a special hotel for Foreign Office officials at Klyazma, forty kilometres outside Moscow.

There, father told us about his new job. He had been appointed Director General to the Foreign Office, working directly under Litvinov. Although he was no longer an active Chekist he remained on the reserve and was liaison officer between the N.K.V.D. and the Foreign Office. He was not concerned with diplomacy but had absolute power over Foreign Office employees from cipher clerks to ambassadors. He was responsible for the administration and control of all Soviet diplomatic personnel, not only in Moscow but throughout the world.

For the N.K.V.D. trusted no one, not even those who held the highest government posts. Father's job was to see that everyone kept to the party line. If they made one slip, he put through an order for their immediate recall and banishment. He had become one of the most powerful men in Russia, but even he, in his turn, was not free from surveillance.

I will never know whether this was done on purpose but, as if to remind us that we were not entirely free, we were given a twelve-roomed villa at No. 22 Botkinskaya Street, Klyazma. Until a short time before, it had been the home of Nikolai Krestinsky, Litvinov's deputy, who had just been arrested for treason. The significance of this was not lost upon father in spite of all his Chekist discipline.

Whenever anyone is arrested like this in Russia his house is shut up and red seals are placed on the doors by the N.K.V.D. When we arrived at the house we had to break the N.K.V.D. seals to enter. As we walked through the rooms we found Krestinsky's suits still hanging in the wardrobe. So were the dresses of his wife, a physician in charge of the hospitals for women and children in Moscow. We explored the two-storied wooden house, then the three of us came down into the hall and looked at each other. Father said with a grim smile:

"Touch wood. I hope we don't follow Comrade Krestinsky!"

Next day we packed up the clothes of the Krestinsky family and the N.K.V.D. came and took them away. Shortly afterwards Vladimir Potiomkin was announced as his successor.

Father's new position made us one of the most favoured families in Moscow. His appointment had been approved by the Seventh Department of the N.K.V.D. who made all the high appointments in the Soviet Union. As well as the wooden villa, we were given a five-roomed Foreign Office flat just outside the Red Gate metro station. We were also given a special Kremlin ration book which enabled us to buy the finest food from the

Kremlin Gastronome near Lenin's library. This special ration book also entitled us to have cooked food sent from the Kremlin kitchen. The servants would bring back a complete dinner, soup, chicken, meat and ice cream in special containers. In addition to his salary from the Foreign Office, Father as a reserve N.K.V.D. official, received a State pension of 500 roubles a month. He was allowed six weeks on the Russian Riviera, the Crimea, and in Caucasia, all expenses paid. Another privilege was that Moscow publishers, four times a year, sent us a list of their new books. We could buy as many as we wanted at reduced prices.

Litvinov had just moved out of the block of Foreign Office apartments to his official residence at No. 17 Spiridonovka and even here in our Moscow flat the previous resident had not escaped the attentions of the N.K.V.D. He had been a member of the Foreign Office Collegium and had been shot just before we arrived in Moscow. At first we were only allowed to occupy two of the rooms until the N.K.V.D. had finished their search among the condemned man's possessions. But as soon as they had left we had the whole flat decorated and we never spoke of the previous owner again. Father's new position made him a most sought-after person, for Foreign Office officials and members of the diplomatic staff could achieve nothing without his authority. He made a point of remaining aloof and because he was unapproachable many people tried to get me to intercede on their behalf. We had not been in our Klyazma *dacha* at Botkinskaya Street very long before I had my first experience of this.

Rizhansky, Soviet representative in Latvia, had been recalled and was living in the diplomats' hotel with his wife while enquiries were made about him by the secret police. He had already guessed that something was amiss and his wife had tried to find out from Father what had gone wrong. But, as usual, he refused to discuss the matter.

One evening I was sitting in the lounge reading alone when Mme Rizhansky came up to me and said, "You're a stranger here, my dear, have you just returned from abroad?"

I told her I'd only come from Stalingrad and she smiled.

"Ah, then, you must be the daughter of the new Director-General? I've heard a lot about you. Why don't you join me for supper?"

Not wishing to offend her I accepted the invitation but the next morning Father heard what I'd done and severely reprimanded me.

"I suppose she asked you to invite her to come round to see us one evening?" said Father.

"No, of course not," I stammered, "She wouldn't be so rude as to invite herself like that. Mme Rizhansky would wait until she got a proper invitation." I never told Father his guess was right and of course no invitation was ever sent. Within a week both she and her husband disappeared from the hotel and I found out that they'd been arrested.

It was always impressed upon me that I must remain in the background and one summer evening I nearly sent Vladimir Potiomkin sprawling by running down one of our garden paths without looking. Potiomkin, later Ambassador to France and Minister of Education, had visited Father to discuss some matter or other and they were both so deeply engaged in conversation neither heard my approach.

Father was about to scold me but when he saw the other man smile he treated it as a joke just as he was doing, for as he stumbled to right himself, Potiomkin said, "Ah, a very pushful young lady, one might say."

After we arrived in Moscow the Soviet held the first elections since the Revolution. The night before election day, 12 December, 1937, Stalin said in the Bolshoi Theatre that the elections would be the freest ever held in any country in the world. He added: "History does not know of another such example. They are much more democratic than elections in any other country."

Stalin may have been right. All I know is that there were 1,143 candidates described as "Communist and non-party". What that means exactly, no one dared to enquire. Every candidate was elected as there was no one else to vote for. Our family recorded our vote in the former English Club near one of the British Embassy residences by the Red Gate metro. The elections may have been free, but the N.K.V.D. terror was everywhere. Soon after the voting something happened in our own household which reminded me once again that the secret police never slept.

Father had a Foreign Office chauffeur, a dark, curly-haired young man of twenty-eight, named Nikolai. I had just begun my studies at Moscow University, where I was specializing in foreign languages in the hope of being a Soviet diplomat. Nikolai, the chauffeur, used to drive me to the university and sometimes we would stop for a few minutes and he would bring out his mouth organ and play arias from operas on it. He was a brilliant player and if I closed my eyes I could imagine I was listening to an organ.

One day when I walked out of the house to go to the university, a grey-haired, elderly man opened the car door for me.

"What's happened to Nikolai?" I asked.

The new chauffeur replied: "The N.K.V.D. have taken him. He has been denounced as a Polish spy."

That night at dinner I asked my father about him.

"But surely, it isn't true?" I said.

Father put down his soup spoon, shrugged his shoulders, and answered: "If the N.K.V.D. say he is a spy — he is a spy."

Next day I heard that Nikolai had been shot.

Sergei, the new chauffeur, had worked for the Foreign Office for several years and had been a chauffeur in Soviet embassies abroad. When he drove us on picnics Father would invite his wife and two boys to come with us. After he had been with us for some months, I was waiting for Father outside the Foreign Office when Sergei's wife came up to me in tears. Between sobs, she said:

"They arrested Sergei last night. They say he is a spy. I am his wife and I know it is all lies. You must speak to your father about it, as he is the only one who can help us."

I promised that I would, but I never did. Several times I screwed up enough courage to speak but at the last moment I did not say anything. I knew it would be hopeless as his attitude was always the same: "If the N.K.V.D. say he is a spy — he is a spy."

Often, when I walked into the Foreign Office, I used to see Sergei's wife lurking near the entrance looking ragged and dejected, obviously trying to speak to me. I was ashamed of myself, but I used to avoid her and scurry quickly into the building. Eventually, one day, she too disappeared and I never saw her again.

The Moscow Foreign Office is a corner building in the Kuznetzki Most opposite the N.K.V.D. headquarters in the centre of Moscow's official district near the Kremlin. The big building was divided into two parts. There was one wing for domestic purposes with a nursery for diplomats' children, a clinic for the Foreign Office staff and officials of foreign embassies. There was also a club and a library, hairdressing saloons, a tailor's shop and a food store. The other wing contained suites of offices and flats for officials. Father's office was on the second floor with three large French windows overlooking the N.K.V.D. headquarters. Beneath these headquarters is the famous Lubyanka prison.

Father's office was furnished with a large Persian rug and a wide, mahogany desk facing the window. Beside the desk was a huge safe, its combination known only to Father and the N.K.V.D.

On the desk were five telephones. One telephone, with a red button on the dial, was connected on a special line to the Kremlin Secretariat and a buzz on the button produced an immediate response from Stalin's office. Another phone, with a white button, was linked with the N.K.V.D. There were no flowers or pictures in the office, except a big portrait of Stalin. On another of the half-panelled walls, the top half of which were painted duck-egg blue, was a large map of the world. There were four comfortable leather chairs for visitors and a divan on which Father could rest when working late.

One of the first jobs Father did was to carry out the directive from the Politburo in January 1938 to close all foreign consulates in Soviet Russia. Father ordered his staff to close them and bring all the furniture which was left behind to Moscow.

This was as a result of an order issued by the Soviet Government on 12 January, which informed other nations that they could only have the same number of consulates in Russia as the Soviet had in foreign countries. This meant the closing down of foreign consulates in Moscow and Leningrad by Germany, Italy, Japan, Poland, and Great Britain. Consulates in other parts of the Soviet Union were also closed. The German attitude towards the matter annoyed Father. Hitler had officially complained of "Continual chicanery with our consulates in Kiev and Novosibirsk, which in spite of repeated representations had not been stopped and can only be regarded as a deliberate disturbance of our consular activities." I imagine Hitler knew what he was talking about. This was the time when Troyanovsky was ambassador in Washington and Maisky was in London. They came under Father's surveillance.

One evening my father invited a man called Slavutsky and his wife and daughter to stay with us. Slavutsky was waiting for a diplomatic appointment. After he had been with us a few days he returned home in high spirits and said:

"I saw Stalin today; I am going to Tokyo."

We had a special party that night to celebrate his new position as Soviet Ambassador to Japan. He was delighted with his new job but, like so many others, he was soon recalled in disgrace. Father never mentioned his name again, and he was never again invited to our house.

It was about this time that I began to realize the significance of the Foreign Office country mansion at Klyazma where we stayed when we first arrived in Moscow. It was a luxury transit camp for diplomats awaiting appointments, but it was also used as a hotel of open arrest for those who had offended Stalin. There were many of them there.

One Sunday afternoon when we went to the hotel I was sitting on the verandah. Father was lying in a hammock when a woman came running up the steps screaming.

"Vassily Savvich," she cried, throwing herself at my father's feet, "save my husband. Save him."

My father jumped out of the hammock in a rage.

"Get out," he yelled at her. "Get out. Never come near me again."

The woman stumbled away, sobbing loudly. I recognized her as Mme Karsky, Professor of Mathematics at Moscow University, whose husband was the Soviet Ambassador to Turkey. He had been recalled a day or two before and the N.K.V.D. had arrested him. My father threw himself back in his hammock and went on reading a book. I did not tell him I had recognized the woman. What was the use? There was nothing I could do.

We had not been long in Moscow when Father came home one evening with a big parcel in his arms. I asked him what it was, but he rushed past me up to his bedroom. Half an hour later he called my stepmother and myself into the room. We both gasped. He was wearing full evening dress, complete with a top hat. He looked so strange after all these years of wearing uniform, and we examined the white tie and the patent leather shoes excitedly.

"The Minister told me I must get one," Father chuckled. "It's a change from the Chekist uniform, isn't it?"

The partisan fighter of twenty years ago had come a long way. Several nights a month he would take my stepmother to diplomatic receptions and banquets given by Litvinov at his home at 17 Spiridonovka. They used to return in the early hours of the morning and tell me about the famous foreign ambassadors and their families they had met. They met Sir William Seeds, the British Ambassador, and Joseph E. Davies, the American.

One summer evening I had a great thrill. My stepmother arrived home with a long cardboard box. In it was a white evening dress — my first! This was exciting enough for a young girl, but I was even more excited when she told me we were going to a diplomatic reception at Litvinov's house that week.

When the great day arrived I was told to be on my best behaviour for the reception was to be the most brilliant held in Moscow for some time.

When our car arrived at the old mansion, we were shown into a spacious room with tapestry-covered furniture. It was crowded with men in white ties and tails, and women in beautiful evening gowns from the fashion houses of the world. I was only nineteen and I had never seen anything like it before. Father mingled with foreign diplomats as though he himself was an

78

ambassador of the old school. Several of the famous ambassadors of the Western powers were pointed out to me, including Joseph E. Davies, the American; and I was proud to observe that none of them were any better dressed than Father in his immaculate Moscow-made tails!

It was a warm evening and I spent a lot of time walking in the garden, under the trees festooned with fairy lights. More tapestried furniture was scattered around the lawn so that people could sit in the open if they wished. There was an orchestra playing swing music — the first time I had ever heard it — and ten kinds of wine for supper with caviar, ice cream and chicken. The menus all had the hammer and sickle printed on them.

I was so delighted with the new Western music that I danced till four o'clock in the morning.

It was a tired and happy young girl who drove home as dawn broke over the spires of Moscow.

CHAPTER VII – "MODERN MOSCOW"

Within a few weeks I had settled down to my life in the Russian capital and I moved about the city streets like any other hardened Moscovite. In contrast to Stalingrad, a new Russian city, Moscow had large numbers of old and shabby buildings with peeling frescoes and cracked plaster. I was soon warned that during the thaw in April and May it was much safer to walk on the outside of the pavements so as to avoid jutting cornices and other parts of the ornamental stonework which would suddenly break off beneath the snow's weight and fall on to the heads of passers-by.

Summer is always welcome in Moscow and in May the weather gets milder, the gutters gurgle with thaw water and great round chunks of ice slide out of the drain-pipes while men and women clamber overhead on the roofs, pushing off blocks of grey and black snow. In early May, Moscow is nothing but water and slush, but after a fortnight the streets are dry again, the trees covered in young leaves and mimosa from the Crimea is on sale at the kiosks. By the end of the month the sun blazes down and there is a stream of sun-bathers to the river.

The sales of ice-cream soar and the fruit drinks are in great demand. All the fruit stalls are decorated with mimosa and the flower lasts much longer in Russia than in England for there we make a special point of putting the flower in warm water and keeping it in a warm room. It always lasts longer in warmth. Moscovites seem to prefer synthetic fruit flavours which the stallholders sell in preference to the real thing. And ice-cream is sold all the year round. Even in the depths of winter, when the frozen snow crunches sharply under foot, ice-cream vendors still flourish on the Moscow streets.

At times the cold is so intense that when you first enter it your entire nose aches and throbs. The pain continues for ten minutes until the nose warms up or the rest of the face gets cold. Handkerchiefs freeze in the depths of your pocket, even in a fur coat, and the whiskers on a man's beard will freeze solid.

Half an hour in a Moscow street in winter is enough to make it hard for you to talk; even to frame simple words is an effort for lips and mouth become too cold to function properly. Maybe this is why the Russians have never made great conversationalists! But Moscow keeps itself several degrees warmer than the surrounding country and it is not uncommon for freak thaws to occur in January and February, the coldest months of all. But they never last long and when the frost returns the streets are more like skating rinks than ever. And Moscow streets were the busiest I had ever seen.

The trams were packed to the buffers and they would never clank along at more than five miles an hour. Even the comic paper *Krokodil* used to make jokes about them. In wartime, tram-rides became nightmares for many Russian women because of the danger of robbery. It became a favourite trick of agile youths to jump on them and slash strap-hangers' wrists in order to snatch the bracelets, wrist-watches and other jewellery they might be wearing.

I had expected to find the Russian capital full of big shops and restaurants, but apart from the three major hotels, Metropole, Moskva and National, the only first-class restaurant was the Caucasian Aragvi, in Gorki Street. Here, for a minimum of 50 roubles (£1) up to 400 roubles, one could get a first-class meal. The Aragvi remained open during the war and, although food was at its scarcest in most of Moscow, this restaurant was providing good soups and *shashliks*, smoked salmon, *boeuf* Stroganoff, broiled sturgeon, caviar in all its varieties, with fruits, wines and *gâteaux* for anyone who had the money to pay for them.

Russian clothing is very shoddy stuff compared to that of the Western world, and during the war foreigners with *propusks* (permits) for the diplomatic shop in Kuznetzki Most used to pass them on to their servants because of the poor quality of the goods. One of these permits was worth as much as 800 roubles in the black market.

Even before the war it was a rare thing to see a woman well-dressed by Western standards walking along the streets of the Russian capital. The visiting foreigner finds overalled women and carelessly-dressed men in their ill-fitting suits, a drab lot. And one of the first things I noticed about the men and women in the streets of England was their rosy cheeks and animated faces. You won't find such health in Moscow. Lack of proper housing forces the citizens to live, as in most of the cities in the Soviet Union, in squalid wooden shacks and rickety tenements which they keep closely sealed throughout the six or seven months of winter. Precise figures for tuberculosis are never published in the Soviet Union, for if they were made public, they would disclose a lamentable failure in the Kremlin's housing plans. It is a secret as closely guarded as the atom bomb experiments.

In all the new industrial projects which have taken place in the Soviet Union in the two five year plans, the main concern of the Kremlin planners has been to establish factories and production plants. In all such projects workers' homes receive a very low priority and, in many cases, are non-existent. It is true that some huge blocks of workers' flats have been erected here and there and they look fine in the propaganda magazines, distributed abroad by the Soviet Union. But many are mere empty shells, without lifts or adequate plumbing and sanitary arrangements. Gas pressure, on Soviet stoves, is usually so low it takes an hour to boil a kettle. I was quite startled when I first turned on a gas-ring in London.

And to get a worker's home even in pre-war Russia was much more difficult than here in England today. One girl I knew who had a good job as a translator-typist at Tass, the official Soviet news service, considered herself very lucky to have a place of her own. She showed it to me once, a triangular space under the staircase on the ground floor of an old block of flats near the site for the Palace of the Soviets.

Here she ate and slept in a space four feet by six feet with a roof starting at 8 inches and sloping to six feet. In any western country it would have been a store-place for brooms, pails and cleaning rags, but Zena had put in a tiny divan, table and a small packing-case for a book-shelf. Her wardrobe was six nails on the wall. She used to steal wood and give it to the caretaker to augment what little central heating there was, but she usually relied on her own small electric fire. Zena used to talk proudly about her apartment and with some justification, for even having that tiny living space to herself was an achievement.

The overcrowding in Moscow is so bad that only the highest party officials have a flat to themselves.

Soon after I arrived in Moscow I had an invitation to call on some friends who were living in a block of flats in the Kuznetzky Most, the Regent Street of Moscow, and I was excited to think I should be visiting such a fine apartment house.

On my arrival I found there were no lights on the staircases; the bulbs had been stolen. But by striking matches I finally found the right floor and I knocked on the double doors of the flat. An old woman opened it very cautiously and when I gave her the name of my hostess, she let me in and I followed her along a corridor illuminated by a single electric bulb. There were six doors on either side of the corridor and I thought to myself "What a grand place to live in."

The old lady knocked at door No. 4 on the right and my friend appeared. "Ah, *Zdrastvui*! Norochka!" she cried. "Come on in." I followed her into a small space curtained off from the rest of the room, from which I could hear much laughing and chattering. In the space where I stood was a little electric hotplate, a sink, a packing-case converted into a cupboard for food and an odd bucket. A towel hung from a nail on the wall.

Everything was spotlessly clean. This impressed me more later when I realized that this woman, her mother, two children, husband and sister-in-law, all lived in the same room. And their pattern of living was repeated with variations in each of the dozen rooms lining the corridor. By casual questioning I gathered there were some fifty people living in this apartment, and they all shared one water closet at the end of the corridor.

As I began to know people in Moscow, I began to realize what a privileged life I had led. The problems of accommodation, food and clothing did not affect us as they were all solved for us by the State. But for the unprivileged millions, life in the Soviet Union is no Utopia. After the outbreak of war, there was so little food in the capital that people had to start queuing at five in the morning even in the depths of winter, with the temperature several degrees below zero, in order to get their bread ration. The shop would open when the bread arrived from the bakery, which might be any time between 8 and 10 a.m. In less than an hour the stock would be sold out and those who came late would go without.

The same applied to sugar. If you were rich enough you went to the open market and bought a loaf of bread for 50 roubles (£1) and compared with this, your rationed loaf was indeed cheap at 2 ½ to 5 roubles. It was actually forbidden to sell either bread, sugar, or coupons to obtain them on the open market; the penalty was a spell in a labour camp. But this did not deter Moscovites from trading in these commodities, and at the enhanced prices bread and sugar were certainly profitable goods to handle. You find these open markets all over Russia and one of Moscow's liveliest spots is the Central Market, covering several acres just north of the city centre. At heart, we Russians are a friendly race, and even in the grip of the secret police we find time to joke among ourselves. You can't walk through the Central Market without hearing some typical Moscow back-chat.

Here's a story current in the capital during the war. It is a fair illustration of the good-natured banter to be found among the workers:–

Militiaman: "You had some sugar in your hand, Babushka" (every old peasant woman is "Babushka" in Russia).
Babushka: "Who me? No, my boy, I am waiting for my friend."
Militiaman: "Now come along. I saw it myself."
Babushka: "Impossible. I have already used my sugar for my daughter's child. Oh, how I wish I were a younger woman! "
Militiaman (intrigued by this odd tangent of the argument): "What's that got to do with the sugar?"
Babushka: "Well, if I were younger, I'd love to marry a fine young man like you."

83

Militiaman: "Oh, would you?" Pause. "Would you make a good wife, d'you think?"

Babushka: "Oh, yes. I'm a wonderful cook."

Militiaman: "Hm. But would you do everything I told you?"

Babushka: "Of course I would; everything!"

Militiaman: "Would you sell sugar on the open market if I told you to?"

Babushka: "Certainly not! "

Militiaman: "Well, you're no good to me. Go away!" and off he strolled, leaving the old woman to the general sympathy of the crowd.

The Moscow winter is terribly hard for elderly people, but the old women stand it better than the men. Even in the backbreaking job of chipping away the ever-forming ice on the main streets and squares, there are always more women at work than men. This job is performed with iron rods and wooden shovels and is paid for at the rate of 300 roubles a month. It is an integral part of the official running of the city during the winter months and everyone below a certain employment grade has to give a hand. Shop assistants, typists and everyone not in the heavy worker class has to take a day's turn in chipping the ice off the main roads, but on most of the pavements the snow is left to be trampled down into solid black ice until the following May when it starts breaking up into black slabs sometimes six inches thick.

There are no paving stones on Moscow's pavements and walking on the frozen asphalt is a tricky business. The surface is bumpy and uneven and people fall about all over the place. There are no iron gratings over open basements, drains are sometimes left open and it is very common for pedestrians to fall and break an ankle. Even on busy main roads, manhole covers are often misplaced and left out of position for days. People of Leningrad have always regarded Moscow as an overgrown village, and in many respects they are right.

Although not an ardent Communist, one of my first sightseeing seeing trips was to visit Lenin's tomb in Red Square. Here, the workers of Russia queue to see the founder of the Revolution lying in state and there is little doubt that their pilgrimage provides an outlet for much of the inborn religious fervour of the Russian people. Men, women and children begin to queue two or three hours before the red and black marble mausoleum is opened. Lenin is on view all the year round and by the time the little metal wicket-gates are opened by the guards the queue often stretches for a mile around the Kremlin walls.

The tallest and smartest of the Kremlin guards maintain their vigil of the tomb day and night. They also marshal the queue as it trickles, one by one, down the black polished stone steps into the vaulted chamber where the body lies. No one is allowed to take a package with them, even handbags are taken away at the entrance. And no one is allowed to linger by the illuminated glass enclosure in which lies the earthly remains of the man who founded the Soviet Republic.

He looks quite small compared with the pictures one has seen of him which usually represent him as a stockily-built man. His features glow in a strange orange light and the lower half of his body lies beneath a heavy scarlet cloth. The corpse has been dressed in a simple, khaki gabardine uniform. The face is peaceful with the high cheek-bones of an Asiatic. Magnificent blooms line the inside of the glass coffin round Lenin's body. These are changed daily.

The embalmed corpse is inspected regularly by a staff of experts. For to Russia Lenin is a saint, and in the peace of his tomb his followers escape from the roar of the Russia outside to pay homage to the man who they know planned a vastly different future for them than the life they now endure. In the grim eerie atmosphere that surrounds his bier, the hopes of millions have been buried. And, a stone's throw away in the Kremlin, Stalin and the rest of the Politburo are determined that these hopes shall remain buried, and the police state goes on.

No account of the life of Moscow would be complete without a reference to the theatres, where the standard of production compares with any in the world. The Bolshoi Theatre Ballet Company, even during the war had a *corps de ballet* of over a thousand and all the male dancers were classed as being in a reserved occupation. When Moscow was evacuated the company went with all their scenery and equipment to Kuibishev, but when the Germans were flung back they returned in triumph, bringing their "props" up the Volga in a barge.

I paid several visits to the Red Army theatre to see some of the shows produced by the soldiers. Nothing is spared in the Soviet Union when it comes to the army, which has the best of everything, and the shows they put on are magnificent entertainment. The curtain swings up on a stage crammed with soldiers in their best walking-out clothes, shiny black peaked caps, red cap-bands and the Soviet star. With red epaulettes and navy blue breeches they sit upon tiers reaching high up to the back of the stage. Over a hundred and fifty men take part in these concerts, four rows of the choir, another of brass instruments, twenty of balalaika players and, in front, nine piano-accordionists. The massed singing is superb but it is always the dancing which really brings the house down. Each troupe has its own speciality dancers and when the time comes they leap around the stage spinning and jumping like fire-crackers. In a grand finale every man on the stage joins in, each doing something different in the way of clever footwork.

In addition to the theatres, there are of course plenty of cinemas, though there is a vast difference in comfort between Russian cinemas and those in England. The seats are of hard wood, but as the show seldom lasts for more than two hours and Moscow citizens are inured to a hard life no one seems to worry. From eight in the morning, when the first queues begin, till ten-thirty at night when the cinemas close, there are always crowds milling round the entrance.

It is always a struggle to reach the box-office of a Russian cinema. It is everyone for himself and the continual wrestle to get near the box-office always attracts the pick-pockets. During the war Soviet servicemen had priority and they used to edge in round the scrum nearest the box-office pushing everyone aside in order to get in. Four average sized Russian cinemas would fit quite comfortably into an English one; they seldom seat more than five hundred, usually only two or three hundred. The big film is always preceded by the Soviet newsreel, but by European standards it is a very dull production.

The film "Klyatva" (the oath), showing how Stalin carried on the Revolution from the death of Lenin, was screened in every Moscow cinema for months during the war. Soviet press reports claim this film to be a sensational success but, in actual fact, film audiences found it mediocre and boring. But despite this, state cinemas kept it on their screens for months. One war-time film which genuinely drew the crowds was "Lady Hamilton" with Laurence Olivier and Vivien Leigh. There are few things Russian women enjoy more than a good weep and Lady Hamilton gave them this. Cinemas were cheap in Moscow — 5 roubles would buy two hours' warmth in spite of the hard seats. Smoking is forbidden.

Towards the end of 1938 I attended a film at the Foreign Office club cinema called, "If tomorrow there is war". It was the biggest propaganda effort of the Soviet film industry up to that time and it was shown throughout the Soviet Union.

The film was a clever documentary portraying the armed strength of the Kremlin and there were innumerable shots of planes, tanks and soldiers. The film was the talk of the country and a special march was composed to run through the commentary as a strident martial background.

This march was also called "If tomorrow there is war" and later, when war had already come to the rest of Europe, the story is told that Molotov sang the opening phrase at the banquet given by Hitler in his honour after the signing of the non-aggression pact with Ribbentrop in Berlin in 1940.

Hearing Molotov start, Ribbentrop lost no time in joining him. Only his song was different — and significant. It was still a Russian one, "Moscow is my beloved town".

One of my first adventures in the Russian capital was a trip on the suburban electric railway to Perlovka to see a school friend. I'd never been on the Russian metro before, and I soon understood why so many workers prefer to share rooms in crowded Moscow rather than live in more comfort outside the city. A journey on the Russian metro is full of hazards and you have to be tough to survive. Later I made this trip so often I got to know the routine backwards. Like cinema-goers Moscow tube travellers don't queue for tickets and there's always a crowd round both the ticket booths and the automatic machines, though the latter are seldom in working order. Escalators take passengers to the platforms but Moscow tube passengers always push whether the trains are empty or full. The train guard never waits for passengers to get on or off, but starts whenever her time schedule says she must leave, hence the frantic fight. Every train has a special coach at the front for children and women with babies in arms and, during the war, wounded soldiers. This is the only carriage you can enter without a struggle.

It's quite a common occurrence to be carried past one's stop, the passengers are packed so close together. Once off, the traveller must search for the next train, but the indicators are seldom much of a guide as Russian trains often start from platforms other than the ones shown.

After finding the train, the Moscovite must wait behind a crowded barrier until the porters think fit to let everyone through with a rush. It is quite normal to see old women and children bowled over in the stampede.

Not even the attendants on the train itself ever seem to know whether the train will be stopping at the station you want. I once got into a train having been assured it would stop at the place I wanted and found myself in a siding with two hundred other people outside the Moscow terminus. We all got out, walked back and started asking again. Russian trains have wooden seats but on the big long-distance runs you can hire cushions and rugs. There are seven stations between Moscow and Perlovka and throughout the journey there were always cries of "Move up, Citizens, Citizeness Olga is falling off," and the most frequent shout was "Let me in, comrades, my hands are freezing." But certain comrades can be remarkably deaf on such occasions.

In the summer, Moscow train journeys are more dangerous than ever. The citizens go out to their allotments after they finish their work, taking spades and rakes. By law, the metal parts have to be covered to prevent accidents but they are still unpleasant travelling companions. Smoking is fortunately prohibited. During the war the English made a joke about their trips on the Moscow suburban metro. They never asked one another "Is your journey really necessary?" It was always, "Is your journey really possible?"

But Moscow's underground stations must be the most beautiful in the world; each one is architecturally different and patterned in a variety of multi-coloured marble, tiles and mosaics. But a Londoner would miss the advertisements.

On the trams the conductress doesn't move about among the passengers but stands in her position and waits for them to hand her the fare. No change is given or asked for, and those nearest her work as hard as she does, passing on other people's money and sending back their tickets in return.

One evening I went with a party of students from the university to a boxing show. The event was held in the House of the Unions in the centre of Moscow. It was the first I'd seen and I wrote a long description of it to a school-friend in Stalingrad. The ring had been built on a platform normally used by concert artists and looked a little grotesque in the pillared hall with its glittering chandeliers. The wall behind the ring had been draped with a red velvet backcloth; it was all very beautiful, and not a bit like the usual prize-fights elsewhere. British or American fight fans would have felt strangely out of place, no blazing arc lights, no pressmen round the ring, no big cigars and no hubbub. It could have been a pianoforte recital in the Albert Hall and the crowd as well behaved as any other Moscow theatre or ballet audience.

Most of the fighters were from the Moscow Dynamo Club or the Wings of the Soviet which draws its members from aircraft factories around the city. The fighters, of course, were all amateurs. There are no professional boxers in the Soviet Union, and you will never hear the ballyhoo announcements which are sent roaring over the heads in Madison Square and Harringay Arena.

In Moscow the announcers say simply, "Master of Sport, Alexander Kitlovy, weight 90 kilograms." Clever fighting is mildly clapped, but when one of our party forgot herself and shouted "Hit him, Kolya," everyone turned round, stared and smiled. Hers was the only shouted encouragement of the whole evening and she was most embarrassed.

There was so little to relieve the monotony of war-torn Moscow that I think even the stony hearts in the Kremlin must have realized this for, throughout the time I was in Moscow, women could always get their nails painted. It meant queuing but the queue was a comparatively orderly one and we could always find plenty to chatter about. The painting was done by a small corps of white-coated girls in the larger establishments, and sometimes one could also get a perm.

Lipstick was a rarity; it didn't look well on cold lips anyway, but painted finger nails at least provided a dash of colour in the greyness of life in Moscow.

Though there were always the red banners spread across the buildings, "Greetings to Stalin the Great War Leader", "All for the Front", and "Work Harder for the Victory". On national holidays, such as 7 November, 1 May or on New Year's Day (Christmas Day does not exist in the official calendar), Soviet buildings are decorated with great portraits in colour and in black and white of Lenin, Stalin, Marx and Engels. These four always had pride of place in Moscow, strung across the columns of the Bolshoi Theatre.

Along the front of the Moscow Hotel, reserved exclusively for Red Army generals and the highest political bodies in war-time, were the portraits of members of the Politburo, Malenkov, Voroshilov, Kalinin and the rest, with Stalin in the centre. On the modern semi-skyscraper opposite, the House of the Council of People's Commissars, the same portraits appeared with the same forbidding look. Stalin's portrait or bust was in every shop window; there was so little else to put in them. Stalin is indeed the god of all Russia, and woe betide any misbelievers caught blaspheming him. Hallowed was the name of our father who lived in the Kremlin. Even so, a popular joke when I arrived in Moscow was that Stalin was the father of too many children. Russians regard their leader as a great lover.

The only thing ever advertised in war-time in Russia was the Government, there was no point in advertising anything else, the goods simply did not exist for the mass of the people.

Yet, by street loudspeaker, in the press, on the cinema screen and on the stage, we were daily told that the new Soviet citizen was better off than anyone else in the world.

It was difficult not to believe it as we had no easy means of discovering the real truth and it was extremely dangerous to try to find out. All we knew about England was that it was a country where a few fabulously rich, usually fat aristocrats, held complete sway over the starving workers. It was, so we were told, a land where hordes of little children roamed barefoot in the slums.

We were assured, however, that the masses were slowly but surely gaining in strength and that the time would come when they would overthrow their cruel masters and join hands with the freedom-loving peoples of the Soviet Union. Most of our reading about the English scene was restricted to

89

Dickens, Sir Walter Scott, Jack London and the odd uncomplimentary report in the daily press about Britain.

For all Russia knows, Dickens's London still exists. No one ever told us that the social evils described so vividly in *Oliver Twist* and *Great Expectations* are now a thing of the past. We were led to believe that prisoners still rotted in Newgate gaol and poor little paupers were still flogged in cold, dark work-houses.

But this state of affairs did not seem to be borne out by the English people I was later to meet. The Englishmen at the Embassy wore good quality clothes and I was vaguely puzzled when I saw them. The quality of Soviet-made goods was never as good as the furniture and household articles in my mother's home. In Moscow's commission shops, the furniture, vases, pictures and other ornaments made in Czarist Russia fetch fabulous prices. Soviet manufactured clothes have little wear in them. For example, the summer weather is usually hot, broken only by thunder storms and torrential showers so that within a few minutes gutters are overflowing and there are big puddles everywhere. Shoes are a precious possession, and when caught in one of the sudden downpours, Moscow women whip them off and run barefoot to shelter rather than risk ruining them.

In the winter we were better off with our *valenki*, long felt top boots made of pressed wool. Worn with goloshes they keep the feet warm and dry.

Religion is still permitted though officially it is discouraged. As I have explained, my own generation have received no religious instruction and the church has become one of the vestiges of the old days to which only the older and country people still cling. A familiar sight at Easter-time outside the big cities is the procession of farm workers in their Sunday best carrying their Easter cakes neatly wrapped in white cloths for the priest to bless at the village church. There were some four hundred churches in Moscow before the Revolution and although most of them have fallen into decay or have been converted into workshops and tenements, a few still carry on. At Easter-time and on New Year's Eve they are packed to the doors which have to be kept open so that the overflow can mass outside.

In the depth of winter, the heat generated by the packed worshippers causes drops of condensed moisture to patter down on their heads from the high roof. Most of the women wear white woollen shawls over their heads and shoulders and each one carries a lighted candle. The droning voice of the bearded old priest, clad in full vestments, is often interrupted by subdued scuffling as someone's shawl is set on fire by the candle behind. The collection is taken in great brass platters and if one cannot spare more than a rouble or two it is quite in order to put in a note and take out the change.

What do people drink in Russia? Vodka is still the staple alcoholic beverage. Bottles of it are placed on restaurant tables just as water is served elsewhere. The name means "little water", which it resembles in everything but taste and smell. It is distilled from either potatoes or grain and the latter variety, practically tasteless, is the better quality. Russians drink many kinds of vodka, pepper vodka, flavoured with red peppers; bulovka, a Polish mixture flavoured with a particular kind of grass; hunter's vodka which looks like cognac but, according to my husband, tastes like floor polish; lemon vodka and pink vodka flavoured with angostura bitters. Vodka is easily flavoured by dropping small pieces of fresh orange peel into the bottle. Russians also enjoy Soviet-made champagne, both red and white, and the State also makes gin and whisky. But vodka remains the nation's national drink and confirmed vodka-drinkers, like Pernod addicts, will go to any lengths to maintain their supply.

One evening I noticed a crowd round a militiaman near Moscow's Arbat metro station and when I reached it I found a woman pleading with the official to find her husband. He asked her what he looked like but her description wasn't of much help to him. Finally, he asked "Anyway, what are you so worried about? Surely he can look after himself?"

"That's just it," cried the wife, "he's a little drunk and now that all his money has gone he'll freeze to death trying to buy some more vodka."

"Freeze to death buying vodka — how's that?"

"Why," said the woman, "you don't know him like I do — he'll sell his trousers! "

These interludes are quite common on the streets of Moscow. The average Soviet citizen is a good-natured fellow who enjoys a joke and likes to have an audience around him.

When a new wing was being added to the Lubyanka gaol during the war the English and Americans made a little joke of it among themselves and called it "the Anglo-American wing". As usual this filtered through to the Soviet Foreign Office and from then on the Russian officials joined in the joke and used to delight in nodding across at the gaol in the presence of the English and American colleagues and drawing their attention to the progress being made on their future home.

On another occasion the personnel of the U.S. Embassy formed a dance band of their own which used to play at semi-official functions. The Americans called their orchestra "The Kremlin Grows". But the title found

91

disfavour with the Kremlin and a polite hint was dropped at one of these dances that the name of the band was not altogether approved. Anxious to please, the Americans said they would of course change the name of their dance orchestra. At the next dance the same band played under a different name. Their new title? — "The Purged Pigeons".

In general, Russian humour is unsubtle and simple. Here is a typical story which used to get roars of laughter whenever it was told:—

A man borrowed a large pot from his next door neighbour but when asked to return it he made a number of excuses. Finally, the owner got so angry he arrived at the man's house prepared to rescue his property by force.

"Ah," said the man who had borrowed it, "Don't distress yourself, but you see there's been an increase in the family and your pot now has a little baby pot." And he solemnly returned one large pot and a small one.

The owner was delighted and some days later when asked to lend it again he did so willingly. But he soon regretted the action for the man kept it longer than ever, and when he finally insisted on its return, he was told, "You can't have your pot back, it's dead."

"Dead?" said the owner, "but how can a pot die?"

"Well, Comrade," said the other, "you were quite ready to believe it could give birth to another pot — so why shouldn't it die?"

I have told earlier of the many sudden disappearances and purges which take place daily throughout the Soviet Union. But none of these events are ever reported in the Soviet Press, unless the culprits are given public trials and this is seldom the case, and Russian newspapers are dull, dreary publications compared with English or American daily papers.

Like all good party-men, Father read and believed every line of *Pravda* and *Izvestia*. He also took the *Bolshevik*, monthly organ of the party and *Krokodil* (Crocodile) a cartoon paper which lampoons the West.

It is strange for me now to pick up a Sunday morning paper and find it filled with the private life of a murderer or crammed with the confessions of a lawyer or sportsman. We do not have such informative articles in Russia! The Russian Press is filled with items of news only found in the trade papers of other nations; the latest production figures of a tractor plant, crop prospects in the collective farms and the number of tons of coal mined during the past month.

92

All these items get big headlines in Russian newspapers and having been brought up in this atmosphere I find it strange to get used to English ones. As all Russian papers are owned by the State, they only give the State viewpoint. I remember once hearing that before the Revolution there were independent newspapers in Russia representing different political opinions. When I asked my father about this he was quick to point out the folly of such a system.

"After all," he said. "Why have different newspapers when there can be only one story to tell? The correct, official version which is what you always get in our newspapers today."

You hear the same exhortations from the State every day on the radio. Day and night there are calls for the workers to do better, to increase output and to report slackers to the heads of the factory. Miners who have broken records with their output of coal are brought to the microphone to encourage others. The Soviet citizen is never allowed to forget how lucky he is to be living in a Communist State when he cannot be exploited by capitalist enterprise.

But Russian newspapers are never slow to criticize, though foreigners find it hard to understand how State-run newspapers can criticize State-run industries and municipal services. Here is an indictment which pulls no punches against the municipal services of Kuibyshev. It appeared in the town's own paper *Volzhskaya Kommuna*:

"Kuibyshev has grown and people visit it from all over the country. A brigade of *Volzhskaya Kommuna* investigators set out to discover how the town greets its visitors.

"They established that the National Hotel and the House of Collective Farmers have been leased to an incompetent crowd, quite unable to maintain even the most elementary tidiness.

"The director of the National Hotel, Kuznetsov, is a guest in his hotel and cares not at all that the hotel is unheated, dirty and thoroughly uncomfortable.

"The food administration looks after everything and everyone except the hotel clients who are obliged to wait several hours for their dinner. All this must be changed immediately.

"Visitors arriving in the town should be given clean, warm rooms and appetizing meals.

"A man arrives in town and at the station is told the name of the local hotel. He arrives at a beautiful house, called National Hotel, only to be informed by the desk-clerk that there is no room vacant for the moment.

The visitor waits in the vestibule until the small hours of the morning and maybe, at 2 a.m., a room becomes vacant. Unfortunately, however, the desk-clerk has now gone off duty and has forgotten to leave a message about the visitor, who is lucky if he can obtain the key of the vacated room by 5 a.m., having waited for exactly twelve hours.

"But, once installed, the visitor wonders whether it would not have been better to have stayed downstairs, for the room is filthy, the floor is littered with cigarette-stubs and bits of paper (no ash-trays or wastepaper baskets are provided), and he has to make up his own bed with the sheets which have been dumped on a chair. These sheets must last for his entire stay, even if he is there for six months!

"There is no heating and people have to sleep fully dressed, because the central heating system is out of order and no one has bothered to order any fuel anyway.

"Visitors who have been staying in the hotel for several months have fixed up electric heaters in their rooms regardless of the posters exhorting them to save electricity.

"There is snow on the walls of the rooms, the lavatories are filthy, and most of them are flooded and the walls and ceilings are peeling. Rats run freely about the rooms and all the doors can be easily opened with the same key.

"The director is never to be seen and is always on business, though it surely is not connected with the hotel.

"Visitors to a town judge it by its municipal services and hotels. The National Hotel is indeed a very poor advertisement for Kuibyshev and the town authorities should do more for its visiting workers."

Reading this you can quite understand that if the popular Fleet Street dailies and weeklies appeared on Moscow newsstands one morning the Russians would be dumbfounded and dismiss them all as rubbish. Russian and Western thinking are worlds apart.

CHAPTER VIII – DEATH OF THE TYRANT YAGODA

One morning at breakfast Father threw a ticket over to me. It was a pass to go to the third public prosecution of traitors in the Soviet Union. "You should go and see it, Nora," he said. "It is necessary for your education to see what Russia does to traitors."

At this trial, which started on 2 March, 1938, twenty-one Soviet leaders were accused of murder, treason, espionage and plotting to overthrow the Soviet Government. I had a particular interest in the proceedings before a Military Tribunal of the Supreme Court of the Soviet, because I had heard a great deal about two of the accused. One of them was Henry Yagoda, for fifteen years head of the N.K.V.D. and Father's late chief. Father always had a picture of him at home. In the dock with Yagoda was Krestinsky, Litvinov's former deputy and before that Ambassador to Germany, in whose house we were living. The prosecutor again was Vishinsky, now Soviet Foreign Minister.

It was ironic that Yagoda should be sitting in the dock as he was the man who had collected the evidence against Zinoviev and Radek, chief figures in a former traitor's trial. Radek, chief editorial writer of *Izvestia* and the voice of Stalin, had laid information against Yagoda a year before. His allegations were investigated by the N.K.V.D. and, although he was their chief, he was arrested. He had been imprisoned for several months before the trial began.

Judge Ulrich, who had presided at the former prosecutions, was again the judge. I was very interested to watch the trial, despite my misgivings concerning Stalin's previous purges. I felt that he was justified in bringing these men to trial, for had they not publicly admitted their guilt?

At eleven o'clock in the morning I sat in the centre of the House of the Trade Unions. It had been specially decorated with flags and slogans for the occasion, so that it looked more like a political meeting than a criminal court. Above Judge Ulrich, and the other three uniformed judges, was a banner bearing, a portrait of Lenin. On either side of the courtroom were the arc-lamps of movie cameras and at the rear of the raised judges' platform were large trees in tubs. The judges sat on the dais looking grim and unsmiling, and below them at a small table was Vishinsky wearing horn-rimmed spectacles.

At a word from the Judges he rose and started to scream into the radio microphones. His speech was a torrent of hate against the twenty-one men who sat dejectedly between armed soldiers in the dock. They had no defence lawyers.

Most of the men in the dock did not move as Vishinsky demanded they should be shot. Some of them leaned back in an almost bored fashion, gazing at the plaster mouldings of dancing girls on the ceiling.

Everyone listened to Vishinsky's speech in silence. Then one after another the accused men stood up in the dock and made a full confession of the crimes which the prosecutor had alleged against them. First to confess was Yagoda himself. White-haired, with his moustache still black, he stood up on his bandy legs and admitted ordering the death of Maxim Gorki, the famous Russian novelist, two years previously.

The head of the Kremlin hospital, white-haired Doctor Levin, confessed that he had killed Gorki and several others on the same day at Yagoda's instigation.

At the end of his statement Levin said:

"I loved Gorki and was sickened by the thought of losing him. I am a coward and should have informed against Yagoda but he threatened my family."

For several days the confessions went on; each one more fantastic than the other. Our former householder, Krestinsky, pleaded guilty to plotting to assassinate Molotov. Perhaps the most fantastic story of all was told by Rakovsky, formerly Ambassador to Great Britain and France. Talking into the microphones he said that while he was Ambassador in London he had been forced to work with the British Intelligence Service and had continued to do so until his arrest.

He said that while he was in London two British Secret Service men came to the Soviet Embassy and produced documents saying that he had served with the German secret police in the first World War. These papers were forgeries, but he became frightened when they threatened to denounce him to the Kremlin. So foolishly he agreed to their demands to spy for Britain. After his return to Moscow he said that Lady Muriel Paget had come to him and acted as a liaison officer between him and the British Secret Service. Lady Paget denied this in the British Press, but Vishinsky based most of his case against the former ambassador on this alleged confession.

These unbelievable statements went on and on, the accused in the dock repeating them tonelessly like gramophone records. Then, ten days later, at four o'clock in the morning, Judge Ulrich sentenced them all to death except three. The main defendants, Yagoda, Rakovsky and Krestinsky were shot.

The verdicts were popular in Russia, particularly the death sentence on Yagoda, who had created the slave camps and armies of forced labourers. He had become a revolutionary when he was a schoolboy of fourteen and was appointed head of the Cheka in 1920, three years after the Revolution. It was he who had arrested Trotsky and exiled him in 1928. He was a strange, wiry, little man with a peculiar aesthetic side to his character, because his hobby was growing roses. He claimed he grew the best roses in Russia. He also built the 142-mile long canal from the White Sea to the Baltic with slave labour. He had a quarter of a million men under him and turned the secret police into a separate state inside Soviet Russia with its own army, factories, prisons, camps, orphanages and schools. His spy network extended all over the world, and in the north of Russia and in Siberia his men controlled large tracts of territory to which entry was forbidden without a pass from the N.K.V.D.

In the early days his secret police, which became the N.K.V.D. in July 1934, had no right to sentence people, only to question them, as the police do in Western countries. Two months after Lenin came into power, corrective labour camps were set up in the Soviet. At first these camps were run in a humane manner and prisoners received trade-union rates and overtime for manual labour. They were even allowed to smoke. But as soon as Yagoda took over in 1920 he changed all that. The prison population, which was 57,000 in 1922, rose to 122,000 five years later. It must have increased greatly later, although accurate figures have never been published.

One of Yagoda's pet projects was the organization of Russia's first labour camps in 1923 in the Solovetsky Islands in the White Sea. By 1930 over 662,000 people were imprisoned in the islands. The canal from the White Sea to the Baltic, built by Yagoda, was constructed with slave labour from the Solovetsky Islands' camps. More than 300,000 slave workers were employed for three years building the canal. Many of them died, but those who survived called it "a hell of ice".

This was the record of the mild-looking little rose-grower who now confessed to plotting against the State. He was shot shortly afterwards.

After his execution, even more amazing stories of his life came to light. He was said to have embezzled more than a million roubles from the N.K.V.D. coffers and to have given wild, drunken parties with money stolen from the State. One of his mistresses was instrumental in his downfall as she had become the joke of Moscow with her wild extravagance and crazy wardrobe. It gave me a peculiar sensation when Yagoda was sentenced to death because he had been Father's chief. His downfall rocked the N.K.V.D.

97

from top to bottom and we were thankful Father had now retired from it and was employed by the Foreign Office. The revelations of Yagoda's life perturbed Stalin and he ordered a new purge of the highest N.K.V.D. men in Moscow. Yagoda's successor, Nikolai Yezhov, rounded up fifty of them and they were imprisoned in the Lubyanka.

There was one further order after the trial was concluded, that all books written by the accused were to be destroyed, and Soviet history books were amended accordingly. When the order came out father spent a whole day going through our library. Not only did he throw out everything they had written, but he also ripped pages out of other books in which they had been named. I offered to help him, but he said:

"No, I am the only one who can do this."

He was a Chekist to his fingertips.

All the time we were living in the beautiful wooden house at Klyazma life was perilous and uncertain. Nearly every day men and women were being arrested, shot or sent into exile. You could never escape from the atmosphere of intrigue, misery and sudden death. It was a strange and sinister atmosphere for a young girl to live in, but somehow one just accepted these things as part of life. One evening, when I was going to dinner at the diplomats' hotel, Dasha, the cloakroom attendant, came rushing up to me and said:

"Something terrible has happened to Mme Yakubovich. Come and help me."

I remembered the name because I had seen in *Pravda* a reference during the trial to Yakubovich as a friend of the accused men. He had been recalled from a post abroad and was ill in hospital. I went with Dasha to a ground floor bedroom. On the bed lay Mme Yakubovich with her mouth open and her eyes glazed, dead. There was an empty glass and a bottle beside her with a note which said: "I am better dead, I haven't the strength to fight the shame of these untrue accusations against my husband."

The day after this happened the student son of Yakubovich came from the provinces on a visit to his family. His stepmother was dead and he was not allowed to visit his father in hospital because Yakubovich was a doomed man. No one ever heard of him again.

About this time a tall, grey-haired, quiet-spoken diplomat came to share our country house with us. His name was Gregori Isaacovich Weinstein. He was a great friend of my father's and head of a section of the Western Department in the Foreign Office which handled all diplomatic business with England and America. He had lived for twenty years in America and England and had been specially picked for his knowledge of the Western way of life.

At this time Soviet foreign policy was to woo English and American sympathy, and Weinstein, who was an Anglophile, did a great deal to further the aim. He used to tell me stories of his life in Western countries and how happy he had been there. He loved England and America and it was inevitable that he should be purged when the Soviet foreign policy became anti-Western. His deputy was Sergei Belko who had been Secretary to Mme Alexandra Kolantai; the only Russian woman Ambassador, she represented Stalin in Sweden. Daughter of a Czarist general, Alexandra Kolantai was a great favourite of Stalin's, but even this did not make her immune from the supervision of the N.K.V.D.

Her husband, Dybenko, was purged and shot, and only the personal intervention of Stalin saved her from a similar fate. She always brought Father cigars and cigarettes whenever she returned from Stockholm. She was one of the most important people in Russia because she was one of the few who could speak direct by phone to Stalin.

Her ex-secretary, Sergei Belko, although he was still at the Foreign Office, was already in trouble. When I met him he had lost his Party ticket and was living with his beautiful blonde wife, Ina, in the notorious hotel in Klyazma. I talked to him sometimes but he was strange in his manner and his eyes were red-rimmed with fatigue. He told me that every night after he had finished at the Foreign Office the N.K.V.D. questioned him about his life in Sweden. They accused him of making anti-Soviet remarks at a diplomatic ball. His hands trembled when he told me this story.

"Of course it is all lies," he said. "But they have got it in for me, so what can I do?"

My conversations with Belko, for whom I felt sorry, got me into trouble with Father. One evening I met him near my home and he walked along with me. It was just about the time Father was due back for dinner and I was terrified he would see me talking to Belko. He had already warned me to have nothing to do with the diplomats staying at the hotel. He had said:

"They are all under suspicion, keep away from them."

But Belko kept telling me his troubles and he was so upset that I did not like to make an excuse to leave him. While he was talking, I heard the sound of a car coming and it passed me before I had time to walk away from him. Inside was Father and Weinstein. They did not look at me but when I got home they were waiting for me in the house.

Father was white with rage.

"I saw you talking to Belko," he stormed. "I will not have you talking to these men. You must know they have been working against us and they are all staying here until they are punished."

He was right about this because shortly afterwards Belko was arrested and sentenced to five years in prison. I saw his lovely wife, Ina, for a moment after the trial and she said:

"I have just seen Sergei. He has asked me to wait for him and of course I will. I will wait for ever."

I am afraid that Ina did not keep her good resolution. The next time I saw her was in 1942 in Archangel when I was trying to leave Russia. We met in the Archangel Intourist Hotel and I hardly recognized her because she had dyed her blonde hair black. She told me that she had remarried. She blushed when she told me who her husband was; he was an N.K.V.D. colonel, a member of the organization which had sent her first husband to gaol.

CHAPTER IX - MOLOTOV ARRESTS MY FATHER

Our two great friends from the Crimea now had big N.K.V.D. jobs in Moscow. At this time Stanislav Franzevich Redens, Stalin's brother-in-law and Father's chief in his early days, was now head of the Moscow N.K.V.D. and Semen Ankadievich Arnoldov — or Arnold as he was generally called — was one of Stalin's *aides* and accompanied him everywhere. He was always in every picture taken of Stalin because he was more than a mere *aide*. He was in charge of the N.K.V.D. men guarding Stalin and was personally responsible for his safety. Stalin was fond of Arnold and would often pose for photographs which appeared in the Soviet press with Arnold's little daughter, ten-year-old Nadezhda.

When we arrived in Moscow I called on Arnold. His wife Elizaveta, whom I called Aunt Liza, was pleased to see me but a little distant. She told me he was away in Vladivostock visiting his brother, another N.K.V.D. chief. I called once or twice again and each time she said he was still away. Then on one visit Elizaveta suddenly broke down and told me the truth.

"He has been arrested in Vladivostock," she said. "He will never come back."

I pressed her for more details but she could not tell me anything. All she knew was that his arrest had followed the court-martial of Tukachevsky, second-in-command of the Soviet Armed Forces. They had been great friends, with adjoining country estates. Again, like so many other people, she asked me to help her.

"Would you phone Redens for me?" Elizaveta asked. "He and your father are great friends of my husband's. Perhaps he will help me."

She gave me the number and I dialled it while she stood at my elbow. After all, I thought to myself, Stanislav Redens, although he has been head of the Moscow Region N.K.V.D. for fifteen years, had known Arnold for years; surely he would help. When I got through to the N.K.V.D. headquarters I asked to speak to Redens saying that I was Nora Korzhenko, daughter of Vassily Korzhenko of the Foreign Office. I had not spoken to him since the old days in Leningrad, but I recognized his strong voice as soon as it came on the line.

"Hullo, Nora," he said. "How are you? You must be a big girl now. Eighteen, eh? We must find a husband for you. You must come along and see us very soon."

We chatted like this for some minutes. At the end of every sentence the woman at my side kept nudging me.

"Ask him now," she whispered. "Nora, you must ask him!"

Just before Redens said good-bye, I managed to get it out.

"Oh, I nearly forgot," I said. "I saw Mme Arnold this morning and she asked me to enquire if there was anything you could do for her now that her husband has been arrested. She has no money and is very worried."

Redens' thick voice oozed charm at the other end of the phone.

"Certainly, Nora, tell her to get in touch with my secretary straight away."

I hung up, delighted, and told Elizaveta what he had said. She hugged me with joy.

I caught the train home feeling very happy. How silly, I thought to myself, to have imagined there would have been any trouble; of course Redens was anxious to help the wife of his old friend. No man could have been more considerate.

But when I reached our house my mood changed and I felt a cold chill in my heart. The house seemed strangely quiet and no one answered my knock. I had to fumble for my key, and when I went inside the house was in darkness except for one room. As I tip-toed past the open door I saw Father sitting there in his shirt sleeves, his face tense and stern.

"Come in here," he called when he saw me. For a moment he stared at me in silence, but his hands were shaking and there were little pulse throbs at his temple. He tried to speak but the words would not come. His rage was cold and frightening. Then suddenly it all tumbled out in a torrent of invective.

"You have been talking to Redens, you slut, how dare you," he shouted.

"I only spoke to him about Uncle Arnold," I stammered.

He came towards me and I stood paralysed. His hands clutched at my throat.

"How dare you," he muttered, through gritted teeth.

"Uncle, indeed, he is no uncle! He's an enemy of the State!"

"Father, stop it, you are hurting me," I managed to choke out. But he took no notice. With one hand on my throat and one on my shoulder he shook me until I was dizzy.

"If Redens tells what you have done, we are finished," he said. "You must never see that woman again. Do you understand? Now get out and go to bed."

I lay in bed that night and cried myself to sleep. I kept thinking of Uncle Arnold in the old days in the Crimea. It seemed a strange way for my father to treat a man who had been his friend for so long. Arnold was sentenced to eight years' imprisonment. I did not dare to speak about it to my father, but I

102

called on his wife many times, although I had to do it secretly in case Father found out.

It was events like this which first led me to doubt my father and led to my final break with him. All my life I had accepted our strange privileged position without question. But now I was becoming a grown woman and was beginning to wonder about the atmosphere of fear and suspicion which surrounded us.

I had never been interested in political matters. My membership of the Young Communist Organization had been very half-hearted and I only attended meetings spasmodically. Also I had never joined the Communist Party.

Because I could not appreciate the N.K.V.D. outlook there were constant scenes and quarrels and the domestic atmosphere became very strained. Ursula, my stepmother, in particular, was always trying to make trouble because of my lack of political fanaticism. She had always been jealous of me, and now she had presented Father with a boy, Felix, she seemed to hate me worse than ever. She was always criticising my attitude towards Communism and what she termed "lack of co-operation in family matters". She meant by this that I did not seem to appreciate Father's high position in the Soviet Union. My life was rapidly becoming unbearable because wherever I went and whatever I did I was spied upon. Maids and waiters in the diplomats' hotel, and even N.K.V.D. people seemed to delight in reporting all my movements. It was a terrible feeling to know that you were being watched all the time and reports were being made about you. It was even worse to know that these reports were going to your own father.

The whole business boiled over one night when Father shouted:

"You are no daughter of mine."

My stepmother agreed and said:

"We do not need a daughter like you."

That night I packed my bag and left. The next day I went to see my father at the Foreign Office. He was cold and business-like, and arranged for me to have one room in another flat in the building.

I never lived at home again but I continued to study at the university. I was now nineteen and still hoped my father would help me into the diplomatic service.

The university training was directed entirely into one channel: that all nations outside the scope of Marxist philosophy were decadent, and their whole policy was to destroy the U.S.S.R. Any student who doubted this ideology, which was thrust down our throats by every professor, had to be

103

very careful to conceal it. Otherwise they would find themselves in a camp for a special re-education course. The most notorious of these was Kem-Solovki in the White Sea area. Naturally, no one wanted to go to these camps so everyone was very careful. I had to be particularly careful as I was living alone without a Party ticket, and I was entirely dependent upon Father's protection. I had no income other than my university allowance of 150 roubles a month which was hardly enough to buy food in the students' canteen. Every student at the university could draw this allowance, but in return they had to agree to give the first five years after graduation to the service of the U.S.S.R. This does not sound unreasonable, but in reality it meant that students had to leave homes and families to go wherever the State ordered.

Nora's Moscow University identity card 1937

After I left my father I began to mix more with the ordinary people of Russia. It was a relief to get away from the mutual suspicion and regimentation of life in the N.K.V.D., but when I began to walk through the streets of Moscow I received a shock. Among officials one naturally never heard any criticism of the regime, and I had always thought the ordinary people of Russia felt the same way.

Yet, as I went about the streets, I was amazed to hear people openly criticizing life under Stalin. Everywhere, men and women were saying things which, if they had been overheard by the N.K.V.D., would certainly have led to their arrest. It worried me a great deal as I knew that even to listen to such remarks was to run the risk of arrest. Also it was impossible to decide whether the person who was complaining was a genuinely disgruntled person or an *agent provocateur*. There was one man in a café who was obviously genuine as he had already been in exile and he didn't care who heard about it. I was embarrassed to hear him shout in a loud voice:

"Communism? Communism hell! You can't tell me Stalin has to sit up all night waiting to buy a pair of shoes and a shirt."

It was this sort of remark that made me realize that life away from my parents was very different from what I imagined, looking at it through the rose-tinted spectacles of the N.K.V.D. A lot of people knew what my father's position was and they lost no time in telling me how they felt about Stalin's rule. I became so confused and worried by the remarks that were hurled at me that I decided to take a few days' holiday and visit Leningrad. I wanted to get away from Moscow and think things over.

I went to say good-bye to Father. By a lucky chance he was alone in the house. It was the first opportunity I had had for years to speak to him without my stepmother being present. He was lying on the bed, looking tired and worried. When I came in he looked up at me and said a little sadly:

"Forgive me, Nora, if I have failed you as a father. Someday you will understand everything."

I sat on the bed and we talked. He said suddenly that he would like to retire from public life and take up his earlier ambition to be a writer. I was astonished to hear this as it seemed to me he had everything that a Soviet citizen could desire. Then he told me something which made my heart stand still.

His room at the Foreign Office was being searched in his absence. He had suspected it for some time and had set little traps among his papers, a paper-clip over a certain word, or a thread of cotton across a manuscript, and next morning they had been moved. This meant that someone was examining his papers during the night. It could only be the N.K.V.D. because his safe had been opened and only the secret police knew the combination apart from Father. The implication was all too obvious. He was under suspicion.

It was with a heavy heart that I said good-bye to him.

On the way to the station I met a professor, a friend of mine, who was in charge of the Soviet International Law Section. He had just returned from

Washington where he had advised the Soviet Embassy on certain negotiations. He was full of enthusiasm for America and the wonderful six months he had spent there. He told me of the fine shops and the many presents he had brought for his wife and child. Although a man of fifty, he gabbled away like a child telling about his first visit to the circus.

When I returned from Leningrad, I met his wife. Her home, her American presents, everything had been confiscated and the professor was now an inmate of the dreaded Lubyanka prison. He had committed one of the major crimes against the Soviet Union, he had praised the outside world too much.

Going to Leningrad, I only had enough money to travel third-class in a coach with wooden benches. It was a twelve-hour journey and straw mattresses were available but there were no blankets and no heating. When I arrived I was worn out. I immediately went to see my father's brother, Constantin, which was one of the main reasons why I had gone to Leningrad. He had been a captain in General Wrangel's White Army and had never agreed with my father's politics. He seemed very relieved to see me.

"Thank heaven you've come," he exclaimed. "Your father has been phoning for you all night. You must go back to Moscow at once."

It so happened that on the train to Leningrad I had met a young flying officer and had given him my uncle's telephone number. While I was trying to think how I would get back to Moscow quickly this young officer rang up. When I told him that I had to go back at once he said that he would see his commanding officer and help me to get a first-class ticket and a sleeping berth on that night's train. He met me at the station and we went to get some papers and magazines. We glanced at the headlines which said: "Litvinov Leaves Foreign Office — Molotov New Foreign Secretary."

"This is good news for you," said the young officer. "No doubt your father will get promotion now."

I agreed excitedly. After all, Father had been a good servant of the Soviet and I felt sure under the new rule he would be suitably rewarded. I had told Uncle to telephone Moscow and tell Father I was coming back. As I stepped off the train I looked eagerly along the platform hoping that he would be there to meet me.

I waited for an hour but there was no sign of Father nor was there an official car, which he always sent. I rang Father's office, thinking he might not have got my message, owing to the pressure of work caused by the changeover. When I gave my name over the telephone there was a pause and a voice said:

"Your father is very ill, Citizeness, very ill indeed."

106

I immediately dialled K 1-25/24, the number of our Moscow flat. My stepmother answered the phone and for a few seconds I could not understand what she was saying as she was weeping so much. Eventually I understood from her incoherent phrases that Father was very ill. I said I would come home at once, and rang off.

When I arrived at the flat I went straight to my stepmother's room. I found her hiding under the bedclothes, babbling unintelligible nonsense. I thought she had gone crazy. I rushed into my father's room but his bed was empty. My grandmother, who was still living with us, came into the room while I stood staring at the empty bed.

"Your father is in the Lubyanka prison," she said. "Molotov has had him arrested! "

CHAPTER X – THE BLACK RAVEN CALLS

Molotov's appointment caused a purge from top to bottom of the Soviet Foreign Office. First to go was Litvinov who was perhaps the best known Russian in the world, apart from Stalin. The suddenness of his dismissal was typical of the way they do things in Russia.

He had been Soviet Commissar for Foreign Affairs for ten years. Before that he lived for ten years in England and married an English girl, Ivy Low, niece of the late Sir Sidney Low, a British Tory. Our family came into contact with the Litvinov's many times, particularly on official occasions. We called her Ivy Walterovna, according to the Russian custom. Her father's Christian name was Walter, and she was always known in Soviet official circles as Ivy-the-daughter-of-Walter.

She was Moscow's most famous English teacher and taught many Soviet diplomats her native tongue before they took jobs in Britain and America. The Litvinovs had two children, a boy called Mischa, and an adopted girl, Tania, who was studying medicine. Litvinov, a benevolent-looking stout man with smiling eyes, was the most popular chief of the Foreign Office that Russia had ever known. He had no time for guards or N.K.V.D. spies.

For years after the Communist Revolution Russia was discredited in world politics, but Litvinov, a great international figure, put the Soviet back on the map. He brought Russia into the League of Nations and was a great advocate of collective security for which he coined his now famous phrase: "Peace is indivisible." It was inevitable that such a man must go when Stalin decided to woo Hitler's Germany.

The sudden departure of Litvinov was a great shock to diplomatic circles in Moscow because he was one of the few high-ranking Russians who knew the outside world. In spite of his geniality he had one curious foible. He had an unreasonable fear of being touched by any one. Foreign Office employees and foreign ambassadors were warned to be careful not to hold his arm while they were talking to him and only to give him the briefest of handshakes when it was absolutely necessary. If anyone overlooked this warning and touched him suddenly, he would shudder for a second or two as though he had a fever.

Apart from this peculiarity, he was a very easy man to meet. I remember on one occasion he came into my father's office while I was there and asked me about my studies at the university. When I told him I wanted to enter the diplomatic service, he gave a broad grin and turning to my father said: "She'll be an ambassador like Madame Kolantai. Just you wait and see."

This was the man who on May Day 1939, stood with Stalin, Molotov and Voroshilov, Commander-in-Chief of the Red Army, on the roof of Lenin's tomb, watching the march past of the Soviet troops and workers. My father also took part in this parade, standing with the British and American ambassadors.

No one had the slightest suspicion that while the leading men of the Soviet Union were talking amiably amongst themselves on Russia's Bank Holiday that Stalin had decided to sign a pact with Germany. On the same day, as he watched the parade with Litvinov, he dismissed him from his office as Foreign Secretary. There was a midnight announcement forty-eight hours later which told of Litvinov's "resignation". But, before the news was made public, he had already left his luxury home in 17 Spiridonovka and moved with his family into a three-room tenement flat.

The ten days that followed the dismissal of Litvinov were a time of great confusion in the Soviet Union. Not even the highest officials seemed to have any idea of what was happening. For instance, Vladimir Potiomkin, Litvinov's deputy — he had succeeded the disgraced Krestinsky — was still in Turkey carrying out Litvinov's policy of trying to rally the Balkans against German aggression. A few days later Potiomkin flew to Warsaw and happily assured the Poles that Russia would support them if Germany attacked. While he was there the Moscow radio announced that Litvinov's resignation would not affect Soviet foreign policy. But already, in the secrecy of the Kremlin, Stalin had decided otherwise. Litvinov's resignation had followed Stalin's approval of Voroshilov's policy that the Red Army would not fight Hitler over Poland.

This change of policy led to the liquidation of many loyal members of Litvinov's staff. Litvinov himself was too important a man to suffer the same fate, although he remained unemployed and in disgrace. When he asked to go to Vichy two months later to take the cure the N.K.V.D. refused him a visa, presumably imagining that he would never come back. Two years later, in 1941, Litvinov was forgiven his diplomatic mistakes. He was sent to Washington as Ambassador for the Soviet, but this was only because Stalin again wanted to be friends with America, because of the German attack on the U.S.S.R. In 1943 he was replaced in Washington by Gromyko and returned to the Foreign Office in Moscow as Molotov's deputy. He resigned for good in August 1946. If you understand Soviet foreign policy, the reason for his second resignation is quite clear. The war over, Stalin dropped his mask of friendship for his former Western allies, and Litvinov was therefore no further use to him.

An old man over seventy, Litvinov no longer takes any part in public life although he has been granted a State pension. He is never consulted by the leaders of the Soviet Union, but he is still treated with a certain amount of respect.

His wife, the former Ivy Low, still teaches English in Moscow, and in March 1949 she was named as Editor of the English section of a new English-Russian dictionary. The Litvinovs managed to escape the full fury that usually follows a dismissal by Stalin. In most cases it was followed by banishment or even death.

My father's story was a very different one. After the May Day parades, before anyone knew of the sudden switch in Soviet policy, he was just about to start dinner in his Moscow flat. He had just heard the news of Molotov's appointment, and was rather excited about it because he thought, as I did, that it might lead to further promotion for him. The telephone rang and he was told that Molotov, the new Foreign Minister, wanted to see him at once.

He left his meal untouched, called for a car, and drove immediately to the Foreign Office. He told my stepmother to keep his meal warm for him, as he would only be an hour or so. Several hours passed, and she became anxious. But she did not dare to ring the Foreign Office as she imagined he was in an important policy conference with Molotov.

Five hours later, at midnight, there was a knock on the door. My stepmother rushed to open it, thinking that he had returned. Four N.K.V.D. men pushed their way past her. They refused to give her any information and started to ransack the flat. They pulled open every drawer and cupboard in the house, examined every piece of paper they could find. Then they put their red seals on every drawer and door.

They left one small room open for my grandmother, my stepmother and her seven-year-old son Felix. At the same time as they were doing this, other N.K.V.D. men were conducting a similar search at our country house at Klyazma. The secret police hardly spoke to my stepmother except to turn to her suddenly and ask where I was. She had the presence of mind to say that I had left home, and was no longer living in Moscow. They seemed quite satisfied with this reply and did not appear to know of my one room in a Foreign Office flat which Father had given me.

I pieced all this story together when I returned from Leningrad. I managed also to pick up some more details of my father's arrest. When he had arrived at the Foreign Office he went to Molotov's room. Molotov received him with a stony stare, told him to hand over the keys to his office. Molotov then dismissed him with a curt nod. As he walked into the corridor, two N.K.V.D. men stepped forward and gripped his arms.

"You are held for investigation," they said. He was driven away at once to an underground cell in the Lubyanka Prison.

My stepmother did not like my staying in the flat. She kept repeating through her tears: "The N.K.V.D. are looking for you. You will not be safe here. Go at once."

I decided to chance it and return to my room in the Foreign Office building. I could not sleep all night because I knew it was only a matter of time before they started looking for me. As the daughter of a secret police official I knew the formula only too well. Under Article 58 of the Soviet Penal Code the arrest of the head of any family was always followed by the detention of his relatives.

The next night a long black limousine drove up to Father's flat. Again the uniformed men asked for me, and again Ursula, my stepmother, said that I no longer lived there. They searched the house again. Next day, at eleven o'clock at night they returned. This time they had with them a Black Raven, the Russian Black Maria.

The N.K.V.D. officer said to my stepmother: "Get a blanket and a pillow." She knew what that meant, a cell in the Lubyanka. They hustled her out of the house into the police van. Three N.K.V.D. men stayed behind in our flat and remained there until the following morning. They searched everywhere, slashed pictures, cut open mattresses, rolled up carpets, unpicked linings of clothing, poked down bathroom and kitchen pipes, they even cut open loaves in case anything was hidden inside them. They snatched a thousand-pound solitaire diamond from my stepmother's finger before they took her away in the Black Raven. They also took my grandmother's earrings.

When I called next day my grandmother told me this story. She said that she and my half-brother, Felix, were completely without money or food. By this time I was quite fatalistic as I felt it would only be a matter of time before they took me too. I decided to remain living in my room and even to attend the university. It was the only thing to do, because I ran a greater risk of being picked up if I was found wandering round the streets.

I had to get food for my grandmother and Felix. Father's special ration card was still good for two months' supplies, so I boldly took it along to the Kremlin stores. I ordered everything I could think of and told them to charge it to my father's account. My gamble was successful. The official machinery had not yet struck Father off the ration list; they had not been informed of his arrest.

My greatest problem was my half-brother Felix. I knew that the usual procedure in cases like this was for the N.K.V.D. to send him to an orphanage as a child of the State. I didn't want this to happen if I could help it. So I phoned Uncle Constantin, in Leningrad, and he came on the next train and took Felix away with him.

The next few days were a nightmare. Desperate for news of my parents, I took time off from the university and hung around the Foreign Office as so many unfortunate women had done before me. I had to be careful not to be too conspicuous, but I took terrible risks trying to get information.

My heart was full of hatred for Molotov. And every day I passed the private entrance and saw Molotov's men riding about in the cars which belonged to my father. The news was not generally known, and the sentry at Molotov's private entrance grinned and gave me a jaunty salute every time he saw me. I felt I could have hit him.

Several employees of the Foreign Office saw me lurking there but they passed me with averted eyes, just as I had once done to other women whose families had been imprisoned. But my heart leapt when I saw a familiar figure approaching along the street. He was the barber who always attended my father in the Foreign Office. I thought that he was bound to have some news. I approached him with a smile, but there was no answering recognition. I tried to speak to him but he walked away rapidly, hissing out of the side of his mouth: "Go away. I don't know you any more, you daughter of an enemy of the State."

Only one man was kind to me during this terrible period. A day or so after my father's arrest one of the heads of the university sent for me. I thought this summons would mean the end of my university career as the N.K.V.D. were bound to have given him a full report of my family's misfortune. I stood before him with my eyes downcast, waiting for him to tell me to leave.

"I suppose you know why I have sent for you, Nora," he said.

"Yes," I replied, hardly able to speak. "You want me to go."

He got up and put his arm round me. I could hardly believe my ears when he said: "No, Nora, you are quite wrong. I want you to stay. You see, I spent ten years in exile myself under the Czar, and I have children of my own. I have nothing but sympathy for you."

He shook my hand warmly and added: "Keep your courage up. Carry on here. I am sure it is what your father would wish."

112

But I found it very difficult to concentrate on my studies because my fellow students were not so friendly. By now the news was all over the university and most of them carefully avoided me. I did not mind that so much, it was the ones who came up to me and made insulting remarks who nearly broke my spirit. They had always been jealous of me because of my father's position and I tried to tell myself this, but their jeers often reduced me to tears. If it had not been for an occasional student who came to me with words of encouragement and sympathy I would have left the university. As it was, I decided to stick it out for as long as possible.

But there was a further blow on the way. A few days after my uncle had returned to Leningrad with Felix, he wrote to say that he could no longer be responsible for the boy as his presence was endangering his own family. He asked me to collect Felix at once. I could hardly blame him in a way because, owing to his connections with the White Russians, he was always in semi-peril from the Party. And harbouring the child of an enemy of the State was just the sort of excuse the N.K.V.D. needed to send him to prison.

So I sold a few trinkets to raise the fare and took the train to Leningrad. When I arrived I discovered my uncle had already boarded the boy out in a village outside the city. I went at once to collect him. The cottagers were only too anxious to get rid of him as they, too, knew that his father had been arrested. They practically pushed both of us out of the door as soon as I arrived.

CHAPTER XI – THE SECRET POLICE SEND FOR ME

It was getting dark as Felix and I wandered along the road, not knowing where to go or what to do. The poor little chap was tired and kept whimpering. At midnight we found ourselves in a wood in the middle of a gipsy camp. Everyone was asleep in their crude, dirty looking tents, but I woke one of the gipsies and they brought their leader. In Russia, the gipsies play a peculiar role, apart from the regimented life of the ordinary Soviet citizen. Even the N.K.V.D. do not interfere with them, and they are allowed to roam about the country unmolested. They are so wild and dirty that the Russian child was taught to regard them as bogey men.

As soon as little Felix saw the leader he gave a cry of terror. The leader was a most terrifying figure — aged about sixty, with a black beard down to his chest and his hair hanging loose over his shoulders. He was dressed in typical Russian fashion with a red shirt loose over faded baggy blue trousers tucked into high boots. He allowed us to stay in one of his tents. We shared this with his wife, a filthy old hag, dressed in tattered and patched garments. Felix kept whimpering about bogey men but I was too tired to care about anything and shortly we both fell asleep.

Next morning I walked through the camp to talk to the chief again. It was a frightening experience. I was still carrying my small suitcase, and some of the ragged women looked as if they would snatch it out of my hand.

The chief was shoeing horses. I told him I was penniless but wanted to get back to Moscow. He pointed to my suitcase and said if I would sell something to him he would give me some money. I gladly opened the suitcase, which contained a few dresses and odds and ends I had thrown together in my haste to get to Leningrad. He examined the contents and said that he thought he would be able to give me enough money; in the meantime we were to stay as his guests and none of the gipsies would harm me.

I lived for four days among the gipsies, eating with them by dipping into the communal pot. Sometimes it would only contain a few herbs, other times there would be a lamb or a fowl, according to what the gipsies had been able to shoot or steal. The greatest delicacy was the leg of a horse which they roasted on a spit. After supper, guitars and tambourines would be produced and girls would get up and dance. They were a merry people, although pitifully dressed. They managed, however, to get some colour into their rags by sewing brightly-coloured cloth on their garments, which gave them a crazy fancy-dress appearance.

Mostly they were good-humoured, but every now and again a fight would start, particularly among the women. They were always fighting over men, and if one glanced at another's boy friend a row would break out. Soon there would be a bunch of clawing, spitting women, rolling on the ground with more joining in every few seconds.

Once one of the women drew a knife and threatened to stab another. Felix crouched close to me in fear, but the chief stepped in and with a few well-directed slaps sent the women reeling. This was the only time I ever saw a man interfere in a women's fight. Unless a knife was drawn, they would stand around enjoying the forest strip-tease as the women tore the rags off each other's bodies.

But mostly the women spent their time round the communal fire, cooking or gossiping. At night the gipsies went into their tents and lay on a pile of dirty cushions, huddling for warmth like sheep. Every day I asked the chief if he had managed to get any money for me but he only shook his head. I began to be afraid that he had just stolen my clothes and the suitcase. But on the fourth day he called me and told me to get ready to go that evening. He handed me some roubles and one of his men led me through the woods to where the Leningrad bus stopped.

I had neither papers nor permits and I was afraid that I would be tapped on the shoulder any minute and asked for them. When I told the gipsy chief about this he laughed as, like all his clan, he travelled everywhere without official papers. He told me that few people would suspect a girl carrying a young boy and that I would easily get back to Moscow.

When I arrived in Leningrad I dashed on the train just before it started. All the way to Moscow, Felix and I sat close together almost afraid to look round. We arrived without incident and I took him immediately to my grandmother's room in my father's old flat. By a miracle the old woman had managed to keep some Dresden china and one or two other valuable articles away from the eyes of the N.K.V.D. and she was living by selling these. I went back to my flat in the Foreign Office, but I did not return to visit Felix for a long time as two new officials of the N.K.V.D. had taken over the rest of Father's flat and I could not risk meeting them.

Strangely enough, no one seemed to bother about me in my one room which was in a five-roomed flat with a communal kitchen, bath and lavatory. Housing accommodation was so short in Moscow that it was quite customary for several families to share a flat like this. One of the other occupants of the flat was a secretary from the Foreign Office who lived there with his wife and mother. The old lady lived in a boxroom without windows. I did not talk

115

to this official much as he was not very friendly. He was a tall, grim-faced man with glacial blue eyes, who had been six years in the Foreign Office.

After the purge he was given a better job. His name was Feodor Gusev and he later became a well-known figure in international diplomacy. My fellow lodger was to become Soviet Minister to Canada and succeed Maisky as Ambassador to Great Britain. He lived the grim, joyless life of a Soviet official and never seemed to smile. The Gusevs lived like Spartans. Their bedroom contained only two desks with green-shaded lamps, a metal bed and a wardrobe with no mirror. The walls were lined with books. Gusev and his wife were two of the most serious Communists I have ever encountered. They sat up every night until 2 a.m. reading books on the Marxist ideology.

Mme Gusev was one of the cleverest women in Moscow, and was quite unlike her gloomy-looking husband. Only in a country where there is complete equality between the sexes could she have held the position she did. She was Professor of Political Economy at Lenin's Military Academy. To the rest of the world it must have appeared strange that this little Jewess with greying hair and a lisping voice should have the unique responsibility of being the political watchdog at the Soviet Sandhurst. She had the responsibility of educating the future generals of the Red Army in Marxist theories. In spite of this, she was a human little woman and up to the time of my father's arrest we were very friendly.

Even before that I was short of money and I had to sell one or two things to live. She bought several books from me. I never thought when she handed over the money for them that the books would one day adorn the bookshelves of the Soviet Embassy in London as the property of an ambassador's wife.

Once she came into my room and noticed that my wine and blue carpet was no longer on the floor.

"What have you done with it, Nora?" she asked. "Sent it to the cleaners?"

"No," I replied, "I have sold it."

"How much did you get for it?" asked Madame Gusev. I told her two hundred roubles.

"You silly girl," replied the little Professor of Economics, "It was worth much more than that. I would have given you four hundred roubles for it myself."

Seven months after my father's arrest, in December 1939, we were all woken up in the night by Mme Gusev calling out. She was in labour. I got out of bed to see what I could do but her husband — her pet name for him was Fedya — had already telephoned for an ambulance. He went with her to hospital and next morning he told me he was the father of a baby girl called

Nina. Even when he told me this happy news Feodor Gusev hardly smiled. He was the perfect Soviet official.

Most of my spare time, while I was living in this flat with the Gusevs, was spent trying to get news of my parents. I went daily to the Kommandatura, the Bureau of Passes, at 24 Kuznetzki Most, where rich and poor gathered trying to get information about their imprisoned relatives. I found that I could arrange for my parents to buy cigarettes, spring onions (for vitamins) and bacon rind at the prison shop. I had to find seventy-five roubles a month to provide them with these pitiful luxuries, and I did it by selling my books.

All over Moscow at this time were official posters which said: "Collaborate with the N.K.V.D. — denounce the enemies of the State".

I often wondered when I saw these posters who it was who had denounced father, but I never found out. One day I met one of the Foreign Office staff who had been in charge of catering. He had been arrested at the same time as Father but had been released. He whispered to me that Father was in solitary confinement and was being questioned daily.

"Don't stop sending him money, Nora," he said. "Believe me it is all he has to live for. May he be spared! "

The N.K.V.D. men were still checking and counter-checking all his activities with the Foreign Office. It was customary when an official had been arrested that Party members met in the Foreign Office club to hear allegations against him. This had nothing to do with the crimes they were alleged to have committed. The meetings were to decide whether they would be expelled from the Communist Party. Even if they were acquitted of the charges brought against them, they would still be expelled from the Party.

These meetings, an integral part of every Soviet factory and institution, were held frequently. To a spectator, they had the appearance of a Boy Scouts' rally, but the men and women who attended them were deadly serious.

Father's case came up several times, but they could not collect enough evidence to expel him from the Party. Leading Foreign-Office officials packed the hall on the second floor, where cinema shows were usually held, and the Party officials sat on a raised platform facing the audience. Everyone attacked their late chief. The most trivial things were alleged against him. A lift man said that he had seen him reading an English newspaper — he could not read English. A cipher clerk said that he had spoken disparagingly of Hitler, now our great comrade-in-arms.

Only one man spoke for him. It was his closest associate and friend, Gregori Weinstein. At these meetings he repeated again and again: "I can say nothing against Korzhenko. He is no enemy of the State."

But it was no use. Finally, at one of these Party meetings, the decision was made. My father, a man who had given his entire life to the Soviet Union, and now a lonely prisoner in an underground cell of the Lubyanka, was expelled from the Communist Party. Shortly afterwards, Weinstein also paid for trying to save his best friend. I was queueing outside the Lubyanka jail to send my father some money when someone tapped me on the shoulder. I turned round and looked into the eyes of Weinstein's wife. For a moment we did not speak and then she said, "Yes, Nora, they have taken my husband, too."

Weinstein was the last of Litvinov's associates to go. He was arrested in August, 1939.

It was about this time I experienced two incidents which both reminded me of the kind of treatment handed out by Father's captors. One of Father's administrative officers in Stalingrad had been an Italian aristocrat named Kirzelli who had become fired with Communist doctrine and left his own country to assume Russian nationality. In due course he had been posted to the Moscow N.K.V.D. taking his Russian wife with him. She was a tall, blonde Ukrainian whom I at once recognized in the street one morning and when she had asked after my family and heard what had happened to them, she took me to the room where she was living and explained that Kirzelli too had been arrested some months previously. He had been taken from their bed at two o'clock in the morning, kept in the Lubyanka for ten months, where he was grilled nightly, and in the end sent to a concentration camp in Siberia.

From there he had somehow managed to scrawl a note in pencil imploring his wife to help him. By some means or other he had managed to get the letter smuggled to her. Mme Kerzelli took the tattered piece of paper from under a floorboard and gave it to me to read.

"My most beloved darling Tina," the disillusioned Italian had written, "God knows if this will ever reach you, but if it does you must help me. You will never know me if you ever see me again. I was beaten raw all the time I was in the Lubyanka. I cannot walk, my hands and wrists have no strength in them and I can hardly write, as you see. In God's name try to get me out of here. I've only a few weeks left on earth. I would so like to die away from here."

There was a dark brown stain across the pencilling. Mme Kerzelli saw me look at it and she nodded.

"Yes, it's blood," she said and burst into a fit of hysterical weeping.

The poor woman went from court to court to try and secure her husband's release but she never succeeded and she never saw him again.

The second episode showing how the Soviet State treats its prisoners happened one day while I was waiting in the Bureau of Passes at 24 Kuznetzki Most where I'd gone to arrange for my parents to receive some money. I was sitting on the bench awaiting my turn when a young Russian air force officer limped up to me on crutches. His face was swollen and his hands were bruised. He looked what he was, a wreck of a man and I at once made way for him.

"That must have been a pretty bad smash you were in," I said. "You're lucky to be alive."

The man looked at me quietly before he replied.

"Yes, Citizeness, I'm lucky to be alive. There were times when I thought it would have been better to have died."

I looked at the man questioningly but he made no sign and stared silently ahead. Soon my turn came at the window and the air force officer shambled on his crutches behind me.

"Do you know someone under arrest?" I asked him.

"Thousands," he said. "But I can't help them, only myself. You see, they let me out yesterday, said it was all a mistake and that's why I'm here. To collect my papers and start again."

He looked down at his twisted foot and spat on the floor.

"That to Russia," he said, and took his turn at the window..... for a fresh start.

Soon after this I gave up attending the university. I felt like an intruder there, with the constant daily insults that were whispered to me, or the people who passed me as if I were a leper. Yet it was not that which made me take the final step and sever my connection with the university; it was that the lectures had lost their meaning. Professor after professor would stand up and rant about the great Communist ideology where all men were equal and no man was oppressed. As I listened to their slavish text-book speeches, I thought of my father and my stepmother eating bacon rind and spring onions to try and keep alive in their cells in the Lubyanka. One day I could stand no more of it. I walked out of this citadel of self-delusion, never to return again.

After I left the university I sold my books and clothing bit by bit to raise enough roubles for Father and Mother to have a few extras in their cells. I continued to live with the Gusevs. It was an extraordinary position, but the all-seeing N.K.V.D. seemed to have lost track of me; at least so I thought.

As a daughter of a disgraced official, I knew I had little hope of securing any job in the State, so I lived quietly selling a book or a blouse to buy myself a meal. Yet I was foolish to imagine that the N.K.V.D. had either forgotten or forgiven me. One morning a letter arrived which made my heart nearly miss a beat. It was on official N.K.V.D. notepaper and told me to report the following evening at seven o'clock at their headquarters opposite the Foreign Office.

I read and re-read the letter. There was one faint ray of hope, and that was the time I was told to report. I knew that most serious inquisitions began after midnight when the accused people were tired and more "pliable." Even so I tidied up my room and packed my clothes because I felt sure I would not be coming back. Then I walked across to the Lubyanka with my knees trembling. A wooden-faced sentry at the gate looked at my letter and passed me on to another man. The letter was checked and re-checked and I was escorted to a lift, a steel-plated cage with armed guards. I was so frightened I could hardly stand because for the first time I was meeting the N.K.V.D from the other side of the fence. Father, disgraced, dishonoured and unwanted by the State, lay imprisoned in the cells beneath us. I was no longer the daughter of a Foreign Office official. I was a Soviet citizen suspected of being an enemy of the State. Anything could happen to me.

Everything about the N.K.V.D. headquarters was calculated to unnerve anyone about to be interrogated. The whole place had the silence of a vast tomb. There were sentries everywhere, and they were stern, unsmiling and silent. The ceilings were low, the walls were sound-proof, as you walked along your footsteps were muffled. When you spoke, your voice sounded flat and dead in the sound-proofed rooms. The N.K.V.D. had studied human nature for twenty years and they knew their job. They knew how to terrify you before they asked their first question.

I was full of these disturbing thoughts as the lift sped silently upwards. When it stopped, I was shown into a corridor and told to sit on a bench and wait. Then a door opened and guard signalled me to walk into a large bare room. Sitting behind a table were two uniformed men, a captain and lieutenant, dressed in navy-blue uniforms with a red stripe down the trousers. Above their heads was, as usual, a large picture of Stalin. They told me to sit down and immediately began firing questions at me. They kept jerking backwards and forwards, rasping questions, like two sinister dolls. Their lips seemed hardly to move as they spoke, their eyes were steely, their hair close-cropped.

The questions seemed harmless enough but the atmosphere in the room was so ominous that even there the most harmless-sounding questions seemed to be full of hidden pitfalls. They shot the questions at me like machine-gun fire. I had hardly answered one, when another was barked at me. "How did your mother die?" they asked. "Is it true she was poisoned? What do you know of your father's love for your governess?"

They knew the whole of my family life in the greatest detail, but I shook my head at all their enquiries. I was too young, I told them, to know the answers to these questions. It was all so long ago.

Without pausing for breath their talk turned to political matters.

"Did your stepmother accompany your father on official tours?"

"Did they ever discuss Trotsky?"

"What was your father's attitude during the Zinoviev trial?"

This was something that I was prepared for. I knew the answers to this sort of questions. I looked my two inquisitors straight in the eye and said:

"I can only speak what I know to be true, Comrades. My father and stepmother were devoted servants of our great and glorious State."

With a superhuman effort, I managed to mutter as an afterthought: "They were loyal servants — just as I am."

At this one of the mask-like faces leaned forward and a voice rapped out: "We are not concerned with you, Citizeness — at this stage."

This remark, with its implied threat, robbed me of my self-possession for a moment. The other man leaned forward with a ghastly smile and said: "What is the matter, Citizeness, are you frightened of us?"

I muttered, half to myself, that I expected to be put in the cells.

The smiling mask replied: "Not yet, Citizeness — maybe next time."

He pressed a button and a sentry appeared and escorted me out. I went down in the steel lift in a daze and when I got to outside the building, I leaned against the wall drinking in the sharp, frosty air of the Moscow evening. I could hardly believe I was still free.

CHAPTER XII – THE FORGOTTEN EXILE IN ASIA

Friendless in Moscow, I drifted more and more towards the queues outside the Lubyanka enquiry office. It was only there that I could find sympathy — from others as miserable as myself. Day after day I talked to men and women, old and young, rich and poor, all levelled to the same sickly fear by the arrest of their relatives. An ambassador's wife stood side by side with the daughter of a disgraced shop steward; a general's daughter talked to the wife of a purged factory hand. I learned the heartaches of a thousand lives in that queue. My mind went back to my youth in Stalingrad when I used to come home from school and see the files of pathetic, shabby women standing outside our home in the N.K.V.D. headquarters. I had brushed past them carelessly as they miserably clamoured for news of the men the secret police had arrested. I had always been taught that they were the womenfolk of crooks and dangerous villains who were to be despised and ignored. I knew different by now as I stood in line outside the dreaded Lubyanka.

Let me recommend a visit to the enquiry queue at the Lubyanka prison for any would-be citizen under Communist rule. Let me suggest that he stands there as I did, watching the dull faces, the tear-filled eyes, the hopeless patience of the women who wait and suffer under the great freedom of Soviet Russia. They keep calling, filling-in forms, asking to see the prisoner, knowing that they will never be allowed to. The officials of the Lubyanka never give any information. You cannot be sure that your loved one is still there. You pass money over, not even sure it will be used to help your relative in jail. From time to time I sold my possessions, such as were left, at the State pawnshops, the Commission Stores. Luckily, I had plenty of books and was able to sell them for fairly good prices. Books were one of the few extravagances my father had allowed. He thought they would be an investment for my future. He little knew that I would sell them one by one to buy him a little bacon rind to nibble in prison.

One day I got a letter from the Estate Department of the Foreign Office, raising my rent from eighteen to two hundred roubles. In Russia rent is paid according to one's income, not on the value of the house. You pay less rent while you are working; this is one of the privileges of a Soviet citizen. It had been reported to the Estate Department that I was no longer at the university and therefore was a useless drone. I went to the official and pleaded with him, telling him I was living on the sale of my books. This did not impress him in the slightest. He told me that everyone had to conform with the law and work to live. He added that I was very lucky that my rent had only been raised. I could have been evicted as an unemployed person.

He knew as well as I did that as the daughter of an enemy of the State I could not find employment. Like every other Soviet official he was completely heartless and told me to pay or get out.

The Soviet citizen is far too afraid of the secret police to risk endangering his own position by giving a so-called undesirable, such as myself, a job. Although I tried everything, no one would give me any sort of work for which my education fitted me. I had to go round hotels, cafés or private houses, pleading for the chance to earn a few roubles by doing a day's charing or dishwashing. Sometimes I earned a little money, but often I spent the day hungry, tramping the streets, unable to find any work.

I was returning from one of these treks one day when I felt a bit dizzy, it was possibly lack of food, and slipped on the escalator in the metro. Someone helped me up and as they did so a voice said in my ear: "Don't give any sign you can hear what I am saying. Just follow me until I sit down."

A tall, well-dressed man then pushed past me and stepped off the escalator a little ahead of me. I recognized him at once. He was A.F., a Foreign Office official who had been in my father's employment, one of the few who had escaped the purge. He did not look back as I trotted dutifully behind him, a few paces to the rear. He walked quickly through the Moscow streets from the Kirov station to a public park.

He sat down on a park bench. I approached him timidly, feeling rather scared. He turned and said quietly, with a smile: "Sit down, Nora, we can talk here."

As soon as he spoke I knew I had nothing to fear. He told me he was present when Molotov had ordered my father to give up the keys of the Foreign Office. He heard Molotov say to him: "Citizen Korshenko, there is to be an enquiry into your work here. You will consider yourself under arrest." Then he had seen the guards lead my father away.

A.F., as we sat on the park bench, told me he thought that Father's German connections might account for Molotov's attitude. This seemed very puzzling as it was an open secret that some new political deal with Hitler was in the offing and Father would have been useful to the Foreign Office in a matter like this. We all spoke German fluently, but how this could have endangered the Soviet State I can't imagine.

As the N.K.V.D. men had escorted my father out of Molotov's office, he had managed to speak to A.F. and ask him to look after his family for him. A.F. held a responsible position in the Foreign Office and as he talked to me in gentle, friendly tones, I realized why my grandmother and young Felix had been allowed to remain in my father's flat and I had kept my one room in Gusev's apartment. Obviously, unknown to me, this kindly man had been pulling a few strings on our behalf.

He gripped my arm as we talked and said urgently:

"It was very lucky I met you tonight, Nora, because we cannot protect you much longer. Things are warming up again and the N.K.V.D. are asking about you. It would be as well if you left Moscow for a time."

He pressed a few hundred roubles into my hand and we arranged a secret method to contact him without the N.K.V.D. knowing. As all telephones at the Foreign Office were tapped, he told me to dial his personal number and when I heard him answer, hang up. He would then be at our agreed meeting place in exactly one hour.

One morning when I telephoned, as arranged, he came to see me. He was obviously in a state of great excitement.

"It is just as I thought, Nora," he said. "It sounds crazy, but Communist Russia is about to play host to the representatives of our greatest enemy, Nazi Germany. Ribbentrop arrives in the morning."

He gave me some more money and said: "If you want to see history in the making, look out of your window tomorrow morning."

The next day I peeped through my window and saw a row of long black cars arrive at the entrance to the Foreign Office. Several people got out and I recognized one of them at once from his photographs, a man with a pale face and protuberant blue eyes. It was the dapper, smiling Ribbentrop, who had come to Moscow that August day to sign a pact of nonaggression with Stalin which would enable Hitler to attack the Western countries. He walked briskly past the N.K.V.D. sentries who swarmed over the Foreign Office since Molotov took over.

Every day I remained in that little room in the Foreign Office I felt would be my last. Any moment I expected a tap on the door which would mean I would be dragged away to prison. I decided to leave because I would be safer away from the shadow of the new regime. It was amazing they had allowed me to escape for so long. One day, in a café, I met a fellow unfortunate, the Russian wife of a Yugoslav who had been exiled to Siberia. She was living in one small room with her fifteen-year-old daughter. There was hardly any furniture in the place, but it was clean. When she heard of my plight she offered to take me in for thirty roubles a month. It was more crowded than my room but it was somewhere to hide. I would feel safer there so I leapt at her offer. That night I packed my bag and walked out of the Foreign Office, past the stony-eyed sentries, for the last time.

I continued my daily visits to the Lubyanka, hopelessly trying to get news of my parents. One December day, in the depths of winter, I trudged through the snow-bound streets with the roubles I had scraped together, to pay to the prison officials. When I handed them over the counter to the clerk he shook his head and said: "No more money can be accepted."

This meant only one thing. They had been moved. Frantic, I pleaded with the clerk to tell me more, but he turned his back on me and would not answer.

The news so upset me that I felt I must talk to someone who would sympathize with me. My landlady had been very kind but she had her own troubles and could not be expected to waste much time listening to me. I could not go and stay with my grandmother because of the N.K.V.D. men who were staying in her flat.

Suddenly, I thought of my mother's parents. I knew their address but I had never met them. My grandfather was still alive so I wrote to Poltava in the Ukraine where he lived, asking if I could come and stay with him. A.F. lent me the fare and told me that the N.K.V.D. were still investigating me. He agreed that it would be a good thing for me to leave Moscow, even if only for a short time. So, in December 1939, I returned to my birthplace, the Ukraine.

My grandfather, a retired post-office official, who had lived most of his life in the Far East, welcomed me as the daughter of his dead daughter. He was an old-fashioned Russian with a long, white beard who seemed pleased to see me and listened sympathetically to all my troubles. He would not waste sympathy on my father and reviled him as one of the men who had destroyed the beautiful Russia he knew. He stood in the centre of his one-roomed cabin and tears streamed into his beard. I could not argue with the old patriarch when he cursed the Communists because I realized he was speaking the truth. He flung his arm towards the ikons in the comer and said: "I suppose you have been brought up to despise these?"

"Not to despise them grandfather," I replied. "Just not to know of their existence."

The old man buried his face in his hands and sobbed.

"Russia," he exclaimed. "Holy mother Russia! What have they done to her?

"Look outside, see what the Ukraine is today. I can remember before these new rulers came when we had laughter, songs, wine and happy peasants. They talk of the Czar as a criminal, but when I was a young man under the Czar the people of the Ukraine had a good life.

"Don't you remember, Nora, even in the early days of the Revolution I could send your mother food parcels. The Ukraine is one of the richest places on earth, and what have they done with it?"

He stood up and started to shout: "I am an old man now, they can't hurt me any more, but they can hurt the Ukraine. God curse them!"

The old man raised his clenched fist and shook it under the smoke-stained rafters.

"This is all a clenched fist has ever meant," he said. "Anger and hate and war, that is all the clenched fist has ever brought to Russia. Come with me and I will show you what the clenched fist has done to the Ukraine."

Together we walked round the little town. He showed me the bread queues, long lines of people waiting patiently for hours.

"Look at them, Nora," cried the old man. "Look at your people; for they are your people. They are the men and women of your birthplace. Now they look like refuse which has been swept up from the gutters.

"They bind their feet with rags. They have lost the habit of changing their clothes, for they have no others. The songs of my youth died under the Red Banner.

"Once we supplied grain for the whole of Russia, now the Ukrainians queue for loaves hardly fit to eat. Under the Czars bread like this was given to the pigs."

We passed a hoard of beggars on the cathedral steps whining for a few kopeks. My grandfather pointed to them and said: "Did your university teach you about these things? Stay with us, Granddaughter, and see the things your learned professors dare not tell you."

We walked back to his shack and I met his housekeeper, an old woman of sixty who had been a farmer's wife and had brought up ten children.

Her name was Vera and as we sat by the stove, drinking tea, she told me how she had lived in the Ukraine all her life and her husband, working hard, had built up his own farm. But the new Communist state rated him a property owner and the order came from the Kremlin to clear out the *kulack* class of independent farmers and turn their property into communal farms to be run by the State. To understand her story it is necessary to know a little about this period in Soviet history, for the order to liquidate the *kulacks* caused a great deal of misunderstanding and unnecessary victimization.

But the Kremlin have only themselves to blame. Few of the *kulacks* were rich; they were in fact small farmers whom the Communists had themselves set up, when they confiscated all the large estates after the Revolution and divided them up among the peasants. Indeed, under the Czar, the village

126

money-lender was called the *kulack*. Many villages reported back to Moscow that they hadn't any members of the despised class. The men in the Kremlin replied that all villages had *kulacks* and solemnly circulated the official description — any man who owned more than six chickens.

Naturally the despised but successful farmers fought to retain their property. Many of them burnt down their homes and cut the throats of their cattle rather than see the state move in. But even so, thousands of them were rounded up by the N.K.V.D., given a few hours to pack and then herded off to the labour camps of Siberia which was then being developed in view of the Japanese threat in the Far East.

The liquidation of the *kulacks* began in 1929, continued till 1934, with the result that by 1937 Russia had just under 250,000 collective farms employing 93 per cent of the nation's peasant families. Just what the farm workers thought about all this is summed up by the fact that in 1941 only 19 per cent of the Communist Party membership consisted of farm workers.

Yet the Communist Party Congress of February 1934 had been solemnly assured that the Soviet peasantry had definitely and unalterably come under the Red Banner of Socialism. The peasants of Russia may have come under the Red Banner, but it was quite apparent their true feelings lay outside its shadow.

After the liquidation of the *kulacks* the men in the Kremlin had hoped to find thousands of men and women whom they could train as factory workers for the first five-year plan. In actual fact most of the peasants who were not absorbed into the collective farms were quite unable to handle the foreign machines with a result that production sagged, inflation increased and large numbers of Party officials were liquidated because their plant hadn't fulfilled its production target.

Rationing was introduced and a national system of shopping. Industrial workers could buy goods at pre-inflation prices but food ration cards were only available for city workers. Men and women working on the land had to find their own. The *kulack* class has now been entirely absorbed into modem Russia, though thousands of them are still living in exile like other political offenders. Their exile means that they must live as best they can in the large wastes of uninhabited Russia and it is forbidden them to visit any principal towns or cities. This, then, was the background to my visit to the Ukraine and although I well knew the story of the *kulacks* this was the first time I'd ever spoken to anyone who'd ever had practical experience of their liquidation. Tears streamed down the face of the old woman as she spoke about it and this is the story she told.

"I remember the day as though it was yesterday. I had just settled down to serve Ivan and the children with their mid-day meal when from outside there came a great noise of horses and shouting. One of the children came running in from the yard, his face white with terror.

"'Mamma,' he said, 'they're here. They've come to take Papa.'

"In the yard I could hear a man shouting.

"'Ivan Ivanovitch,' he called. 'Pack your things. We have come for you.'

"I recognized the man's voice at once. He was the chairman of the local district committee. My husband jumped up from the table, grabbed a gun and rushed upstairs to the attic. He had only just left the room when the door burst open and in came a number of peasants and O.G.P.U. men.

"'Where's your husband?' said the chairman. 'Don't lie, we know he's here.'

"The children sat at their places pale and silent. I said:

"'What do you want him for; he's done no wrong.'

"'Done no wrong, indeed? Ah, that's a good one. You know as well as I do he's just a dirty *kulack* who has been living on the profits of the sweated peasants in his employ.'

"The men started searching the house and I noticed one of them was one of our own cow-hands.

"'My husband is a peasant just the same as you,' I said. 'Ask Gregory here, he has worked for us for fifteen years. Ask him if he has been exploited, as you call it. Ask him if he has any complaint of the way he has been treated by my husband.'

"The chairman of the committee called the man over.

"'Well, Gregory,' he said, 'what have you got to say to a *kulack*?'

"And Gregory spat in my face.

"Overhead I could hear the heavy tramp of the men's boots as they pulled open doors, looked under beds and probed into closets in their search for my husband. Then suddenly there was a cry and a mad rush of feet. The door was flung open and my husband rushed in. He was unarmed and helpless but one of the O.G.P.U. guards levelled his revolver and shot him at point-blank range. I ran to him and caught him in my arms. His blood covered me as he sank to the stone floor. And there in the kitchen of his own home he died.

"His murderers left him there but the next day they came back, rounded up all our cattle, livestock and equipment and took it into the committee headquarters for distribution among the peasants. Then they came back and ordered me to pack up my personal belongings and leave. I asked them what would become of my children and they said the State would take care of

128

them from now on. My eldest boy was twenty and fortunately was away from home on a visit to relatives with one of his brothers. I never knew what happened to them but I know that after I was taken away the rest of my children were put into State orphanages. In my own case I spent five years in prison and was then released to work on a collective farm. My only crime was that my husband had been a successful farmer.

The three of us talked about these old days for hours that night. Then we all went to sleep in the little shack. Grandfather lay down in his usual corner and the old lady curled herself up on top of the stove. I woke up in the middle of the night to hear a soft moaning. It was the old woman weeping. The talk about her husband's death had brought back so many sad memories that she could not sleep. The moans turned into big, choking sobs and I turned my face to the wall and gritted my teeth. It was a dreadful thing to see such grief in an old woman whose whole life had been ruined by the Soviet.

After staying for a few weeks with the old couple, I returned to Moscow. This was in January 1940, just about the time when Russian troops invaded Finland. I went to the post office to see if there were any letters for me. I found a card from my stepmother. It said:

"I have been given five years administrative exile in Kazakstan. Will you please come and see me and bring some warm clothing. I am leaving Moscow any day now."

I had never liked my stepmother because she had schemed against me for many years, but my heart went out to her when I read this pathetic little note. Administrative exile meant she would have to stay in Kazakstan Province, a wild, lawless place, inhabited by Asiats and Kazaks, few of whom even spoke Russian. Even among people like this she would be forbidden to take any employment other than the lowest menial tasks. For an educated woman like her it was a dreadful sentence. I had no bitterness left in my heart as I rushed around trying to collect a few warm clothes which she could take with her into exile. Then, with my little bundle, I went to the Butirki prison where she had been taken to await exile. I showed the sentry outside the red-brick building the letter from my stepmother. I showed the officials my identity card and received my permit to visit the prisoner.

I was led into a large room and saw my stepmother behind bars. Two guards stood on her side of the partition, two more on mine. I hardly recognized her at first, her eight months' imprisonment had aged her so much. She was pale and thin and her hair was streaked with grey, but she still wore the green gabardine raincoat which she was wearing when the N.K.V.D. men had bundled her into the Black Raven. Her lips trembled when she saw me and tears came into her eyes.

"I knew you'd come, Nora," she said. "Though I would have understood if you had stayed away. I haven't been much of a mother to you, have I?"

I tried to speak but I couldn't find words. I could not find it in my heart to dislike her in spite of everything that had happened; she looked so frail and old and frightened in that grim room. The guards stood motionless and on the wall was a prison notice warning visitors against discussing politics. It added: "Only personal matters can be talked about here."

I remembered how, when trouble came, she had refused to tell the N.K.V.D. where I was. I will always be grateful to her for that. I tried to smile and tell her that five years was not a lifetime. She asked for news of Father and I tried to cheer her up by telling her that although he was in the Lubyanka prison he was well.

"As he has not been tried yet," I said, "there is a good chance he might be freed."

"I don't think so," she said, sadly, "but if you manage to see him, tell him I am innocent......"

There was a rough shout from one of the guards:

"Citizeness, the time is up."

I leaned over and pressed her thin hands as they gripped the bars. "Look after little Felix," she said in a choked voice.

Then the guard put his hand on her shoulder and as she turned to follow him back to her cell, there came a little whimper as though from a dog that had been beaten. It was the last sound I ever heard from her. Sometimes when I wake up in the night I hear it still. It is a sound I shall never forget until I die.

Soon after this I had a letter from the Supreme Military Collegium of the Soviet Union. It told me to present myself at their headquarters where I would be officially informed of my father's fate. This was the first time I had heard any news of him since I had been told that I could no longer send him any money. I was in the waiting-room half an hour before the time given on the notice. I need not have hurried because I had to wait for six hours.

The room was full of people who, in accordance with the Russian law, had been summoned to hear the sentence which had been passed on their arrested relatives. Next to me was a little girl of ten; near-by, an old man of seventy. We all sat there, not speaking, not looking at each other. After I had been there an hour or two a middle-aged man came in waving a telegram.

"Where can I go? What can I do?" he cried. "Look at this! My brother is to be shot in twenty-four hours. How can I save him?"

He kept waving the telegram at us. No one bothered to look at it because we all knew his mission was hopeless. Eventually a guard told him to be quiet and he sat there like the rest of us with his head in his hands, occasionally muttering. At 11 p.m., when I was almost asleep with exhaustion, a sentry prodded me.

"Your turn, Citizeness," he said. "Come this way."

I followed him down a long corridor, through a heavy door into a room where a uniformed man sat at a desk. I recognized him as one of Vishinsky's assistants. For Vishinsky was still the Public Prosecutor responsible for all State prosecutions, including my father's. The man at the desk hardly looked at me. He held out a well-manicured hand and said: "Your identity card, Citizeness."

I put the document on the desk, he flipped it open, nodded, and gave it back.

Then he picked up a card from a heap on the desk in front of him. Reading from it he said: "It is my duty to inform you that your father, Director-General Vassily Savvich Korzhenko of the Foreign Office, has been found guilty. The court has sentenced him to ten years' imprisonment with full confiscation of goods. He is degraded from his rank and privileges and is forbidden to receive or write letters."

The voice stopped. The man's lips moved again but I could not understand what he was saying. I could not see him, my eyes were blurred with tears.

But I did manage to stammer: "Please, may I see him?"

"Certainly not, he's an enemy of the State."

"Can't I send him something?" I faltered "I know he has only his summer clothes, the grey suit he went into prison with."

"That, Citizeness, is not our concern."

He nodded to the guard behind me and, looking down at his desk, said: "That is all, you can go."

The guard took my arm and somehow I found myself outside in the street. A wave of despair ran through me, the whole world seemed to be spinning round. I leaned against the railings, half fainting, holding them to prevent myself from falling.

How long I stood like that I have no idea. The next thing I remember was a man's voice which said: "Are you all right? A young girl like you should not drink so much. Let me take you home."

His words brought me back to my senses.

"It's all right," I said faintly. "I'm not drunk, it's just that I'm terribly upset."

The man looked at me suspiciously. Then he glanced at the building I had just left and raised his eyebrows sympathetically. I nodded. He shook his head sadly. He understood.

I have never heard from Father since. It is ten years ago since he was arrested and to this day I haven't the slightest idea what he did wrong. No charges were specified in my interview with Vishinsky's department. Letters I have written to him have never been answered, perhaps they were never delivered. I did hear a story from one N.K.V.D. man that he had been shot, but it is impossible to find out. You can never find out about the fate of political prisoners in Soviet Russia. But I know that he was alive when I went to hear his sentence. I had proof of this from my grandmother. She was still living in the Moscow flat and occasionally I used to call on her when I knew that the N.K.V.D. men were not there. She told me that a man had been continually phoning to try and contact me. The number, K 1-25/24, was known only to a few intimate friends of Father. The man said he wanted to speak to me personally and would not leave a name.

One morning, while I was there he phoned again and I answered it. He asked me to be outside the N.K.V.D. headquarters at midnight. He said he would be wearing the uniform of the secret police and carrying a newspaper under his left arm. I suspected a trap but was so desperate for news of Father I decided to keep the appointment. The man was standing there. When I spoke to him he thrust an envelope into my hand and said: "This explains itself. Good luck."

And he hurried off into the night without another word.

When I opened the letter I found it was addressed to the Foreign Office Accounts Department and signed by my father. It asked them to pay me five hundred roubles of his Chekist pension which were due to him. Next day I presented the letter at the Accounts Department, but when he looked at it the clerk shook his head: "The date is wrong," he said. "It is a month late. It is now February and we can't pay January bills. Perhaps you could get your father to send another one."

I just picked up the letter and left. Perhaps it was late because the man had been a long time contacting me. Or perhaps the prisoner in the Lubyanka had lost all sense of time. Anyway, I knew I would never get another letter.

At the time of my father's sentence, I was still living in the one-room tenement behind the Red Army's Central Theatre, sharing a room with the

132

Yugoslav's wife and daughter in a three-roomed flat. The other two rooms were occupied by a factory worker and his family. He lived with his wife and nine-year-old daughter in one room. The woman had just been released from a lunatic asylum where she had been sent after developing homicidal tendencies following the birth of her last child. She spent most of the day screaming vile abuse about her husband, but apart from her screaming she was harmless enough. In the third room lived one of her married sons with his wife and child and her daughter with her husband and child. So there were twelve of us in three rooms, and no bathroom.

I received no news of my parents after my interview at the Military Collegium on the twenty-sixth of March 1940, until one day I received a letter from my stepmother. As an exile, she was allowed to write occasionally, even though she had a terrible story to tell. She was marched out of prison one night and packed with many others into a railway truck. For three weeks they travelled across Russia, sometimes being shunted into sidings for days. As the train trundled slowly across the Soviet Union the men and women in it were packed like cattle. They were forced to relieve themselves in the trucks, and the guards robbed the better-dressed prisoners. Everything of value was stripped from my stepmother.

One night the train pulled up and she was pushed off with a crowd of other unfortunates without food, water or money. They were dumped in Chiili, near Kzyl-Urda, in the desert wilderness of Soviet Asia. When the guards pushed her out of the truck her hair was matted, her skin filthy, her clothes in rags. She looked more like a baboon than an educated woman who had once been employed in positions of trust by the Soviet.

It was a long letter and I wept as I read it. She had managed, after terrible hardships, to find a home with some Asiatics who let her live with them doing odd jobs like cleaning out their pigsties. Without papers, she dare not go near a town to look for work. Eventually, she found a slave camp where the workers were toiling away at an irrigation project. Here she got a job, scrubbing floors and cleaning out latrines. One day while she was cleaning the office of the manager of the irrigation works she heard him talking about the muddle his book-keeping had got into. As former chief of the German section of Voks (the society for cultural relations with foreign countries) in Leningrad, book-keeping was an easy job for her. She asked the manager if she could help him out and he agreed although it would have to be in secret, because no enemy of the State could be employed in such a responsible position.

So my stepmother, a graduate with honours of a university, became at the age of thirty-eight a lavatory cleaner by day, a secret accountant by night.

I continued to get occasional letters from her right up to the time I left Russia. When Hitler invaded the Soviet and Moscow was evacuated, my grandmother managed to scrape enough money together to pay the train fare to this remote place in the Asiatic wilderness. She had decided to share her daughter's exile and take my stepbrother Felix with her. They managed, after months of suffering, to join my stepmother. I lost nothing by their departure. On the one occasion when I had gone round to ask her for shelter — it was forty degrees below freezing — she had refused to let me in. With the door on its chain she had screamed at me in German, "Get out, you Russian swine, I have nothing more to do with you Korzhenkos." And she slammed the door in my face.

After her arrival at Kazakstan, however, there was an almost continual flow of letters addressed to me at the *poste restante*, Moscow. Both Ursula and her mother asked for money, food and medicine; anything that could be spared. I sent what I could and I still have their letters with me. Of course they were heavily censored and I don't believe that my stepmother really meant me to remain "faithful to the high ideals of our Socialist society." The phrase had been included as a sop to the censor, nothing more.

Here is a letter from my stepbrother, Felix, sent when I was in Archangel awaiting my freedom:

"Your letter has made me very sad for it means we have to say good-bye, perhaps for ever. Thank you for thinking of us out here with money and parcels, because we have nothing. I have grown out of everything. My clothes have been mended over and over again, and now they are only rags. I am walking about in Daddy's old jack-boots — I look just like Puss-in-boots. But of course there are others far worse off, as I am reminded when I think of what this dog's devil, Hitler, has done to the whole world.

"I am going to school and I have been admitted to the Pioneers. Soon, with Mummy, I shall dig the earth and plant vegetables. We have all been ill, one after the other, but now we are well again for the sun has begun to warm the desert.

"Take care of yourself, Norochka, and never forget me, just as I will never forget you. I shall remember you always, darling sister. Good-bye, I kiss you, your brother, Felix."

He was just eleven years old and doubtless Ursula helped with the composition.

I also received one letter from Ursula's mother:

"We have nothing and look like ragged beggars," she wrote. "The clothes I wore from Moscow I shared with Mamma and now they are all finished. It is impossible to buy anything here. It is hard enough to produce the miracle of a piece of bread daily — let alone anything else. It is a wonder we are still alive and impossible to believe in our hunger, cold and privation, my daughter and I were once in positions of responsibility and treated as human beings. How much I yearn for my own little corner in the home we used to have.

"Home! I cannot even imagine it any longer — did we ever have a home and live like clean and decent people? It is like a dream, but reality is one long nightmare.

"Do not forget us, I was not much of a grandmother to you as a little girl, and God forgive the way I used to treat you. In my heart I regret that and ask your forgiveness. Perhaps God will let us meet again."

One of the last letters I received from Ursula told a pitiful story. Her sentence meant she was forbidden to live in any civilized town and had to carry on as best she could in the barren desert near the Afghan border. I have kept this letter with me for eight years and every time I read it I realize that only a miracle saved me from a similar sentence.

I had managed to send her some money but she wanted more as her mother was ill and it was impossible to obtain medical attention:

"Bubik (German for 'little boy') is well but thin and weak and the only thing which may save us from starvation is to get a goat for milking." She wrote, "This is an agricultural area and there is no other source of livelihood. I've nothing to sell and the goat will cost 1,000 roubles. I can raise 300 roubles by the end of January (the letter is dated 4 January, 1942), but if you have the money please telegraph it as it would otherwise take a long time to get here and prices are soaring. Send it *poste restante* as the people with whom I live would steal it if they knew I had it, but you can send letters direct.

"We were surprised to hear you were in Archangel but I am sad your fiancé is not Petka, Vanka or Vaska... instead he is John, but then everyone to his own taste. My only worry is Felix; he is doing well at school and I hope one day he will grow out of the bad habits he has picked in our terrible life. If you can get a permit to send any parcel, please send him milk and sugar but don't involve us with the British Embassy. If the food is from them we don't want it."

I showed John this letter and he sold his watch to send her the money. But Ursula never got her goat — the owner refused to sell it and instead she invested the money on fencing and seeds for a vegetable patch. They used to sleep on the floor of their shack covered with rags, and their daily diet was less than a pound of rice between them a glass of milk and some bread. When milk rose to 14 roubles a pint they lived without it.

"We exist as animals except that we can talk," she wrote.

She asked me for soap, matches, medicines and bandages. All three of them worked in the fields and when she received my final letter saying I was leaving Russia she replied that she would rather go naked than see me leave the Soviet Union. But here again she could only have meant those words for the censor.

This then was the life of Ursula Korzhenko, her mother and her son. Her only crime was that she had married a man who had risen to one of the highest positions in the Soviet Government and had then been dismissed. None of us was ever told what he had done wrong, but under Soviet law his family had to be punished too. As far as I know Ursula and her son are still in exile but it would be a comfort to know of their escape — even if this means their death.

CHAPTER XIII – THEY ORDERED ME TO BE A SPY

The spring of 1940 was one of the unhappiest periods in my life.

The Soviet war against Finland had ended with an armistice on 12 March. Although the European war between Germany and the Western European countries continued, Soviet citizens did not dream they would be involved. They thought the pact between Stalin and Hitler would keep them out.

Life continued smoothly in Moscow for the troubles of the rest of Europe did not concern Russia. But my own life was far from smooth. I became an outcast with my father in gaol and my mother in exile. I got through that winter scraping together a few roubles by selling books and doing odd jobs. But no job lasted more than a few days, for as soon as they found out my background I was instantly dismissed, and the only reason I got them at all was because I began my employment before I had filled in the necessary form. I worked in the Moscow Foreign Library, issuing books in the German Section, as an artist's model in an art school, and as a manicurist and receptionist at a beauty salon. By living frugally, without buying clothes, I could manage on 300 roubles a month, and for a few weeks I got a job as a children's nurse. I had only one thing to be thankful for, the N.K.V.D. left me alone. The only friend I had was Anna Mironova, a girl I had met in a queue in the Lubyanka prison. She had come from Vladivostock where she had been working in the agricultural department as a secretary. She was trying to find out what had happened to her mother whom she had left behind in the capital. She discovered she had been arrested by the secret police at three o'clock in the morning, but it took many calls on the N.K.V.D. before she found out that her mother had been sent for ten years to a concentration camp where she was now working as a slave labourer in a coalmine behind the Urals.

I had taken Anna to live with me in my Foreign Office room and at times we were so hungry we used to suck our fingers for comfort. Anna's husband, an engineer in the Far East, had been arrested, and on her return to Vladivostock she sent me 2,000 roubles. She continued to write to me fairly often at the *poste restante* in the Moscow Central Telegraph Office. Here, too, I received the letters from my stepmother.

When I was down to my last change of clothing I used to go to the State bath-house in Hunter's Row where I would give in my clothes to be cleaned and pressed. Here you could have a *sauna*, the Finnish bath, for which you stay as long as you can in a hot room full of steam while a woman attendant

137

beats you with branches of birch. This is followed by buckets of cold water. Sometimes, when I could afford it, I would treat myself to the luxury of a shampoo and set.

One day, after leaving the *banya*, I was standing in the queue at the post office waiting to see if there were any letters, when the man in front of me seemed to be in difficulty with the post office clerk. He was a tall, distinguished, white-haired man and obviously a foreigner. He did not speak any Russian and the clerk stood blank-faced and unhelpful while the man spoke to him in French, English and Italian. There was a pause and then the tall foreigner began to speak in German. When I heard German spoken something seemed to happen to me, because German was my second language, taught to me by my stepmother. Before I could stop myself, I stepped forward and offered to interpret. I knew that it was a capital offence for a Soviet citizen to speak to a foreigner but I did not care any more. I was sick of the Russian regime which had rewarded my father for a life of service with imprisonment and turned me into a pariah. Although I had never been outside Russia in my life, I felt instinctively that the rest of the world must be different. I felt the need to speak to someone from the outside world; some one who did not live in terror of the secret police.

When I addressed the man in German he gave me a charming smile and thanked me for my offer of help. I explained to the clerk that he wanted his letters, and within a few minutes a girl arrived with a bundle of correspondence. The man stuffed them into his pocket and waited for me while I asked if there were a letter from Anna. We walked together into the street, and he introduced himself as a Hungarian nobleman, Doctor F., who was on a diplomatic mission to Moscow.

He was a cultured man, interested in the art galleries, museums and cathedrals of Moscow. The Soviet Government, with their usual generosity, had offered to provide him with a guide, but he had no wish to be shepherded by an N.K.V.D. informer. He explained this to me as we walked along the street in the spring sunshine. He spoke as if we were old friends. As he talked I took a decision which was to change my whole life. In a hesitating voice I said: "I know Moscow, let me be your guide."

Dr. F., my new friend, looked at me enquiringly, with a quizzical smile. "Why should you want to show me around Moscow?" he asked.

I blushed. "Because I'd like to, and because I need some money," I said. "I'm hungry."

The Hungarian smiled understandingly, we shook hands. He was very business-like about my offer and arranged to pay me a fee of five hundred roubles. I asked if he could pay it in small amounts every day. He looked startled at this, but somehow I felt I could trust him so I told him who I was and what had happened to my family. He listened in silence, and at the end I added: "I think it is only fair that you should know the truth. And now, I suppose, you won't want me as a guide."

I turned to walk away, but he touched my arm and said. "This will make no difference to me. We will meet tomorrow."

During the next few days I took him all over Moscow showing him places of interest. One of the first places we visited was the Saint Vassily Cathedral outside the Kremlin in the Red Square. As we wandered round the vast building, suddenly, without any embarrassment, my friend knelt down to pray. Having been brought up an atheist, I had never seen anyone kneel down to worship God before, except as a little girl in Leningrad. I just stood and fidgeted, gazing into the distance, while he finished his prayers. Then he got up, dusted his trousers, and looked at me. I blushed slightly but he made no comment.

Next day we visited the Tretyakoff Gallery and went to the section where there is a famous painting of Christ. The Soviets had kept it for the beauty of the painting but insisted that it had no other significance. When I look back at this episode now I realize that my kindly friend deliberately led me to this painting. As we stood in silence before it Dr. F. said: "You know who this is, I suppose."

"Yes," I replied. "But I don't believe it."

Dr. F. smiled — a gentle, sweet smile — and said: "No, no, of course. You are an atheist."

As we walked out of the gallery he started to talk about Christianity. I quickly silenced him with the maxims I had learned at school that "religion was the opium of the masses" and other phrases. I knew them by heart, because I had been brought up on them, and my father had believed that every good Soviet citizen should be an anti-Christ. Yet, as I repeated these words to this kindly man who seemed to understand me so well, my voice faltered. The words seemed empty and meaningless, and very soon I became silent.

"Have you finished?" asked Dr. F.

Then, very gently, as we walked along the streets of Moscow — the citadel of atheism — he began to tell me the story of the man at whose picture we had just been looking. His words had a disturbing effect on me. I went back to my room that evening full of strange thoughts.

For several days after this we talked about religion, and, although I never admitted anything. Dr. F. knew that in the midst of my unhappiness I had found some hope. I could tell by his manner that he was a happier man because, among the millions of Russians, he had discovered one girl who had become a convert to an older creed than Communism. I grew to respect Dr. F. more than anyone I had ever met in my life, and I shall always be grateful to him for the help he gave me in my darkest hour.

At that time he held a responsible post in the government of his country. Today the long red arm of Communism has stretched out and has him in its grip. His country is Communist-dominated, and he has been stripped of his possessions, his position and his family, and is living in penury. It is my dearest wish that one day I shall meet him again and thank him for the spiritual help he gave me. Perhaps he too may be better able to face the tribulations of the materialist modern Communist state, because he brought one Russian girl to God. The Communists always preach that hunger and misery are the best breeding grounds for their materialistic philosophy, but the hunger and misery they brought to me had the reverse effect. After my talks with the Doctor, I became a Christian in my secret heart. Not only was I grateful for Dr. F.'s spiritual assistance, but the money he gave me for guiding him changed my life. For the first time since my father's arrest I was able to buy myself some new clothes and a few little luxuries.

One evening I was sitting in my room, happily planning my next day's tour with Dr. F., when there was a knock at the door and someone asked for me. It was a Russian naval officer who said he had come from Vladivostock with a message from my friend Anna. He handed me an envelope containing some money. A note inside said she could afford it as she was back home. She also suggested that I take her naval officer friend out and show him the city; it was his first visit and I was a Muscovite. I was a little startled when he suggested we went to the Metropole Hotel, one of the best in Moscow. It was one of the few cosmopolitan hotels left in Russia. Soviet citizens seldom went there as it was too expensive, but the naval officer said he had plenty of money and had always wanted to go to the Metropole. I had just bought myself a new dress with the money that Dr. F. had given me so I was delighted to accept his invitation.

Most Muscovites shun the Metropole because it caters especially for foreigners and the N.K.V.D. are therefore apt to look with suspicion upon anyone who frequents it. As I had already been escorting a foreigner around Moscow I thought I might as well take a further risk, and have an evening in the half-forbidden hotel. So I put on my new dress and we set off.

Anna's naval friend was a gay young man and soon we were enjoying ourselves, dancing and eating caviar, which I had not tasted since my father was an official. Half-way through the evening a silver-haired, thick-set man, who had been watching me dancing and laughing light-heartedly, came across to our table. He bowed and, with a smile at my naval friend, said something in a language I did not understand. Knowing he was a foreigner I asked him in German what he wanted, and he replied: "A dance." I turned to my escort and interpreted the man's request. He stood up and bowed agreement.

When the band struck up again the stranger came over to claim his dance and, while we glided over the floor together, I learnt he was an Englishman from the British Embassy. We only had that one dance together; this strange Englishman and the little Russian girl who spoke no English. It was an innocent enough episode and I hardly thought about it afterwards. Yet, unknown to me, this dance was to lead me into a terrifying new adventure.

A week later, after I had been showing Dr. F. round some museum, I was just getting ready for bed when there came another knock at the door of my room. When I opened it, I found myself faced by two smart young men.

They bowed stiffly and said: "Good evening, Citizeness Korzhenko. Would you like to come for a moonlight drive with us?"

I thought at first they were friends of Anna's naval officer, but then I realized they could not be, so I replied angrily: "Why should I? I don't know you. Who are you?"

One of them looked me straight in the eye and said in silky tones: "Perhaps we have not made ourselves clear. This car ride is not an invitation — it is an order."

He flipped back the lapel of his jacket. Beneath it was the badge I knew only too well — the badge of the N.K.V.D.

"They have found out about my association with Dr. F.," I thought to myself as with trembling hands I put on my coat to go out with them. I had no alternative; one doesn't argue with the secret police.

Outside in the street was a gleaming, black Zis saloon car, the Russian Rolls-Royce. A chauffeur in civilian clothes was sitting at the wheel and in the back seat was a third man. He was a swarthy, clean-shaven, well-dressed man, who hardly looked at me as I sat down beside him. He rapped on the glass partition and ordered the chauffeur to drive along the government road to Himki. This is a well-known beauty spot on the Moscow-Volga Canal. The citizens of Moscow are very proud of Himki with its gigantic waterworks and riverport. Perhaps some day someone with a conscience will dedicate it to the slave labour that built it.

The car drove smoothly along the motor road — and my mind was in a whirl. I was only relieved that the N.K.V.D. man had not ordered the car to go at once to the secret police headquarters. As we drove out of Moscow the men introduced themselves as officers of the Special Branch of State Security dealing with foreigners. The two men who had called for me said they were Captain B. and Captain N. Their companion said nothing. He sat smoking a cigarette, and gazing out of the window at the dark countryside flowing past.

"But what has the Special Branch dealing with foreigners to do with me?" I asked, apprehensively, although I knew.

The third man turned to me and told me that he was Major Kirilov. He looked me full in the face and his dark eyes seemed to peer into my mind.

Then he said: "Well, Citizeness, what do you think you have been doing?"

"Nothing," I gasped. "Nothing at all."

"Indeed," he said, lighting another cigarette. "Then perhaps you would be good enough to explain what you mean by escorting a foreign diplomat all over Moscow for the past fortnight without authority.

"We know who you are, Citizeness. You of all people should know what a serious offence it is for an unauthorized person to talk to foreigners."

I did not reply because I could not think of anything to say. My silence seemed to infuriate him. His calm dropped from him like a mask and he pushed his face up against mine and shouted: "And how dare you dance with these capitalist swine without permission?"

"But," I stammered, "I have never danced with Dr. F."

"It is not Dr. F. whom I am talking about," he retorted angrily. "I'm speaking of the Englishman — the man who held you in his arms in the Hotel Metropole."

"But surely," I said, "there is nothing wrong with that. I don't know the man and I have never seen him since. I was there with some friends and he asked me for a dance. I accepted and that's all."

The three men gazed at me in silence — and for the first time I began to feel really frightened. I realized how foolish I had been and I thought of what had happened to my father and stepmother. I was completely in their power and I thought that I would never leave the car alive. My fear must have shown in my face because the dark-eyed major smiled for the first time. He offered me a cigarette. But I told him I didn't smoke.

"Come, come," he said soothingly, "You are very young and we all make mistakes. Maybe you can be of use to us."

142

"Me? How can I be of use to you?" I repeated, puzzled.

Major Kirilov looked at his companions and said: "What do you think, gentlemen? Was I right or not?"

The two junior officers nodded agreement as the major said: "We require your services — by helping us you may be able to help your father. If you refuse it will be bad for you — and worse for him."

As the car rushed through the night the three men put their proposition to me. The major said I was a girl of intelligence and good education. It was unfortunate that my father had been found to be an enemy of the State but as his daughter I could make retribution for his crime. I could speak German and therefore it would not be difficult for me to talk to foreigners. I had been seen with Dr. F., an important foreign diplomat. If I were sensible I could have security.

"But how?" I asked. "What have I to do?"

He looked at me for a moment and then he told me. At first I could not believe it — but he said it again.

He wanted me to spy for Stalin.

CHAPTER XIV – PERMITTED GIRL

The secret police then told me what they wanted me to do. I was to continue to meet foreigners, but I would report everything they said to the N.K.V.D. Anything I wanted would be provided by the secret police, they would give me every help. I realized this was no proposition but a command. There was an alternative, but it was an alternative that no one could take. They said the N.K.V.D. did not like people who would not co-operate, and it would be too bad if I had to follow my parents to prison or into exile. When they had outlined their scheme to me, they ordered the car to go back to Moscow. As we neared my tenement room, the major said: "Well, Citizeness, what is your answer? Are you going to return safely to your room or are you coming to the N.K.V.D. headquarters with me to be questioned as an enemy of the State?"

I knew I had no choice, and so did he. I said that I would work as an informer. The men told me to report to Room 413 at the Hotel Metropole in two days' time for further orders.

As the major opened the door of the car for me, he said: "You have made the correct decision, Citizeness."

I lay awake that night thinking over the sinister interview and wondering what new perils were ahead. It seemed a grim twist of fate that I was being forced to work for the very organization my father had served all his life and which had repaid him by denouncing him as a traitor!

One thing I decided was that I would never see Dr. F. again. I was not going to involve a man who had been so kind to me. I would tell the N.K.V.D. that he had refused to see me any more. That, at least, was something over which they had no control. In the morning I went to a public call box and rang up the National Hotel where he lived. I was afraid the N.K.V.D. might be tapping the line but I was determined to let Dr. F. know that I would not be seeing him that afternoon — or any afternoon. As soon as I heard his voice, I said very quickly that I could no longer act as his guide.

"But why not, Nora?" he asked.

"I'm afraid I can't tell you that either. I just want to say thank you, and good-bye."

Dr. F. must have understood, because he replied: "I have an idea what you are trying to tell me. Good-bye, Nora — and God bless you."

I hung up the receiver, deeply moved. It was the first time anyone had ever said such a thing to me in atheist Russia. That night I knelt down, and prayed for the first time.

Next day, according to my instructions, I presented myself at Room 413 in the Hotel Metropole. When I knocked at the door a voice said: "Come in." As soon as I heard it, I knew who was waiting for me, it was the major of my midnight journey. Kirilov was sitting on a sofa in a well-furnished suite. After I had closed the door he at once became brisk and business-like. He took it for granted that I had not dared change my mind and started to brief me at once for my new job as a spy. It was to contact a Mr. William Bagshaw, an Englishman. He gave me no instructions as to how I was to get into touch with him, but he said I was to ingratiate myself with him in every possible way. I was to train myself to make a mental note of every little point of our conversation together. Nothing was too trivial to be memorized, and from time to time my masters would communicate with me for my report. I was to make this mysterious Englishman take me to restaurants and hotels which foreigners frequented, and introduce me to his friends.

I pointed out that I had never been to a restaurant or hotel frequented by foreigners, except for the one visit with Anna's naval officer friend. The major replied: "No, of course not. I am glad to hear it, Citizeness, because no patriotic Soviet Citizen would be seen in such places except on official visits. Now it is your duty to go there because you are on official business."

We Russians are a fatalistic race and already I was quite resigned to my new job. In fact, I thought that perhaps I might as well get something out of it before it was too late. So I pointed out to the major that in view of the way I had been living my clothes were hardly suitable for the type of place he was asking me to visit. I badly needed new clothes to mingle unobtrusively with the smart foreign women whom I had seen on my first visit to the Metropole. The major gave another of his wintry smiles when I put this suggestion to him.

"I will give you plenty of money once you have contacted Bagshaw," he said. "When I am informed that you are taking afternoon tea with him at the Metropole, then I will give you some money.

"You will be known as Swallow. When you work for us you are to forget your own identity. Swallow will be the only name you will use. Any telephone calls will be made in this name. All information and letters that you send us will be written in the third person. Everything you describe will be 'Swallow did this — or Swallow did that'.

145

Nora in Moscow 1941

"Any message you send will not be signed. We will know who it is from by the description of Swallow's actions.

"If we send you any written instructions you will burn them as soon as you have memorized them. Your communications must be undated and nothing must be sent through the post. We will arrange your means of communication."

The major, who had been lying on the sofa while he told me all this, suddenly sat up and looked at me, saying: "Remember, we have eyes and ears everywhere. Do not try to double-cross us because once you have joined us there is no escape. Now repeat your instructions three times so I know you have understood them."

He produced a statement which he asked me to sign. I read it through with a sinking heart. It bound me body and soul to the N.K.V.D., to obey their instructions implicitly and not to divulge to anyone that I was working for them. He made me write at the bottom that I understood the full consequences should I break faith with them. The punishment, he informed me, was simple enough, I would be shot.

After I had signed this document, Major Kirilov blotted it carefully and put it in his breast pocket. Then for the first time he gave one of his grim, unexpected smiles.

"Remember, little Swallow," he said, "you are now one of my birds. There are many others. Some try to fly away, but they don't get very far. I advise you not to follow their bad example."

Having had his little joke my sinister acquaintance then gave me details of my first assignment as a secret police spy.

"You will talk to him about the weather, horses and sport generally. Englishmen love to talk about such subjects. Then lead the conversation round to discover if he has any pet subjects. But no political discussions — political discussions are barred.

"It is all very simple," added the major. "It is a very easy job because you are new to the work. All you have to do is to get nice and friendly with Bagshaw and have a good time with him. You will hear from us in due course."

I listened to all this amazed, especially when he gave me Bagshaw's telephone number at the British Embassy and told me to ring him up.

"But I can't ring up a man I don't know," I said. "Why should he see me? Who is this Bagshaw, anyway?"

"He's no stranger to you," said the major. "He's the man from the British Embassy with whom you danced at the Metro pole. He is secretary to the British Naval Attaché."

I walked out of Room 413, clutching the telephone number in my hand. I was too afraid of the N.K.V.D. not to start work at once. I immediately dialled the number and asked to speak to Bagshaw. He seemed very surprised when I told him who I was, but agreed to meet me the following afternoon for tea.

I went to the Metropole to meet him, feeling ill at ease — and it was not only my shabby clothes which made me so. Perhaps my nervousness communicated itself to him because the meeting was not much of a success. He was a much more experienced man of the world than I had known and my nervous chatter seemed to make little impression upon him. Eventually, after about an hour, he paid the bill and politely excused himself.

He did not offer to see me again. I sat at the table after he had left, wondering what would happen to me if I failed in this assignment. But I wasn't very surprised when an elderly woman came over and joined me. Without any preliminaries she said: "Well, how did you get on?"

I pretended not to understand although I was quite civil to her, and after a few minutes she left. As I got up to leave the waiter pushed a note into my hand. When I was alone I opened the note, which told me to report to a room in the Hotel Savoy in an hour's time. When I arrived I found one of the captains who had accompanied me on the midnight car-drive.

"We are informed you did well," he said. "Just carry on as you are and don't worry. We will keep in touch with you. If you obey orders you will be all right. Now tell me, did he say anything interesting?"

I gave him a detailed account of our conversation. It was so trivial that I thought he would realize that the meeting had not been a success. But he nodded his head several times and seemed satisfied.

"And what about the woman who came up and sat at your table afterwards?" he asked. "What did you tell her?"

"Nothing," I said.

"Yes, I know, she is one of our agents, of course, a very good one. But she might not have been, so be very careful what you say. If you carry on as you are, you will make a good agent too."

"That's all very well," I said. "But all this intrigue frightens me. I don't know how long I can stand it."

"Stop that nonsense," answered the captain. "You must keep a clear head and find out what we want. You must learn how to handle all types; answer

148

them back if they are rude to you, but make sure you never insult them first. All these foreigners are insulting. They know nothing about culture. Now listen carefully. Next time you meet him I want you to take him to the American Bar at the Metropole. There you will meet Michael, one of our men, who'll be in civilian clothes. He is coming here presently to meet you." Soon there was a knock at the door and two young men entered and clicked their heels. The captain introduced the taller of the two as Michael and we shook hands.

"We have an assignment on Friday at 11 o'clock."

"What do you want me to do?"

"It is all quite simple. You have to bring Bagshaw to the American Bar at that time. You will be drinking and I will come up and ask you for a dance. Then you will introduce me to your companion and I shall be able to talk to him in English. What could be simpler than that?"

"But what if he doesn't come? He is such a difficult man."

"Your orders are to bring him in."

The men stood up; the interview was over. Next day I called Bagshaw at his villa in Mali Haritonievsky Pereulok and his housekeeper answered the phone. She told me he was out but would be in for dinner.

Later I rang again. "What is it?" roared Bagshaw.

A little frightened at the reception, I told him that I would like to see him.

"I'm busy. I can't see you; phone me later."

"But it isn't tonight, it's tomorrow night."

"What isn't tonight but tomorrow night?" he said suspiciously.

"Oh, nothing, it's just that I'm going to bed early tonight but I thought we might meet tomorrow."

Bagshaw seemed satisfied with the explanation and agreed to meet me outside the Metropole the following evening.

It was a cold night and it had already turned eleven o'clock before Bagshaw's navy-blue Buick pulled up. Immediately he stopped, a black Russian Ford drew into the kerb some distance behind and two men in black coats got out. I guessed at once who they were; N.K.V.D. underlings whose job was to trail Bagshaw wherever he went. Every foreigner, whether he likes it or not, is followed by N.K.V.D. men in the U.S.S.R. for his "personal security"; the Soviet Union believes in looking after its guests.

I walked over and Bagshaw smiled a greeting.

"Hop in," he said, "I'll take you to the Nationale."

"No, please, not tonight. I'm so cold, now that you're here let's go into the Metropole."

Eventually he agreed and I entered on his arm. The bowing commissionaire greeted him and we left our coats in the foyer. I suggested going to the bar but Bagshaw remembered that I didn't drink and was at once suspicious. Just then the cigarette girl passed and he bought a packet of Troika. Not having any change he went off to the bar to get it and at the same time ordered drinks from the German barmaid.

We sat on high stools and the first thing he said to me was, "Well, here we are, as you wanted. What next?"

I didn't know what to say I was so nervous, but I managed to chat away in German and though I kept looking about me there was still no sign of Michael. But, just as Bagshaw was suggesting we should have a meal in the restaurant, a strange young man came up and asked his permission to dance with me.

"Go right ahead," said Bagshaw, glad to get rid of me.

The stranger held me in his arms as we half danced to the current foxtrot hit "Katusha".

"Michael wasn't able to come," he whispered. "Don't worry, we wanted to know if you could carry out our orders. You have done as we asked; there'll be another time soon."

I was mad and relieved at the same time, but in the case of Bagshaw there was no next time as far as I was concerned. The N.K.V.D. must have found out what they wanted to know by some other method. But I was not to know this then, and when I rejoined the Englishman at the cocktail bar, he puffed at his cigarette, looked me straight in the face and said,

"Listen, why do you keep bothering me? I know you are only one of the Mozhno girls who work for the N.K.V.D."

I choked over my drink. I did not realize that foreigners had so much knowledge of the Soviet system of espionage. It was evident that he knew that the only girls allowed to speak to foreigners in the Soviet are "permitted" girls who are known as Mozhno girls. They are agents of the N.K.V.D. authorized to mix with foreigners in return for information they give the secret police.

I pretended not to understand what he was saying, and after several drinks he became more relaxed. He smiled and said: "A young girl like you won't get much out of me. I suppose you would like to know where the British Fleet is? Or would you like to know how many submarines we've got? Or perhaps the type of torpedo we are using? Or what about aircraft? Would you like to know the secrets of our latest bomber?"

I laughed as if he was talking the greatest nonsense in the world. Yet, all the time, the thought of my secret police masters was at the back of my mind. So I took another drink and pretended to be gay and happy, as if I hadn't got a care in the world. This must have made an impression on Mr. Bagshaw because he became more friendly and said: "You are a funny little thing. Even if you are a spy, you are quite amusing. Perhaps we ought to see more of each other."

Before he left he casually mentioned that there was to be a party at his flat next day to welcome a new British Embassy official.

"Would you like to come?" he said. I was so worried about his unexpected knowledge of the workings of the Soviet spy system that I did not realize the significance of this invitation and mechanically accepted it.

When I reported to Major Kirilov that night at his hotel suite, I mentioned the invitation. To my surprise he jumped up from his seat and put his arm around me.

"Good work," he said. "This is really good work, my little Swallow. This is what we have been waiting for. There is a man in the Embassy whom we are anxious to keep under surveillance. This is where you really go to work."

I walked home thoughtfully after leaving the major, wondering what strange new path the N.K.V.D. were forcing me to tread. Who was this mysterious Englishman whom the secret police were so anxious to track down? I laugh sometimes when I think about it, because that man is now my husband, John Murray.

CHAPTER XV – A SPY'S LIFE IN MOSCOW

Major Kirilov was so excited about my invitation to the flat of a British Embassy official that he asked me to come and see him next day. As usual, he told me to meet him at another hotel. I was never allowed to go to the same hotel twice running. This was all part of the secrecy of the N.K.V.D. Although I was one of their informers I never went to their headquarters. All the meetings were in hotel rooms which the officers took for a few hours in order to interview one or two agents. My appointment next morning was at the Hotel Metropole where I usually worked in the evening. Major Kirilov opened a cardboard folder which contained a detailed dossier of the Englishman I was to contact. He told me that this record was the result of two years' shadowing by secret police agents.

In the folder were photostatic copies of the Englishman's passport, and other documents which showed he was an importer and tobacco merchant living in Riga, in Latvia. These papers had been secured in the usual N.K.V.D. manner, by a hotel servant abstracting them for the secret police to photograph while the visitor was out. Few foreigners escape this surveillance. The major said that the N.K.V.D. now had confidence in me and wanted me to have the fullest information about their suspect. He said they believed this mysterious Englishman was not the simple businessman he pretended to be.

"In fact, little Swallow," said the major, "we have very good reasons for thinking this Englishman is a secret agent employed by the British. His job in Moscow, as secretary to the British Air Attaché is only a blind."

When he told me this I accepted it as part of the all-powerful knowledge of the N.K.V.D. Later I was able to laugh at all their silly suspicions. John Murray was no more a secret agent than the man in the moon.

I did not know this when I arrived at Mr. Bagshaw's flat off Kirov Street, near the Red Gate underground station. The flat was in a villa owned by the British Embassy. Mr. Bagshaw greeted me at the door and I discovered I was the only woman guest. There were only four of us. But there was plenty to eat and drink, black caviar, vodka and cocktails — a western drink I had never tasted before.

Mr. Bagshaw introduced me to a quiet unassuming young man whom he called John. As soon as he told me that he had just come from Riga I realized that this was the man in whom the N.K.V.D. were interested. He spoke German and we talked in a friendly way, but he seemed a bit stand-offish.

Before I left, I met Mr. Bagshaw's housekeeper. She was a middle-aged woman, called Rachel, who had gone to England with her parents as a child twenty years ago. She had worked in a British bank and used to live in Finchley Road, London, but in 1939 she had made the mistake of returning to Russia to look for her relations. The N.K.V.D. arrested her and put her in prison for a year. She had no idea why this had happened, even when they released her without papers or money. Practically destitute, Rachel had gone to the British Embassy with her story and they had given her a job on the permanent staff as a housekeeper. It was a typical, meaningless Soviet episode as she told it. I had heard many such stories and no one is ever able to fathom them.

While I was talking to Rachel, the party broke up. John, the man from Riga, was just leaving when I managed to speak to him and ask if we could meet again. He obviously thought I was a little forward in suggesting this and made a noncommittal reply.

Next morning I dialled K5 24-13, the number of the Foreign Section of the N.K.V.D. I was rather elated at having contacted my quarry so quickly even though I did not appear to be making much headway with him. I was not unduly depressed about this. I put it down to the insular temperament which makes Englishmen rather shy and offhand at first meetings. When I heard Captain N.'s voice on the telephone I said with a laugh: "This is your little Swallow speaking." I expected a chuckle at the other end of the line, but none came. He told me to keep contact with John, and if I could not see him by arrangement I was to go to the Metropole every evening.

That night I made my way to my usual table in the rococo restaurant of the hotel. This restaurant, which was opposite the Bolshoi Theatre, is famous all over the world. There is a circular pond in the centre filled with fish. Tables are grouped round the pond and there is dancing to an orchestra in evening dress which plays the Soviet version of the latest dance hits. There is a girl singer who croons in several languages. At that time the Metropole was run by a well-known Russian *maître d'hôtel*, Gabbiridze. He had worked in London for years and he spoke perfect English. As I watched him walking among the rosewood tables, beneath the glittering candelabra, I had an illusion that I was not in Soviet Russia at all, but in a luxury hotel of a Western country. Gabbi, who came from Georgia, like Stalin, greeted me as usual. I had hardly sat down at my table when a man in foreign naval uniform came across and bowed.

"Forgive me, Mademoiselle," he said. "The general has asked me to give you this."

153

I had no idea who the general was, but I slit open the envelope and read the note inside. It was an invitation to join a party a few tables away. The signature, written in a foreign language, was illegible. I dare not leave the table without N.K.V.D. approval, but as usual one of the secret police was nearby. I put the envelope down and glanced across at him. He took his cigarette out of the corner of his mouth and blew a smoke ring. That was my signal. Everything was in order. I walked across to join the other party.

Four men at the table stood up when I approached. One of them, a white-haired, friendly man in his sixties, introduced himself as General Constantin Sanatescu, head of the Rumanian delegation to Moscow.

"I hope you will forgive my troubling you," he said. "But I noticed you were alone, Mademoiselle, and — well — so are we. So I thought you would do us the honour of joining us for dinner.

After dinner the German-speaking general, who had been Military Attaché in London and Paris, asked me if I could show him something of Moscow. When I replied that I could not agree until I had considered the matter, he gave me a wise smile.

"I understand perfectly," he said. "You will have to get — how shall I put it — an authority to be my guide. Let us hope you will be successful."

He rose, kissed my hand, and said good-bye. As I walked out of the restaurant I passed the N.K.V.D. man sitting alone at his table. He gave me the briefest of nods. But it was enough; he had watched and approved.

Next day I went to see Major Kirilov and he agreed that I should become the official guide to General Sanatescu, later Prime Minister of Rumania.

"You were doing very well, little Swallow," he said. "He is an important man, and this is a grand opportunity for you to serve the State. Let us know everything you can."

I spent the next few evenings dining with the general at the Metropole. His *aide*, a naval officer, and a monocled man, his adviser, remained discreetly out of earshot at the next table. As we sat talking together in German I could feel my prestige rising in the restaurant. Gabbi and his staff now gave me deep bows as I walked in. And even one or two of the N.K.V.D. men sitting around glanced at me with approval. What none of them realized was that almost at once I had a complete understanding with the general. He was well aware of how the Soviet system worked, and he knew that any girl who talked to him must have the approval of the secret police. Almost as soon as we were alone together he said: "How did you manage to get mixed up in this sort of business?"

I knew it was no use trying to bluff him, so I decided to tell him my story. It was a reckless thing to do, perhaps, but then I was not a very good spy. The information I gave to the secret police seemed to me to be a mass of trivial details. I was just a cog in a machine built by Stalin to ensure that no foreigner, not even a Communist sympathizer, would be able to move about Russia without surveillance.

Let no visitor to the great free Soviet Union imagine otherwise. Every step they take, every word they utter, is reported faithfully to the secret police. Waiters, maids, chauffeurs, shop assistants, are all part of the N.K.V.D. web. This network of secret informers threatens every Russian and enmeshes every foreign visitor.

The position I found myself in — talking to this foreign general in the Metropole — may seem bizarre to anyone in the outside world. But in Russia everything is possible. I was just one of the many thousands, trapped by the N.K.V.D. organization. No one works for the N.K.V.D. as an informer unless he is forced to do so. It is even more depressing to realize that while you work for them you are helping to prop up a system which has denied freedom to the men and women of Soviet Russia today. The general sat in silence while I poured out this story to him. I told him about my family and how I was penniless, hungry and unwanted, how I had never joined the Communist Party, and because of my father's disgrace there was no employment for me.

I spoke in rapid whispered German. When I had finished he said: "I will try and think of some way out for you."

He never referred to the incident again and I continued to show him around Moscow. We saw Pushkin's ballet "Bakhchisarai Fontaine" at the Bolshoi and also visited the famous little gipsy theatre called the "Romen" off Gorki Street, where the all-gipsy cast have even set Shakespeare to their own music. I took him to Moscow's book stalls where he purchased volumes of the Russian Academia edition of the world's classics. His pet name for me was Kickernase — German for snub-nose. From time to time I reported back to Major Kirilov and his *aides* on Sanatescu's movements. Every step he made and every place he visited was known to the secret police. I realized, of course, my own share in this shadowing was very limited and that having confessed to the general my true position he knew he had nothing to fear from me. Any indiscreet remark he might make against the Soviet, or any expression of opinion against Communism which might be of use to the N.K.V.D. would certainly not reach them through me. But I was quite sure there were many others at work on the general and his staff and none of them would have similar scruples.

The general had come to Moscow to discuss a new boundary line between Rumania and Russia. One evening I kept my usual appointment with Major Kirilov and he told me I was to sound Sanatescu out on his own personal reactions to a new war in Europe.

"This is very important for us all," said the Major. "It would be of great assistance to know what line the Rumanians are likely to follow. Of course, we know all about their official attitude, but a man like Sanatescu is important. It's his personal feelings that matter, he's a man of influence and there are plenty who follow him. Just wait till you get the chance and then introduce the subject of Germany and Russia into the conversation. Very often a man will slip and give himself away without realizing it."

I went home and thought over what the major had said. I had no wish to trap my friend and I decided to repeat my conversation word for word. At our next meeting I explained to him what had happened and asked his advice.

The general laughed. "Yes," he said, "I can well imagine your friend's anxiety. Most of Europe would like to know half as much."

"But what shall I tell him?"

"Tell him — let me see — tell him that I'm a great admirer of Switzerland .... and leave it at that."

I duly reported this back to the major who grunted and said, "Oh, well, it was worth trying."

On another occasion the major told me I was to effect an introduction between the general and a German-speaking Russian oil-expert from Baku.

"This man will come up to your table at the Hotel Metropole and greet you like an old friend," explained Major Kirilov. "He will remind you that he knew your father in Stalingrad and that he is now on a short holiday in Moscow. His name is Igor Petrov and he'll be carrying a black brief-case. He's a short, stocky chap with a black moustache; you'll know him at once."

"But what shall I tell the general?"

"Oh, nothing — just make the introduction and suggest he joins your party. You can leave the rest to Petrov."

The following evening I explained to the general what was likely to happen and he smiled.

"Oh, yes," he said, "I've heard of this one — he's a mining engineer all right, but of a very special sort. After he has joined us you'd better go home, Nora, then you won't be involved in any way."

Just then Petrov came threading his way across the room to our table. He flashed a big smile and went through his routine. The general at once invited him to join us and as soon as he was settled I made an excuse and left.

The next time I saw General Sanatescu he made no mention of the oil-expert from Baku but as I was curious to know what had happened, I asked him about it.

"It was all rather amusing, really," he said. "He stayed with me for over two hours and we talked about everything under the sun until he finally got round to the one topic on which he had been told to question me, oil. Of course, I was ready for him and every time oil cropped up I made quite sure it was always Russia's we talked about — not Rumania's."

The general chuckled.

"You know," he said, "this N.K.V.D. of yours are a very simple lot."

A few days after this incident he came to me and said:

"I am sorry, my child, I have to return to my country. But I will not forget you, although I cannot do much for you at this stage. Try and get over the border. Then send a message to me at Constanza. I will give you freedom if you can reach me."

Freedom! His words were like a shaft of sunshine.

As a Russian girl born and bred it had never occurred to me to try and escape from the Soviet. Yet I reasoned that if an important man, a foreign statesman like Sanatescu, thought I could, I should take his advice. From that moment I had only one thought in my mind — to escape from Soviet Russia.

Meanwhile the N.K.V.D. were pressing me for further information about John, the Englishman from Riga. Spurred on by their pressure I rang him up almost every day but I could never persuade him to come and meet me. I began to think that the N.K.V.D. were right and that he was a dangerous secret agent who had seen through that naive, unpractised little spy, Swallow. My life for months had consisted almost entirely of mixing with foreigners except for my brief interviews with the N.K.V.D. One morning, however, I was reminded that I still had some friends among my own countrymen. I went to the Moscow *poste restante* to see if there were any letters for me and found an envelope in the rack. It was from A.F. who met me in the park and assisted me after my father's arrest. He had escaped the purge and was still working in the Foreign Office. His letter asked me to meet him that night at our usual park bench. I managed to slip away from the Metropole without being followed. It was a bitterly cold evening in December 1940, and A.F. was muffled in furs. He told me he had asked to see me because he was very worried. It was his last night in Moscow; he was leaving in the morning to go to Berlin with Molotov to sign a non-aggression pact with Hitler.

"You know what this means, Nora?" he said. "It means we are finally slamming the door on Britain and America. It may mean a complete break with England at any moment. They may even close the British Embassy here.

"If they do, the N.K.V.D. will have no further use for you; you have been too friendly with the British. You will no longer be able to work as a Mozhno girl. That is why I have come to see you. You must get out of Moscow as soon as you can."

It began to snow but we sat on the park bench talking. A.F. was also anxious about his own position.

"I think something has gone wrong," he said. "I have a feeling they may purge me. This may be our last meeting."

When we parted I knew I was saying farewell to the last Russian friend who knew my family. In the morning A.F. left by air for Berlin with Molotov. I never saw him again. And I never heard what happened to him. I rang him at the Foreign Office several times, and a strange voice answered.

I was not able to take his advice; firstly because I was too afraid of the N.K.V.D. and secondly, because travel had become extremely difficult. For me, of course, it would have been quite impossible to get the necessary N.K.V.D. travel permit. The war, though still remote, was making itself felt in Russia. There were checks and counter-checks at all railway stations and the country was in the grip of an even more feverish spy mania than usual. Even legitimate travellers with papers were stopped, questioned and turned back. So there was no escape for me yet.

I did decide, however, to move out of my room in the tenement. I had become friendly with a girl called Tania, a Jewess from Gomel. She worked in a restaurant as a cigarette girl, and as she often came into the Metropole on the arm of a foreigner, I assumed that she was an N.K.V.D. informer like me. However, I took great care not to mention my suspicion to her for it was a strict rule of the secret police that their operators must not recognize each other. This girl suggested that I move in with her. I was so tired of my noisy flat, with no room for anyone, that I accepted her invitation gratefully. I decided to sell everything except my camp-bed and trunk so that I could be completely mobile if I ever saw a chance of escape.

I had not seen Tania's house, but when I arrived I regretted my decision. Tania had two rooms for herself and a maid but she had no intention of letting me share them. I was given a corner of a large room which I had to share with a woman, her two daughters and her mother. The woman had lost her husband in some minor factory purge and was earning only a hundred and fifty roubles a month as a charwoman. I thoroughly disliked my new accommodation and the people there hated me. It was not long before one of the women denounced me to the house committee as an undesirable. She said I was a daughter of an imprisoned Soviet official and not the kind of person who should be allowed to live in the flat of "good, honest, decent folk." They held a house meeting about me and decided that I had to go. Tania did not lift a finger to help me as I staggered into the street carrying my trunk and camp-bed. Life was a struggle for a long time after this for, each night, I had to be at the Metropole as the secret police instructed me. But, luckily, I had a few roubles with which to carry on. I had given up my room with the Yugoslav woman for 3,000 roubles "tea money" — as premiums are called in Russia. An old woman had offered this to me saying she had dreamed of a room to herself all her life. Penniless as I was, I was only too happy to let her have it, and I had also had two payments of 500 roubles from the N.K.V.D. for my work as an informer. But I still had no permanent home.

Moscow citizens used to hire out spare beds from ten to thirty roubles a night but they were hard to find because few Russians were willing to take the risk of opening the door to a stranger who, in most cases, was on the run from the police. Sometimes, when I had the money for a bed but couldn't find one, I used to hire a taxi and order the driver to cruise round Moscow while I dozed on the back seat. I couldn't stay in an hotel without police authority and I received no help from the N.K.V.D. for informers were not officially part of their organization. One night I balanced on a plank across two chairs in the kitchen of a ruined house but the rats frightened me so much I couldn't sleep.

If you have never lived in Russia, you cannot appreciate the plight I was in. Every room in Moscow is controlled by the housing manager of the building. There is also a house committee composed of people living in the premises. There was a great housing shortage and workers always had a priority, so, unless you were in a job, there was little chance of a room. This led to a gigantic black market in property with rooms changing hands for as much as forty thousand roubles. Even when you found a room, the housing manager went to the local police with your identity card. They made a note of where you lived before, your occupation and salary. This information was passed on to the N.K.V.D. who are more than likely, if they have got anything against you, to order the house manager not to admit you. I had no chance of obtaining forty thousand roubles for a black market room so I had to live wherever I could. When I had a little money I bribed people to let me stay a few nights with them. Other times I drifted around Moscow, sleeping where I could.

One of the people who befriended me was a fellow Mozhno girl, Helga Mueller, who lived with her mother in a small flat in Gorki Street. Helga's mother worked as a charwoman in an engineering factory and her daughter had become friendly with a young Englishman named Simon who worked at the British Embassy. Sometimes I used to sleep at the Muellers' flat and she used to let me have the key. When I opened the door one night I was faced with two N.K.V.D. men in uniform.

"Well, who are you?" one of them asked.

I gave them my name and said I was a friend of Helga's.

"All right, come on in and sit down — but keep still."

As soon as I got inside I saw what was happening; cupboards, mattresses, furniture, the whole place was being turned upside down. The men said nothing and I sat there from ten-thirty to eight the following morning trying to comfort Mrs. Mueller. When it was all over one of the secret policemen tore a piece of paper from his notebook and dictated a statement to the effect that I'd seen nothing unusual and heard nothing unusual during the whole time I'd been in the flat. He ordered me to sign it and put the paper back in his pocket.

"You will not talk about this to anyone, Citizeness," he said. "We shall soon know if you have been foolish enough to discuss the matter."

The N.K.V.D. then told the old woman to pack a bag, and, one on each side, they marched out to their car. Just as they were bundling her in, Helga arrived. I rushed up to her and told her what had happened. Helga stood there without understanding while I ran across to the N.K.V.D. men and asked them to allow Helga to say good-bye to her mother. The young girl threw herself on the floor of the car and clutched her mother's knees.

"Mamochka," she cried, "why are they doing this to you — what have you done?"

The old woman burst into a fit of wailing and her escort pushed Helga out of the car. Later she received official notification that her mother, who was quite illiterate, had been found guilty of stealing plans from the factory where she was employed as a charwoman. She was sentenced to eight years' imprisonment.

Simon did everything he could to help Helga obtain her mother's freedom, but it was no use, and as if to punish him for trying, the N.K.V.D. next instructed her to break off her friendship. The Englishman came up to me one day, asked if I'd seen her and said she'd been missing four months. He was very worried about her and feared she might have followed her mother to prison. Some weeks later, however, I saw Helga again; she told me she had been goaled and I noticed one of her front teeth was missing.

"Yes," she said "they did that too. They've let me out on condition I have nothing more to do with Simon."

And, despite every advance by the young Englishman, Helga kept her part of the bargain.

By now I had received several payments from Major Kirilov and his henchmen and I'd been able to buy myself some new clothes. I went to the Metropole every evening under their instructions and a table was reserved for me. Sometimes one of the N.K.V.D. men in civilian clothes would join me. From them I began to pick up the current gossip of Moscow's diplomatic world. It was soon quite plain to me that the N.K.V.D. had enrolled a number of girls like me to help them in their job of shadowing foreigners. English, American, French and other European diplomats used to come into the restaurant nightly with Mozhno girls on their arms. Doubtless they had all been warned by their own governments to be careful of foreign women, but even so few appeared to realize that their friends were N.K.V.D. agents.

Anna, the girl who had shared my Foreign Office room, had now returned to Moscow from Vladivostock and I was glad of her company. I had been worried about her because I hadn't received any letters from her except one which said she was in hospital.

"What was the matter with you?" I asked her when we met one night in the Metropole.

"Oh nothing," she said. "I wasn't in hospital, I was in gaol. They put me there for five months for being late for work."

For lateness, three times in succession, is a criminal offence in the Soviet Union.

Anna's boy friend in Moscow was a Russian whom she called Vladimir. At least we all thought he was a Russian — he spoke the language perfectly and wore Moscow-made suits. He used to take Anna to eat at the Hotel Nationale restaurant and sometimes I would join them. One night I was Vladimir's guest at the Hotel Moskwa when he gave a big shout and invited a pair of shabbily-dressed Russians to join us.

"The party's on me," he cried. "Let's have some fun."

The two workmen helped themselves to food and filled their glasses.

"That's it," said Vladimir. "Have what you like. I know you get little to eat in this confounded place."

His words surprised me and Anna, for we had accepted him as a fellow Russian. But he took no notice of our stares.

"You Russian workers think you are well looked after," he said loudly, "but you ought to visit Germany to see what real democracy is. The Politburo is fooling you. You don't know the meaning of Communism here. You had a good man in Trotsky, but you let Stalin and his gang kick him out."

The two men sat in silence. They were obviously frightened, and so was I, by Vladimir's outburst. I nudged Anna and said "Let's get out of here, the man's crazy to talk like this. We shall have the N.K.V.D. after every one of us."

But Anna just shrugged and finished her drink. Then Vladimir turned to me.

"I know what I'm saying all right — so there's no need to sit there like a lot of dummies. Anyway, what the hell. You think I'm a Russian but I'm not, see. There — how do you like that?"

And Vladimir threw on the table a German passport with its eagles and swastika. He jumped up, clicked his heels and raised his arm in a Nazi salute with the cry of "Heil Hitler".

That was enough for our two Russian guests — they fled. I heard afterwards that Vladimir was a colonel in the German Army and was in the military attaché's department of Hitler's Moscow Embassy. His unexpected outburst made me determined never to be seen in his company again.

Moscow at this time was a dangerous place at night. People were constantly being attacked and robbed, even stripped of their clothes. There were organized gangs who roamed the streets specializing in this kind of crime. It became so bad that the whole Moscow police force was deployed to try and stamp out this after-dark reign of terror. It was months before the thugs were captured, and no wonder. One of the ring-leaders was caught in a round-up one night and when he arrived at the police station he was found to be Captain Antonov, a Moscow police chief.

I began to look upon the Metropole, which I had at first dreaded entering, as a place of refuge. I was at least able to get something to eat and drink there and to meet people. The signing of the non-aggression pact, for which my friend, A.F., had flown to Berlin with Molotov, was immediately followed by a large number of Germans passing through the Russian capital. A great many of them stayed at the Metropole and I was introduced to Karl Hagenbeck, the famous German zoologist.

I received N.K.V.D. approval to show him round the city. By this time I was so depressed that eventually I also told him my story. Like Sanatescu, he was sympathetic and promised to help me if I could ever get across the border into Germany. Assistance awaited me now in two countries on the Soviet border, but escape seemed more impossible than ever.

One day in desperation I decided to confide in Tania who, although she had been most unhelpful about accommodation, was still a friend of mine. Once I had broken the ice I did not seem able to stop myself. I told her the whole story of my conversations with Sanatescu and Hagenbeck. Next day, in the Metropole, Captain N. of the N.K.V.D. approached me.

"We want to see you tomorrow afternoon," he said. "Report at three o'clock punctually."

When I arrived I found Major Kirilov and the two captains waiting for me. During the past few months, because they thought I was developing into an efficient informer, they had seemed quite pleased to see me. This time as soon as I walked through the door I realized the atmosphere was different. All three of them glared at me in a hostile manner and Major Kirilov suddenly barked at me: "You have been babbling. We know everything. You have placed yourself in a very unfortunate position through your own stupidity."

My heart sank. I knew at once what had happened. Tania, a loyal N.K.V.D. girl, had betrayed me.

I stood there white-faced waiting for Major Kirilov's next words. He did not go into any further details but said: "This is your last chance. I am tired of having you roaming round the Metropole babbling to foreigners and not doing your duty. You must make further contact with that Englishman. He is the one we are after.

"We have been patient with you long enough. You have exactly a week to make a friend of him. If you don't succeed in this time we shall finish with you. And you know what that will mean."

I did indeed. Without their backing I would be lost. I would be rounded up and sent into exile as an undesirable. I simply had to contact the Englishman again. And this time I could not afford to fail.

The interview with the N.K.V.D. was a few days before New Year. On New Year's Eve I sat amid the streamers and excitement of the Hotel Metropole, surrounded by foreigners laughing and talking. They were welcoming the year 1941, which was to change the destiny of Russia and the world. I did not share their gaiety. I was a lonely, sad little Russian girl who perhaps would not live to see the end of the year. I noticed Tania enjoying herself as usual. She took no notice of me as I sat at my table alone. The week that the N.K.V.D. had given me was nearly up and I had achieved nothing. I had dialled the Englishman several times and he still refused to see me.

In desperation I decided to have one more try. I went to a phone booth and dialled the flat of Mr. Bagshaw, with whom John was now living. John himself answered the telephone. When he heard my voice he immediately became cold and distant. He tried to hang up but I said: "I must see you. I must. It is very important."

Something of the frantic anxiety in my voice must have conveyed itself to him for, to my relief and amazement, he hesitated and then said: "All right then, you'd better come round — but only for a few moments as I am just going out."

Scarcely believing my good fortune, I rushed out of the hotel and ran through the snow-carpeted streets. John opened the door. There was no one else in the house. He told me that Mr. Bagshaw was at a party with Walter Duranty, the American journalist, who was then in Moscow for the North American Newspaper Alliance.

John was about to join them but he showed me into the flat and said: "I can give you a few minutes. Now tell me, what do you want? Why are you always pestering me?"

I looked at this strange, quiet Englishman who had resisted every overture I had made. Something in his demeanour made me decide to chance everything in a last gamble.

"I am here to beg you to help me," I said. "I am in terrible danger and only you can help me."

He gazed at me in astonishment. "But how can I help you?" he asked. "I don't know you."

"Just let me see you, that's all," I pleaded.

John smiled. "I think I understand," he said. "You want to see me so that you can report everything back to the N.K.V.D.?"

At his words I just slumped into a chair. I felt that there was no more I could do. If this calm Englishman was so sure of my mission, he must be a secret agent as the N.K.V.D. said.

This was the end of the road. I could go no further. I saw my life stretching in front of me — the Lubyanka, Siberia, perhaps death. I was completely lost. I leaned my head against the arm of the chair and burst into uncontrollable sobs.

When I managed to look up and gaze at John through my tears I saw that his face was sympathetic.

"Look," he said, "I know you are an N.K.V.D. girl. I can't help you. You go back to your bosses and tell them they are wasting their time. But first of all have some tea."

I dried my tears and we began to talk in a more friendly way. I blurted out my story to a foreigner for a third time. I told him that I had no wish to spy on him but for my own safety it was essential that I should be seen in his company.

"From time to time I will report to the N.K.V.D.," I said. "But they will be innocent reports. I don't care what you're doing, I won't let you down."

"Are you suggesting that you would betray your country for a foreigner?" he asked with mock severity.

"On the contrary," I cried, "it is they who have betrayed Russia!"

He looked at me for a long time without saying anything.

Then, quietly and simply, he said: "Nora, I very seldom trust people but I will trust you. I'll do my best to help you, here's my hand on it." As we clasped hands he added: "I never break my word as you will find out. And now, before we go any further I think you ought to know my story, too, and then you'll see that you're not the only one who has had experience of the N.K.V.D."

He didn't tell the whole story then, but I know it now. John had left England when he was seventeen and arrived in Riga, capital of Latvia, where he became an accountant in a Greek tobacco factory. After four years in the Baltic countries he opened his own factory in Riga in 1933, Latvias Tabakas Sabiedriba, the Latvian Tobacco Company. At the end of 1937 he sold out to the Latvian Government and went to Finland where he opened an import-export business. When Russia invaded Finland in 1940 he went to the British Legation in Helsinki with a view to returning to England, but he was advised to remain in view of his knowledge of the Baltic States and he became a diplomatic courier. He worked for the British Legations in Sweden and Norway until the Germans overran the latter country and one of his last jobs there was destroying British diplomatic papers in the Oslo Legation. He escaped from Oslo to Stockholm and was then sent with despatches to Helsinki, to the Estonian capital, Tallin, and on back to Riga.

John was in Riga, capital of Latvia, staying at Krisjan Baronu Street, when the Russian troops occupied the rest of the country. Nearly all the foreign legations and consulates had been closed and as one of the few Englishmen left in the country he was asked by the British authorities if he would be willing to go to Moscow as civilian secretary to Wing Commander (later Group Captain) Halliwell, the British Air Attaché.

John accepted the post but he could not quit Riga without a permit from the Soviet Government. Frequent application produced nothing. Instead, he was visited by two Russian members of the Latvian Ministry of Interior Security, the Latvian equivalent to Russia's N.K.V.D., which the Red Army had set up in the country. One of them spoke English, the other German, and they first of all pretended they had called to ask his advice about restarting the Government tobacco factory. But this was only a blind, they arranged to see John again and it was soon obvious from their conversation that they knew a great deal about him and his activities in the Baltic as a diplomatic courier. Finally, they admitted they also knew he was waiting to go to Moscow and work in the Air Attaché's department in the British Embassy. One of the Russians then offered John the opportunity of working for the Russian Intelligence. He was told it would be quite simple for the Soviet to arrange payment for his services in any country in the world in any currency.

John told the two men he would have nothing to do with their proposition. The men were indignant, but when they saw he was adamant, they got up and left. But they had not yet finished with him, and for the next two months other Interior Security men came to see him regularly. On other occasions he was told to report at their headquarters. At all these interviews, the Russians subjected him to a merciless grilling on his activities in the Baltic. They accused him of being a German spy and no amount of persuasion on his part would alter their attitude. Meanwhile, the British Embassy in Moscow were puzzled by his non-appearance. They telegraphed him, but his reply that he was being held up never reached Moscow. Instead, the Embassy sent Geoffrey Wilson, then secretary to Sir Stafford Cripps, Britain's Ambassador in Moscow, to find out what was happening. John told Wilson the whole story and he went with him to the Prefecture to find out why they'd not yet given a permit for him to take up his appointment in Moscow. As soon as they saw Geoffrey Wilson, the Russian officials blandly assured him the whole matter was a mistake and a permit to leave Riga was issued that same day.

On his arrival in Moscow John saw Sir Stafford, made a full report which the Ambassador asked him to sign. The matter was taken up with the Russians but their only answer was that John had been mistaken and could have left any time.

The little that he told me that night made me understand Major Kirilov's interest in this Englishman who had joined the British Embassy from Latvia. He had obviously received a full report of the incident and, such is the spy mania in the Soviet, he was still anxious to keep the newcomer under complete surveillance.

When John finished he had quite forgotten about his party and now that we both knew one another's history we talked for a long time and eventually agreed on a plan to save me from the N.K.V.D. John spoke good German and I was to call upon him early each morning to teach him Russian, when we would have coffee together.

"Anyway, I want to brush up my Russian," he said with a wry grin. "Perhaps I can get something out of this as well."

But he absolutely refused to meet me in public at night, to do so would jeopardize his own position with the Embassy.

Next day I reported to Major Kirilov. He received me grimly, but when I told him that I was going to meet the Englishman every day his face broke into a smile.

"You see, little Swallow," he said, "It was only a question of trying hard enough."

CHAPTER XVI – THE HEART OF A SECRET POLICEMAN

Shortly after I started meeting my Englishman regularly I was again reminded of the long arm of the N.K.V.D. From my earliest days I had always regarded my father, Uncle Arnold, and Redens the head of the Moscow N.K.V.D., as inseparables. Father and Arnold had been purged but Redens had outlasted them. I thought it was because he was Stalin's brother-in-law, but eventually even this did not save him. About the time I met John Murray, Redens fell out of favour at the Kremlin. He was removed from his post as head of the Moscow secret police and followed my stepmother into exile to Kazakstan in Asiatic Russia. He was given a nominal post as N.K.V.D. chief there. But as all the inhabitants, except for nomadic tribesmen, were political exiles who had been declared enemies of the people, it was obvious that there was no work for him.

It was not long before the motive in sending him to Kazakstan became evident for he was soon arrested on some pretext, given a secret trial, and disappeared like so many others. His wife, presumably because her sister had been married to Stalin, managed to escape the full wrath of the Soviet tyrants. After her husband's death, she was allowed to return to Moscow with Felix, her child. She was given a small room in a block of tenements. The last I heard of her she had resumed her maiden name of Anna Allilujeva and was earning a precarious living by writing the life story of her father, Stalin's father-in-law.

I am afraid the news of Redens' disgrace did not interest me unduly, as it seemed the inevitable end of all N.K.V.D. chiefs. My daily Russian lessons with John were progressing satisfactorily, and every day I reported my conversations with him to Major Kirilov. Once I asked the major if he could find me anywhere to live. He refused at first but eventually he booked me into a small hotel, the Hotel Europe. I told him I was afraid to stay there without papers but he said I needn't worry.

"This is one of our own establishments; no one will ask any questions."

I stayed in the Hotel Europe for three weeks, they gave me a shabby little room but at least it was better than nothing at all. While I was there, the major asked me to compile a complete report on John Murray.

"Take your time over it," he said, "We want every little detail you have found out about him. Even the most trivial fact may be of use to us."

168

I saw John the next morning and told him what I'd been asked to do. He chuckled and said, "Well, that's up to you, but at least you ought to be able to give them something to think about."

That evening I set to work, and the report, duly written in the third person as I'd been instructed, gave a brief history of his life in the Baltic States before leaving Riga and joining the British Embassy. Since all this was already known to the N.K.V.D. there was no harm in letting them read it all over again. I also added some facts about his life in the north of England and explained that he was an acknowledged expert on aeronautical matters, which, of course, he wasn't. The whole report covered four pages and by the time I had finished it was an impressive document.

I made a rough draft then copied it carefully in my hotel bedroom and addressed it to Major Kirilov. The next time I saw him he congratulated me on it.

"Very excellent work," he said, "I'd no idea you were so observant."

On several other occasions I was asked to put specific questions to John and report his answers back to the N.K.V.D. On the face of it they seemed innocent enough but it was quite apparent that they fitted into a general pattern and that the secret police were compiling a daily dossier on the happenings inside the British Embassy. The questions usually dealt with arrival of personnel at the British Embassy, their full names, time of arrival and where they would be staying. It was quite obvious the major required this information so as to be able to arrange for one of his Mozhno girls to contact the newcomers, just as I had been instructed to contact John when he arrived from Riga.

Another time I was asked to find out what kind of reports were being sent back to England by Wing Commander Halliwell, the Air Attaché, on the strength of the Soviet Air Force. They were, it seemed, particularly anxious to know his assessment of their planes.

"No difficulty in finding out for us, surely, my little Swallow," said Major Kirilov. "After all, your boy friend is the secretary to this man."

When I told John what the major wanted to know he laughed and said, "That's something you'll have to work out for yourself."

And in my next report to the major I said that Halliwell thought the Russian Air Force unconquerable!

In all my dealings with the secret police I was always very careful to give nothing away. At the same time it needed a great deal of ingenuity to produce answers which would have the appearance of being authentic. But somehow I succeeded and although I was unable to produce any shattering secrets of the

British Embassy I was at least able to give the impression to Major Kirilov that it wasn't through want of trying.

Soon the time came for me to leave the Hotel Europe and I was still without a permanent home. John had helped me to satisfy the N.K.V.D. but I did not wish to worry him further with my own troubles. It was enough that I had met him and escaped a Siberian exile.

Every day when I left him and reported to the N.K.V.D. I began my ceaseless search for a night's lodging. That winter was particularly hard, even for Russia, and one night, covered in rags, I was forced to sleep in a cemetery. I chose this spot because I did not wish to be picked up by the police and I thought that I could rest there undisturbed, if nearly frozen. Next morning I awoke stiff and shivering after a few fitful hours of uneasy sleep. When I walked into the street I collapsed. The wife of the grave-digger picked me up and carried me to the one room she lived in. She called a doctor who diagnosed pneumonia. For six weeks that old woman, short of food and money, nursed me although I had hardly a rouble with which to repay her.

Ill as I was, I was happy to be with her because she and her husband typified the kindly spirit of the old Russia. Her humanity and gentleness reminded me of the bearded old man in the Ukraine, my mother's father, who had ranted so much against the inhuman regime which my father had helped to found. She treated me like a human being. It was the first time it had happened to me since my father's arrest. At great risk to herself she managed to get a message through to the British Embassy to tell John that I could not continue his Russian lessons. I did not send any other message except to say that I was ill. I thought perhaps he would be glad to be rid of me and my worries about the N.K.V.D. But I was pleased when one day the old woman brought me a parcel of food and some money.

"From your friend at the British Embassy," she said with an understanding smile.

John had not forgotten his little Russian girl and nearly every day afterwards food and money arrived for me.

One morning when I was recovering, although still weak, there was a knock at the door. When the old woman opened it a voice said: "You have a woman named Korzhenko here."

"Yes," said the old woman. "Who are you?"

"We are from the N.K.V.D.," said the man in an authoritative voice.

"Come in," replied the old woman, " But don't blame me if anything happens to you afterwards."

"And what is likely to happen, you silly old woman?"

"Nothing very much, except that Citizeness Korzhenko has smallpox.

There was a silence after this remark. Then the sound of heavy boots walking rather hurriedly down the stairs. Even in my weak state I could hardly repress a chuckle. The N.K.V.D., however, are not as easily disconcerted as that. A few days later they returned and gave the old woman instructions that I was to report to them as soon as I was well.

Not until spring came was I strong enough to go out. John sent me food, flowers and badly needed medicine. When I became well enough, we went out for walks in the spring sunshine. I hoped the N.K.V.D. were watching; it proved that even though I was convalescent I was still doing my duty. As soon as I was well enough I reported to the N.K.V.D. When I was announced I was shown into Major Kirilov's office. He did not ask about my illness. Before I could open my mouth he shouted at me: "So ... the little Swallow at last returns."

"I have been ill," I said. "I could not get to see you before."

"You are too late, Citizeness," he replied. "Now the spring has come we have other swallows. We do not need you."

I repeated that I had been ill and that he must have known about it because his officers had tried to see me.

"They have seen you all right," said the major and flipped open a folder. Then he read me out a list of dates and times of my meetings with John. He knew where we had been and what we had done. The spy had been spied upon.

"All that is absolutely correct," I said. "But what are you worrying about? The Englishman has been kind to me when I was ill. I needed help and he was the only one who took any interest in me. And anyway it was you who suggested I met him in the first place."

Major Kirilov looked at me coldly and said: "I am not concerned about your illness; we are not running a hospital. You had no right to meet him without informing us.

"We tell you when to see these foreigners, you don't meet them just when you think. You didn't even bother to report that he had come to see you."

I stood there amazed. This was the last thing I had expected, but then the N.K.V.D., as I had learned, were never grateful to the people who worked for them.

The major was annoyed by my silence.

"What is the matter with you?" he stormed. "Are you in love with this foreign swine?"

For a moment I could not say anything. Then from somewhere my courage came back, a courage that I thought the secret police had extinguished for ever.

"This foreigner has been very kind to me," I said. "I have sunk pretty low, but not so low as to betray every movement of a man who has shown some decency towards me. I have done my duty, you cannot ask for more."

Major Kirilov's face became grim.

"It is exactly as I thought," he said. "You have no further use for us? You prefer the Englishman? Well, we have no further use for you."

He flung a paper across the desk at me. A glance showed me that it released me from all N.K.V.D. work. This should have brought me relief but in fact it frightened me very much. It meant that I could no longer rely on even the dubious protection of the secret police. I looked at it appalled.

"Go on, sign — sign," shrieked the major, working himself up into a fury.

With trembling fingers I wrote my name and walked towards the door.

"Go back to your hero," sneered Kirilov as I walked away. "See if he can look after you now. Remember, Citizeness, you are a Russian."

I realized as I left him exactly what the paper meant. Up to now my N.K.V.D. work, slight as it was, had saved me from following in the steps of my father and stepmother. Now it could only be a matter of time before I, too, was exiled. I felt an odd sense of relief, like a person who knows there is no more reprieve. I telephoned John and asked him to meet me. I explained what had happened and he said there was only one thing for me to do, to get out of Moscow at once. He lent me the fare and I caught the night train to Leningrad.

I could not stay with Uncle Constantin again as I knew that he was now thoroughly frightened of the secret police. As the train rumbled towards Leningrad I suddenly remembered Nina, an old friend of my father's who had known me as a small child. She had been friendly with my father's family in Czarist days when Leningrad was St. Petersburg, the Imperial capital. In those far-off days she had been a well-known cabaret star.

I found her still living at her old address. She had a well-furnished room and told me she was working in a factory canteen which gave her accommodation as a worker. In addition, I discovered that she was an N.K.V.D. informer, but she was very kind to me in spite of my history and I felt safe with her. However, when N.K.V.D. men came round in the evening I felt an embarrassment to her. She introduced me to an old friend of hers, Fanny Akimovna, a dear old lady to whom, almost without thinking, I told

172

my story. When I got to the part about John, she nodded her head wisely and said: "An Englishman? They make good husbands I understand."

She said it in such a knowing way that I looked at her and said joking: "Surely you have never been married to an Englishman?"

"No, I have not," she said with a smile. "But my daughter has — and still is."

"Your daughter?" I queried.

"Yes, my daughter Tamara," said the old lady. "She ran off with an Englishman. They tell me is the editor of an English newspaper. His name is Bill Rust."

The mother-in-law of the late editor of the *Daily Worker* realized my difficulty in staying in a house where there were constant visitors from the N.K.V.D. She introduced me to a woman with snow-white hair who had just returned from five years in a concentration camp.

Lydia Koslova was in her mid-thirties but she looked twenty years older. I stayed with her for some time and the stories she told me of the horrors she had undergone made me more determined than ever to remain hidden from the N.K.V.D. She had been a book-keeper in an industrial plant and her arrest had followed an enquiry into suspected sabotage. In her position she had no access to any machinery, and to accuse her of damaging any of the plant was ludicrous. But Soviet Russia is full of such situations. She had been arrested in her home, taken to the Kresti prison where she was kept in solitary confinement and questioned daily by relays of uniformed secret police.

"I cannot describe the terror and humiliation of those days and nights," she told me. "I was dropping with fatigue and exhaustion all the time I was there. They never let me sleep properly and I never knew when the key would turn in the lock and they would drag me out again to face the inquisitors. Over and over again they stood me in a little white-washed room with a bright light from a naked bulb overhead while two of those N.K.V.D. swine sat at a table.

"I used to stand there numb, half-dead with fear and exhaustion. And always the men would keep shouting at me the same questions: 'Who paid you to wreck the plant?' 'Name your fellow conspirators,' 'Confess you're a Trotskyist.' 'Admit everything and you will be freed.'

"I had no solid food, only thin soup. Towards the end I lost the power of my legs and I could only shuffle. Several times they dragged me from my cell and made me stand naked before them. Finally, when I was just a helpless mass of shambling limbs, without proper control, over either my brain or my body, they succeeded in making me sign a fake confession that I

173

had been working against the State. They left me alone after that and a doctor examined me. Then one day I was brought before another line of N.K.V.D. men to receive my sentence; five years exile. I went with several hundred other poor wretches on a three weeks' train journey to the Urals.

"We were packed in open trucks, under armed guards, and our life when we arrived still gives me nightmares so that I wake up screaming. As a so-called intellectual I found I was far worse off than any of the other prisoners. The guards used to delight in brow-beating any educated man or woman and they made a special point of giving such people the most degrading jobs they could think of."

Lydia Koslova's story broke down several times as she told it. She was still suffering from the effects of her imprisonment and the memories of it reduced her to tears. There are thousands of men and women in Russia today with similar tales and even the threat of the secret police cannot stop them from telling them. It is as though their experiences are too heavy a burden for them to carry alone and they try to escape their past by confiding in others.

Now that I was in Leningrad I started to look up some of my old friends from my childhood. I have already told how I again met the Morton family and after visiting them I decided to call on another family I knew that lived in the same block of flats. This was Sergei Zhupakhin, son of the chief of police for the Leningrad region, whom I had known when I was a little girl in the Crimea. His father had been purged and shot the year before and he was now living with his young wife Irena Zernova — she had retained her maiden name on marriage and was the daughter of Kirov's deputy. I had known Irena when we were schoolgirls in Leningrad and although I had heard of her father-in-law's fate I had no idea of her own personal suffering.

But as soon as she opened the door I knew she too had been a victim of Stalin's rule. Although only twenty-two, her hair was streaked with grey, her face lined, and she looked like an old woman. She was pleased to see me and we talked over old times.

I saw at once she wasn't the gay, carefree girl I had known in my teens and eventually Irena, too, told her story.

After Kirov's assassination, her father and mother were shot in the big purge that followed. It is Russian justice to punish the children of any man or woman convicted of plotting against the State, and although she was only sixteen, Irena and her twelve-year-old sister were banished to a concentration camp where they became slave workers on a road-making project.

"Believe me, Nora," she said, "you have no idea what goes on in this terrible country. Look at me — I'm just a broken husk of a woman. The things those swine did to me makes me sick. For months I used to vomit at the mere thought of a man. It is only Sergei's kindness and understanding that has brought me back to some semblance of sanity."

Irena choked over her words and I gripped her arm to soothe her.

"I can't wash myself enough," she said. "I'm so unclean. The things my sister and I had to do in that camp make me retch when I think of them. We slept on the floor in filthy huts unfit for dogs. We were covered in lice, and the rest of the prisoners had already turned the place into a urinal. We lost all shame, we did as they did.

The guards weren't even human — we were both raped by them the first night and from then on they took us whenever they felt like it. There was no escape, there was nothing we could do. Our only crime was that we were the children of Zernova."

Irena's story was so frightening I kept it to myself, but knowing Russia as I do I have no reason to disbelieve her.

While I was still in Leningrad I stayed two nights in the home of Dr. B., whose wife was the woman who had once asked me to hand her hidden store of *valuta* over to my father.

Mme B. was delighted to see me but when I enquired after her husband she told me he was in his second year at a concentration camp. Someone had denounced him as a Trotskyist. I saw her again before I left Russia and she told me her husband had returned to her unrecognizable. People who had known him well were quite unable to place him. He had been ruthlessly tortured in the Kresti prison before the secret police finally broke his spirit and obtained a confession. Even so he told his wife he had withstood their water torture, drips of ice-cold water on his naked back, for two hundred hours. Torture and drugs form an integral part of the N.K.V.D.'s methods of obtaining confessions at both secret and public trials.

Soon after my father's arrest in Moscow I met a woman doctor whose husband had served under him in Stalingrad. Her name was Alla and she lived at No. 19 Kutznetsky Bridge. Alla was of Mongolian extraction with black hair, slant eyes and thick lips. She took me back to the communal flat in which she had a luxuriously furnished room and told me she was now separated from her husband. I was in need of friends at that time and for the next few weeks I often visited her. But my calls were always in the early evening as she was never up before midday and regularly every night at ten-thirty, she would get up, put on her coat and pack her bag of medical instruments saying she was off to work. One evening I asked her what her work was and she gave me a sly smile.

"Haven't you guessed?" she said. "Where else would I be going at this time of night? I work at the Lubyanka."

Alla and her little black bag at once had a new significance, for I knew just what her employment meant in the Lubyanka gaol, and the next time I saw her take the glistening hypodermic needle from her bag and shoot a few drops of liquid into the air I could not suppress an involuntary shudder. The N.K.V.D. doctor caught the movement.

"So," she said, "Nora doesn't approve!"

I said nothing and Alla spun round, her eyes blazing.

"Well," she cried, "do you think I like it? Do you think it's any easier for me going there night after night to help them in their wretched inquisition? Look, what do you think these are?"

She flung a cupboard open. Inside she had stacked rows and rows of empty vodka bottles.

"That's my secret, Nora. That's the only way I can carry on, and God alone knows what I've been through."

She started to weep and I did what I could to comfort her but it was no use. In any case I kept telling myself that it was doctors like her who went to work every night on my father in the underground cells of the Lubyanka gaol. Perhaps Alla herself was trying to extort a confession out of him. All N.K.V.D. questioning is done at night into the small hours of the morning when the human spirit is at its lowest ebb, and Alla did not have to tell me any more. I knew at once the explanation for her luxury flat with its fine Persian carpets, grand piano and white bearskin rug.

I never called on her again.

I remembered this last meeting with Alla as I heard the fate of the men and women I had been looking forward to see once more in Leningrad. It seemed that everywhere I went I was to be haunted with these stories of arrest, torture and concentration camps. And each sad tale kept stabbing my mind with the thought that my own father had now joined the millions who were suffering under the Communist regime. And now, of course, the N.K.V.D. were after me. Every day spent with Lydia Kosloff I lived in terror of being traced.

I hadn't long to wait for one morning there was the usual knock on the door and the police asked for my registration papers.

I had to admit that I had not registered in Leningrad, so the officer asked me to accompany him to the police station. I wondered how the police could have tracked me down so quickly but when at the police station I was immediately handed over to an N.K.V.D. man, I realized what had happened.

Nina, my father's friend, had done her duty as an informer. She had given me away to the secret police.

I was kept in a cell and at 8 a.m. they began to interrogate me. This continued until six o'clock at night. No brutality was used towards me but again and again my inquisitors asked the same questions.

"What are you doing here? Who is this Englishman? Why are you friendly with foreigners?"

I knew as soon as I heard these questions that Nina had given me away, but I parried them and persisted that I was a student in Leningrad on holiday. I said that I had invented the story of knowing an Englishman and told it to Nina in order to appear as a glamorous girl from Moscow. This did not go down too well but it puzzled them slightly and they went away. A few minutes later they were back, asking the same questions again... again... and again. I realized that probably the questioning would go on all night and sooner or later I would break down and tell the truth. I was already feeling rather faint from hunger, and dizzy from questioning.

Suddenly one of the N.K.V.D. men, a major, had an idea. He picked up a telephone and said: "If you come from Moscow, they'll know about you there. I'll have a word with them."

My head was aching and I could have collapsed on the floor, but I had an inspiration.

"Fine," I said. "Just tell them you have picked up the Swallow."

I realized, of course, he would never have heard of me but it was enough to identify me with the N.K.V.D. The major banged down the phone and his expression changed at once.

"But, Comrade, this is different," he said. "Why on earth didn't you tell us this morning as soon as we started questioning you?"

"You know as well as I do that we cannot disclose our identity. I shouldn't have done it now, I suppose."

It worked. He believed me. If he had phoned Moscow they would have repudiated me at once and said I was no longer working for them. That would have been the end of me. Instead the N.K.V.D. man slapped me on the shoulder and said: "I am sorry, Citizeness, I thought you had no right to be here. Now I know better, let's go and have dinner."

Next day a message came telling me to report to the major again. I thought my best move was to do this because I knew if I tried to hide they would only pick me up. I decided to report at once and try to keep up the bluff. But I need not have worried because it was obvious after a few moments' conversation he still thought I was an N.K.V.D. agent. So even the secret police slipped up sometimes.

He said: "All travel will be banned at midnight. Can you finish your secret mission by then?"

I had no idea what secret mission he was referring to but I said airily: "I don't think so, because the Englishman I have to meet hasn't arrived yet."

"Ah," said the major as though I had supplied the clue he was waiting for. "It seems that your Englishman has been detained in Moscow. I think it is better that you should return there. I will reserve you a seat on the last train."

I did not dare to enquire why travel had been banned at midnight. But I soon discovered, as the train stopped and started to let troop trains go through, that there were big movements between Leningrad and Moscow. The date was 22 May, 1941, a few weeks before Hitler invaded. Obviously Stalin had received some secret information about German troops massing on the Russian frontiers and decided to make his preparations.

When I arrived in Moscow the city was full of troops. I had nowhere to go so I went to the Metropole. After all, if the N.K.V.D. wanted me, they would find me soon enough. So I might as well walk into the lion's den brazenly.

Yet my stomach turned over slightly as I walked through the ornate doors of the famous hotel. I flinched when I got inside the door because someone tapped me on the shoulder at once. I was afraid to look round, but it was only Gabbi, the *maître d'hôtel*, smiling at me.

"Where have you been, Citizeness?" he asked. "An important gentleman has been making quite a fuss at your absence. It is a good thing you came here tonight because he is here waiting for you. I will take you to him."

Perplexed, I followed him across the room, ready for anything. We came to a table in the corner and Gabbi bowed. Sitting there was one of the last people I wanted to see, Captain N. who knew my record with the N.K.V.D. Gabbi pulled out a chair and I just dropped into it. I was too frightened to speak when Captain N. ordered a meal for two of borsch, meat, caviar, with a bottle of wine. He seemed delighted to see me and was strangely exhilarated. He poured out a glass of wine for me and said:

"You have been a very naughty girl. We have been trying to find you everywhere, but never mind that now, at last we are together."

I had had far too many dealings with the N.K.V.D. to question this extraordinary change of front, so I just ate and drank and said nothing. Eventually, overcome by this strange meeting, I became bold enough to say: "Why do you want to see me?"

He drained his glass and leaned towards me in a confidential way. "No, not here," he said. "Don't ask those questions here."

He got up, called his car, and told the driver to go to Himki. I sat back in the darkness beside him remembering the last time we had travelled together, along the same road nearly a year ago! At the end of that journey I had become a spy, and as the headlights of the car stabbed the road ahead, I sat wondering what awaited me this time. We were out of Moscow before he spoke. Then he leaned towards me and whispered: "I am afraid this is going to be our last meeting. You will know why very soon. The whole world will know it soon. Russia will be at war in a month's time."

As the car drove along this grim-faced, stern N.K.V.D. officer became a human being. He offered me a cigarette and said: "Tomorrow I am off to my regiment. It will mean freedom for me. It will mean the end of ten years' repulsive work. I'm not a Chekist at heart, though I knew and admired your father.

"I am a bridge builder by trade and a good Communist. It is because I was such a faithful member of the Party that they put me into the N.K.V.D. I had no choice.

"I have never liked it, but I have done my best. I have never wanted a life which meant making war on fellow Russians. For ten years I have had to hound innocent people, sometimes just to cover up someone's clerical error."

He became full of the traditional Russian melancholy.

"You see in me one of the men who has destroyed Russia," he said. "Today we are as rotten as we ever were under the Czars. The country is choked with informers who would sell their own mothers with a false smile. The Politburo know this but they are very clever. They know the N.K.V.D. cannot rebel. When we are no longer useful to them we will all be liquidated just as your father was. My end will be a bullet. I only hope it will be from some honest Russian boy as an expression of what he thinks of his rulers. For I must tell you, Nora, that even in the army I cannot escape. I will remain an N.K.V.D. man, spying on my fellow soldiers. There is no escape from the secret police. I am sick of it. I wanted to be a honest soldier, but I dared not refuse because I have a wife and children. If I did, it would have been the end of me. You probably think I have been very hard on you, but really I have been your friend in secret. Time and again I was sent to arrest you in your room in the Foreign Office but each time I have deliberately arrived when you had gone.

"Nearly everyone you have been mixing with is an N.K.V.D. informer. My advice to you is to speak to no one, because no one is to be trusted. Beria (now head of the N.K.V.D.) has given orders that you must be brought in for good but I have not passed the order on. So no one outside my office knows you are no longer one of our informers."

The car was driving back to Moscow and as we approached the city he suddenly leaned across and pressed some money into my hands.

"The only thing for you to do is to get out of the capital and lie low," he said. "The best of luck, Citizeness."

The car roared away into the night and I walked slowly along the Moscow streets. Captain N. had given me plenty to think about. Up till now I had always imagined that my own astuteness had saved me from being picked up by the N.K.V.D. Now I realized that it was not my own cleverness but Captain N.'s helping hand which had saved me — and now he had gone to join the army. I considered my position. I had no job and was not registered with the police and at any moment I could be picked up and put into prison. By this time, after living the hunted life for so long I had gained a sort of animal cunning. Captain N. had told me that my dismissal by the N.K.V.D. was known only to a handful of men in his office. I had also had an experience in Leningrad of the N.K.V.D. making a mistake. With troop trains pouring in and out of Moscow and every civilian traveller being questioned, I felt that Captain N's advice was bad. I would be picked up if I ever approached the railway station.

I decided to pursue my usual bold course which had led me to meeting Captain N. I made up my mind to visit the Metropole Hotel just as though nothing had happened and I was still accepted by the N.K.V.D. I knew the ordinary police made routine checks in the hotel but I could manage these. The restaurant staff were not afraid of them like they were of the N.K.V.D. and always seemed to know when the raids were coming. They always tipped me off before the raids began. The N.K.V.D. do not work in collusion with the ordinary police, and the restaurant staff probably thought they were helping an informer by getting me out before any formal questions were asked.

One night after being warned of a raid, I slipped out of a side entrance of the hotel and hailed a passing taxi-cab. As the taxi started, a police car swung alongside and two policemen told me to get out. They were ordinary police officers, not N.K.V.D. men, and they drove me in their car to the police station for questioning. I was not very worried as I realized that the ordinary police have little power, so at the police station I told them that I had to come to Moscow to see a boy friend. The new travel regulations had stopped me leaving the capital but all I wanted to do was to get back. I gave them the address of the woman with whom I had stayed in Leningrad. I also said that my handbag with my identity card had been stolen from me. The raid on the Hotel Metropole was a normal police check and I had aroused suspicion by rushing out too quickly.

The police sergeant listened to my story and said:

"We will look into this again in the morning, Citizeness."

That night I again slept in a cell. Next morning I was lined up with several more people to await my turn for re-examination. When they took me into the charge room I repeated the story with more assurance than I had the night before. I demanded that they should find the man who had stolen my handbag and arrange a return ticket for me to Leningrad.

The sergeant swore at me for my impertinence and told me to get out.

"Don't let us catch you hanging around Moscow again," he said, "Or you'll get a trip somewhere else — and it won't be to Leningrad."

I did not dare go to the Metropole after this as I was now known to the local police and did not want to be rounded up by them again. One night I was walking along the street when a policeman stepped out of the shadows again and asked for my papers. I told him the same story as before but he wasn't satisfied. He said I had better come to the police station with him. He seemed an amiable sort of man and when I said I didn't fancy a night in the cells without something to warm me up he agreed to come and have a drink with me. This was not surprising as it was a cold, wet night with a threat of snow. We went together into the café and after a few drinks the policeman became rather amorous. He said he would let me go if I would meet him in an hour's time when he came off duty. I agreed to this, but of course I never saw him again.

I was still free but it was a precarious liberty. I felt the net was closing in. One more casual questioning and the prospect of exile or imprisonment loomed very real indeed. Again my Russian fatalism came to my rescue and I decided that I would face up to what life had in store for me. I had not worried John with my troubles but now I decided the time had come to say good-bye to him.

When I met him for our morning coffee, I must have talked rather gloomily about my future and I think he imagined that I was going to commit suicide. He tried to joke with me but nothing would relieve my depression. Eventually I stood up and held out my hand to say good-bye. When he gripped it I felt something cold and metallic pressed into my palm.

"That is the key to my flat," he said. "Go round any time and let yourself in. I will see about getting you appointed as official housekeeper to myself and the man I share the flat with."

At first I could not believe that his generous gesture was seriously meant. He explained that the flat was within the environs of the British Embassy at No. 14 Sophiiskaya Embankment. A number of Embassy employees lived in the outer buildings. The British Embassy would bring me immunity from the secret police, I would be on diplomatic ground. As soon as I had left John I hurried to the flat which spelt freedom for me. The building is quite near the Kremlin and was securely guarded by sentries and N.K.V.D. men. No one could enter without an official British Embassy permit to show they worked there. Every time I got near the gate a sentry turned towards me. It was a most nerve-racking experience to be within sight of a safety and yet unable to reach it.

I walked for hours round the building like a hunted creature, looking for my opportunity, praying that no police patrol would pick me up. Every time I went near the entrance, a guard approached and I dodged away. I stood in the shadow of a wall nearby. I realized my only hope was for the guard to turn his head for a few moments, then I could slip past him into the Embassy. It was not until nine o'clock at night, after ten hours of waiting, that my chance came. The guards stood and chatted for a moment away from the gate with their backs towards me. The entrance was unguarded. I dashed across the street like a shadow and with three tip-toed steps I was within the sanctuary of the Embassy. I flitted down the drive silent as a phantom. Any moment I expected a loud challenge which would drag me back into slavery, but none came. I slid through the passages until I came to John's flat, and opened the door with the key. He had told me where the housekeeper's room was and I opened the door and went in. It was a plain little room with a bed, dressing-table and a chair. When I saw it, my heart overflowed with joy. I walked to the bed and sank on my knees in prayer. I was free.

CHAPTER XVII - KIDNAPPED

A few hours later John came in and was astonished to see me there so soon. I do not think he had realized quite how desperate my position had been. He explained in a rather perturbed voice that staff could only be employed at the Embassy if they had a permit from the N.K.V.D. All Embassy staff were approved by the secret police. When he told me this, he patted me on the shoulder and said: "Don't get alarmed. I will manage it somehow. I will not hand you over to your friends."

I met the woman who had been cooking for John and his companions. She was a big, robust Latvian who, as soon as I spoke to her, made it plain there was no welcome for me in the flat. I could not leave the house because I would have to show a permit as soon as I walked out. Next day I paced up and down the rooms like a caged animal. Even in freedom I was still a captive. It was only a day or so before the N.K.V.D. made their first move. They asked the Embassy that I should be removed from the house as an undesirable person who had not been certified by them. The Latvian cook, an N.K.V.D. informer, had of course reported my presence at once. When the first request for my dismissal was ignored innumerable others followed but the Embassy took no action. They did not seem to realize what the position was. They regarded me as an ordinary Mozhno girl who had been employed by one of their staff. There were about fifteen Russians working in the Embassy premises and all of them had N.K.V.D. approval and permission to work there, except me. This approval was a Russian system. The Embassy did not seem to appreciate that every Russian on their staff was a Mozhno man or woman who reported everything that went on back to the N.K.V.D.

At this time Sir Stafford Cripps was the Ambassador. Occasionally I saw him walking past John's quarters across the grounds to the main building. I used to see him early in the morning taking a brisk walk, a tall, thoughtful, intellectual man, who always seemed to be working out some abstruse problem. I often wondered just how much this British Ambassador knew about the Soviet system which surrounded him, and the conditions under which his Russian employees had to work. For example, a switchboard girl or a receptionist obtained her job because she was a good linguist. As these jobs brought her into contact with foreigners she was carefully screened by the Security Branch of the N.K.V.D. The girl had been taught from childhood that foreigners only came to Russia to take advantage of the U.S.S.R. She has no way of knowing anything different. So when she accepted a post which brought her into contact with people from beyond the Iron Curtain she had to sign the oath of secrecy and loyalty to the N.K.V.D. This meant that she reported anything that she thought would interest the secret police.

This may appear sinister to a foreigner but there is nothing remarkable about it to a Russian, it is just part of the system.

A switchboard operator may lead an uneventful life for years reporting in a routine way to the N.K.V.D. Then something may happen which immediately opens the dark door to exile or even death. A handsome foreigner may begin to speak to her. She has been forbidden to make dates with foreigners or meet them outside her employment. But perhaps her emotions rise above the strict regimentation that Stalin's regime has instituted. This little girl may find strange feelings welling up in her breast. She may find that she is in love with this stranger from another world.

The N.K.V.D. have a formula for this too. She must report the matter at once and accept official guidance as to how her love life should be conducted. Yet even Stalin cannot control the oldest of human emotions. Often, against her will and her training, the girl enters into a secret understanding with the stranger whom she has been schooled to hate. She makes secret assignations with him but he is never able to understand her secret terror that one day the N.K.V.D. will find out the true position. One day her pitiful little romance is discovered. She has been betrayed by an informer. She has broken the law of the Soviet by having a secret contact with a man from the outside world which she did not report to her masters, the N.K.V.D. The penalty for this crime is several years in a correctional camp. There she will learn to love Stalin, and not any stray foreigner whom she may happen to meet. If the man is important enough the N.K.V.D. may instruct her to capitalize on her love and act only under their instructions. For the sake of her freedom, she often agrees to become a full time spy for the secret police. Once she does this, all kinds of paths are open to her — all selected by the N.K.V.D. She may find that she is ordered to go out with somebody quite different from the man she loves. By this time she is so frightened that she obeys.

The N.K.V.D. also work the situation a different way, as they did with John. Once they discovered that the Embassy was not willing to give me up to their sinister machinations, they decided to try another angle. John was bombarded daily with a persistent flow of females from beautiful blondes to qualified housekeepers. They were sent to take my place. He refused all these offers as he knew they were N.K.V.D. women, instead he chose me. I was lucky because the N.K.V.D. usually succeed in breaking up a friendship between a Russian girl and a foreigner by one means or another. Many young

Englishmen and Americans, innocent and decent young fellows, must have wondered what happened to their girl friend when she did not turn up one night to meet them. They probably thought they had been jilted. They did not know Russia; she had been sent to a correctional camp.

The war years brought many young Russian girls into contact with foreigners for the first time. Some succeeded in making happy marriages, but for most of them it only brought heartbreak, tragedy and bitterness. You would not think that the men in the Kremlin would bother about a small thing like the love affair of a Russian girl and a foreigner. But nothing is too small for them. To them people are only pawns, their feelings do not matter. The guilty men in the Kremlin do not mind the hatred of the world. Like gods, they regard themselves as above such things.

The case of the Soviet war brides typifies their attitude, for, as you know by the newspapers, every now and then a deputation of unhappy husbands protests to the Soviet Embassy in London about their wives not being allowed to join them in their own country. They never get any satisfaction and it is doubtful if they ever will.

It must be made clear that not one of these Russian girls could have mixed with the men they married without the approval of the secret police; they would not dare. It is still a capital offence, punishable by death or exile in the Soviet Union, to associate with foreigners of any nationality. Everyone of these girls had to report to the N.K.V.D. Under secret police terror, they had no alternative.

I am not suggesting that all my sister war brides did this willingly. But some of them did; like the two brides who came to London and then went back to Moscow. These two, Nina Brand and Natalya Clarke, were cold-blooded, fanatical Communists. When they returned to Russia they said in *Pravda* and over the Moscow radio that London was "a dreadful prison." Stalin knew this would be their reaction, and that is why he let them go. He and his secret police arranged the whole business for propaganda reasons before they left. He knew these women would not disobey.

All the Soviet war brides are not in this category. Some are innocent girls who became friendly with foreigners during their work. Once they were seen with them the N.K.V.D. interrogated these girls and instructed them to report the movements and conversations of their men friends.

I have told how I worked as a member of the Moscow spy ring which the Kremlin maintains to shadow foreigners. It was the only way to see the man I loved. I know of other Russian girls who did the same and some very bravely refused to act as N.K.V.D. spies.

Anyone who tries to flout the all-powerful Soviet system is in grave danger. That is why in February, 1949, Mr. Hector McNeil, Minister of State, announced that the British Ambassador in Moscow had privately advised two of the Russian wives to divorce their husbands in their own interests. They were being persecuted by the Soviet authorities and had threatened to commit suicide. I can well understand this because I know how terrible this persecution can be.

These two wives, Mrs. Lola Burke, wife of an Ealing accountant and Mrs. Rosa Henderson, married to Patrick Henderson, formerly of the Foreign Office, now in Toronto, were employed, as I was, in the British Embassy in Moscow. And another Russian wife, Alexandra Greenhalgh, has been sentenced to two years' imprisonment for "not conforming with the registration formalities."

There are still twelve women waiting hopelessly in Russia to join their English husbands. Among them is Clara Strunina, married to Alfred Hall, a former Press officer of the London County Council. It is painful for me to have to say this but the plain truth is that most of these twelve women must have agreed at one time or another to carry out some sort of spy work for the Soviet. Otherwise, they would not have been given permission by the N.K.V.D. to marry foreigners. For, even the marriage certificate has to be issued by the secret police. Moscow's N.K.V.D. have numbers of men and women on their books whom they can detail to ingratiate themselves with foreigners and fellow Russians for the sole purpose of gaining their confidence so as to be able to report their activities back to the secret police.

When the N.K.V.D. found that all their women did not persuade John, nor were the Embassy very impressed that I was an undesirable person, they tried another form of attack.

John, as secretary to the Air Attaché, had to spend some time away from his quarters. As soon as he had gone, the secret police tried to entice me out of the safety of the Embassy into their clutches. I nearly fell for one trick. One of the old gardeners came and said John wanted to see me urgently at a place outside. The old man seemed perfectly sincere but by this time I had become so suspicious that I decided to telephone John. As I suspected, he said that he had never sent any such message. He pleaded with me never to leave the Embassy grounds, no matter how urgent the message seemed. Some time later I managed to talk to the old gardener. He admitted shamefacedly that he was a spy from the N.K.V.D.

"What have I ever done," I enquired bitterly, "That you should want to trap me into leaving here and being arrested and perhaps tortured by the secret police?"

The old man bowed his head and tears came into his eyes.

"Citizeness," he said. "Forgive me. I have done ten years in Siberia and I do not want to return. These N.K.V.D. beasts know this. They know they have me just where they want me.

"They appear to be friendly and meet me once a week. They buy me gallons of vodka and tell me to do just what they ask. If I didn't, you know what it would mean?"

And he drew a finger across his throat.

Mr. Bagshaw, who was living with John, was about to be posted away from Moscow and they decided to throw a party to celebrate his departure. He was the same man who had asked me to dance at the Hotel Metropole. And now the Russian girl, who had never met an Englishman before, was a maid serving cocktails at his party in the British Embassy. I was given a black frock and a white apron for the occasion. Mr. Bagshaw had invited all his friends and the party was gay and noisy. At 3 a.m. after everyone had gone, I was helping to clear away the dirty dishes and glasses when I heard a strange noise coming from outside the Embassy walls. It was the howling of dogs and it seemed as though every dog in Moscow had joined in. The blood-curdling wail went on for some time. It was quite frightening.

The noise woke up John who shouted to us that he was going over to the Embassy to see if there was any news, as the international situation had become tense.

He was back within a few minutes.

"The Germans have invaded Russia," he said. He sat down heavily, hardly able to credit the news.

"It's war," he kept repeating. "It's war."

The date was 22 June, 1941.

My mind went back to my conversation with Captain N. when I drove with him to Himki. He had been right almost to the day. Russia had become Britain's ally. I wondered where Captain N. was now?

Soon a new sound filled the Moscow sky. It was the howl of sirens. Then there was the crackle of gunfire and red flashes lit up the night. Yet I will always remember the day Hitler declared war against Russia by the uncanny howling of the dogs. By some strange instinct they almost seemed to know of the tragedy which had already reached the Russian border. Each whine

187

seemed to be a canine prophecy of the agony that Russia was to undergo during the next few years.

Next day at noon Molotov spoke on the radio. He told us the cowardly Nazis had bitten the Russian hand of friendship, so generously offered to them. All good citizens, he said, would resent this vile act of treachery. Russia would unite to teach the traitors a lesson. Radio loudspeakers in every corner of Moscow blared out the news and worked up the city into a frenzy of foreboding.

A host of official announcements followed. Bank withdrawals were limited to two hundred roubles a month. All radios were to be handed over to the police. Russians were only to be allowed to listen to news broadcasts linked with the state controlled radio stations. A censorship of all civilian mail was set up, and overnight foodstocks disappeared from the shops. Citizens walked up and down the crowded streets talking excitedly to one another, retelling rumour after rumour.

In the British Embassy I escaped the ban on listening to foreign broadcasts. I was able to use an Embassy radio to listen to the German broadcasts which Hitler was directing against the Russian people. Renegade Russians, mostly Czarists, were enlisted for these "Russian to Russian" tirades. Their message was brutal and to the point.

They said: "This is Germany calling. Citizens of Russia the time has come for you to arise and overthrow your rulers. The men who promised you freedom have given you slavery. Your country is riddled with secret police, concentration camps; rise and strike your oppressors down."

Thus Nazi Germany, speaking to Soviet Russia. The irony of it was almost unbelievable. I, who had suffered under the N.K.V.D., but also knew something of the German methods, realized it was one slave-state reviling another. There was nothing to choose between either system.

My meeting with Captain N. had prepared me for the coming of the war. There is no doubt that the German attack had been long expected by the higher Soviet officials. But it certainly came as a tremendous shock to the man in the street.

Yet Captain N. had been sent to join his regiment exactly a month before the German attack. There must have been millions like him all over Russia. Hitler's massing of troops along the Soviet frontier had not escaped unnoticed, and both Britain and America had informed Stalin of Hitler's intentions.

The first Russian reaction to the war was typical. A great purge was ordered and there were roundups everywhere by the N.K.V.D. Military tribunals were set up throughout the Soviet Union. They ordered the wholesale arrest and banishment of thousands of innocent Russians. As the Nazi troops pushed onwards over the frontier, large numbers of political prisoners were shot in the concentration camps and places of exile to which they had been sent. Stalin was taking no chances; he did not want a single person to help the invaders.

Stalin himself came on the radio and said in justification of this: "We must organize a ruthless struggle against all disorganizers of the rear, deserters, panic-mongers and cowards."

He called upon every loyal Russian citizen to turn over to the military tribunals all cowards and panic-mongers "whoever they are and wherever they may be."

In Moscow the city authorities set about turning the capital into an armed camp. The city rocked to the noise of trucks and armoured cars trundling to the front. Call-up boards were set up throughout the Soviet Union and millions were mobilized. Yet when Stalin admitted that Hitler's panzers had overrun Lithuania, part of the western Ukraine, and a large section of White Russia, it struck a chill into everyone's heart. The news did not surprise the various service attachés within the British Embassy. But to a Russian, to me, it was unbelievable that our great country of two hundred million people was reeling back before the German onslaught.

The war threw Moscow into chaos although I saw little of it. I was still a prisoner within the Embassy. Mile-long queues appeared outside the shops. When I heard about them I was thankful for my diplomatic sanctuary. The metro stations were used as shelters for women and children only. Most of the population had to rely on their own cellars and ground-floor rooms.

Shortly after the war broke out Sir Stafford Cripps was joined at the Embassy by the British Military Mission, headed by General Mason-MacFarlane, who was later knighted. The general, an imposing six-foot man, used to stride along the Moscow streets every day, wearing shorts or battle-dress.

Soon, in August 1941, there came news of the evacuation of Moscow as the German troops advanced. We now moved to a flat in a building near the Red Gate metro station and where I had lived with Father. Although it was no longer in the Embassy grounds, it still came under Embassy protection. The Latvian cook and I went along in a diplomatic car, and soon several English refugees from Bucharest joined us. They lived in the rest of the villa.

I was worried by this move but John assured me that as long as I remained on British property I was safe from the N.K.V.D. We were joined there by

189

another servant, a *petite*, pretty girl called Nina who had been employed at the German Embassy. She told me that when war broke out all the Russians on the German Embassy staff were rounded up within forty-eight hours and sent to Siberia. As they all spoke German, Stalin was taking no chances. I could not understand why Nina had escaped the N.K.V.D. round-up. But I was not long left in doubt. She had been spared so that she could be employed on a new mission for the N.K.V.D.

Her new task was simple enough, to break me down. She gave me no peace, day or night. She engaged me in a personal vendetta of hatred and did everything she could to make my life unbearable. There were many times when I would have cheerfully torn her to pieces, to silence her constant gibes against my father and myself whom she constantly called traitors. One night I was so incensed that I flew into a temper and threatened to attack her if she did not leave me alone. This must have frightened her because next day she left; possibly to report to the N.K.V.D. that I was incorrigible. The next day the gate keeper came to me and said the local police had been round enquiring why I had not reported to No. 66 District headquarters of the Kirov district to receive my ration card.

I did not suspect a trap as the local police did not always work with the N.K.V.D. They had probably asked me to register as part of the routine. I could hardly believe the news, because once registered and in possession of a set of ration cards I could no longer be re-arrested on sight. The N.K.V.D. probably had so much to do in the stress of war that they had lost interest in me. After all, I was not very important.

My appointment with the police was for 6 p.m. I left the flat after tea to walk there. I had only walked a few yards along the street when someone tapped me on the shoulder.

"Excuse me," said a polite voice. "Could you possibly tell me the way to the metro?"

I turned round and suddenly two arms gripped me round the waist. A hand was clapped over my mouth from behind. I was dragged across the pavement and bundled into a large black saloon car.

CHAPTER XVIII – RESCUED FROM A MOSCOW CELL

My kidnappers threw me on the floor of the car. One of them knelt over me, putting his hand over my mouth. The car shot forward. A few minutes later my head jolted heavily against the driver's seat as it stopped. The men pulled me to my feet, dragged me across the pavement into a police station. With my eyes still blinking under the harsh light, I was pushed in front of a muscular woman police officer. When she saw me her face broke into a savage grin.

"So, Citizeness," she said, "We've got you at last, have we? You filthy tramp. How dare you think you could get away!"

She slapped me hard across the mouth. It was a powerful, spiteful blow and her nails ripped my flesh. I clenched my hands in an effort to stop myself from retaliating. I knew only too well the penalty which awaited me if I should lose control of myself and smash my fist into her sneering, sardonic face. It would only mean that I would be tied up and tortured by this same woman, and I would not be able to use my hands then. I tried to appear as calm as possible.

"I was told to come here with my papers in order to register," I said coldly.

"Register! register!" shouted the amazon. "The only place you'll register for is Siberia."

She snatched the identity card which I was holding in my hand and drew a thick black cross through it. By cancelling my only means of identification she had robbed me of the only way I could prove I was still a Soviet citizen. Without that card I would be a person with no official existence. I consoled myself by thinking it probably did not matter as I would be sent to Siberia anyway. She confirmed this view by reaching out, snatching the ring from my finger, the watch from my wrist.

"You'll have no need of these where you're going," she said. "Let's see if your English friends can get you out of this."

Just then a superior officer came in. Her attitude changed at once. She stood to attention and motioned me into another room. The only occupant of this room was a weedy-looking clerk checking papers. Then I saw a telephone on his desk.

"Could I make a phone call?" I asked him with studied casualness.

The man was too immersed in his papers even to look up. "Of course, Comrade, help yourself," he said.

Within a few seconds I was through to the British Embassy and managed to get a German-speaking secretary on the line. Speaking in German, quickly I told her where I was and what had happened.

"Tell John," I said. "Tell him straight away. Otherwise I am lost."

I hung up the phone hastily as I heard footsteps approaching. My woman guard entered the room and spoke to the clerk.

"This citizen is held for interrogation," she said. "See that she speaks to no one."

The clerk looked up terrified, remembering my phone call. Then he saluted and said: "Very good, chief."

He sat back at his desk and worked, cocking an apprehensive eye at me every few moments. I sat on a bench in the corner with my head in my hands. A siren wailed. German planes were approaching Moscow. The woman police officer returned at once with a guard.

"Take her to the cells," she said. I was taken down a flight of stairs and pushed into a cell. It was completely dark and I stood motionless trying to see through the gloom. The heavy footsteps of my guard were resounding down the corridor when a voice whispered out of the darkness:

"What are you here for, Citizeness?"

I said I didn't know, sat down on the floor and burst into tears. A slim arm was pressed across my shoulders.

"Don't cry," said the voice. "Cheer up. I've been in and out of these places for the past two years. It's not so bad really."

I asked my unseen companion on what charge she had been arrested.

"Prostitution," she said.

Even in the cell the roar of the barrage thundered and echoed. The guns of Moscow were giving the Nazis all they got. The little cell shook every few moments with the noise of guns or bombs. Every now and again a gun flash or a searchlight beam would flicker across the gloom through the barred window. It was cold in the cell and the prostitute snuggled against me for warmth. When the noise of the guns died away for a few minutes, there was a strange scuffling in the cell and the flicker of bright little pinpoints in the dark.

"Rats," said my cell companion philosophically. "The gunfire has disturbed them. They are all right — it's the human ones you have to worry about."

I sat in the darkness for hours trying to realize that at last I was in a prison cell. My struggle against the N.K.V.D. had failed. They had me where they had always wanted me. I was beaten. Ahead of me lay only exile — or worse.

192

The girl in my cell slept, but I lay awake with tears coursing down my face. Eventually I must have fallen asleep. Suddenly I was conscious of a bright light stabbing into my eyes.

"Korzhenko, come out," said a voice. "Walk ahead."

As I stumbled out of the door a voice whispered out of the darkness: "Good luck."

Before I could answer, the heavy cell door banged and the guard shoved me along the corridor in front of him. I never met my cell mate again. I never even knew her name.

I climbed up a flight of steps and stood blinking under the naked lights of the room where I had made my telephone call. Standing there, looking white and worried, was John. I broke away from the guard, ran to him, and put my arms round his neck. He stroked my hair.

"You see," he said. "I came at once. Come on."

He led me out of the police station into a waiting car. The thunder of the guns started again, interspersed with the thud of bombs and the whine of aeroplane engines overhead. As the car crept through the darkened streets, we could hear the tinkle of shrapnel falling in the roadway. I flung my arms round John and clung to him.

"Frightened?" he asked.

"Not of the air raid," I whispered. "I don't think I shall ever be frightened of air raids. They are nothing compared with the N.K.V.D."

John held me tight and said: "You needn't be frightened of them any more."

As the car swung on British Embassy ground again I lay back without speaking, unable to believe my good luck. I had managed to escape the N.K.V.D. again. Then in John's room, a cup of tea in my hand, he told me how he had managed to obtain my release. When he had come back, he had found me missing. The gatekeeper told him he had seen me bundled into a car. John realized what this meant, but the air raid had already started and it was quite impossible to grope his way through the streets. He remembered a bottle of whisky he had tucked away for an emergency. He called the Embassy duty chauffeur, opened the bottle of whisky, and offered him a generous draught. Most Russians love to drink and the man was fascinated by the fiery taste of the whisky, which he drank neat. John plied him with several more until, without any prompting, the chauffeur kept protesting that he would do anything for his brave allies and courageous comrades-in-arms, the British.

193

"Would you drive me through the barrage to the police station?" John asked.

"Comrade," said the chauffeur with drunken solemnity., "I will drive you anywhere in any barrage. It is the least I can do for England."

John realized that if I had been kidnapped I would be taken to the nearest police station. He hoped that the sudden air raid had prevented them sending me on to the N.K.V.D. He rushed into the police station, followed by the chauffeur, full of drunken enthusiasm. He said that he was from the British Embassy and demanded the chief.

The chauffeur said: "You had better bring the chief. This is a very important man from the British Embassy."

When the chief appeared John said: "I know you have Citizeness Korzhenko here. I must see her at once."

The police officer pretended to be surprised. He denied all knowledge of my existence but John sat on the corner of the man's desk and said: "I know you have her in the cells below. Bring her up or it will be the worse for you. You will be in more trouble than you realize if you don't."

The drunken Russian chauffeur, still full of pro-English feeling, kept interrupting. "He is a very important man, Superintendent. You don't know who you are dealing with. He's from the British Embassy — the Embassy of our great ally. He's next to the Ambassador himself."

The chauffeur went on and on, talking volubly in Russian, impressing the superintendent with John's importance. He began to look very worried and eventually admitted that I had been brought in for questioning. He promised to release me in the morning.

"In the morning?" shouted John. "What do you mean 'in the morning'? How dare you speak like this to me. It is an insult that a woman in my household should be persecuted in this way.

"I regard it as an affront to the British Embassy. I will now place the whole affair on a diplomatic level, and God help you."

He reached for the telephone but the police chief agitatedly put his hand over it and said: "No, no. Don't do that. I would like to help you but I am only carrying out orders. Please understand my position."

"Whose orders?" asked John.

The police chief hesitated. Then he muttered: "The orders of Beria."

Beria, head of the N.K.V.D., was one of the most important men in Moscow.

"Very well, then," said John. "Telephone Beria. This woman is a British Embassy employee and you are violating all diplomatic agreements by

194

holding her here. I insist that you telephone to Beria and tell him who I am and why I am here — and that I demand her release."

The superintendent, a bureaucrat to his fingertips, did not like John's attitude. He did not dare to phone Beria because such an important man would order him to be purged at once if he made a mistake. And this strange Englishman appeared to know all the answers. He spoke to a guard who disappeared. A few moments later I came stumbling up the stairs, blinking in the unaccustomed light. There is no doubt that, but for the air raid, I would have been taken to the headquarters of the N.K.V.D. in the Lubyanka prison, never to be seen again. The air raid saved me — that and John's quick-wittedness with a bottle of whisky. The N.K.V.D. work in secret and, at this time, when the U.S.S.R. was posing as the friend of Britain, they could not afford a diplomatic scandal. If my arrest and detention had been officially reported by the Embassy they would have had to reveal the way the State treated Soviet citizens. So they had to let me go.

But five days after I had escaped from the police station I received a notice to appear before one of the military tribunals which had now been set up throughout Russia. I was told to report to the office of Judge Gribkov, deputy chief of the military courts in Moscow. As this notice had been sent quite officially and the N.K.V.D. did not seem to be involved, I decided that it would be better for me to obey it. I took the precaution of showing John the order and telling him exactly where I was going. I felt that there could not be much danger. The military tribunal might even clear me in view of the pressure of war, now at the gates of Moscow.

When I arrived I was shown into a room where Gribkov sat alone at a desk. When asked for my identity card I showed him the one which had been scored through at the police station. He nodded grimly when he saw the black cross through the document and produced a typewritten statement which he asked me to sign. I read it through. It was a confession. It said that I admitted that I had broken the law by failing to register, had not tried to obtain a job, had been dismissed from the N.K.V.D., and had had illegal contact with foreigners.

"But I am not going to sign this," I cried. Judge Gribkov glared at me and thumped the desk with his big fist.

"Quiet, Citizeness," he shouted. "We don't care if you sign or not. The case is closed. We have only brought you here for Sentence."

"Sentence?" I exclaimed, bewildered. "What sentence?"

"The sentence is," said the judge, "that you must leave Moscow within forty-eight hours. You can go anywhere you like but all cities and towns are forbidden to you."

This was the favourite Russian trick of getting rid of unwanted citizens — exile. They did not dare to give me a harsher sentence in case the British Embassy interfered. Presumably they hoped to bamboozle the Embassy into believing that I had only been sent out of Moscow to be safe from the invading German forces. As I stood in front of the judge's desk a soldier came in with a message. The judge hastily walked out of a back door. The soldier had his back to me. I saw my opportunity, grabbed my identity card from the desk, and slipped quickly out of the building. I raced breathlessly out of the room and slipped past the guards, pretending to walk. I managed to hail a passing taxi. I realized why it was so easy to escape from the building; it was because no ordinary Russian would have tried it. They would not have gone far before they would have been picked up by the police.

In my case it was different. I gave the driver the address of the Embassy flat and lay back trembling. I realized that this was the most serious thing I had ever done. Now, if I were caught, I would be shown no mercy. I was an escaped criminal.

I realized my only hope was that as the Germans were getting nearer to Moscow every minute, my defiance of the military tribunal sentence would remain unnoticed. One thing at least was certain. I would only be safe as long as I never put foot outside the Embassy grounds. I decided I would never leave them again, on any pretext whatsoever.

CHAPTER XIX - TO ARCHANGEL WITH FORGED PAPERS

Shortly after my rescue from a prison cell, Stalin decided to evacuate Moscow. By September 1941 the Germans had already reached the suburbs and Moscow was a front-line town. Most of the important party officials had left the capital. These favoured ones were given permits to allow them to travel in trains or in their own cars. The power and water supplies were interrupted frequently as the city was bombed daily. Winter was approaching but there was no fuel to heat homes. Moscow was filled with the wildest rumours. Stalin had been assassinated, a fifth column had overthrown the N.K.V.D., Moscow would be in German hands tomorrow. People began to tear up their party cards and burn pictures of the Soviet leaders. In the middle of October the German panzers reached Himki, the suburb where I had driven with my N.K.V.D. friends. Moscow was beginning to fall into chaos. Houses were looted in the blackout and people were staggering through the streets, drunk on vodka.

The German army, a few miles outside the city, flooded the air with propaganda broadcasts from their front-line transmitters. Sometimes a man's voice speaking fluent Russian urged us to overthrow our Red tyrants. At other times a woman would call to the mothers of Russia to stop "this senseless war and massacre of innocent children."

The Germans boasted in these broadcasts they would crush us in six weeks. History has already shown that they did not do this, but even to me it seemed to be a very bold prediction. For years the Germans themselves had helped to build up Russian industry. German experts and German machinery were in our factories from the early thirties. The potential strength of the Soviet Union in manpower alone was three times that of Hitler's hordes.

In September 1941, a small, round-faced gnome-like little man arrived at the British Embassy from London. He was Lord Beaverbrook, who headed the English section of the Anglo-American mission. He was followed by Sir Walter Citrine with a delegation from the British Trades Union Congress. The British trade-unionists, who were accommodated at the National Hotel, had come to meet Soviet workers' representatives in Moscow. Every night the anti-aircraft guns flashed and roared. After nine o'clock no one could strike a match or use a flash lamp. After midnight you were not allowed on the streets without a special police permit.

On Wednesday, 15 October, 1941, Moscow Radio confirmed that the Red Army was fighting the Germans in the suburbs of the capital. Stalin issued a decree that Moscow was to be totally evacuated to give the army full scope to defend it street by street.

A Kremlin decree ordered foreign Embassies to leave and make arrangements tor their nationals to do the same. The British Embassy staff were ordered to go to Kuibyshev, five hundred miles to the east. John told me of this decree and silently I helped him pack. There was no question of my going too. This was one time when the Embassy could not protect me. I was still a Soviet citizen.

It was a sad night, the night all the English left me. It began to snow and I watched Sir Stafford Cripps, the Ambassador, leading his airedale, Joe, Sir Walter Citrine, and the rest of them, go. They got into their cars and drove through the blacked-out streets to catch their special train from the Kazhan station. John was one of the last to leave. I said good-bye and told him, without much conviction, that I would be all right. As I watched him step into the long black car, the roof already mantled with snow, I pressed my face against the cold window pane of the Embassy building. The car disappeared into the night and I sat for hours alone in the empty house, the loneliest woman in Moscow.

A few Soviet employees were left as caretakers of the Embassy and John had given me a certificate appointing me official caretaker of his flat. The Americans, who were not yet in the war, took over responsibility for the British Embassy property. Among the people left was Nina, the N.K.V.D. girl. The night that the British left she walked out of the Embassy. I thought she had gone for good, but next day she returned with a small, slant-eyed little man who she said was the first secretary of the Japanese Embassy. She packed her trunks and left with the little Japanese. John told me later that he saw her with the Jap in Kuibyshev. She was wearing jewels and furs and obviously had got herself a new job, spying on the Japanese.

I remained in Moscow, miserable, frightened and forlorn, wandering through the empty corridors of the Embassy flats, eating the tinned rations which the British had left behind. I lived mostly on tins of asparagus. I barricaded my door at night, and awaited the arrival of the Germans. Only a few thousand civilians were left in the city, which day and night trembled with gunfire and the rumblings of armoured cars and lorries taking men and supplies to the front. The Germans were only twenty miles away. They had already passed Himki and the front line crept nearer to the centre of Moscow.

John's last gift to me was a little amber madonna which he pressed into my hand.

"Take care of her and she'll take care of you," he said with a catch in his voice. Every night I took out that little madonna and prayed.

One day the barrage died away slightly. I looked out of the window and I saw lorry after lorry of strange troops rumbling along the streets. They did not look like Russians at all. They were tall, slant-eyed men, like larger editions of Nina's Japanese boy friend. They were regular battalions of the Army of the Red Banner, the Soviet force on the Manchurian frontier. They had come to relieve the volunteer worker detachments who had been helping the Red Army to defend Russia's most sacred city. These battalions of fresh troops stemmed the German onslaught. I did not know it at the time. For days afterwards I waited anxiously in the Embassy flat expecting any moment to see tanks painted with swastikas arriving in the Moscow streets. But those Mongolian men turned the tide for Russia. From mid-October onwards, the German air raids became less, the firing began to recede and a few frightened civilians appeared on the streets.

I remained firmly at my post as caretaker of John's flat, even though I was getting a little tired of asparagus. One night, less than a month after John had left, the phone rang in his flat. It was a call from Archangel. I could not believe my ears when I picked up the receiver. It was John's voice. I was wildly excited, but his first words threw me into the deepest despair.

"I am leaving Russia for England," he said faintly over the telephone. "I have been posted home. Don't despair. Stay in the Embassy and you'll be quite safe. I'll come back for you somehow."

For a second or two I could not take in what he meant and said: "What are you doing in Archangel?"

"I am sailing from here," he said. "I am going back to England."

Then his voice faded and all I could hear was a whisper amid the buzzings on the line.

"Can you hear me, John?" I shouted desperately. "I will get through to see you. I must say good-bye to you — I may never see you again."

The line still buzzed and then his voice came through quite clearly.

"Nora, don't be crazy," he said. "You would never get through. The war is still very near Moscow. I implore you to stay where you are. You will be much safer."

I could not sleep all that night. I tried to work out how I could join John before he left Russia. My first problem was to get myself a new identity card. I still had the old one with the telltale cross scratched through it. I knew it would be impossible to travel with that. In the middle of the night I had an inspiration I decided that the situation needed a desperate remedy. I decided to gamble everything on the fact that the war might have made the police a little careless. Many people's identity cards must have been destroyed in the air raids. I would go to the police station next morning and tell them that mine had been lost in this way.

Early next day I sat on a bench awaiting my turn in the police station. When a policeman called me over I told him my story. He gazed very intently into my face and then said: "Come with me, Citizeness."

Had he recognized me? I soon knew the answer. He led me away out of earshot of the other people waiting and whispered very quickly: "Every policeman in Moscow is looking for you. I know who you are — I knew your father. You are on the list for liquidation. Get out of here quickly before you are spotted."

I didn't need to be told twice. I ran back to the safety of the Embassy flat. But I wanted to see John more than I feared the N.K.V.D., and felt there must be some way round the situation. Then I had another brainwave. I remembered a Russian employee at the American Embassy whom I knew. He had always appeared friendly and sympathetic at the treatment father had received. I phoned him and he came to see me. I explained the situation and he said he might be able to help me out but it would cost money. I said he could have anything he liked out of the flat and he chose a bookcase, two leather suitcases, a trunk, some china and some clothing. In return he agreed to get me to Archangel, six hundred and fifty miles away.

"I will come and see you in two days' time," he said. On 20 November he came back. He pulled an imposing-looking document out of his pocket. It was typed in Russian on official American diplomatic notepaper, headed "The Foreign Service of the United States of America." In one corner was a big red seal.

"Have you got a photograph of yourself?" he asked. I pulled one out of my handbag and he left me to go back to the U.S. Embassy. When he returned my photograph, the U.S. Embassy stamp across it, had been fixed in the right-hand corner.

"There you are," he said with a smile, "that should get you to Archangel."

I read the fake letter carefully. In imposing language, the document said I was an employee of the British Embassy travelling on an important diplomatic mission to Archangel. Scrawled across the bottom was the forged signature of a secretary of the U.S. Embassy. It looked so impressive that even I could not believe it was not genuine.

While I was reading it, my friend asked: "How are you going to get to the

THE FOREIGN SERVICE
OF THE
UNITED STATES OF AMERICA

AMERICAN EMBASSY
АМЕРИКАНСКОЕ ПОСОЛЬСТВО
Москва, СССР.

20-го Ноября 1941 г.

УДОСТОВЕРЕНИЕ.

Настоящим Американское Посольство
Удостоверяет, что гр-ка Коржeнко Нора Васильевна
является служащей Великобританского Посольства
и направляется в данное время в г. Архангельск
для встречи сотрудника Великобританского Посольства
г-на Мурей.

Гр-ка Коржeнко имеет постоянное место-
жительство в г. Москве по Мало-Харитоньевскому пер.
дом № 3 на территории Великобританского Посольства.

Г. Ф. Райнхардт
Секретарь Посольства.

Forged US Moscow Embassy Document 1941

station? You can't walk through the streets with a document like that. You
must have a car. It would be suspicious otherwise."

201

"Could you manage a car?" I faltered.

The man snapped his fingers and said with a grin: "I will not only get you a car but it will have a special flag on it, too. Leave everything to me."

That night he came round in an American diplomatic car and with a sleeping-car ticket for the five days' journey to Archangel. He kissed my hand and wished me good luck as the immaculate chauffeur started the car to drive me to the Northern Station. I hardly dared to breathe as we pulled up at the platform where the Archangel train was waiting. My Russian chauffeur lifted out my luggage and I walked boldly up to the barrier. The N.K.V.D. men patrolling the station gave a smart salute when they saw the American flag. Yet my heart was in my mouth as I walked to my compartment. No railway platform ever seemed as long as that one did that night on Moscow's Northern Station. I felt that everyone was looking at me and that I would be stopped at any moment, but no one took the slightest notice. The chauffeur followed, carrying my luggage.

When I reached my reserved berth I found the train jammed with men in uniform. They were all N.K.V.D. officers, serving under Beria, the man who had given orders that I was to be arrested. I was terrified in case any of them should recognize me as the policeman had done. The chauffeur in the uniform of the American Embassy made them respectful. An N.K.V.D. colonel pushed forward and saluted. He and a major took my baggage from the chauffeur. He loaded it into my first-class sleeping-berth where I had two bunks to myself. I sat on the bunk, still not believing that my bluff had succeeded. The train gave a sudden lurch and puffed slowly out of the station. I was on my way.

I was the only girl in the coach so it was inevitable that the officers should come into my compartment for a little friendly banter. They were all front-line officers and N.K.V.D. men, but they accepted me as an authorized traveller. None of them questioned my right to travel to Archangel, although all that night and for several nights afterwards, I could hardly sleep as the train rumbled along. Every sudden creak made me imagine someone was coming to question me. At a town called Vologda the train stopped. The local N.K.V.D. men came through checking identity cards and travel documents. I began to tremble slightly as their voices came nearer and nearer. My compartment door was pushed open and in came a young, handsome N.K.V.D. officer. I steeled myself to remain calm.

"Good evening," I said nonchalantly.

"Good evening, Madame," he replied, gazing at me curiously. I leaned back against the cushions on the sleeping berth and carelessly lit a cigarette.

"I am sorry," I said. "I forgot. Perhaps you would like to smoke too?"
I handed him a packet of American cigarettes which my Embassy friend
had given me. He took one gratefully, so I said: "Look, have the lot. I don't
suppose you get much chance of smoking this sort of cigarette."

He thanked me with genuine gratitude and as he was talking I said with a
great show of boredom: "Oh, yes, I suppose you've come to see this?"

And I produced the fake letter of authority with the U.S. Embassy seal on.
He glanced at it for a moment then he gave me a knowing smile. He thought
he had discovered my secret and was very pleased with himself. He imagined
that I was an N.K.V.D. girl working against the Americans. I smiled back but
I am afraid it was a forced smile, because at any moment I thought he was
going to ask for my identity card. If he did so, I was lost. Instead he lit one of
my American cigarettes and prepared to have a sociable chat as one N.K.V.D.
employee to another.

Then another N.K.V.D. man called from outside: "Is everything all right
in there?"

The young man called out: "Everything is in order."

Then he gave me a smart salute and a sly wink.

"It has been a pleasure to know you, Madame," he said. "I hope you have
a pleasant journey."

The N.K.V.D. men left the train and it began to chug slowly northwards
again. At last we drew into the station at Archangel. When we stopped, my
worries began again. Would the American document deceive the N.K.V.D.
check at the platform barrier? I felt certain that this time they would ask for
my identity card.

But the N.K.V.D. officers on the train with whom I was friendly
unwittingly helped me to deceive their own officials. An N.K.V.D. colonel
came to my compartment and asked me if he could assist me. I thanked him,
and he and another officer picked up my bags and we walked along the
platform together. I walked through the barrier between the two of them. No
one suspected me in such illustrious company. No one stopped me. We
walked out of the station together, across the frozen river Dvina, to the
Intourist Hotel in Archangel. When we arrived at the hotel I asked the
receptionist for John's room number.

"An Englishman?" she said and thumbed through the register Then she
put her finger to his name and said: "He's gone. He left the other day."

"Gone?" I repeated blankly. "Gone where?"

"To England," she said. "His boat has left."

CHAPTER XX – THROUGH THE FORBIDDEN ZONE

When I heard the news of John's departure I was stunned. I booked a bed in the hotel and sat down on it to try and think. In the room, No. 9, there were three beds. In the other two were two Esthonian women. I could not speak their language nor could they talk mine, so I went miserably downstairs again. I cross-examined the receptionist rather hopelessly to make sure that John had really left. There was no doubt about it and the receptionist noticing my misery said: "Cheer up, I will introduce you to some of the people staying at the hotel."

She introduced me to General Michael Gromov and I joined his party for supper. General Gromov, a Hero of the Soviet Union, who had flown across the North Pole, was returning with his co-pilots from a six months' tour of the United States. They were a fine type of man — they would probably have been called gentlemen in a bourgeois society — and if I had not been so upset I would have enjoyed myself. The general was anxious to talk to me because he wanted to hear how Moscow was surviving the air bombardment. I was able to give him a first hand account, although I omitted any personal details, except that I was on official business. We spent a long time talking about Hitler's defeat outside the city. He was anxious to see his baby and he gave me his address and asked me to call on him when I returned to Moscow.

Next morning when I met the general in the lounge he turned his back on me. He had obviously heard that my father was a disgraced and exiled Foreign Office official. I had been fortunate to dine with the general that night, but if I wanted to eat any more I had to have food permits. So I went to the British Military Mission in Archangel and told them I had arrived with John's property from the British Embassy and was therefore on official business. An official gave me food and residential permits for five days. This gave me the right to remain at the Intourist Hotel and to eat at the Sovtorgflot, the Soviet Merchant Fleet House, which had a restaurant for foreigners and Russian servicemen.

That evening I sat at the same table as an Esthonian sea captain who spoke Russian. He ate a hearty meal but when the bill came discovered he had no roubles, only foreign currency. He was most apologetic and said: "I wonder if you could possibly settle the bill for me. I will repay you later."

I was short of money but I paid it and we walked through the frozen streets back to the Intourist Hotel. When he asked me what I was doing at Archangel, I hesitated for a moment and then told him some of the story.

He suddenly interrupted and said: "I know the ship your friend is on. It is the s.s. *Temple Arch*. It has been held up by the gale. It was to sail in convoy to England — but it won't leave until the weather gets better."

His next words made me almost beside myself with joy. "The ship is still lying in the river," he said.

He went on talking but I did not listen. All the time a little voice inside me kept saying: "He hasn't sailed ... he hasn't sailed. I may reach him yet! "

Then I came back to earth and asked: "How can I get to the ship? What passes do I need?"

"You will need a pass from the Security Police to get out to it," the captain said. "If you try them in the morning, they may give you one."

I could have hugged him for joy. He had more than repaid me for buying his dinner. He went on to give me instructions how to get to the ship, which was lying down river some way out of Archangel at Economia. I had to go to the Port Authority and ask for the Commander, an N.K.V.D. major. He was the only person who could give a permit for the restricted area outside Archangel.

At nine o'clock next morning I was in the Commander's office. I told the clerk that I was a special envoy from Moscow and I was at once shown in to the Commander. I talked fast and produced my forged American Embassy permit. When I gave him precise details about the convoy and the names of the ships taking part — the Esthonian captain had briefed me well — he was obviously impressed with my knowledge. I was able to keep control of the conversation and stop him from enquiring about my identity card. Without any hesitation he gave me the necessary authority and said he would warn the guards that I was on my way.

A two-hour journey by tramcar took me outside Archangel. Then I had to walk. It was a bitterly cold November morning; it had been snowing heavily. The snow came up to my knees as I stumbled along. Then it began to snow again. The only people I saw in that wild, windswept country were groups of ragged forced labourers, who were staggering through the scurrying snow urged on by armed guards. They were used as slave labourers for tree-felling. Despite the blizzard, I carefully followed the directions given by the N.K.V.D. major and at last I found myself at the door of a two-storied wooden building. I was grateful to get inside into the warm hut. Standing by the stove was a grim-faced woman N.K.V.D. officer. Beside her, stretched out on the floor, were two powerful Alsatian dogs. They were the "restricted area" patrol.

"Well, Citizeness?" enquired the N.K.V.D. woman harshly as the dogs rose and stretched themselves. "What is your business?"

I told her I had an important message for someone aboard the s.s. *Temple Arch*.

"He hasn't left yet, has he?" I asked.

"No," the woman replied, "the ship's still here."

I showed her my fake letter of authority and she eyed the imposing red seal suspiciously. She read the document through carefully, glanced unsmilingly into my face to check the photograph, and sat down at her desk. She picked up a pen and wrote my name on a green form and handed it to me.

"That authorizes you to get through the final check point to the ship itself," she said.

She insisted that I should take an escort with me as it was already 3 p.m. and the light was fading. This escort was not offered out of suspicion. She said I might lose my way and become a prey to the wolves which roamed the trackless waste. But I did not relish the company of the N.K.V.D. and managed to convince her that I would manage to get through on my own. I stumbled out again into the snow storm. The wind was so fierce that I had to lean against it as I pushed on. The blizzard was blinding but at last I arrived at the restricted area. It was surrounded by an electrically wired fence and at every corner were wooden watch towers from which armed sentries could overlook the whole area. Before I banged at the gate I crossed myself and breathed a prayer. The N.K.V.D. guards took my papers and asked me into their little hut while they were checked. I stood rubbing my hands by the stove while they read them. The N.K.V.D. green pass was enough. They stamped it and told me I could proceed.

I pushed on through the heavy snow drifts, alone in the blinding expanse of white. Snow began to fall again and it was getting dark. There was no life anywhere. The N.K.V.D. had given me very vague directions, telling me to keep following the river. Somewhere along that river I would find John. The cold was intense. I had eaten nothing all day and my limbs were numb. I felt that I would never make it when I saw some lights, the powerful lamps of a timber camp. The shapes of men loomed up at me but I was afraid to talk to them, because they were slave workers and might have been dangerous. Then out of the gathering gloom I recognized one of them as a woman.

"Where is the English ship?" I shouted at her.

She jerked her thumb over her shoulder. "Over there," she said. "Straight ahead."

She would have given me more explicit directions but an armed guard shouted to her not to dawdle. I trudged on, nearly collapsing with fatigue and cold. Suddenly in front of me I saw a loading-yard flooded by arc lamps. At first I could not make out what was happening. There was a lot of noise with men running about and shouting. Then I realized what it was all about. They were kicking a ball. I knew I was in the right place. Only the English could be so crazy as to play football in the snow.

"Is John Murray here?" I asked the nearest Englishman.

Before he could answer there was a shout from the ship.

"Nora," a voice cried. And down the gang-plank came the sound of running boots. John rushed up to me and I fell exhausted into his arms.

"You crazy girl," he said. "you came after all. How on earth did you get here?"

CHAPTER XXI – ESCAPE IN THE BLACK-OUT

I walked up the gang-plank, arm in arm with John. As we arrived on deck there was a noise from the shore. We both turned our heads. Dogs were barking and there were shouts from uniformed N.K.V.D. men. The woman secret police officer must have got suspicious of me and sent a patrol out. But they were too late. I was already aboard.

Immediately John took me to the captain and said: "This is the girl I have been telling you about, Captain. This is Nora. She has managed to get here from Moscow — God knows how."

The captain, who saw how cold and fatigued I was, ordered tea and brandy. As I sat sipping it on his bunk, I told the story of how I had managed to escape from Moscow.

"What is going to happen to you now?" asked the captain. "You'll never get back."

"I hadn't thought as far as that," I said. "All I wanted to do was to come and say good-bye to John."

"You crazy, crazy girl," said John as he put his arm around me. "You should never have done it. What are we going to do about you?"

Suddenly I burst into tears and cried: "Take me with you. Take me to England — take me to freedom."

Both John and the captain shook their heads solemnly.

"It's more than I dare do," said the captain. "You have no passport and there is a war on. You could never land in England. It would cause an international incident."

His next words chilled me to the heart. He was a kindly man and it obviously upset him to say them.

"You will have to go back," he said. "I am sorry for you, my girl, but you must not stay on this ship."

I had not set out from Moscow with the idea of escaping to England but now I was aboard a British ship, past the N.K.V.D.'s final check point in the forbidden zone of the docks, I could think of nothing else. Freedom seemed very near, and only imprisonment or death awaited me in the country of my birth. I pleaded with the captain but he told me he was powerless. I had to go back. By this time it was 8 p.m. and quite dark. The long journey through the snow back to Archangel filled me with foreboding, apart from what probably awaited me at the other end.

John, resourceful as usual, said that he did not think I need worry about the N.K.V.D. for the moment. He got the captain to agree to telephone the British Military Mission in Archangel reporting my arrival aboard the ship. The message also added that I was returning to report to the Mission. He knew the telephone message would be intercepted by the N.K.V.D. and he reasoned that once my arrival had been recorded on a high level the N.K.V.D. would not interfere. They were afraid of a diplomatic incident. The best move was to go back to Archangel.

Some of the English crew located a sledge loaded with timber which was going to Archangel that night. The driver agreed to take me for a few packets of cigarettes. I was a most miserable woman as I lay, covered with sacking, on a pile of timber. The sledge driver whipped up his horses. It was very cold and I thought I would be frozen alive, but it did not seem a very terrible fate compared with capture by the N.K.V.D. and on the sleigh I stood a much better chance of avoiding the guards. It was nearly midnight when I arrived back at the hotel. I was stiff and sore and very cold, and I walked in very apprehensively. There had been no N.K.V.D. enquiries for me so I decided to have a good night's sleep. I did not care much what happened the next day. I was making my way stiffly up the stairs when I heard a voice call out my name. I thought that the cold had given me hallucinations because it was John's voice.

I turned round as he came bounding up the stairs.

"The most marvellous thing has happened, Nora," he cried. "After you left I was so desperate that I telephoned the whole story to Group Captain Bird of the British Military Mission at Archangel.

"I didn't think that anything would happen but almost immediately a message came back telling me to report to the British Military Mission here. Not only that but they sent a car out for me. I am to stay in Archangel until further orders — and here I am."

It had been such an exhausting two days that I just sat down on the stairs and wept.

"Now stop that," said John with mock severity. "We've no time for that, we're having champagne for supper." But the meal seemed tasteless, the wine flat.

"I have caused you an awful lot of worry," I said between tears. "I think it would be better now if you forgot about me. I will wait here until the N.K.V.D. come and I will take whatever medicine they have to give me."

I realized that I was beaten. I had been very foolish to follow him, and said so again. John put down his champagne glass, reached over and held my hand. He looked into my eyes for a moment with a half smile and said: "Nora, you are looking at the biggest fool you have ever met. I should have thought of this a long time ago. When I saw you today staggering across the snow towards the ship I realized what you meant to me."

I listened in silence, too tired and worried really to understand what he was saying.

I repeated dully: "John I must have no more to do with you. I am a Russian. This is my country for better or for worse."

"For better or for worse is what I mean," said John. "Nora, you need not be a Russian any longer. You can be British."

I looked at him, still not understanding.

"Nora," John said, "will you marry me?"

"Marry you, John?" I said amazed. "I can't marry you. I am an unwanted Russian girl and I am no good to you. Please forget about me."

"I want you," said John. "Will you marry me?"

"John I would marry you tomorrow but it is a silly dream," I said. "Even if I did I could never leave Russia, the N.K.V.D. would never let me go. And your home is in England."

"Look," said John with a tender smile, "I am not going to ask you again — will you marry me?"

I leaned my head against his chest and, before I realized what I was saying, I whispered: "Yes."

The rest of the evening passed like a dream. My heart was full of love and gratitude to John for wanting to transplant a lonely little Russian girl, hated and hounded in her own country, to a better life.

Next morning John was waiting for me in the lounge of the hotel. When I saw him standing there, for the first time in many months there was hope in my heart. I was still worried about the N.K.V.D., but John said they would never dare offend the British or the Americans while the war was on. To prove this he took me to the local N.K.V.D. chief and asked that I should be registered and issued with an identity card as I would shortly be marrying him.

The head of the secret police eyed me rather strangely and I knew that he had already been informed of my history. His attitude made me cling to John like a lifebuoy. The N.K.V.D. chief was very courteous, but he kept glancing towards me in a most unfriendly manner. For a time he prevaricated but when John pressed him he said he would look into the situation. As we left the office, I could tell that he intended to do nothing. I thought John had been oblivious of the sly glances given to me by the secret police chief. But when we got outside he told me that he had formed the same impression. He insisted that I lock myself in my room every night and refuse to open the door to anyone.

"The only thing they can do is to break down the door," he said. "And they won't dare to do that. It would cause too much of a scandal with their allies."

Every morning after breakfast, John took me to the Military Mission Headquarters and I stayed locked in a room there. I talked to several officials at the British Military Mission and they all agreed that as long as I remained under their protection I would be quite safe. By this time I had become a well-known character in Archangel. Most of the Russians refused to speak to me; they had obviously been warned. But the foreign colony, who did not even speak a language I could understand, were excited and curious about my romance. They plied me with questions and wished me luck.

Nora and John in Archangel 1941

During my stay in Archangel I began to hear news of wartime Russia.

In the hotel one day I met a woman who had somehow managed to slip through the German blockade of Leningrad which was to last two and a half years.

She was surprised to see dogs still running about in Archangel, they had nearly all been eaten in her own city. She told me cats were the tastiest to eat, they tasted like hare. Dogs were similar to mutton. Later I heard of one little girl who had survived the siege being asked if she liked dogs.

"Of course," she said solemnly, "especially fried."

John was working in the same room as Lieutenant-Commander Fisher, an expert on submarines, who was acting as an interpreter. When the commander heard our story he said he would do everything to help us. He was as good as his word and he went to see Ivan Papanin, a member of the Supreme Soviet, who was the Kremlin representative in Archangel. Papanin received the British commander courteously, listened to what he had to say and added with a smile: "I am afraid I can do nothing."

This Russian attitude was not followed by the high-ranking British officials. The head of the British Shipping Mission at that time was the Honourable John Scott Maclay, who authorized my staying on the premises during the day. I spent two worrying weeks in Archangel living this life of a semi-prisoner, a refugee from my own people. The British, however, obtained the impression that the N.K.V.D., although not friendly towards me, would not do anything to offend my foreign protectors. In fact the N.K.V.D. chief in Archangel came to life one day and told John that if I were to take the matter up in Moscow it would probably be satisfactorily settled. When John suggested I would need a travel permit and identity card, he replied that I could probably travel to Moscow as I came, particularly as I was under the protection of the British.

The N.K.V.D. chief pointed out that I could never obtain an identification certificate unless I returned to Moscow. After consultation with John I decided to chance it. I had really no alternative as without an identity card and official papers I could never be married.

John booked me on the train and kissed me good-bye on the platform without a secret policeman in sight. For three days the train rumbled slowly across the snowy wastes of Northern Russia. I was just congratulating myself that the chance I had taken had worked out better than I expected, when the train stopped at Nyandoma. The N.K.V.D. men started coming through the coaches checking everyone's papers. I had a premonition that this was the end of my romantic adventure, but when they came to the door of my carriage I gaily produced my fake letter of authority from the U.S. Embassy. The secret police officer hardly looked at it.

"You are travelling illegally without papers," he said. "You are under arrest."

He motioned two guards who were standing by with fixed bayonets. They stepped forward with military precision, told me to pick up my luggage, and escorted me to the station waiting room. I stayed there for fifteen days, sleeping on the floor without bedding. Day and night an armed sentry stood outside the door. After a few days I was half dead with the poor food they gave me and the lack of warm clothing.

When the N.K.V.D. officer came on his rounds, I demanded that he get in touch with the British Military Mission in Archangel and explain what had happened to me. His only retort was to turn round on me and snarl: "You seem to think that you can run around the Soviet Union just as you like. Now we're going to teach you something different."

I was used to the technique of the N.K.V.D. and was not particularly frightened by his remarks. And, after days of cabbage soup and sleeping on the hard floor I felt I had nothing to lose by pressing him. So every time he came on his tour of inspection I asked for an interview. He listened reluctantly as I threw in the name of every important British and American official I ever heard of — I even took the name of Sir Stafford Cripps in vain! Anyone listening to my conversation would have thought that I was the British Ambassador himself. I realized that all my desperate boasting was hopeless but I still kept on. Even Siberia seemed preferable to that hard cold waiting room floor!

One morning when I approached the officer to give him some more details of the important people I knew he said: "Listen, you miserable creature, I've got some news for you. I've just had a message that you are to be put on the next train to Moscow. You will be under guard and a man has been detailed to meet you there."

The train seemed like luxury after the station waiting room and I sat back gratefully. We arrived at the Northern Station in the black-out. When the train drew into the station my guard motioned to a uniformed Moscow policeman who was sitting on a seat.

"Here is the prisoner," he said. "Take her away."

The policeman took a firm grip of my arm and guided me into the darkened streets of Moscow.

"Where are you taking me?" I asked.

"Where do you think?" said a detached, unemotional voice out of the darkness. "I am taking you to the N.K.V.D. of course."

I had become an expert on detecting even the smallest note of friendliness in the voice of an official. And somehow this man in spite of his cold, crisp attitude, did not seem to be such an enemy as usual.

"I can't think why you are taking me to the N.K.V.D.," I said. "After all it was only a little mistake."

"I have my orders," he said. "I am not interested in what you have been doing."

We walked a few more hundred yards in the blackout. All the time I was trying to think up something which would convince him of my innocence. Then he said: "What have you been up to anyway?"

"That's a funny thing," I replied. "When I got on the train at Archangel I discovered that I had lost my identity card."

"Is that all?" he said. "You'd think the N.K.V.D. would have enough on their hands in the middle of a war without bothering about a thing like that. Still, those are my orders."

I began to sense real antagonism in his voice so I went on talking about the way I had been interrogated at Nyandoma. He listened without a word. Then suddenly he began to rail against Stalin, the secret police and everything for which Communist Russia stands.

I saw my chance and said: "If you feel like that — why are you arresting me?"

Instantly he became the official again and said: "I must obey orders, Citizeness."

Almost without thinking I pulled my arm away, kicked him, and ran away into the Moscow night. I heard him shouting behind me but I ran and ran. The Moscow black-out saved me. An hour later, at 3 a.m., I managed to grope my way towards a familiar building. It was John's flat in the premises of the British Embassy. I still had a key and I opened the door. I fell into the hall and slammed the door.

CHAPTER XXII – A SOVIET WEDDING

Next day I made myself known to the British staff of the Embassy. A lot of them had returned as the war had drifted away from Moscow. I discovered that most of the British and American diplomatic staff knew my story. And they welcomed me like an old friend. Just as their compatriots had in Archangel, they said they would do everything they could to help me.

One day General Mason-Macfarlane came to the flat on a routine tour of inspection. He asked how I was getting on. And before I could stop myself I was pouring out the whole story. He listened in silence. When I had finished he held out his hand and said: "We will do what we can for you. Meanwhile just carry on living here."

Soon after this visit, a telegram came from John at Archangel saying that an arrangement had been made for me to go to the police about my identity card. As we were officially engaged, this gave him a great deal more authority in pressing my case, so I had no qualms about approaching the Moscow police headquarters. I thought the telegram might have been another trap, but when I reported they said they had been expecting me. Without a word they gave a me a letter authorizing the re-issue of what was the most precious thing in my life at that time, a Russian identity card.

I carried this letter in my hand, gazing at it every few moments, hardly believing it was true. I took it round to No. 66 District Area Police Station where I had been in the cells. The first person I saw was the hard-faced policewoman who had interrogated me. When she saw me her face lit with an unpleasant smile.

"Well, you slut," she greeted me, "What have you been up to this time?"

She followed this up with a stream of filthy words, but in the middle of it I silently handed over my letter. She picked it up and as she read it she became very quiet.

Finally she put it down and said: "It's a forgery, you pig."

As she said this her superior came into the room, looked at the paper and said: "Oh, yes, I know about this. What's all the trouble about? Give Citizeness Korzhenko her new card."

"Oh, certainly," said the policewoman. And without another word she filled in my name and handed it to me.

I went back to the flat in the Embassy. I could hardly realize there was nothing to stop me returning to Archangel. For the first time since my father's arrest I was no longer being hunted. An Englishman who had only

215

been a short time in Russia had been able to achieve the impossible. I was an established citizen again. My papers were in order and I had no need to hide in alleyways to avoid the police. I walked through the snow-laden streets with my new identity card safe in my pocket and looked at the onion domes of the Kremlin. I remembered how excited I had been when I had first come to the capital as a young girl. I watched the citizens scurrying through the frozen streets. I was leaving Moscow perhaps for ever, I was going to a strange country, and would never see my native land again. I tried to imprint the white snowy roofs in my memory for ever but somehow they did not seem quite real.

Only the Kremlin seemed permanent. It had seen the Czars and it had seen Stalin. The Czars had gone, never to return. One day Stalin would go, and one day I might be able to return to Moscow under a new regime. It was a cold snowy morning when I left Moscow for the last time. Now that I was an official citizen again I travelled first class without any difficulty. In the same compartment were two naval officers. I was tired by all my adventures and was dozing when suddenly a remark made by one of them jerked me back into wakefulness.

"Have you heard about the Russian girl who wanted to marry an Englishman?" one said. "She's been sent into exile of course."

"What's happened to the Englishman?" asked his companion.

"He's had to go back to England," the other said.

I had listened to their conversation and there was no question that they were talking about me. I pretended to sleep but I felt a certain satisfaction that, in spite of all the precautions and secrecy of the N.K.V.D., my adventures had somehow reached the ears of the man in the street. The naval men went on talking — most of their information was inaccurate — but the main story was correct. I did not dare to reveal my identity during the long journey back to Archangel. And several times they told me the romantic story of the Russian girl who had tried to flout the N.K.V.D. According to them she had not escaped her just punishment. It seemed to me that the N.K.V.D., unable to stop rumours, had decided to try and end them by saying that I had been sent into exile. I did not wish to disillusion my carriage companions in case my luck changed — and the secret police came and really banished me.

I arrived in Archangel on New Year's Eve, 1941. Even in Communist Russia the death of the old Christian year is still a time for rejoicing. The Intourist Hotel, decorated with paper streamers, was filled with foreigners. Archangel, normally an obscure Russian port, had become a busy cosmopolitan town during the war.

As a hallmark of its new-found sophistication, Gabbi, the *maître d'hôtel* of the Metropole in Moscow had been transferred to take charge of the Intourist Hotel. There were many English people staying there and a large number of Poles arriving from concentration camps. They had been sent to these camps by the Soviet before Russia entered the war on the side of the Allies. After Germany invaded Russia, Stalin had agreed to release them to serve with the Free Polish Forces in England. Archangel was their embarkation port for Great Britain and the hotel was full of their noise and gay laughter.

All the foreigners, both Poles and English, gave John and me a great welcome. Our story was the sole topic of conversation in Archangel. Everyone greeted us like old friends and in order to be alone with me for a short time John ordered dinner in his room. We sat drinking champagne at the candle-lit table but there was no privacy for us on this New Year's Eve — the gayest I have ever spent in my life. Every few moments hotel guests kept coming in to drink our health. Eventually we gave up all idea of having a quiet evening together and joined them in seeing the New Year in; a New Year which was to make the greatest change in my life.

But in the middle of all the gaiety there was one worry in both our minds. Would the Russians give us official approval to be married? John had received no objection from Sir Stafford Cripps, the British Ambassador, to our marriage, but this was not enough as I was still a Russian living in Russian territory. We decided to visit the Archangel N.K.V.D. together next day. It was useless. All the senior officer said was: "No." When John protested the man suggested that we should see the Registrar of Marriage, Z.A.G.S., so we went along to him. He obligingly read through the marriage code several times for our benefit. But it always amounted to the same thing.

No Russian could marry a foreigner without N.K.V.D. permission. In other words the two officials were just passing us from one to the other. As a Soviet citizen, nurtured in bureaucracy, this seemed quite natural to me, but as an Englishman John found it more than he could bear. One day, without telling me, he stormed into the office of the Archangel N.K.V.D. chief and told him what he thought of the prevarication which had gone on. He had not the same fear of the secret police as I had. He was able to lose his temper without any fear of being sent to Siberia. The implacable attitude of the police chief infuriated him so much that he said: "If you don't let me marry her, I'll come back and shoot you!"

The N.K.V.D. chief must have thought he meant it because when he came back to his room in the Intourist Hotel he found all his belongings turned upside down as though a burglary had been committed. N.K.V.D. agents had been frantically searching through his luggage for the one thing he needed to put his threat into action — a gun! As John never carried a gun, their search was fruitless.

We laughed about their frenzied suspicions although all our romantic ideas had been frustrated by the secret police. John began to worry that one day the N.K.V.D. would come and take me for good. Finally we decided to do a crazy thing. It seemed the only chance left. John wrote out a telegram addressed to Beria, head of the N.K.V.D. in Moscow.

It was a simple message, the plea of a man and woman in love. It ended: "I sincerely love her, and she loves me. Please let us marry."

After we had sent it off we both agreed that it had been foolish; the immovable bureaucratic heart of the N.K.V.D. was hardly likely to be touched by such a human plea. The telegram was dispatched on the 15 January, 1942, and of course we heard nothing. Day after day passed and we did not dare even to hope any more. A week later, in the middle of the night, there was a loud knocking on my door. When I opened it, sleepily, a maid outside said: "Come quickly there's a phone call from Moscow for you."

When I picked up the telephone a man's emotionless voice came over the line saying: "Citizeness Korzhenko? This is the Moscow N.K.V.D. speaking. I am instructed to tell you that we have sent an authority for you to wed your Englishman. Permission has been sent to the police at Archangel. It should be there now."

Then he hung up the phone and I stood with the receiver still in my hand trembling. The little maid had stood wide-eye at my elbow while I was speaking to Moscow. She plucked me anxiously by the arm as I stood there, white-faced and dazed.

"Are you all right, Citizeness?" she asked, anxiously. "Is it bad news?"

"No," I said, suddenly realizing what had happened, "It is not bad news. It is wonderful news. The N.K.V.D. have told me I can marry John."

Almost as soon as I had spoken the girl dashed away and within a moment she was back followed by a sleepy figure in a dressing gown.

All I could say to him was: "Darling, we can be married."

Somehow I managed to babble out the story but he was not convinced. I think he thought I had been dreaming!

"Are you serious, darling?" he asked. "You are sure it is not a joke? Let's go to the police station to find out."

As we walked through the snowy streets of Archangel, we held hands hardly daring to look at each other. When the officer in charge of the police station heard our story he picked up some papers. The suspense was ageless. Then he put his glasses on his nose and peered at one of the documents.

"Yes," he said slowly, "That is quite correct. You can be married. Here is the message from Moscow. When are you going to have the ceremony?"

Two voices answered as one: "Today."

The officer, who regarded it as just another routine affair, said: "Very well, I will tell the Registrar that Moscow has given approval."

It was three-thirty in the morning when we left the police station. We walked along arm in arm, oblivious of the snow, back to the Intourist Hotel. As we neared the hotel entrance John said: "Do you realize what day this is?"

"Yes," I whispered happily, "It is our wedding day."

Next morning, as soon as the Registrar opened his office John was on the doorstep. Registrar Zudov shuffled through some papers, confirmed he had received an authority from Moscow for the wedding, and the time was fixed for two o'clock that afternoon.

Already the story had got round the hotel. It seemed as if the whole of Archangel had heard about our wedding. When we walked through the hotel lounge people rushed up and showered congratulations upon us. Those who were most kind were the British and American sailors who had come into Archangel with convoys, carrying lease-lend goods. These men from the other side of the Iron Curtain had become very popular with the Russians. They in their turn liked the Russians they were allowed to meet. They seemed delighted that a Russian girl was marrying an Englishman; the first war bride to cement the friendship between two great wartime allies. Yet in the midst of all this celebration John had a frown on his face. I could not understand why until he confided his problem to me.

"I want you to have a wedding ring," he said. "I want this to be a real wedding, although we can't have a church ceremony until later."

I knew better than he did that it was impossible to obtain a wedding ring in Archangel. The Soviet State lays it down that such symbols are bourgeois. Therefore few Russian women wear them. But both of us felt that the ring was important because it symbolized our union. We resigned ourselves to the fact that it was impossible when the Esthonian captain who had done so much to bring us together came up. He overheard our conversation.

"A ring, eh?" he said. "If that's all you want, Nora, you will have it with my blessing."

I looked at him puzzled, as with a great roar of laughter he undid his shirt and fumbled among the hairs on his chest. He pulled a gold chain from round his neck. Attached to it was a ring.

219

"I've carried this round for years," he said. "It has always brought me luck. I hope it will bring you luck too."

After lunch, with John clutching the ring, we drove round to the office of Registrar Zudov. The atmosphere in the office removed any romantic feelings we had. Two grim-faced girl clerks sat at desks flanked by a bust of Karl Marx and a picture of Stalin. I sat down in front of one of them while John faced the other. Almost before we realized it, the unromantic marriage ceremony began with this question.

"Is there any V.D. in your family?"

"No," I said.

"Any T.B.?"

"No."

"Married before?"

"No."

All these questions were written down by both the girls.

Then one said: "What name will you have?"

I replied: "I will take my husband's name."

The girls insisted on pointing out that I had a choice, that I could either keep my own surname or take my husband's. It was simply a question of filling in a form. Finally one of the girls said: "That's all then. If you want a divorce come here any time and fill up the forms. You can have one for thirty roubles."

They pushed a ledger in front of us and said: "Sign here please."

This was the end of our wedding ceremony. It could hardly be called romantic.

As we turned to go, the girls both held out their hands and said: "Congratulations on your marriage."

Outside John and I looked at each other. Then he gently slipped the wedding ring on my finger. There had not been any opportunity to do it before, the ceremony had been far too matter of fact. I looked down at it but could hardly see it because my eyes were blurred with tears of happiness. At last I was married — the wife of an Englishman.

CHAPTER XXIII – A TELEGRAM TO STALIN BRINGS ME FREEDOM

When we arrived back at the hotel we found a wedding celebration had been arranged for us. Gabbi, who knew me from the Moscow days, had arranged everything, including the music. The band, as a compliment to John, played "Tipperary." For me they played a Georgian folk song called "Suliko" and many other Russian tunes. But the nicest of them all was one I had not heard before which went: "Oh, Johnny, how you can love."

Group Captain I. C. Bird, head of the Mission — who later became an air commodore and Britain's Air Attaché in Moscow — proposed my health and I made my first speech in English in reply. It was just a phrase or two which I had learnt parrot-wise from John. It must have sounded rather insincere as I stumbled through it with my Russian accent, but I meant every word of it when I said: "I am most grateful to you all for your kindness. You are the most wonderful people in the world!"

We were married! For some time that was enough for us. But at the back of our minds we both realized we had one more gulf, perhaps the greatest gulf, to cross. John was under orders to return to England but, although I was married to him, I could not leave Russia without permission from the N.K.V.D. For in the eyes of the Soviet I was still a Russian citizen. They had to release me from my Soviet citizenship to enable me to obtain a British passport. We sent many requests in to the N.K.V.D. but each one was met with a firm refusal. Three months went by and I began to worry. Again the position seemed hopeless. John would have to leave me behind, even though I had been married to him with official approval. But he had not my awe of the great figures of the Soviet Union, and he persuaded me to send another telegram to the Kremlin. This time it was addressed to Stalin himself and signed with my name.

The message simply said: "You have let me marry an Englishman. Please let me go with him to England because he is leaving immediately."

Both of us realized that we did not matter to Stalin, any more than we did to Beria, the head of the N.K.V.D., to whom we had sent the first telegram. But we gambled on the fact that if we went high enough up we might get above petty officialdom and reach the men who did not wish to offend our great wartime ally, Britain. It had come off once before by some magical means so we saw no reason why we should not try it again. For days after we sent the telegram we kept our fingers crossed, but without much hope. We knew that if Stalin agreed to release me from Soviet citizenship he would notify the British Embassy in Moscow. And no word came from them.

Then one day General Mason-MacFarlane came on an official visit from Moscow to Archangel. I was presented to him as the wife of an official of the British Mission. This tall, silver-haired, imposing man in battle-dress uniform, took my hand, smiled gently at me and said: "So you are the girl I have heard about? I remember you in Moscow. I have good news for you now. His Majesty's Government have recognized you as a British subject and you are free to go to England. I hope you will be happy there."

Stalin had answered my appeal!

The police next day confirmed I had been released from Soviet citizenship and Group Captain Bird gave me a British passport. I ran my finger unbelievingly over its rough blue cover. It seemed like some sort of talisman.

When I left the group captain's office the first person I went to see was a girl friend of mine called Mme D. She was one of the few Russians who remained friendly with me during my four months' stay in Archangel. She was an understanding woman because her own story had been a sad one. She was the wife of a Soviet diplomat and when he had received a sentence of ten years' imprisonment she had joined him voluntarily in a concentration camp. She had spent seven years there but the sentence was too much for her husband. He hanged himself.

Mme D. knew my whole story and I had

Nora's first UK passport issued by the British Embassy Moscow March 1942

promised to let her know the moment I became a full British citizen. When I rushed into her room she saw at once by my excitement that the great moment had arrived. Without a word she took me in her arms and hugged me. Then she said: "Let me see this wonderful thing, this passport to freedom."

I took the passport out of my pocket and put it in her hand. She held it as though it were a sacred relic and cried unashamedly.

"I would give my soul for this," she said. "What a wonderful thing it is to be free. What wouldn't I give for a moment's happiness away from this sad country of ours where no one's life is one's own, where brother spies on brother and a son denounces his father."

She put the passport reverently back in my hands and said without the slightest touch of envy: "God bless you, Nora, I hope you will be happy. But never forget us, the people you have left behind."

When I went back to the hotel there was a telephone call from the local police. Even though I was clutching my British passport, the cold voice on the end of the line still gave me a feeling of apprehension when it said:

"Major Dritz, Chief of Police, wants to see you. You must come at once. And you must come alone."

The major was sitting at his desk in front of the inevitable picture of Stalin. Standing next to him was another man, a plump little man with cold grey eyes, wearing the dull green uniform of a the N.K.V.D.

The police major introduced him, saying: "This is a major from the N.K.V.D. who has come from Moscow to see you."

The major in the green uniform made no attempt to shake my hand and without any preamble he said: "Citizen Korzhenko, your trials are coming to an end. I have to tell you that our great leader, Stalin, has at last given you permission to leave Russia.

I did not say anything. I did not wish to tell him that not only had I heard the news but the British had already given me a passport.

After he had made this statement in a stern official voice his manner changed and he said a surprising thing:

"I have instructions to apologize for our behaviour to you during the past. We deeply regret any ill-treatment and persecution you may have suffered."

A cheerless smile crossed his face as he added: "You must realize that even the N.K.V.D. makes mistakes and we were misinformed about you.

"I would like to tell you now, Nora Vassilevna, that the N.K.V.D. has always admired you for your courage and determination. In spite of everything you have carried yourself as a true Russian."

He handed me a document saying: "Here is the copy of the special decree of the Supreme Soviet releasing you from Soviet citizenship."

As I took it the major said: "There is one more thing that I must tell you before you leave. Never forget that wherever you are, or whatever you may become outside Russia, you will always remain a Russian.

"You have technically been released from Soviet citizenship but the blood of Russia will still flow in your veins. You must be true to your birthright. You owe it to us and your family never to betray those you have left behind."

The major's cold grey eyes gazed steadily into mine as he made one more remark: "You have seen and heard many things which would be of use to our enemies in the capitalist world beyond the boundaries of the Soviet. We rely on you never to divulge these things. We demand your silence."

Next day John and I left to join the *Empire Stevenson* which was docked at Molotovsk in the White Sea. Molotovsk was a half-built town newly named in honour of Molotov, the man who had dismissed my father. We should have sailed the day after we joined the ship but a broken propeller held us up for months. Already my mind had carried me away from Russia and all the evil memories it had for me. The delay was terrible for me. I wanted to get away as soon as possible from the country of my birth. Every day as the ship remained in port I hated Stalin's Russia more. For here under my eyes was the tragedy, the inhumanity of the Soviet system.

Molotovsk was being built by thousands of men and women slaves. Great gangs of these unfortunate wretches toiled round the docks bullied by armed guards. They were ragged, filthy scarecrows dressed in sacking, blankets, anything to keep out the cold of Arctic Russia. These half-starved wrecks of humanity stumbled around the half-finished city in their thousands. They were building another port for Stalin out of the tangle of scaffolding and unpaved streets. Every now and again, tired of being aboard the ship, we would walk through the streets of the skeleton city. Whenever the guards were not looking, slaves with shaved heads stumbled towards us with arms outstretched, pleading for food or cigarettes. If the N.K.V.D. men saw them they clubbed them back with rifle butts. It made me sick and ashamed to see such behaviour in the country of my birth.

Sometimes we managed to sneak something to these half-human wretches. I remember one incident when a tattered, desperate man said in perfect English as we passed: "Excuse me, but could you spare a little food?"

The man spoke in a cultured voice almost without any accent, and John hastily dug into his pocket for some chocolate. He tried to slip it to him but the guard had already spotted us. He came up and knocked the packet out of the man's hand and stamped it into the snow.

The man bit his lip and said in a gentle voice: "Thank you all the same."

224

The guard hit him with his rifle butt and knocked him into the snow. John and I walked away with tears of rage and mortification in our eyes, powerless to help this unhappy creature. It was one of my last memories of Russia, the sight of this ragged wretch with his pleading eyes, grovelling in the snow. He had obviously once been a man of some position and possibly had visited England. Now like millions more in the Soviet Union he was being treated like any animal. When the guards were slack British sailors would manage to throw a few cigarettes to the slave labourers. If a sailor even carelessly threw a stub away a dozen men would pounce on it, fighting among themselves like wild beasts. They even fought over the garbage emptied from the boat, stuffing potato peelings and stale bread crusts into their mouths with feverish fingers.

On 25 June, 1942, the U.S. ship *Mount Evans* came alongside us and the rumour went round that we were due to move. The propeller had been repaired and a convoy to run the gauntlet of the German U-boats in the northern seas was being made up. The N.K.V.D. boarded the ship for a last check-up. Fulfilling their Soviet principles they diligently searched the ship and all the passengers. Everyone, including the crew, was paraded on deck while the secret police combed their cabins. This inspection took four hours and in the middle of it I was called to my cabin. I found an N.K.V.D. officer holding several documents in his hand. One was a letter from my stepmother sent from her exile in Asiatic Russia.

"You won't need this now, Citizeness," he said. I could understand why; the new Russia does not like such damaging documents to get into the hands of anybody in the outside world. He also took away the letter releasing me from Soviet citizenship. At two o'clock that afternoon the men in the green uniform gave the captain his clearance papers and left the ship. The engines began to throb. There was a rattle as we cast off the chains which bound us to Russia. The ship shuddered slightly and drew imperceptibly away from the quay. I stood on deck gripping the rail with John's arm around me. For the last time I was looking on my homeland. The gap between the shore and the ship widened every second. Then the *Empire Stevenson* turned slowly and headed out into the icy Arctic seas. The grey coastline began to fade. I watched until it disappeared.

It seemed sadly symbolic to me that the last human beings I saw silhouetted against the dark Russian skies, were the ragged slaves toiling to build the new Soviet city of Molotovsk.

My mind went back to the green-uniformed secret police major who asked me to promise never to tell what went on in Russia. For seven years I have kept silent. Now I have not been able to keep silent any longer.

The major was right. The blood of Russia still flows in my veins and I am true to my birthright. Russia is bigger than the N.K.V.D. It is bigger than Stalin, just as it was once bigger than the Czars. The true Russia, that I love, does not need secret police, concentration camps and firing squads, so that a group of men in the Kremlin can keep a great nation in chains.

INTRODUCTION by Peter & Leeroy Murray

John Murray's book *A Spy Called Swallow* was written thirty years after the publication of *I Spied for Stalin*.

In 1972, at the age of 64, John attended Nottingham University in order to study for a degree in History. It was there that he began to write about his wartime experiences and of meeting Nora. By this time, Nora and John had been separated for over twenty years and had not spoken for the majority of this time. The publication of his book sparked in her a renewed interest in his life, and perhaps a realisation that she may have greatly underestimated him.

Reprinting *A Spy Called Swallow* allowed Leeroy and Peter Murray to complete their father's account of his enduring love for their mother - Nora, the Russian spy. The moment he met Nora, John's life changed irrevocably and dramatically. He may well have had girlfriends before, but up to that point he largely kept to himself, protecting his independent, self-determined lifestyle. As a businessman travelling the Baltic states, his suits, shirts and shoes were usually made-to-measure. He carried gold coins secretly hidden in his belt, readily available and easily exchangeable. He also carried his favourite compact Bayard automatic gun. He knew the value of good health having had rickets as a child, which had forced him, for a time, to push himself around on a cart because he could not walk. In his teens he became very active, exercising regularly, running, boxing and lifting weights.

John was worldly in his outlook; earned from his rich experiences as a businessman. He went from an employee at a cigarette-making factory in Kovno, Lithuania to owning his own factory in Riga, Latvia. With his knowledge of languages, he also became a broker for air engine parts, importing them from the UK for clients in Latvia, Norway and Finland. He may even have been involved in arms-dealing. His last business address was in Helsinki when World War II broke out.

Whichever country John found himself in, he was easily accepted as part of the expat community, socialising with others at British Embassy events. He also regularly attended the local community church services. His was a self-contained understated lifestyle. He operated very much beneath the radar, not one for being showy, or to covet attention. His experiences as a courier from 1939 onwards suited his self-reliance and lone-wolf tendencies. It also drew on his ability to mentally shut-down, ignore everything around him and focus on the task in hand. He was not easily intimidated.

When John met Nora, his independent existence took a very different turn, one that later left his life hanging in the balance. His uncompromising commitment to her was made when, one evening in November 1941, whilst leaning on the railing of his homeward-bound ship, *Temple Arch*, docked at Molotovsk Archangel, he watched with incredulity as a lone-figure struggled through the blizzard. Against impossible odds, Nora had made it from Moscow to the inhospitable northern ports of Russia simply to say goodbye. From that moment, with all the energy that his 'steel trap' mind could muster, he made a commitment to Nora...a commitment which never faltered.

Leeroy and Peter's re-publication of their father's book - *A Spy Called Swallow*, is very much a dedication to John - a singular man who was the best possible father his children could ever ask for. A man who always stood by his family despite enduring years of personal struggles, poverty and grief. During his lifetime he experienced the deaths of his younger sister Irene, and of his two younger brothers, Demetri and Nicholas. Later, he suffered the death of his wife and the untimely death of his eldest son, also called John. Never complaining, he simply carried on as the principled, determined and unbreakable man he truly was.

PROLOGUE: A SPY CALLED SWALLOW - John Murray

Espionage is a word that invariably excites the imagination of all who come across it, and rightly so, for the stakes are high and the pay-off in many cases, death.

If there is any truth in the axiom 'All's fair in love and war', the same may be applied to my own axiom 'There's no game like the spy game', by which I mean that the most innocent and unsuspecting of people are considered 'fair game' for recruitment by those who conduct the business of espionage. Whether these are recruited or coerced into the spy game, there is one thing that sets them apart from the dedicated professional spy. They tend to follow their emotional instincts rather than professional rules, and as such in spite of

The author with his parents, baby sister and younger brother Nicholas (left of picture)

all the careful selection and examination into their character and background, confound their selectors by acting contrary to all expectations. The experiences and incidents I am about to relate will bear out this assumption.

To give you some idea of my background, I will briefly outline my history: I was born in Blackpool on 7 January 1908, the eldest son among the four children in our family. My younger brothers, Nicholas and Demetri and sister Irene were also born in Lancashire. My father was Greek, and came from Kythnos, one of the small islands near Pireus, and our family name was Varicopulos. My mother was English of Irish descent and was born in Eccles, her maiden name being Murray. We boys all adopted our mother's maiden name which we found much more convenient to use. My father who had arrived in England during his early teens, refused all invitations to take out naturalisation papers, averring that he was a true Greek and proud of his ancestry. This decision was apt to cause many difficulties when my parents left England, whereas we children with our British passports experienced no trouble whatsoever when travelling abroad.

After the First World War we moved down to London. It was from there in 1925, aged seventeen, I sailed from Hays Wharf on a cargo boat to Riga, capital city of the then newly-formed Republic of Latvia, to take up an appointment as book-keeper to a Greek cigarette manufacturer. The owner of the factory, a Greek tobacco merchant called Mr Asimakis – an old family friend – had paid my fees for a two-year commercial course at Pitman's College which I attended after leaving St Mark's Preparatory School in Fulham. It was a period when England was in the throes of an economic recession that spelt unemployment and misery to millions. At seventeen, I was in good health and being of an adventurous disposition was prepared to tackle anything; besides I also felt that I owed my benefactor something in return for his kindness.

I arrived in Riga at the end of May 1925 and soon made myself indispensable in the years that followed. In 1927 I went to Kovno, the capital of the neighbouring republic of Lithuania, and assisted my employer in the opening of another cigarette factory. It was during my sojourn in Lithuania that I made the acquaintance of a young army lieutenant called Alexsis Balunas, who was an aide to the Minister of Defence. His English was very poor and in the course of our friendship I wrote many letters on his behalf ordering armaments required by Lithuania from the well-known British firm of Armstrong Vickers.

In 1931, my employer suddenly died intestate and his relatives started litigation proceedings over his estate. Legal costs practically brought the factories to a state of bankruptcy and the Riga firm was closed down. The family differences were finally settled in 1932 and I was able to sell the Kovno factory for them. The commission I earned enabled me to leave Lithuania and buy up the factory in Riga which I re-opened. I brought my father and mother, together with my brother Nicholas, to Riga and set about building up the business anew. I was soon employing a work force of over three hundred, and we became one of the largest cigarette factories in Latvia.

It was in Riga that I made the acquaintance of a Latvian ex-airforce pilot who designed and built his own aeroplanes. He knew no English so I undertook his correspondence with Bristol for the purchase of Gypsy aero engines which were the only ones he would use. This association, like that with Lieutenant Balunas, was later to have far-reaching consequences. I was completely unaware at the time that Soviet spies operating in Lithuania and Latvia had reported these connections to Soviet Intelligence who promptly put me on their list for future attention.

Choir of the British Church in Riga, Latvia, Armistice Day 1936.
From left, standing: The author, his cousin Flora, his brother Nicholas, Mr John Watson (reputedly a British Agent), Mr Cox (Union Cold Storage Manager) and Helen Bisseniek. Seated in middle row on extreme right: Mrs Bisseniek whose husband was liquidated during the Soviet annexation of Latvia. Bottom row from left: Miss Bisseniek, the younger of Mrs Bisseniek's daughters and third from left, Anne, cousin of the author.

In 1937 my factory was nationalised together with other British firms by the Latvian government. It came as a shock, the compensation paid was hardly sufficient to cover the cost of the machinery and to make matters worse I could not even take this money out of the country owing to currency restrictions. Furthermore, to make things even more difficult I had my

231

personal employment and residential permits cancelled. My father and brother were asked to remain as consultants to the tobacco industry. As my parents had grown to like Riga and had made many friends there they agreed to remain, but my brother after only a short period returned to London.

King George V's Requiem Mass held in the British Church, Riga,
conducted by Reverend Harrison

I then decided to go to Helsinki in Finland where I had several business acquaintances. I had two reasons for doing this. First it was near enough for me to keep an eye on the welfare of my parents, and secondly I wanted to be near at hand so that, should developments permit it, I would be able to get my money out of Latvia and procure a further indemnity for the loss of the factory. In this I failed, I was never again to see my money or get proper compensation for my factory.

I was not to know this. Nor was I to know that my decision to go to Finland was to result in my being enrolled as a diplomatic courier, and in my travels I was to eye-witness the invasion and annexation by the Germans and the Soviets of one country after another. That I was to escape capture and death by the skin of my teeth. That I was to get involved with a beautiful Russian spy who ended my bachelor days by embarking on a perilous three-month voyage in an Arctic convoy as my Soviet bride. Such is Fate.

PART I - WAR COMES TO FINLAND

Arriving in Finland in the September of 1937 meant starting all over again right from the bottom. But it was not long before I got a job with a Finnish firm of exporters and importers dealing mainly in timber and textiles. The state of the world economy was still very bad and trade suffered from currency restrictions imposed by various European countries endeavouring to maintain their balance of foreign commitments. To offset this my firm transacted business under a barter system that was both unique and interesting and I soon became quite adept at arranging exports of Finnish goods to the Levant and Germany in exchange for consumer goods required by Finland. The director of the firm I worked for was a very distinguished gentleman known as Consul Arvi Paloheimo whose wife was the daughter of Jean Sibelius, the great Finnish composer.

All in all I loved Finland. It was a beautiful country, its forests and innumerable lakes whether in summer or winter held a peculiar fascination for me. It was a country of natural brooding loveliness. The long drawn-out winters with their intensive dry cold weather were similar to those I had experienced in other Baltic States and it suited my temperament.

I made many friends and found that in business they were the most straightforward people I had ever dealt with. I was kept so busy that the first year in Finland passed unnoticed. Politically, I was well aware of what was going on in Europe but it seemed so far away and Finland such a haven of peace, that it was the best place to be in.

During the summer of 1939 I felt particularly honoured to receive a personal invitation to attend the birthday party of Jean Sibelius. Here I must mention that I had written several letters for him in English replying to the many demands he received from the great orchestras in England and America to conduct performances of his works. Although still vigorous, he was reluctant to leave his native country, apart from which he was still occupied on important compositions.

The party was quite a magnificent affair and took place in the gardens of the Paloheimo estate. The set tables gleamed and glittered with a fantastic array of silver and crystalware. There were about two hundred guests and besides all the Finnish notables there were members from almost every foreign diplomatic legation resident in Helsinki. The festivities ended with a splendid fireworks display, a treat that his grandchildren had arranged as a

233

surprise for him. There were so many toasts drunk that I'm afraid that I don't know how I got home that night.

It was not long after this party, 1 September 1939 to be exact, that the whole world was stunned by the news of the German invasion of Poland. Alarmed by what might happen should the conflagration spread to Latvia, which after all was not far from Poland, I left the next day by plane for Riga to join my mother and father and it was on the following day, 3 September, we sat huddled together listening to the radio broadcast announcing Britain's ultimatum to Germany. We looked at one another in stunned silence as the news came through. Finally my mother remarked,

'Well that's it! Let's have a cup of tea.'

I remained with my parents till the end of the month reassuring them that all would be well and not to worry. Life in Riga seemed on the surface to be still running smoothly and my father was quite happy carrying on with his work there — which made things easier. It was during this period I received a letter from my firm enclosing a sealed envelope from the British Consulate in Helsinki. It contained brief instructions from Mr Waite, the Consul, to report immediately to the British Military Attaché in Helsinki and added that it was a decree applicable to all British subjects of military age living abroad. I did not mention the letter to my parents.

I went to the Legation as soon as I arrived in Helsinki and on presenting myself was greeted with the laconic remark,

'I don't think we will send you home Murray, you'll be a lot more use to us this side of the world.'

The interview ended with my being told to stand by for further instructions which would be sent to me in due course.

I returned home that evening bewildered and isolated and spent the time thinking things over. What were my thoughts at the time? All I can remember was the bitterness I felt. Three times since leaving England I had striven to build up a life that would afford some degree of independence and security only to see my efforts come to nought. Now there was a war to be reckoned with. What my part in it was to be I had not the faintest idea. I remembered my uncles Costa and George, both Greek, who had fought with the British forces in the First World War; my cousins on my mother's side, Harold who had come home badly wounded with a gaping hole in his side, and Roland the ever-smiling boy who had gone to the front when only seventeen and had never returned. How my mother had cried when she received the news of his death. They had all been my boyhood heroes, but it all seemed so far removed from what was happening now.

I had learned a lot since leaving England, especially about the Nazis with whom I had come into contact through the Balt Germans. I knew much of the fallacies of communism through my own workers in Kovno and Riga and was well aware of the existence of underground hard-core cells on both sides of the political spectrum throughout the Baltic States. I was never a talker, but always a good listener. Both creeds to me were obnoxious. During the latter years the looming clouds of war had given rise to a general consensus of opinion among our people in the Baltic that war was inevitable, but it would be between the Fascists and the Communists whilst we would sit on the fence and watch them destroy one another. The non-aggression pact however, signed between Germany and the Soviets had now upset the scheme of things and I realised only too well the danger that threatened Britain. As far as I was concerned there was no doubt in which direction my duty lay and having arrived at this conclusion I decided to give up worrying and let the future take care of itself.

At about 9 a.m. on the morning of 30 November 1939, I was sitting deep in thought in a café in Helsinki, having a coffee prior to going to the office, when I suddenly looked up to see the place completely empty. Further, a Finnish soldier carrying a rifle was banging on the window gesticulating to me to leave the place. I got up hurriedly. He grabbed me by the arm and seeing I was a foreigner, kept shouting 'Russky, Russky!' and pointed to the sky. I heard guns booming in the distance and looking up saw scattered puffs of smoke appearing high in the cloudless deep blue sky, with planes glinting silvery in the morning light. I decided that I would go to the nearby flat of one of my friends Fred Bucknall and warn him of what was happening. I arrived at his flat which was on the third floor of the building and found him calmly shaving in the bathroom. 'Have you heard the news?' I cried. 'Yes, it's all right, it's only the Russky's bombing Helsinki!' he said. 'What are we going to do now?' I asked, not having a clue what to do, everything had happened so suddenly.

'I shall go to the office and then on to the bank to see if I can draw some money, if you can take the wife and the kiddy down to the cellar while this is on John, I'd be very grateful. I'll try and get back as quickly as possible.'

His wife and little girl came down with me to the cellar. I emptied a basin of lump sugar into my pockets as we went. The large cellar was crowded with men, women and children and I noticed that it had been hastily shorn up with huge baulks of raw timber. So the Finns had been expecting something

235

like this I thought, and here was me, as ignorant as a coot of what had been happening around me! And I thought I knew everything. I was glad I'd taken the sugar lumps. We could hear the boom of bombs as they exploded mingling with the quick sharp continuous reports of the anti-aircraft guns. All this set the children crying. I went around giving them sugar lumps, laughing and talking to them. It had a good effect. After a couple of hours, the all-clear was given. Fred returned and I decided to make my way to my own office. On the way I had to go past the coffee house. It was a shambles — no windows, and all the tables turned over and chairs in a jumble. The street itself was ankle deep in jagged pieces of broken glass. Before the café lay a tram on its side, a mass of twisted iron as though some giant hand had crumpled it up.

When I arrived at the office no one was there so I returned to my rooms, still wondering what to do next. The next day I went to the office again. This time Dagni, one of the clerks was there. From her I gathered the details of the Russian attack of Finland. Mr Paloheimo had, as yet, not been to the office and she did not know when he would come. The bottom of the world had seemingly fallen out. I decided to go to the Legation. On the way there another raid started. A bomb must have fallen somewhere down the end of the road. I didn't hear anything but all of a sudden, a terrific blast of air lifted me off my feet and I was hurled backwards over quite a distance. Stunned, with my head buzzing, fit to burst, I got to my feet. I felt drunk. Many years afterwards during an Army medical I was told the scars on my ear drums were probably due to blast perforation.

I continued on my way to the British Legation and saw Mr Desmond, the Chancellery servant who I knew quite well. He told me the Legation staff were preparing to leave for a safer place somewhere on the coast. He had to remain as they had to have someone in the building to attend to the postal and telegraph communications that would still be coming in. He said that feeling lonely he would feel happier if I could join him. He had got a fairly good shelter in the basement so I stayed with him, giving him what assistance I could. The days passed with alarms and raids to enliven our existence. All I knew was that the Finns were putting up a good fight, which knowing them, was only what I expected, though I could not see much hope of them winning.

On the afternoon of 4 December 1939, Mr Bamford, the British Vice-Consul suddenly appeared in the Legation and informed me that most of the British Colony was to be evacuated to Stockholm in Sweden and would leave Helsingfors that very night. It was an urgent and imperative order and my name was on the list. I was to report to the British Consul at 7 p.m. that evening. I went to the Consulate at seven and found about forty people assembled. Among them was Mr Beck, Reuter's Finnish correspondent. We more or less teamed up together. I had no luggage, as there had been no time to collect anything. All I had was the black leather briefcase with my personal documents, passport, etc., that I always carried with me. Apart from a few socks, pants and vests I had stuffed into it, there was a little statuette of the Madonna that travelled everywhere I went. I had brought this along to the Legation as a kind of mascot, a gesture that Mr Desmond being a Catholic, warmly appreciated.

Bamford was in charge, and soon we found ourselves on the train for Turku, the Finnish west coast port where we were to embark for Stockholm. We had been travelling for about two and a half hours when the train stopped. The sliding door at the end of the coach opened and in strode half a dozen fully armed Finnish soldiers. Their faces were grim as they walked down the centre of the coach peering intently at the occupants on either side as they passed. As they came to Bamford, who was seated in the middle section, one of the soldiers grabbed him roughly and hauled him to his feet, shouting angrily in Finnish. Poor Bamford looked startled and was not even given a chance to speak as they tried to drag him along.

Beck who knew Finnish fairly well said to me, 'Crikey, they think he is a Russian spy.' We both jumped up and I went forward waving my British passport in the soldiers' faces, shouting 'Leave him alone, he's our British Consul, we are all English here!' Just then an officer appeared and seeing the struggle that was going on gave a sharp order and the soldiers let Bamford go. Then a whole series of explanations followed with Bamford producing his documents. An apology was made and thankfully accepted. It appeared that the Finns had information that a Russian spy or spies had boarded the train. Bamford, who wore a fur cap and long black coat, had aroused their suspicions. We arrived in Turku, which was still burning from an air-raid, just after midnight. Through the rubble we were quickly shepherded to a small Finnish steam packet that had just arrived in the harbour. We sailed almost immediately. Even the upper decks were crowded with refugees. It was one of the most bitterly cold sea voyages I have ever made.

We arrived in Stockholm in the early hours of 5 December. As the ship approached Stockholm, we saw the city with all its lights full on, such a contrast to Helsingfors where a black-out had been enforced. When we docked, all passengers except the British were disembarked. A British Consular official came aboard later and our papers and passports were checked against a list. Beck, some others and myself, were then driven to a small private hotel where some of the lesser Embassy staff lived, and given private rooms with instructions to report to the Embassy later in the day. I remember asking Beck why the evacuation had been so sudden, reckoning that he, as a newspaper man would know something, because we had been given no information at all. He said that a rumour had been circulating that the Russians were going to use poison gas on Helsingfors, which of course they never did.

At the first opportunity I wrote to my parents in Latvia, to let them know I was safe in Sweden and if possible to contact Glynn Hall, the British Vice-Consul in Riga, and get him to transfer some money over to me. Very shortly I received one hundred pounds through the Embassy with a letter from my mother saying they were well and I was to look after myself and not to get into trouble.

Although we had breakfast at our hotel, our main midday meals were taken together with other members of the Embassy at a large restaurant in the centre of the city. It was quite amusing; we used to occupy a couple of large tables, next to us would be a Japanese contingent on one side, and on the other, several tables with German Legation staff. We used to sit down pointedly ignoring them. Sometimes our chaps would draw our attention to several ordinary looking fellows sitting apart whom they whispered were foreign secret agents known to them.

It appeared that quite a number of German secret service agents were operating in Stockholm under the guise of businessmen. I was not surprised at this information, because I had come across similar types in Lithuania and Latvia. They had appeared in the Baltic States shortly after Hitler had assumed power in Germany. They were, in fact, mostly ex-army officers from the First World War and their job was to recruit young Baltic Germans for the Hitler Youth Brigades. How I came to know this was that my brother and I had formerly been members of KSK — a Baltic-German Sports Club — he played football for them and I boxed in the club. As we both spoke German we got to hear about these special visitors from Germany.

I found Stockholm a beautiful and interesting city with many imposing buildings, especially the large royal palace set on the crown of a hill. Waterways seemed to run in and all round the city. Whilst I was there, the newly built Princess Charlotta hospital was opened for public inspection. I went to see it and was very impressed indeed with its lay-out and up-to-date chromium and nickel-plated equipment and the bright silent flooring and sliding doors. I should imagine that at that time it must have been the finest hospital in Europe.

Beck was very restless in Sweden and confided to me that Reuters had been expecting him to station himself on the Finnish front, which for various reasons he had been reluctant to do. His wife who was Finnish had not come with him and his son, although only eighteen, had gone off to volunteer for service with the Finnish Army. His father could not stop him — such is youth! A famous reporter by the name of Walter Durante had arrived in Stockholm, representing World Press News and Beck invited me to go along with him to see the great man who was well known to him. I think he was staying at the Grand Hotel. It was about ten in the morning, and Walter was lying on a large double bed in his pyjamas. The bed was littered with a number of Swedish newspapers. On either side of the bed sat a couple of the most beautiful blonde Swedish girls I had ever seen. There were also a couple of cases of bottled beer. Walter, after introductions, waved with one glass of beer in his hand and the other holding a newspaper, for us to be seated and help ourselves which we did. I followed the subsequent proceedings with some amusement. Walter would point to a caption under a picture in the newspaper and one of the blondes would translate it into English. Thereupon, he would dictate a telegram message for the other blonde to take down and after several such, she would go off to despatch them. His dictation ran as follows:

'From our special correspondent on the Finnish front stop Temperature now 40° below zero stop Under appalling conditions saw...'

and then would follow rehashed texts in journalese from the Swedish newspapers. Beck was quite aggrieved by all this, as Reuters were now using Durante's services. It was a bit of an eye-opener to me, but it did not alter the fact that Walter Durante was nevertheless a great man in the profession as I came to know later. He was a newshound who would go anywhere and was just as tenacious as a bulldog.

Reporting in at the Embassy one day in February 1940, I was summoned to the Chargé d'Affaire's office and told I was to prepare myself for a trip to Oslo as a diplomatic courier. On 9 February 1940, the first secretary handed me an envelope about five inches square, heavily sealed at all corners and the centre, addressed to the British Minister, Sir Cecil Dormer at Oslo. After signing several 'Official Secret' declarations I was told it was to be handed to

239

Sir Cecil personally. I was to guard it with my life etc., etc., I cockily replied that they could safely leave me to carry out the instructions given. The Secretary asked me how I was going to carry the envelope. I opened my jacket, then my waistcoat showing that inside the lining of my waistcoat were two pockets. I had always had my tailors make such pockets which I used for carrying either large sums of money or confidential documents. He nodded his head satisfied. Then he said I was to see the Chancellery servant and get my tickets and reservation forms and leave that night on the midnight express. I had to hang about in the Embassy until it was time to leave. Just before eleven I got my papers. I had no luggage, only the old black leather briefcase filled as before.

Now there were two Chancellery servants in the Embassy, a father and son. The father was the senior and had served the Embassy many years with distinction and had been awarded the OBE for his services. His son was a tall, lanky fellow, always smiling and affable, but too effusive for my liking. The older man, white-haired and portly, was always quite serious in his manner. This night it was the younger man on duty, and the Embassy at this hour seemed practically deserted. I asked him particulars about the trip I was to make, as the journey from Stockholm to Oslo was new to me. I particularly wanted to know the length and time the journey would take and the border station at which I must expect passport and customs control. I had travelled much in Europe, and I knew that this was important to anyone going from one country to another. While he was explaining, he opened the drawer of his desk and took out a big black German Mauser automatic revolver and handed it to me.

'You'll want one of these for your journey.' I handled it gingerly. I had never possessed or fired a revolver in my life.

'Is it loaded?' I asked, trying to look as though handling revolvers was all in a day's work. He took it off me – 'Yes, but the safety catch is on, so it's all right now,' and he pointed it at the passage wall where some coats were hanging. He must have squeezed the trigger as he pointed, because flames suddenly shot out of the muzzle and five shots rattled out one after the other but so quickly, that it sounded like one. He was so shocked he dropped the gun, and people came running into the passage from all directions. There was one hell of a hubbub over the damaged clothes. In the midst of the row that followed I looked at my watch. I had not much time, so I slipped out, caught a taxi to the station, found my train and reserved compartment and settled down. All these events were to be very important to me, though I did not know it at the time. Many years after the war had ended this young

Chancellery servant brought disgrace on his father's name by being found out and convicted whilst still in the employ of our Embassy as a spy in the pay of the Russians. Whether he was a spy for the Germans at the time I was in the Embassy, I do not know.

As I settled down in my compartment I recalled the fate of two other diplomatic couriers. One whose mutilated body had been found on the railway lines, verdict — sad case of falling out of a moving train whilst under the influence of alcohol. The other, whose newspaper photo depicted him sprawled half out of his bunk in a sleeping-car with a knife stuck between his ribs, verdict — suicide whilst of unsound mind. In both cases the diplomatic documents they were carrying were missing and the incidents hushed up to avoid political embarrassment. Musing on these events, I got up and made a quick survey of the first class coach to see who my fellow travellers might be. The coach was empty, I would be travelling alone. The reason was that all the sensible travellers had booked warm cosy sleepers. It was mid-winter and a very cold one at that. I locked the sliding door to my compartment and taking off my overcoat, huddled into a corner and was soon into a kind of half-doze, not daring to sleep. How many hours went by I do not know, when suddenly I became aware of a dark figure looming against the glass of the door, there was a rattle of the lock being turned from the outside, a click, and in stepped what seemed to be a mountain of a man. He had no hat, no coat, no luggage. He closed the door and sat directly opposite me, his knees almost touching mine. I was startled. That door had been locked, only a conductor with a master key could open it from the outside. This man was no conductor. From under half-closed eyes I looked him over. I had made no movement and remained as I was when he came in. I was frightened, I had reason to be. He was a bull of a man, his bulk dominating the compartment. The pair of huge hands with the thick powerful fingers resting on his knees filled me with a kind of fascinated horror. One of those huge hands around my neck and it would snap like a matchstick. I could not help shuddering at the thought.

That he was a foreign agent I had not the slightest doubt. He looked like a German to me and I was doubly alarmed. From under a closely-cropped bullet head, a pair of watery-blue piggy eyes surveyed me with studied calculation and then wandered speculatively to the black leather briefcase at my side and the overcoat I had carelessly flung beside it. The maker's name, Elias Jakobson of Riga, on the ornate label showing very prominently. Questions were tumbling through my mind at an incredible rate. Who was the fellow? Did he know I was a courier? If so, how had he got the information?

241

And, if he attacked me, what could I do? The slightest move on my part might start him off. I knew I didn't stand a cat in hell's chance against a chap like this. I tensed inwardly, watching him for any sudden movement. I noticed his eyes slightly narrowing as though he was doing some thinking. Evidently he was not quite satisfied about something. The Jewish name on the label of my overcoat seemed to draw his attention. It occurred to me that he might have been tipped off that a courier would be travelling on the train, but did not know for certain his identity. I had often been mistaken for a Jew with my dark curly hair and longish nose and I wondered if he thought I was one. All of a sudden my thoughts were interrupted by his addressing me with a guttural 'Good evening!' in English. I looked at him blankly. He spoke again.

'I said "Good evening! " Is it not?'

I shrugged my shoulders and spread my hands out deprecatingly, 'I do not understand what you want of me, I don't understand anything!' I replied in my best German-Yiddish manner.

'*Pfui*! He spat dramatically on the floor of the compartment in disgust.

'*Noch eine verdammte Jude!*' (Another damned Jew.)

And he nodded his head to add emphasis to the words. As for me I had a sudden feeling of relief, blessing the time I had spent many years previously with a Jewish family called Levinson in order to learn German. They taught me Yiddish. Only later when I proudly attempted to air my newly-acquired knowledge with a Balt German called Schwedrup Schwedler, the head book-keeper of the factory I worked in, was I to learn my mistake. He had acted in exactly the same manner.

This sudden change in the situation undoubtedly saved my life as well as the despatch I carried. But I was still worried about the fix I was in, and I could feel the German was not yet sure of his ground. In an altered tone he asked me if I'd ever been in Germany. I told him yes, and mentioned the towns I had visited in the course of business, then I added plaintively that it was a pity the Germans had such a hatred for the Jews, whereupon he went off into a long tirade about the Jews ruining Germany by making money and illegally taking it out of the country, so harming the financial state of Germany. All the time he was talking I was calculating in my mind how soon we would reach the Norwegian border because I knew the passport and custom control officers would appear and it would give me the chance of doing something about the plight I was in.

During a brief interlude in our conversation when I thought the time was ripe I stood up, not even bothering to glance at my briefcase or coat and asked him at which end of the coach the toilets were. He did not know, so excusing myself, I slid the door back and went into the corridor to find them myself. He did not make any attempt to stop me, and I breathed a silent prayer as I went out. Reaching the toilets, I hastily locked the door and with my back to the wall stretched out my right leg to jam the door. I was lucky. Not long afterwards, though it seemed ages to me, the train slowed down and then stopped. Within a few minutes I heard the trampling of heavy boots and my door was tried, then banged upon and a shout bade me open for passport control. I opened the door and five large uniformed officers stood outside. Quickly I showed my passport and courier documents and explained that a German had made an unwarranted entry into my compartment. Without a word they all turned, and went down the corridor to my compartment. I remained where I was. I heard a lot of shouting and banging going on, and shortly afterwards, the officers returned and led me to my compartment, saying, 'Don't worry, you won't be disturbed any more!' When they had gone, I examined my briefcase — it had been wrenched open and the lock was broken.

The rest of the journey passed without incident but I felt terribly relieved when the train steamed into Oslo station. I waited in my compartment until a young man appeared who asked me if I was Mr Murray from the Embassy in Stockholm. He introduced himself and said he was from the Legation in Oslo where he then took me and introduced me to the First Secretary, Mr Lascelles, and to the Minister, Sir Cecil Dormer, to whom I gave the sealed envelope I had been carrying. On being asked if I'd had a pleasant trip, I recounted my experience on the train. Sir Cecil was quite upset, especially over the fact that I had been unaccompanied by an Embassy official to the station in Stockholm. He said it was a breach of the regulations and would send off a complaint immediately to Stockholm. He then asked me to wait whilst they both went into the Minister's private study. I waited thinking that I would be instructed to go on another assignment. After some minutes, Mr Lascelles returned and asked me if I would consider staying on in the Legation in the capacity of night security guard. He explained that they formerly had three, working in alternate shifts, but one of them had met with an unfortunate skiing accident and was in hospital with a broken leg and the Legation urgently needed a temporary replacement and they would be very grateful if I would consider the matter. I did not hesitate and told him I would accept the post and carry on as long as it would be necessary. I signed another set of official secrecy forms and was then introduced to my opposite number, Mr

Gobby, an ex-naval marine with whom I was to share quarters at a private hotel in Oslo.

All I remember about Oslo was that it was a quiet peaceful city. The people were very friendly and kind. There was such an air of calm and a total absence of uniformed soldiers such as I'd been accustomed to see in Germany and the Baltic States, that it almost seemed that I was back in England. The news coming through about the war was not bad. The Navy was keeping the Germans penned in and our troops in France were keeping such a formidable check on the Germans that it seemed the whole business of war might peter out. Such was the general feeling, but all too soon events were to prove us wrong.

PART II - WAR COMES TO NORWAY

On the evening of 8 April 1940,1 arrived for duty at the Legation some few minutes before six, to find several of the staff only just beginning to lock away their papers prior to going home. Normally they were already away by the time I took over from the day officer. It had evidently been a day of quite exceptional activity. By eight o'clock the building was empty except for the Minister who was still in his office adjoining the library. In any case, this was not unusual as his official residence was on the top floor of the building. On arrival I had switched over the telephones at the reception desk, checked my requirements for the night: torch, candles, recording clock, and the handy iron bar which I thought could be useful in an emergency — and watched the remaining staff leave. The last to go were the Naval Attaché and the First Secretary. As soon as they had gone I commenced my rounds of the building, checking all doors and windows and recording on my clock the various key points.

My check times took place at hourly intervals and I'd often wished something would happen to break the deadly monotony of these nightly vigils. Beyond a few phone calls and the occasional appearance of Mr Lascelles for spot checks to see everything was in order, nothing ever happened. It was just after ten when the library door opened and Sir Cecil came out.

'Good evening Murray. Everything all right?'

'All's well,' I answered, and added, 'but you seem to be having a long day of it today, Sir.'

He stroked his chin and nodded.

'Yes, I'm afraid it has been a heavy day.' He sighed and continued, 'I am very tired, Murray, and am going to turn in. Will you please tell any callers that I am not to be disturbed under any circumstances. If you should be in doubt, put the call through to my butler.'

'Very good, Sir. I'll see to it,' I said.

As he turned to go, he added, 'Oh, and by the way, there's a plate of sandwiches in the library. I've told the butler to leave them for you.' He was always very informal and it was such gestures that made working for him a real pleasure. I thanked him and with a final goodnight he went off, little knowing how soon his plans for a good night's sleep were to be shattered. The hours passed slowly by: no calls, no interruptions. It looked like being another uneventful night. At about two o'clock I got up to make another round of inspection and had just reached the end of the corridor when all the lights began to flicker and suddenly went out. I switched my torch on and rushed back to the desk. The sudden change from light to blackness did not unduly perturb me. I put it down to a power failure, especially as glancing through the windows I noticed there was total darkness outside.

I rummaged through the drawers of the desk and found a couple of candles, lit them, and stuck them on the desk. I had no sooner done so and was wondering what to do next, when a series of heavy booms broke the darkened silence. Gunfire! No mistaking the sound. I'd heard it only too often in Finland. But they did not continue. I got up to look through one of the windows — it was still black outside and once again all was silence. Still undecided about what to do, I returned to my desk and a gradual feeling of apprehension began to overtake me. I had the feeling once again that things had been too good to last. Something was about to happen. What it was, I didn't know, but in any case my job was to hang on until there was some definite directive as to my next course of action. The Minister had given me strict instructions he was not to be disturbed and in any case, all was silent now, only the lights weren't working. The sudden ringing of the telephone bell seemed like an explosion in itself. I grabbed the receiver — 'The British Legation here. Who is it please?'

A thick precise voice preceded by audible heavy breathing answered me. 'Please, I must speak with the Minister, it is very urgent!'

'I'm afraid I can't get the Minister for you, he has retired for the night and I have strict instructions not to disturb him, but, who is that speaking, and can I take a message?'

'But please, I MUST speak to him. This is the Prime Minister of Norway speaking. The Germans are invading my country now! Please, I must speak to your Minister!'

'Hold the line Your Excellency, I'll get him for you immediately,' I replied, ringing through at the same time to the Minister's apartment.

Within a few seconds the sleepy voice of the Minister's butler came through, 'What do you want?' he demanded.

'Get Sir Cecil on the line immediately…' as he was about to protest I added, 'I've got the Prime Minister of Norway on the phone, it's extremely urgent.'

Within seconds Sir Cecil came on the line. 'Well, Murray, what is it?'

'It's the Prime Minister of Norway, Sir. He says the Germans are invading his country. I'm switching you through now, Sir.'

I heard a muttered 'Good God' as I switched the line over.

That is how the first news of the invasion of Norway by the Germans was given to our Minister, Sir Cecil Dormer, by the Norwegian Prime Minister, Johan Nygaarsvold.

A few minutes later, there was a click on the switchboard denoting the end of the call and shortly after that I heard the door of the library at the end of the corridor open, and Sir Cecil appeared holding a lighted candle above his head. He was wearing a dressing gown over his pyjamas. He hurried towards me. 'Oh, there you are, Murray. Good. Now listen to me. You know what it's all about. I want you to ring up as many of the staff as you can get hold of as quickly as you can. Tell them to come to the Legation immediately, bringing what valuables they can with them and tell them not to waste any time. Those are my orders! Should they ask any questions, you are not to mention the invasion, just make it plain that they are my personal instructions. I am going to get dressed now, and will be down very shortly. In the meantime, do your very best; we have very little time.'

One by one I got the Service Attaché and the Secretaries, and then the others of the staff. The first to arrive was Mr Lascelles who was already aware of the situation. He gave me an approving nod and hurried to the Minister's rooms. Some of the staff were quick to realise that the call was urgent beyond question; others began to hum and haw, but when I informed them that they were holding things up as I had to contact all the staff, they realised that something really serious was afoot. The Senior Chancellery Servant arrived, and when I mentioned the news, he was visibly shocked — his wife was Norwegian and he had only recently set up home just outside Oslo. He now took over the telephone, whilst I gave a hand in the frenetic activity of destroying all documents likely to be of use to the enemy. The order had been given out that the Legation was to be evacuated immediately, and already part of the staff were busily engaged in loading every available car. Meanwhile the lights had suddenly come on again, which greatly facilitated our activities. By now, of course, everyone knew that Norway was being invaded by German troops. What they did not know, was whether any resistance was being put up by the Norwegians and what was more important, how much time there was left to get out before the enemy arrived on the scene.

In spite of the seeming confusion, everything went as methodically and as smoothly as circumstances permitted. By about three-thirty a.m. on 10 April a convoy of cars began to stream out of the Legation grounds into the deserted road. A notable feature was the arrival of the head of the American Legation, a woman, whose car roof was adorned with a huge American flag, its stars and stripes distinctly visible and covering the whole top of the car. I guessed it was for possible protection from air attack and some sort of protection for the convoy itself, the United States still being a neutral country at that time. It seemed very odd to me that a woman should be holding such a high diplomatic post, but I could not help admiring her courage in undertaking the forthcoming journey with its unknown hazards.

There were now only three of us left – the Senior Chancellery Servant, Jack, Ted, the day security officer, and myself. As we stood silently watching the cars move off, the last one stopped and Mr Lascelles, the Chargé d'Affaires, got out and came over to give us our final instructions. These were to await the arrival of members of the American Legation who would affix United States seals on the building so it would come under their custody. Meanwhile, we were to complete the destruction of the remaining documents, and then make our way to Narvik, which was over six hundred miles away, and might present some difficulty especially as we hadn't even a car. So I asked him if there was any possibility of getting a car.

'I'm sorry Murray,' he said, 'but we've commandeered every car possible and are already overloaded. We've got to join up with the Norwegian Government who have already headed north. I'm afraid you'll have to do the best you can — at all costs keep out of German hands. Best of luck. We'll be seeing you!'

With that he drove off with the rest. We looked at one another, our thoughts as bleak as the grey morning sky overhead. Of the three, I was the best off: Jack, the Chancellery Servant was married to a Norwegian and Ted, who had a Norwegian fiancée living in Oslo, must have also been thinking about her; whilst I had no ties.

'Come on, let's get cracking,' said Ted, breaking the silence.

With that we started collecting all the remaining papers we could find and dumped them in the garden. With a gallon or so of petrol we soon had quite a fire going. I went off to make a final check on all the rooms and returned to the bonfire.

'Look at those bastards over there,' Jack said, pointing to the building on the opposite side of the road some fifty yards away. It was the German Legation, and every room was lit up, and we could see shadows of figures moving constantly behind the curtained windows.

'I wonder what they're up to,' I said.

'Perhaps they're getting ready to attack us,' said Ted.

248

'We'll keep away from the fire, we don't want to be sitting targets should they start shooting,' said Jack jokingly.

But nevertheless, we moved into the shadow of the trees. In the distance we could hear the clang of a fire engine approaching; it gradually grew louder and then, to our surprise, we saw the fire engine appear and draw up outside the gates. The firemen on it jumped down and began hammering on the gates which were locked.

'Go on Jack, see what they want. Your Norwegian is better than mine,' I said. He went off and I could see he was doing a lot of gesticulating. At the same time I noticed the shadows behind the curtains opposite were no longer moving but seemed all bunched together. There was no doubt we were under surveillance. After a while the firemen could be seen remounting their engine and they drove off.

Jack returned. 'It's them Jerries,' he said. 'They phoned up the fire brigade and told them we were burning the place down. I told them they'd got it all wrong and that we were only celebrating an old English custom called Guy Fawkes to ward off evil spirits!'

'Blast them Jerries,' said Ted. 'I wish those Americans would hurry up before they arrive.'

He had no sooner spoken than a car drew up. It was the Americans. We let them in and I told Jack to take them round as quickly as he could and get the sealing-up done, in order that we could get away. It had already gone four o'clock and it was getting lighter every minute. Jack shook his head. 'No, you two go on. I'm going to stay. I'll go back to the missus and we'll hole up somewhere in the mountains. You go. I'll see to the Americans.'

I could see the sense of it at the time. There was no use arguing, and if I'd had a wife like him, I would have probably done the same. Ted was also turning things over in his mind too. They'd both lived in the peace and quiet of Norway for so long, that the invasion did not seem real to them. He said his fiancée would be worrying about him and perhaps he'd be safer joining her.' I reminded him we had been given definite instructions. As an ex-Grenadier Guard (for he was only on loan from the War Office to the Legation for security duties) his habit of strict discipline was the deciding factor, and he agreed to come with me.

'Come on Ted,' I finally said. 'Let's get going.' We exchanged wishes for the best of luck with Jack and made for the gates. As we were unlocking them to go out, a man came running up the road. He was well-built, clean-shaven, had no hat but wore a blue serge overcoat. He stopped in front of us. 'This is the Legation?' he asked in perfect English. I nodded.

249

'Take me to the Minister,' he said.

'Who are you?' I asked.

'Look, my name is Williams and I've got to see the Minister,' he said. I then knew who I was talking to. Mr Williams was one of our 'Hush' men. He was, in fact, a Lieutenant Commander in the Royal Navy sent over on a special mission, dressed of course, in ordinary civilian attire. He'd been expected earlier and I had been informed of this possible arrival though no one knew when he would actually turn up. I explained the situation to him and asked him how he had managed to get to the Legation. He told me that on arrival in Oslo the evening before, he was so fagged out that he had put up in a hotel to get a night's sleep, with the intention of calling on the Legation first thing in the morning. About an hour ago he had been awakened by the sound of banging doors and the trampling of heavy feet with a lot of shouting going on.

'I got up,' he said, 'and looked out of the window and saw a crowd of German soldiers in the street. I didn't wait. I got dressed and slipped out, and here I am!'

'It looks as though we had better get moving quick!' I remarked.

Whilst we were talking another figure arrived on the scene. It was the Rev. Linton, Chaplain to the Legation, and on explaining the situation all over again to him, he was most indignant that the staff had gone off without him.

It was a strange situation. None of us had the slightest idea of how we were going to get out of Oslo. One thing was clear, and that was that we had to get out and get out quickly. We talked amongst ourselves and finally decided that the only thing to do would be to start walking and hope for the best. The idea was to reach a railway station and try and get a train going north. Failing that, to make for the airfields and see if we could fly back to England. In the meantime, we'd try and pick up a taxi or a car to get us out of the danger zone.

With this in mind, we called to Jack, who locked the gates behind us — said cheerio to the Americans who'd practically finished their job of sealing the Legation doors, and started to walk down the road leading away from the city.

It was already half-light. The residential area through which we walked was quiet and deserted. We kept to the shadows of the tree-lined roadway. How long we trudged along, silently, each one busy with his own thoughts, I don't know. One seemed to have lost count of time and we didn't even have any idea where the road led to, except that it was leading us away from the city. Looking back over my shoulder from the way we had come, I saw a car

250

coming. I thought I'd take a chance and try to stop it, so I ran into the road and waved my arms. The car stopped and the driver pulled down the windows as I approached. I could see he was a civilian, and in halting Norwegian I asked him if he could give my friends and I a lift. He smiled and said, 'You are English, aren't you?' I showed him my passport, and seeing that it was unnecessary to struggle along with my imperfect Norwegian, I explained the plight we were in. It was a chance in a million! Within a few seconds we were all in the car and bowling along at top speed away from the capital. He explained that he himself was fleeing from Oslo and was going north to join the Norwegian Army if it was still in existence. He said he'd no doubt the British would be coming to the aid of Norway, and was hoping to fight alongside them. He showed me his Army reserve papers to prove he had been an officer. There was no doubt about his sincerity, and we all had the utmost confidence in his ability to get us out of the scrape we were in. Discussing our plans as we drove along, he said the idea of picking up a train en route would not be feasible as by now, if any trains were running, they would already have been commandeered by the Germans, so it was decided we'd try for the airfield at Fornebu and get a plane. The roads were still clear and we had so far seen no traffic whatsoever. It was already daylight but the sky was still overcast. The Commander sat in front next to Sven the driver, whilst I sat in the back with the Chaplain and Ted, who remained pretty silent throughout the journey and most of the conversation and speculation was left to the other two and myself. At one stage, Sven pointed out the neat and attractive house of the composer, Grieg, and my remark that Solvega would really have had something to lament about had she been with us, really tickled him.

As we approached the airport, we became aware of the growing hum of approaching aircraft. Sven stopped the car and we got out to have a look. In the far distant sky above the road we had just come along, we could see several small groups of aircraft spread out across the sky. 'They're Germans. Come on. Let's get going!' said Sven. We got in quickly and started off at full speed. There were no side turnings to the road so we had to keep straight on. We reached the airfield which was to the left of us. By now, the hum had grown into a roar of indescribable intensity. Sven pulled the car onto a verge by the side of the road under the shelter of some trees overhanging a low wall of a churchyard. We jumped out of the car, spread out and took what cover we could among the gravestones. I dropped behind the first upright tombstone I could find, grabbing it with my hands, hugging it close – squirming my body in a desperate attempt to get as much cover as I could.

No matter how much I contorted my body, I was only too conscious of the fact that it was to be either my head and shoulders exposed, or my behind, and I couldn't help thinking what an awful calamity it would be to be shot in the rear. The first stream of bullets began to phut and zip around us. You could hardly hear them because of the deafening roar of the overhead aircraft. The very ground was vibrating and heaving to the noise. I had a glimpse of the deserted airfield beyond. Near us there seemed to be two tarpaulin-covered anti-aircraft guns, silent and deserted. On the far-distant perimeter I could make out an anti-aircraft gun surrounded by eight or nine moving figures. One moment the muzzle was emitting a series of quick flashes, and the next minute it was enveloped in one huge flash with bodies, earth and metal flying in all directions. I remember shouting to my companions, but the noise was too great for them to hear — a solid black of roaring engine noise. I looked up. I'd never seen anything like it! One gigantic swathe of planes flying almost tip to tip and blackening the sky. On and on they roared in a never-ending stream. The scene was awe-inspiring and frightening. Suddenly I realised what war was going to mean. 'God help the country,' I thought. Still they came on. There must have been hundreds and hundreds of planes. The whole ground was shaking. I'm sure they must have struck terror into the hearts of all who saw them. They epitomised to the full, the power, and might of the German invaders.

As the last of this vast armada flew off into the distance, we got up and scrambled back to the car. Luckily none of us had been injured and the car had suffered no damage. Our sense of urgency was now mounting. After a brief consultation, Sven decided we should carry on and make for Elverum, which meant bearing north-east instead of north-west to the coast.

At the first opportunity we left the main road and climbed the higher mountain roads that were still bedecked with snow. Occasionally we stopped to watch Germans speeding along on motor-bikes on the roads below. The bikes had side-cars with mounted machine-guns, with one occupant and a driver with a pillion rider on the back. They came along in small interspersed batches of six to eight with small carrier cars full of troops accompanying them every now and then. Beyond this, everything was still peaceful. Sven seemed to know his way well. How long we drove for was hard to calculate. We'd sight a small town or village in the distance, stop, and Sven would get out and check the lie of the land, bringing back food and information. It appeared that the Germans had not reached so far in force as yet, so we pressed on.

During the journey I was relating some of my experiences in Finland and Esthonia to Williams who asked me if I'd heard about the escape of the Polish submarine, *Orzel*, whilst I was over there. I told him how I was on my way through Esthonia when the *Orzel*, which had escaped capture by the Germans during the invasion of Poland, had put into the neutral port of Tallinn and had been interned. Subsequently, when I was in Riga, the capital of the neighbouring state of Latvia, I'd heard a lurid account of how the crew had killed the soldiers guarding her and had escaped with the submarine into the Baltic. The German colony's newspaper at that time had been very bitter about it and had accused the Esthonians of deliberately allowing the submarine to get away. He informed me that the *Orzel* was now with the British fleet and had just recently sunk a German ship, the *Rio de Janeiro*, off the Norwegian coast. I got the impression that this had something to do with his being in Norway, but I did not ask him.

It must have been four hours since we left the airfield when we came upon the first signs of a Norwegian resistance to the invasion. A group of Norwegian soldiers manning four machine-guns, straddled the road in front of us and we were commanded to stop and get out. Sven took over at once, explaining who we were and the usual show of passports helped matters. We gave them all the information we could, but before going on, Williams got Sven to explain to them that the position of their machine-guns would be useless against a frontal attack and that they had far better conceal them among the cover of the rocks above, to give a better command of the roadway. They saw the wisdom of this and began to deploy their defences on the slopes above the road. We rode on, and came to one of the villages before Elverum. Here we were made very welcome by the inhabitants who gave us food — I had my first taste of a sandwich made with minced raw meat. They too were eager for information, and in turn warned us that Lillehammer had already been taken by the Germans, who were fanning out southwards across our proposed path. It seemed we would never make it to Narvik.

To me it was now a case of getting out of Norway at all costs, so I asked Sven if he could take us to Sweden, hoping that the Germans would not invade there too. Sven reckoned he could, though it would involve the risks of going back to reach a point on the border which he knew. He said it was Medskogen on the Swedish side of the frontier. Everyone agreed, though we hadn't a clue where it was. So off we went. We could not have picked a finer saviour than Sven; he handled the car magnificently over those mountains and deeply wooded forests. We had arrived just outside the approach to the Swedish border when a car suddenly shot into view behind us, switching its lights on and off, and hooting at us — presumably to stop. Sven stepped on the accelerator and we slightly increased the distance between us. We were expecting to be shot at any moment and crouched down in our seats. We arrived at a long clearing in the forest, at the end of which was a striped red and white barrier manned by Swedish troops. They let us through and commanded us to stop and get out. We were immediately surrounded by soldiers and led to the Commandant's office. Looking back, I saw the car that had been following us had stopped at the barrier. There were German armed soldiers in it, but the Swedes would not let them through. The Commandant listened to our story and took our passports away. I asked him to contact the British Embassy in Stockholm for verification as to our identities. Sven, being Norwegian, was taken away, but not before all had thanked him. I, as an afterthought, asked for a piece of paper and wrote a letter addressed to 'Those British Authorities Concerned', explaining that my companions and self had been aided in our escape from Norway by Sven, who was a Norwegian officer and wished to serve with the British forces in defence of his country. This I signed as Security Officer to the British Legation in Norway, and gave it to Sven. Unfortunately, I never heard what happened to him.

After being held an hour or so, pending enquiries as to our identity, we were informed that everything was all right. We were then escorted to a small hotel, given rooms for the night and told we'd be put on a train for Stockholm the next morning.

Following a good night's rest, we reported back to the Commandant, our passports were returned and we were driven to the station. There was an obvious air of tension in Medskogen and there seemed to be an unusual number of uniformed police about for such a small town.

We were soon on our way to Stockholm, the journey lasting about four and a half hours. On arrival, we got a taxi and went straight to the Legation. The first person I met was Mr Lascelles. I was surprised to see him, being under the impression that by this time he would have been well on his way to England.

He congratulated me on my safe arrival and took me to the Minister to give an account of what had happened. When I had finished, the Minister smiled and said, 'It looks to me, Murray, the war is following you around. I think we'd better get you out of Stockholm before you bring trouble here too!'

I had barely been a week in Stockholm when I received instructions to report to the Secretary of the Legation. He called me into his room and told me to sit down. He himself stood up with a typical gesture that always

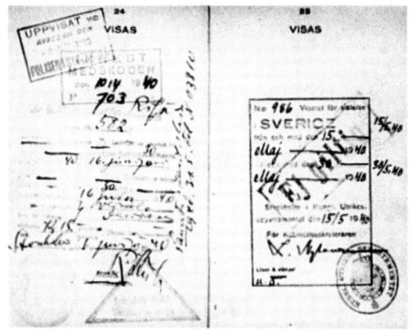

Page in the author's passport, with his Visa to Sweden, on escaping the German invasion of Norway

amused me. He'd stand, legs apart, one hand in his trousers pocket, the other holding a chain with a bunch of keys attached to it, whirling them round and round.

'There's a couple of diplomatic bags that have to go tomorrow — one is to Helsinki, the other to the Legation in Riga. Which one do you wish to take? It's up to you, Murray.'

Now my mother and father were still in Riga and I was terribly anxious to see how they were getting on; to all intents and purposes, it was logical therefore, that I should opt for the Riga run. But throughout my life I have invariably depended and acted upon intuition. It's a peculiar sense which I cannot define, and in some cases it has led me into some right messes, but then again something invariably happens to get me out of them.

'I'll take the Helsinki bag!' I said.

'All right, report tomorrow at eight, Murray, and don't be late. The boat leaves at nine.'

I turned up at the Legation the next morning in good time and was joined by the other courier. I was pleased to find that I had only one diplomatic bag to look after, whilst my fellow courier had eight bulky bags. The diplomatic bags, made of stout canvas, were sealed and studded with large brass eyelets for the purpose of ensuring that they would sink quickly should the occasion arise for throwing them overboard in the event of an impending attack. Our instructions were always simple and to the point: 'Guard them with your life and prevent them getting into the hands of the enemy!'

My colleague and I were driven in the Legation car down to the quayside and we boarded our respective ships. I could not help envying my opposite number. His ship was spanking new. A Swedish liner of about five thousand tons, sleek, dazzling white with shining brasswork. Mine was a Finnish boat, a small five hundred tonner more like an old weather-beaten converted tug.

Our boats sailed off side by side. After a couple of hours' sailing, we had cleared the islands that surround Stockholm and steamed into the open Baltic. As we reached the point where our paths diverged, the Swedish liner bearing south, and my boat heading north, the grey form of a German destroyer cut right across our bows, her heliographs blinking frantically. With many of the Finnish crew standing beside me, we watched the Swedish ship slow down.

'He's after them,' the Finnish officer standing next to me said. 'Here have a look,' and he handed me his binoculars. Peering through them I could discern my colleague on the blind side of the ship to the destroyer, hurriedly tumbling the diplomatic bags into the sea. I saw a small boat with German sailors leave the destroyer and head for the Swedish ship. I did not see the end — we steamed on fast. One thing I do know, my colleague never arrived in Riga!

The rest of the voyage was uneventful. After about eight hours we arrived in Helsinki where I was met by one of the Minister's staff and whisked off to the Legation. After delivering my bag and reporting to the Chargé d'Affaires, I was told to return the next day for further instructions.

I found things in Finland were back to normal, the war with Russia having ended in March, so I went off to Desmond's place to stay the night. He was glad to see me again and looked none the worse for his sojourn in Helsinki during the war, and we had lunch together and swapped yarns. I was very happy to hear that his wife and children had managed to reach England safely and were well. I took the opportunity of visiting Mrs Paloheimo and was shocked to learn that her husband, Arvi, had died from a heart attack during one of the air-raids on Finland. Her son, however, who had been in the Army, was alive and well. I asked her about her father, Jean Sibelius. She told me he was still going strong, although he was now getting old and more crotchety than ever. She asked me if I got the message during the early days of the Russian attack, to go down and stay with them at their country home. She had made all the arrangements to put me up and was really upset I had not replied. I told her I had been staying in the Legation and had been suddenly sent to Sweden, which was the reason I'd not got her message, which had been directed to my flat.

The next day I returned to the Legation, where I was informed that there was a diplomatic bag to be taken to Tallinn, the capital of Esthonia. A seat had been booked for me on a plane that was leaving at six the following morning, and in view of the urgency, I was to sleep in the Legation that night, so as to be ready first thing. There seemed to be a lot of activity that night. Most of the senior staff were working all night. However, I managed to get some sleep, and was up and ready well before six.

I collected my 'bag' and was leaving with one of the staff detailed to accompany me to the airport when one of the secretaries came running down the steps and called us back. It appeared an urgent despatch had just come in from London and the decoding would still take some time, and I was not to leave until further instructions. Whatever it was, it took a further three hours. Additional despatches were put into my bag, it was resealed and I was then told that I was to leave on the cross-gulf steamer at noon. The journey across the Gulf of Finland took the boat about three hours and when we arrived in Tallinn I looked in vain for the Legation official who should have been there to meet me. Not seeing anyone, I hailed a taxi and was driven to the Legation. There was some consternation at my arrival, and I was taken immediately to the Minister, Mr Gallienne.

'Thank goodness you're alive, Murray! How did you get here?'

I told him about my delay in Helsinki, still somewhat mystified what all the fuss was about.

He explained that the last message they had received from Helsinki was that I'd left on the six o'clock plane for Tallinn. They had sent one of their staff to meet me, but had been informed at the aerodrome that the plane had mysteriously blown up whilst flying over the Gulf of Finland. There had been no survivors. It was known that the plane would be carrying French and Japanese couriers as well as myself, and several foreign journalists. My name had been on the list and they had not, as yet, received any signal from Helsinki that I had been re-routed hence their surprise at seeing me.

When I recounted to him what I had seen on the voyage from Stockholm, he said he had already heard about it. My colleague had been captured aboard the Swedish ship and taken off as a prisoner of war. This was one of the reasons why he would have to send me to Riga with duplicate despatches that same night. Later that evening, I was on the train to Latvia looking forward

257

to meeting my parents again, so much had happened since I had last seen them. On the morning of 10 June 1940, I arrived in Riga.

PART III – WAR COMES TO LATVIA

The Soviet Secret Police Move In

I was met at the station by one of the junior members of the diplomatic staff and driven to the Riga Legation. I handed over my diplomatic bag and after quickly finishing with the necessary formalities and receiving instructions to stand by until called for, I hurried off to surprise my parents.

It was quite a reunion. They were relieved and overjoyed at seeing me. Soon I was sitting down again to a home-cooked meal. They were, of course, anxious to know what had been happening to me. I gave them a sketchy account, making everything sound like a normal course of duty. I did not want them to get unduly worried. Latvia was still a peaceful country and as far as outward appearances were concerned, the actual war was still far beyond their borders, though by now I was already beginning to have my doubts as to how long this would remain so.

It was nice to see some of the old faces again and as my passport was completely filled with visa stamps, I called on Glynn Hall the Vice-Consul, to get it renewed. I had known him since 1925 when I'd first come to Riga. In the course of our meeting, I mentioned that since arriving back I had seen a letter addressed to one of my acquaintances from his brother who had left Latvia for Germany and on arriving there had been enrolled in the German Army. His brother had written that he was in Peenamund, a German coastal resort in the Baltic, and his unit were carrying out exercises on the sands in preparation for desert warfare.

The author's passport signed by W. Glynn Hall, Acting British Consul, Riga

259

He did not give this information much credence, however, because at the time it did not look as though Hitler had any thoughts, or reasons, whatsoever, to embark on desert warfare.

A few days later I was called to the Legation for an interview with the Chargé d'Affaires.

'We've received a request from the Embassy in Moscow to send them a secretary for duty with the Air Attaché, Murray. Would you like to go?'

Although taken by surprise at this unexpected offer, I replied without hesitation, 'Yes, I'll go.' My assent must have been expected because I was immediately presented with a series of prepared documents for me to sign. Amongst them was a short form stipulating that as my appointment was a war-time emergency one, I would not be entitled to compensation for disablement or even loss of life incurred during the term of my employment. In other words, I took the job on at my own risk.

On querying this document, I was told that owing to the recent Soviet-German pact, His Majesty's Government could no longer guarantee the safety of its personnel on Soviet territory. I signed. The Legation undertook to procure the necessary Soviet entry visa and Latvian exit permit on my completing the application forms and supplying four photographs. I had always taken the precaution of carrying several passport photographs about with me, so there was no delay in getting that part of the procedure under way. The Ambassador in Moscow, however, had to confirm my appointment, so I was told to call back in a couple of days for final instructions.

It was with mixed feelings that I went home to acquaint my parents with the news. They took it well and we spent most of that evening speculating what it would be like to live in Moscow.

During the morning of 14 June 1940, we had an unexpected visitor — it was Mrs Rhodes, one of my mother's old friends who was married to a Latvian. She was full of excitement and as I let her into the flat she cried, 'Have you heard the news? The Bolsheviks are here. They've invaded Latvia! Oh dear, whatever will happen to us now?' and she began to weep.

I looked at my mother and father. I did not know what to say. I just felt as though the pit of my stomach was dropping out. Suddenly my mother put her arms around her old friend, 'There dear, don't go on so, it'll be all right! I'll make a cup of tea. Sit down now, there's no need to go on so.'

Finally we quietened Mrs Rhodes down. I assured her there would be no fighting and said I would go along with my father to watch the Russians march in, as it was bound to be a peaceful occupation and the Russians were not as bad as everyone thought they were.

260

Deep down inside me, though, my mind was in a whirl — the news was a shock. First Finland, then Norway, then the unbelievable news about France and Dunkirk! England itself threatened and now here, a thousand miles away from home. How was it all going to end?

I asked Mrs Rhodes how she had come to hear that the Russians were coming, and was it really true because everything outside appeared to be quiet and normal. She said she'd been round to see Mrs Bisseniek, an Englishwoman who was also married to a Latvian, who had told her that her husband had been called away in the night and had not returned home. Someone had telephoned her that very morning from the Finance Ministry to say her husband was being kept at the Ministry as the Russians were expected to march into Riga during the afternoon. She had left Mrs Bisseniek in a state of collapse and had come round to tell us the news.

I could well imagine the state Mrs Bisseniek would be in as she had good cause to fear for his safety. George Bisseniek had been the Latvian Consul in Leningrad when one of Stalin's right-hand men, Sergei Mironovitch Kirov, had been assassinated. The date was 1 December 1934. The man who shot Kirov was a Leonid Nikolayev who was said to have received aid from a foreign Consul on behalf of a 'Great Power' in order to carry out the deed. The official Soviet newspaper *Izvestia* quoted Bisseniek as being the mysterious Consul behind the affair. Bisseniek, whom I knew personally, later told me there was no truth in the allegation. What had happened was that following the assassination he had received an anonymous telephone call from a supposed well-wisher informing him that he was going to be arrested by the GPU* (The Soviet Secret Police) and charged with complicity in Kirov's murder. He was told it would be advisable to get out of Leningrad as quickly as possible. Fearing for his life he left by train that very night and returned to Latvia. The next day *Izvestia* published an article claiming that the guilty man was the Latvian Consul who had already fled the country to avoid interrogation and Soviet justice.

Mrs Bisseniek's fears proved to be well-founded, her husband was never to return home again. He was the first of many people I knew in Riga that were later to disappear.

* Readers should note that the Soviet State Security Department came under headings denoted by the following initials:

From 1922-34	- GPU
From 1934-43	- NKVD
From 1943-46	- NKGB
From 1946-53	- MGB
From 1953-onwards	- KGB

Mrs Rhodes stayed for lunch and feeling a good deal better, went off to see Mrs Bisseniek again, while my father and I went off to watch the arrival of the Russian troops.

Everything was quiet in the streets; the shops were open. The only thing that was noticeable was that there were no trams running along the *Marijas Iela* so we had to walk to the centre of the town. There were also no uniformed soldiers to be seen. This was unusual because Latvia had a large conscript Army and there were always quite a number of soldiers to be seen on the streets.

As we reached the end of the *Marijas Iela*, near the railway station, we were halted by a huge crowd of some twenty thousand or more people lining both sides of the street and spilling over on to the green verge to the left of the National Theatre. We were soon parted by the jostling, thrusting crowd, and I found myself being pushed along with the mass of people near the theatre. We had arrived just on time. Cheers and hurrahs filled the air as the first tanks came rumbling by. Over the heads of the crowd I could see the open turrets of the tanks as they swept by in one unending roar. The soldiers standing in the turrets were of small build and had swarthy Mongolian features. They looked neither right or left, staring with impassive faces straight ahead, completely ignoring the waving and cheering of the Latvians. The crowd was constantly surging backwards and forwards, breaking the thin cordon of police strung along the sides of the street. This went on for some time, when without warning, a sudden volley of shots were fired over the heads of the crowd. Those I was with panicked. Gratings surrounding the National Theatre were torn up, and before I knew where I was, I found myself jammed in one of the large manholes. With another volley of bullets spluttering overhead I could not see what was happening, but could still hear the tanks roaring on and the crowd cheering, booing and cat-calling intermittently. The firing stopped and the crowd once again surged forward to greet the tanks, whilst I jumped out of the manhole and searched the outskirts of the crowd for my father. Deciding that he had already gone home, I gave up the search and started off at the double, anxious to get back as soon as I could. To avoid the crowds, I made my way through Verman's Park adjoining the Boulevard. I passed groups of machine-guns manned by tense-faced Homeguards (The *Aizsargi*) lying in the grass, their guns trained on the approaches to the park. What they were doing there I did not know; and from the looks of them, they did not know either. Leaving the park I came into the streets which were this time quite deserted. I began to run and did not stop running until I reached home. I was relieved to find Dad had arrived before

262

me. Sensibly, he had made his way back shortly after we had been parted. We stayed up very late that night, but all was quiet, the people in the surrounding flats and houses remaining indoors.

The next morning Dad went off to work early and I went to the Legation. Life seemed normal and the shops were open as usual.

I found the Legation staff busily emptying filing cabinets and burning documents — it was the Norwegian Legation all over again. From a short conversation I had with the Secretary, I gathered all Legations and Consulates throughout Latvia had been given forty-eight hours to get out by the Russians who were in the process of annexing the Baltic States for their 'protection' as the Secretary grimly put it. When I asked what was going to happen to the rest of the British colony in Latvia, he said Glynn Hall the Vice-Consul would be left in charge, he being the only British official that the Russians would allow to remain until arrangements for evacuation had been completed by our Embassy in Moscow. He also informed me that our Embassy had confirmed my appointment, my visas had been applied for and I would be notified by the Soviet Embassy and the Riga Police Prefectura when they would be ready. All I had to do was to sit tight until I received their notification.

From the Legation I went to the British Club where I thought I might see someone with whom I could discuss the situation. The only one there was John Watson, a British timber merchant. He was a very knowledgeable chap and always seemed one ahead with all the news. He'd heard that the Colony would be evacuated to Vladivostock and thence to Australia. He said he was not surprised the Russians had been welcomed as most of the crowd would be the industrial workers who belonged to the communist-inspired Stradnieku party. He showed me the *Jaunakas Zinios* (the Latvian national newspaper). It gave a lurid account of the previous day's shooting. 'A brutal attack by the Fascist-inspired police against innocent workers who had assembled to greet their Soviet brothers and saviours,' was how they put it. It went on to say that fifteen unarmed workers had been killed before the 'authorities' could take action. 'Justice would be demanded by the workers and they could rest assured that all necessary steps would be taken to bring the guilty fascist police to book for their dastardly actions.' Other articles stressed the united efforts of all peace-loving workers and their leaders to bring the warmongering fascist element of the former government to justice.

When I left Watson I promised to return that evening for a dinner in honour of some of the Legation staff who were leaving. It was at this dinner that I met Mr Reinhardt, a young American cipher officer passing through

Riga on his way to join the American Embassy in Moscow. He had already received his visas and was due to travel with those of our Embassy staff leaving for Moscow. We had quite a friendly chat and I promised to look him up when I arrived there. The next day I went to see them all off, but was not allowed to approach the platform. The railway station was already under close guard and long queues of people with their bags and bundles were waiting about for trains to take them to their various destinations. But only those with special permits were being allowed to leave Riga.

The days passed by. I still awaited news concerning my visas. During this time changes became evident all round. My father told me that the directors in the factory had all disappeared. No one knew what had happened to them. A Commissar had been appointed to the factory whose job it was to organise 'Work Committees' and convene workers meetings. Measures were taken to ensure that the factory worked at full blast. It was compulsory for every worker to attend these meetings at which Marxist principles were expounded and the role of the Soviets in freeing the proletariat were acclaimed. Even my father who could not understand the language had to be in attendance. Marches and parades were also organised with the workers from other factories to take place on the official rest days. They were held to show the populace the solidarity and happiness of the working class. I occasionally took my mother to watch these processions and we'd cheer my father as he trudged along, hanging on to a ribbon streamer attached to one of the many huge banners depicting Lenin and Stalin. In the evenings we would pull his leg about it. But it was a thing he dared not avoid. Workers in the factory who had stubbornly refused to take part in spite of being cautioned, disappeared and were not seen again.

To all intents and purposes the banks were closed and assets frozen. Only the paying of money and limited withdrawals were allowed, while paper money became more evident.

The markets my mother used were no longer filled with innumerable stalls and tables packed with mounds of vegetables, meat, butter and other dairy produce. Instead, they gradually diminished in number and there were now only miserable small portions of everything to be seen.

On the first day the jewellers shops, of which there had been many in Riga, were locked and guarded by roughly-clad civilians wearing red armbands and armed with bayonetted rifles. The shop windows were later emptied of all jewellry and one saw them replaced with one or two shoddy alarm clocks. The big stores, one especially, the *Armijas Ekonomiskas Veikals*, were besieged by Russian soldiers purchasing everything which they

264

could lay their hands on. They seemed to have enormous sums of Latvian paper money in their possession. The stores were soon empty. In the streets quite a large number of Russians appeared, dressed in drab khaki tunics over which they wore a Sam Brown belt and holstered revolver, with baggy trousers tucked into leather knee-length field boots. They looked and seemed to act quite kindly towards the civilian population.

I often saw them sitting on benches in the Boulevard and Parks, quietly discussing and explaining the political situation to groups of ordinary citizens who would gather around them listening intently. These were the 'politicos' whose job it was to smooth over the Occupation. On the surface, life seemed to be proceeding in a well-ordered fashion. Perhaps it was because the working element of the population was kept intensely busy, all factories and industries having been ordered to carry on as usual, with the emphasis on higher production.

During the second week of the Russian Occupation, I received a telegram from Moscow. It simply read, 'Please report without delay for duty at the British Embassy Moscow — (signed) Stafford Cripps.' I decided to take the telegram and go immediately to the Prefectura and Soviet Embassy to enquire about my visas. The Police Prefectura was a large stone building just off the Boulevard and was the centre of Police administration for the whole of Riga and its suburbs. The place was packed, every ante-room was filled with men and women waiting for permits of one sort or another. Some seeking news of relatives who had disappeared; some endeavouring to procure travelling permits, and others identity documents. Armed soldiers guarded all doors and kept the crowds in order. The fact that I was a British diplomatic official counted for nothing. On managing, after much difficulty, to reach one of the inner offices, the telegram was taken from me and I was told to wait. I was put into a small waiting room by myself. After half an hour, a man in officer's uniform came in and said brusquely in English, 'Your papers are being attended to, but you must go to the Soviet Embassy, who will deal with your Soviet visa.' He gave me no chance to discuss the matter but summoned a soldier to escort me out of the building.

The Soviet Embassy was a huge white building set in its own grounds in another boulevard, running at right angles to the main boulevard, which contained many fine, imposing edifices, the former homes of the wealthy. They looked, with their shuttered windows, totally deserted. My reception at the Embassy was similar to that at the Prefectura. An impassive official took my telegram, asked if I spoke Russian to which I said no, and then questioned me in German, which I understood. His answer was brief. 'Your application is being dealt with, call again next week.'

I left and went to the main Post Office and sent a telegram to the Embassy in Moscow stating why I was held up. This was only one of the many telegrams I was subsequently permitted to send to Moscow. Only later was I to find out that the Embassy never received them.

Three days after this, at six o'clock on the evening of 9 July, I was sitting in the flat with my parents having tea when there came a knock at the door. I opened it. Two men stood outside.

They were an unusual looking couple. One was an elderly man of small compact build, grey-haired, clean-shaven, wearing metal-rimmed spectacles behind which a pair of slate grey eyes fixed me with an unblinking stare. His face was long and narrow, the skin ashy-grey, but heavily pitted with pock marks. The other man was younger, about thirty-five years of age, heavily built, with a large full-moon face, also clean-shaven. He had the swarthy look of a Georgian Russian with large round black eyes, longish straight hair which was black and greasy. He wore an ordinary working man's check cloth cap on his head. Both, however, wore grey gaberdine coats, much too long for them, and their shoes were long and very pointed in the fashion of the 'twenties'. They seemed to glide rather than walk normally.

It was the younger man who addressed me, 'Are you Mister Murray?' He spoke English with a heavy American, nasal twang.

'Yes,' I nodded.

'Can we talk with you?' he said.

'Yes, come in,' I invited. I took them in and introduced them to my parents. My mother instantly offered them a cup of tea, but they refused. They sat down with their headgear still on. I asked what I could do for them. It was the younger man who continued:

'Can you speak Russian?' he enquired.

Although I knew a fair amount of Russian, I decided on the spur of the moment to say no, but added, I could speak German besides English. I also complimented him on his perfect English, which I noted pleased him. 'My companion does not speak English, only Russian,' he said, and the other man evidently understanding, nodded his head in agreement. He went on. 'We are from the Russian tobacco industry and heard you have a tobacco factory in this country.'

'I did have, but not now,' I answered.

'But you know about Russian tobaccos, don't you?'

'Oh, yes, I used them in my tobacco blends. The Yalta, Souchoum, Namhun and Kuban are the best Russian tobaccos I know of and they make very good cigarettes,' I replied, wanting to appear friendly. He translated my remarks to his companion and they both smiled approvingly. The younger man then looked at his watch and said,

'We have to go now, but we would like to talk further with you. Perhaps we could have dinner together tonight — Yes?'

Not wishing to appear rude to my unexpected guests, I thanked them for their invitation and although feeling somewhat uneasy, was nevertheless curious to find out what they meant by 'further talk'. We shook hands and as they left, the spokesman for the two turned to me and said, 'Good, we will call for you tonight at eleven o'clock and we shall have a nice evening together.'

After they had gone, my father remarked, 'They're a couple of queer customers, aren't they?'

'Yes,' I said, 'they are queer customers, but they're Russians and things being what they are, it's as well to keep on the right side of them, anyway.'

I explained to my parents that they were Russian tobacco industrialists and that they had invited me out to dinner that night. When I said they were calling for me at eleven, they remarked that it was a pretty odd hour of night for dinner. They would have thought it odder still had they known what I knew! My unease had been caused by the fact that in listing the names of the Russian tobaccos I had mentioned the name 'Namhun' which was a Chinese tobacco leaf and one which any tobacco man would have known was not Russian. They had not even commented on this fact. So, they were not tobacco industrialists.

At eleven o'clock sharp, there was a knock at our door and there were my two guests to take me out. Waiting outside the house was a large black limousine complete with chauffeur. 'This is our car, we'll ride to the restaurant, nice and comfortable, eh!' my companion said. We drove through the by now quiet and deserted streets to the centre of the city and stopped outside the Caucasia restaurant. This was a basement restaurant well known for its cuisine. You went down steps, along a passage leading to a large circular room, surrounded by a series of intimate alcoves across which curtains could be drawn. The centre of the dance floor had a raised platform for the orchestra. The furnishings were rich and lush, the lighting soft. It was a notorious locale for tired businessmen and their lady friends. This night, however, although the orchestra of five performers was playing, the place seemed deserted. We were conducted to an alcove by a very attentive waiter and sat down to a table already loaded with a choice selection of hors d'oeuvres. The remainder of the meal consisted of steaks of fresh salmon with all the trimmings, followed by ice-cream and coffee. The only time my hosts smiled was when I insisted on only drinking tonic water instead of the spirits and wines that were offered.

They really enjoyed their food and were not sparing with the drink either. I enjoyed mine, too, in spite of feeling a bit queasy. In the beginning, the conversation was just a series of commonplace remarks which, in between gaps, had to be translated and relayed back and forth. Nothing was mentioned about tobaccos and I was beginning to wonder what this meeting was all about when suddenly I was asked if I would like to work for the Soviet tobacco industry? To this unexpected question, I replied that much as I might like to, I was already engaged by my government to work at the British Embassy in Moscow and was awaiting daily my visas. There was a long pause and the younger man fixed me with a steady stare. 'We know all about you!' This abrupt change in manner and tone had me non-plussed.

'What has that to do with me,' I countered. 'I don't know anything about you, not even your names.'

He ignored my interruption and repeated, 'Yes, we know all about you. You were in Koenigsberg in July 1930; in December the same year you were in Berlin—' and without pausing, went on to rattle off dates and names of various cities and countries I had visited during the past ten years, many of which I had already forgotten about. The details were amazing. I was quite taken aback at this sudden change in the conversation and was beginning to wonder where it was all leading to. I interrupted him and said, 'Look here, I don't know what you're talking about. Anywhere I have been is my business. What has it got to do with you?'

'No? But I only want to show you that we know all about you. Everything!'

With that he banged the table service bell. A waiter appeared, the older man scribbled on a chit of paper, gave it to him and was dismissed by a wave of his hand. They then both rose from the table, simply said, 'Goodnight,' and left me sitting there. Just like that, one word and they were gone. I wondered what was going to happen next. I looked at my watch; it was already three a.m. I got up and walked out. As I made my way home through the deserted streets, I heard the sound of footsteps coming from some distance behind me. I surmised I was being followed, but try as I would, I could not get a glimpse of my follower. Our house was in a kind of cul-de-sac off the *Artillerijas Iela*. An armed soldier stood on duty at the top of the

268

street. He made no move to stop me as I passed and just gave me a cursory glance. I had a feeling of disquiet, nevertheless, as it dawned upon me that now our street was under surveilance.

Over a week went by and still I could get no news about the granting of my visas and visits to the Soviet Embassy were met with curt dismissals. Once I observed the figure of the elder man framed in a top window of the Embassy watching me when I called. I became aware also that I was being followed whenever I went out. The armed soldier was still evident at the top of the street; even my mother noticed him. I told mother not to worry as it was for our protection. It was an assurance I did not feel. Our house which contained fifteen flats was now almost empty — the occupants had, one by one, been collected on various nights. The procedure had always been the same. At about midnight, a covered lorry would come noisily down the street, six or seven armed soldiers would jump out and enter the house. We would hear banging and shouting through the curtains, and we'd see our former neighbours helped into the lorry – a few bundles thrown in after them and off the lorry would go again. We never knew much about them beyond the fact that they were some kind of civil servants, mostly youngish couples, who kept very much to themselves. The atmosphere was unpleasant and though we did not talk about it, I knew my parents were feeling the strain, and this was one of the reasons why I did not go out much. I was frightened something might happen whilst I was out. The landlord who had always collected the rent personally, also disappeared and in his place a house porter was appointed to collect the rent and live in one of the flats. This man appeared one day with a house book which we had to sign stating name, nationality, place of birth, and place of employment.

I received another telegram from Moscow. It was from the Embassy stating that I should report for immediate duty urgently. No mention was made of my previous explanatory telegram to them. I went to the Post Office and tried to telephone the Embassy, but they said there was no telephone communication with Moscow, but I could send a telegram, which I did, guardedly explaining that I was still awaiting my exit visa from Latvia and the Soviet Embassy's entry visa for Moscow; adding that they should try and hurry things up for me over there. As the days went by, I began to feel despondent. Somehow I knew that my telegrams were not reaching Moscow, but why were the telegrams from Moscow being permitted to reach me? It was a question I could not answer. Every time I went to the Prefectura and the Soviet Embassy I was either deliberately fobbed off with some excuse and passed on from one official to another or requested to call at a later date.

It was an impasse I could not break through. Sometimes I was not even allowed to enter the buildings which teemed with armed military-clad officials.

I called occasionally at the British Club which was also depressing. There were reports that the Club was to be shut down, but the Secretary declared he would remain in residence and never leave, stoutly maintaining it was British property, built on British soil. This was quite true, the English Church and adjoining Club had been built with materials and on soil brought specially over from England many years ago by members of the British Colony to ensure that there would always be a little part of England on the shores of the Baltic.

No one there had any news from the Embassy in Moscow: all communications for the time being dead.

I was returning from the Club one afternoon when I met my two Russians at the top of our street. I greeted them and they stopped me. The young man shook my hand and said, 'We are going to call for you tonight and we shall have a nice dinner, you understand?' The last bit was said in quite an authoritative tone.

I just nodded. I felt more depressed than ever. These were not ordinary people. It was very disturbing and all I could do was wait and see what it was all about.

Again they called for me at eleven o'clock at night. The car was the same and we drove to the same restaurant as before. There was no orchestra playing at the Caucasia that evening. All was silent and deserted. We spoke very little during the meal which consisted of several courses of the most extravagant food, superbly cooked and served. The two Russians were good trenchermen and obviously enjoyed their food. I still refused wine and spirits and stuck to soft drinks which again made them smile. No reference was made to our previous dinner, and I was racking my brain to think up something to keep the conversation going when the elder man, who as usual had hardly spoken a word, turned to his companion and said in Russian, 'Enough, give it to him hard, we have wasted enough time already!' I gave no indication that I had understood what had been said, and waited enquiringly for the younger man to translate what had been said, knowing full well he would not. He sat back, took out a packet of cigarettes, offered me one which I accepted, took one himself, and we lit up. Then, turning to me, said, 'We know everything about you.'

'Well, what of it, you've told me that before.'

Ignoring my remark, he continued, 'You are poor, we can give you much money.' He waved his cigarette expansively, 'Anywhere in the world, London, New York, South America, in any currency you like.' He waited to see what I would say. There was nothing for me to say other than the obvious.

'You say you are going to give me money, eh, and what have I to do for this money?'

He spoke very slowly, 'You are going to your Embassy in Moscow, yes? You will be doing much writing in your work; it is nothing, just simple — you make an extra copy of your work and we shall collect it and pay you much money, anywhere, to any bank you like.'

I felt sick. Then this was what it was all about. I was in the hands of the Russian secret service. I felt cornered, isolated. The proposition was monstrous. I decided to put up a show and brazen it out. I stood up, and fear gave way to an uncontrollable fit of anger.

'See here, I don't want to know what you are talking about. Also, I don't want to know you, and I wish I'd never met you,' I shouted, and with that strode to the curtains and tore them apart to get out. Two soldiers with crossed rifles and bayonets barred my path. The younger man leapt to his feet, towering above me he put one hand on my shoulder and flung me back into my seat, whilst the other calmly got up and drew the curtains to again.

'We are talking to you — you understand? This is not the time for comic operatics. Listen to what I have to say —' I interrupted him,

'Yes, you want me to be a traitor to my country.'

'Your country, pah! You are not even British,' he countered.

'Yes, I am. I was born and bred in England and it is my country.'

'Ah, born and bred in England,' he mimicked. 'If you're born in a stable that doesn't make you a donkey.'

'Well, look at you, you're not even proper Russians,' I countered. He ignored this gibe and spread out his hands placatingly.

'Don't be silly, this is business, a simple business proposition, what is the reason for getting angry about it? Just be calm and think about it. Perhaps you will change your mind. What have you to lose? Your country, Great Britain is finished. The Germans have beaten your armies and soon they will invade your country.'

'No,' I said. 'There are tens of millions of people in Britain, much better than me and they will not only fight, but in the end they will defeat Germany.'

'It is not so, your country is finished. It is us, the Soviets who will smash Germany, and it is so. Only the armies of the Soviet will defeat the German

271

barbarians, and then you English will be our friends! Think again. What have you to lose?'

'I have nothing more to say,' I said, and shook my head and relapsed into a sullen silence.

The two men carried on a rapid discussion in a dialect I could not understand. Finally, the older man took out a piece of paper from his pocket, gave it to his companion who handed it to me with a fountain pen.

'We will not waste any more time with you,' he said. 'You will write down on this paper what I dictate to you and sign it with your name.'

'I am not writing or signing anything,' I said.

'You will do as I say or you do not leave here. Do you understand that?'

I knew that there was no way out of the situation. Besides, I felt tired and sick with worry.

'All right, tell me what you want me to write.'

He dictated slowly and I wrote the following:

'I, John Murray, the undersigned, will not communicate or divulge to anyone the meetings and conversations I have had with the representatives of the Soviet Union Tobacco Industry. Should I do so, then I understand that I will be liable for whatever punishment will be carried out against me.' I paused before signing it.

'Go on, sign your name.'

'No,' I said, 'I will sign it if it is necessary, but first you must promise me that I will get my visas without any more trouble, so that I can join my Embassy in Moscow. As you have said this is a private business matter between us, I won't mention it to anyone — not even to my superiors, and I always keep my word.'

'Don't worry, you'll get your visas, but you must sign the paper now. We are not waiting here all night.'

I signed.

The pock-faced man took the paper, folded it up and put it in his pocket wallet. We rose from the table, the younger man escorted me past the sentries who stood rigidly to attention, and at the door he stopped and put his hand on my shoulder.

'Don't worry, everything will be all right, but think carefully. You love your mother and father; it would not be pleasant for them to be sent to a labour camp. Think about it, and let us know when you meet us again. We shall wait for you in the restaurant at Verman's Park at eight o'clock on Sunday evening. Do not be late!' With that he ushered me out.

My head swam as I walked the deserted streets. It was four a.m. and already beginning to get light. I neither cared nor feared whether I was followed that morning. The whole situation was so unreal, except the threat uttered about Mum and Dad. That was real. I thought about the paper I'd signed — I had really meant it when I said I would tell no one, but would they keep their promise about getting my visas granted?

Once in Moscow I'd have the Embassy to help me, but would they now let me go? Deep down inside I knew the Russians would not keep their promise; the only consolation I had was that it would at least free me from mine. But what could I do? I hadn't the faintest idea.

The days that followed were a nightmare. I jumped at every knock at the door and shivered when a car came down the street. I accompanied my mother every time she went out shopping and waited anxiously every day for my father's return from work. Meanwhile, I had to hide my anxiety from them. They, poor souls, never lacked courage but I did not want to add further to their unspoken fears about the future. Nevertheless, we managed to hold on to our bit of sense of humour, chivvying Dad about his procession, and Mam singing, 'He bore on high a banner bearing a strange device Excelsior, Excelsior!' Sometimes I'd say — 'I don't know what we are doing stuck in this place,' and my mother would remark, 'It's a funny old world John, but don't worry, it'll all come out right in the end.'

We had a Telefunken radio and the news was not always bright, but Churchill's speeches and the link with England gave us great comfort. All radios, by the way, were supposed to have been handed in to the authorities. I said that as we were foreigners and couldn't understand the various decrees that were made, we'd just plead ignorance if anyone came about our set. We were never troubled on this score, however.

It was by now the end of August — the five days to my next meeting with the Russians soon passed.

As I was getting ready to go out that evening, my mother asked me where I was going, and I told her that I had to meet our 'queer friends' at Verman's Park Restaurant. As I was going out, my mother looked at me searchingly, 'Well, John, be careful now, and don't do anything you would be ashamed of afterwards!'

I arrived at the Verman's Park Restaurant dead on time. This was a popular restaurant set in the midst of a small park adjacent to the State Opera House. Though many of the cafés and restaurants were closed, this one was still open. Not surprisingly, there were very few people in it, and I sat down at a corner table and ordered a lemonade. It was not that I was a teetotaller, it was just that a clear head seemed to me the most important thing. I waited. The minutes passed by. It was already half-past eight. I kept a watch on the doors and looked round at the other tables and still my Russians did not appear. I was wondering about this when a very young and most attractive young woman, heavily perfumed, with a glass of wine in her hand, glided up to my table.

'Can I sit at your table?' she asked, in faultless German. 'You look so miserable sitting there alone. Perhaps you would like to dance?' It was so obvious, I guessed at once that she had appeared in place of my two Russians, so I decided to play up to her for the time being.

The dances in those days were the tangos and foxtrots. You held your partner in your arms — close or otherwise as occasion demanded. This was a foxtrot — she held me close, with soft perfumed hair brushing my cheek. Her body was soft. Our steps seemed to match perfectly. Her dress, low cut but long, was of a blue silky material that clung close to the shape of her figure. We returned to our seats and after I had offered her a cigarette, she looked appealingly at me from out of a pair of soft limpid brown eyes, 'I'm so tired, would you like to see me home, we could perhaps have a little drink together?'

So my suspicions were confirmed. I thought it best to get out as quickly as possible. I looked at my watch. 'I'm sorry, thank you for your kind invitation, but I have to meet someone and am late already.' With that, without waiting for any comment, I got up quickly and went home.

The following day another telegram arrived from the Embassy in Moscow: 'Cannot understand your delay in reporting for duty stop you are to proceed to Moscow immediately — Stafford Cripps.' I decided to send an answer, once again explaining my difficulties with my travel permits, and then proceed to the Prefectura to complain about the delay in granting my visas. Arriving at the Prefectura I demanded to see the head of the Visa Department. This time I was told to remain in the waiting room, which was packed with Latvian subjects, mostly poorly clad, some holding small babies and others bundles which I supposed contained all their earthly belongings. From what I heard in the hubbub of conversation going on, many had been waiting weeks for permission to return to their homes in the country. I had to wait nearly two hours before a policeman came to escort me to a room deep in the interior of the building.

We had to pass through endless guarded corridors to reach the room. Before me sat a high-ranking officer at a table on which were a file and a pile of papers. There was also a large black revolver lying on the table to the left of him. He spoke in English.

'What do you want?' he snapped. I told him I was from the British Diplomatic Service and had come about my visa to Moscow.

'You get no visa from here. You are a spy!' he shouted.

'Me, a spy? Don't be ridiculous. You know it's not true!'

'Yes, you are a spy — a German spy, and you will be shot!'

I was shaken. 'If you touch me, you will be held responsible by my Embassy —' I began. But he interrupted me, shouting —

'Yes, you are spying for the Germans. We have the papers to prove you are a double agent and when we have shot you, we will send the documents to your Embassy to prove it. They will be only too pleased to know we have found you out. Do you understand what I say?'

It was my death sentence, I knew it! My knees seemed to be buckling from under me. But the one dominant thought that overrode all others was that at all costs I must not betray the fear I felt.

'Go on, shoot me then. Shoot me now,' I blurted out in desperation.

'No, we'll shoot you when we are ready, not when you want,' he sneered.

'You go home now,' he commanded.

With that I was led out of the building without another word being spoken.

When I got home I went straight to my room and locked the door. I wanted to be alone. I tried to recall all the events leading to the situation I was in. The fact that I could be hauled off at any time, shot in the back of the head and dumped in some God-forsaken hole was terrifying enough, but what of my parents? Poor, innocent, harmless old folk, no one to help them. What would happen to them? I felt on the verge of insanity. I could see no way of escape — only the black horror of it all.

Now I am not religious in the accepted sense. I believe in God. A church of any denomination is to me the same — a place where one goes to commune with oneself in silence. My philosophy from being quite a young man had been that we and everything are one with God; we are part of God and of Him, and we should live according to the light of the conscience we have been given. For those that require ritual, let them be; for those that require hymns and music, let them be; for all is the creation of God's expression. In my case, I had devised a technique, which I used whenever I had reached the uttermost depths of hopeless despair. I had first used it in 1932 to blot out my grief when on returning home I found my sister laid out dead, the first close death that I had ever experienced. It was such a shock, so

275

unexpected, she was gone, never to be recalled. I had recourse to use it again on a winter flight to Finland in 1938 when as a lone passenger in a small de Havilland biplane flying over the gulf of Finland in a blinding snowstorm, buffeted by the winds, we ran into trouble and chances of survival were minimal. The technique I used was to sing silently to myself over and over again my own version of the first two lines of the hymn —

Oh God our help in ages past our hope
for years to come...
For never ending Thou art God and our
eternal hope. Amen.

I sang this continually until my mind was conditioned to a state of mute nothingness, and so I would go on and on until nothing seemed to matter any more. When I returned once again to normality I always found that I could carry on in a kind of ice-cold logical manner that would brook no deviation either to the right or left of the path I decided to take. This may seem in a way callous, but it was the only way I knew of effecting a complete shutting out of all thoughts that could disturb my mental balance. It was a technique I only used in times of extreme urgency. I now called on it again to relieve the pressure I was feeling. 'Don't think about anything, John,' I said to myself. 'Nothing can touch you... Oh God our help...'

Two hours later I felt as if I was another person. I felt a kind of superiority to everyone and everything around me. So, the Russians had broken their promise to me! Now it was my turn. I felt a kind of righteous freedom to act in the way I thought correct. Up to this moment I had been afraid to meet or speak with anyone in case it would precipitate further action by the Soviet Agents and bring trouble to anyone I spoke to. It was for this reason I had avoided contact with any of my friends since the two mysterious Russians had called upon me. I decided I'd go and see Glynn Hall and tell him the whole story. I arrived at the Legation building without hindrance. It seemed deserted, so I banged hard on the door. It was opened by Mrs Glynn Hall herself. She looked very distraught and her eyes were puffed with recent tears.

'Oh, Mr Murray, I'm so glad to see you. Come in,' she cried.

'Can I see Glynn? It's very important,' I said.

'But he's ill, very ill. Oh I'm glad you've come. I don't know what to do with him.' And she burst into tears.

I followed her into one of the rooms. It was bare with just one long table in the centre. In the far corner of the room, crouched and doubled up, swaying from side to side, his hands clasped around his head, was Glynn Hall. He was whimpering, 'Don't let them get me! Don't let them take me away!' On and on he repeated the same words. I went over to him and patted his shoulder. 'Don't worry old chap, it's only me, Murray – no one will get you.' His eyelids were moving up and down in one continuous flicker – he could not look at me as he kept repeating the same thing until his voice dropped to an unintelligible mumble. He did not even recognise me. It was unbelievable! I saw that it would be hopeless to try and get any normal response from him. I turned to Mrs Hall and asked her how he came to be in such a state. She told me that some weeks previously, two strange men had called upon them. They were closeted with her husband for some time. When they left, she had found him in a state of collapse. Since then he had attempted to commit suicide and she had to watch over him all the time. I asked her if anyone from our own people had called, and she mentioned John Watson who had been very helpful and was a constant visitor. As he was what I called a 'senior member' of the British colony in Riga, I knew she was in good hands. Then I asked her to describe what her two visitors looked like. Her description fitted that of the two Russians I'd got to know so well. I comforted her as best I could, saying that it was all right, the Embassy in Moscow would protect them, so she was not to worry.

I went home and tried to think things out. To me it was evident that they had attempted to recruit him too, and he had broken down under the strain. Whatever it was, by the time I had got home, I realised that I would have to do something other than just sit around and wait. Mrs Hall's mention of Watson had struck a chord in my memory. I knew John fairly well. Many years ago when I had first met him, it was whispered to me that besides being the manager of a Riga plywood mill, he was also a British secret service agent who had served in the First World War. It was not the thing in the British colony to speak or ask further questions about, you just accepted it. I decided I would make an attempt to contact him before it was too late.

We lived in a street called *Dainos Iela*, which was really only half a street. At the back of our house and at the end was a derelict building site. That evening I waited until after midnight and crept out of the flat along the corridor to the back window of the house which overlooked the building site and got out. Luckily, it was a thundery and overcast summer's night, and quite dark. Even now, I don't know how I managed to make that journey to

Tornakalns, which was a suburb some two miles from where I lived, without being picked up by the night patrols. But make it I did.

It was about three a.m. when I reached the quiet suburb of Tornakalns where Watson lived. After some prolonged discreet tapping on the front windows the door was opened after I'd whispered through the letter box who I was.

'Christ Almighty man! What brings you here at this time of night?'

'I'm going to be shot so I thought I'd better see you first.'

He looked at me incredulously and then said, 'This calls for a drink. What'll you have?'

Over a couple of stiff whiskies I told him my story, beginning with the visit I had had from the two Russian so-called tobacco men, and my recent call on Glynn Hall. John said he knew about Glynn Hall's condition. He had, in fact, managed to get a permit for him and his wife to leave Latvia for Sweden, but on the way to the aerodrome Glynn had become unmanageable and had attempted to commit suicide by throwing himself out of the car. I then explained why I had not been around for fear of implicating other people in my troubles. I said that if he could somehow get a message through to Moscow about my plight, I'd be very grateful. I also added that in the event of my disappearance, would he keep an eye on my parents for me, and lastly, should any documents turn up incriminating me as a double agent and German spy, would he see that it was made known that they were forgeries. He told me not to worry. I did not stay long as I had to get back before daylight. On leaving he bade me keep a stiff upper lip and wished me the best of luck, promising that he would see to things for me.

I got home safely and felt that a great load had been lifted off my shoulders — my troubles were at last shared. I slept solidly for twelve hours — the first real sleep I'd had for months.

The next three weeks passed by without anything untoward happening. I made no further attempts to approach the authorities concerning my visas to leave the country. I knew it would be useless. I rarely went out and if I did, never went far from home. The news over the radio from England was far from heartening, but we were all convinced that everything would come out all right in the end and Churchill's broadcasts really bucked us up. How were things in Riga at this time? To me they seemed passably normal.

On the whole, food was still available, but gone was the super-abundance; it was noticeable that all canned goods had disappeared and small queues were beginning to be evident in the shops. The services ran normally in Riga itself. Travelling by train was, however, very restricted. The streets had lost that bustle of humanity. Noticeable was the lack of younger men, where before one had seen young conscripts mingling among the populace, now there were none to be seen. Most of the cafés and restaurants were closed but some were still open and patronised by nondescript middle-aged people. The only time I saw younger people, was when they turned out in organised demonstration marches, and these were the workers. I often wondered what had happened to the tens of thousands or so of young military conscripts that had been under arms at the time of the Occupation.

The newspapers — the Lettish *Jaunakas Zinas* which was the largest and most popular one, the emigré Russian *Segodnya Vyecherom* still appeared but in a much reduced tabloid form. They now no longer dealt with the normal newsy topics, instead they were filled with articles extolling the might of the Soviet Union, the brotherly co-operation of the Lettish people, their security from war under Soviet protection, eulogies to Stalin; the constant achievements of the workers in industry and on the land. It was all so childishly written and repetitive that many papers lay in the kiosks unsold.

As I reviewed the hopelessness of my situation, the dominating fear of what would happen to my parents once the Russians had dealt with me, gave way to a bitter rage. That they would shoot me I had no doubt whatever, and I determined that when the time did come I would not be taken like the Letts I had seen, bundled helplessly into a truck to be carted away for slaughter, if I was going to die, then I'd take as many of my would-be executioners with me. I knew it was not their way to collect victims in broad daylight, this kind of work was left to special squads — lorry loads of armed soldiers at midnight.

I already had in my possession a small but deadly Belgium automatic pistol which I'd thought it wise to acquire whilst in Norway after the Nord Express incident. I decided to use this and made plans accordingly. My bedroom was at the end of the passage in the flat, so one evening after my parents had retired for the night I fixed up a photo flash in front of my bedroom door that would light up the passage for just a split second, it was all I needed. I then left the front door off the latch so that entry would present no obstacle, put out the lights and waited, half-concealed in the bedroom doorway. I reckoned that I could rake the passageway with at least one burst of fire aided by the flash which I hoped would put the soldiers off guard for a second or two. It would be all I required. I took up this vigil night after night, from the moment my mother and father retired until the hours of early dawn. Somehow I derived a feeling of grim satisfaction with the role I had adopted, even taking a flash picture of myself at the ready and fixing my camera so there could be one picture of the final scene when it transpired. As far as I

279

was concerned it was to be 'Custer's Last Stand'. But it was not to be. The unexpected happened!

At ten a.m. on 19 October 1940, a car drew up outside our house. The man who stepped out and came into our flat was Henderson, the official interpreter to the British Embassy in Moscow. He informed me that Sir Stafford Cripps' private secretary, Geoffrey Wilson, together with another member of the Embassy had just arrived and were staying at the Rome Hotel. He had been sent to fetch me there. I was so relieved I could have wept. In next to no time I was in a room in the 'Rome' and being introduced. 'We hear you've been having trouble, Murray, tell us all about it and we'll draw up a statement which you'll

The author at the start of his long vigil in Latvia

sign,' were the first words addressed to me by Geoffrey Wilson.

I gave them a brief account of what had happened to me since the Soviet Occupation. It was written down whilst I recounted my experiences. I signed it, then Wilson said we would go to the Prefectura at once. On arriving there, we were immediately shown into the presence of the head of the Visas Department. I've always had a sense of humour and I really saw the funny side of the interview view that took place. The official that we spoke to was Russian. Before he could say anything, Henderson adopted a bullying tone. Speaking in Russian, he said it was contrary to all regulations for a British subject, and member of His Britannic Majesty's Government to have been denied a visa to join his Embassy, and the Ambassador in Moscow would be compelled to make an official protest to the Kremlin. He mentioned nothing, however, about the incidents I had recounted. The Prefect we saw said he was sorry but the whole thing was due to a mistake on Mr Murray's part. He had certainly filled in the application forms, but had done so incorrectly, and furthermore Mr Murray did not need a visa but was free to travel to Moscow any time. All Mr Murray had to do was to submit his passport for stamping. In fact if he had it with him, the visas would be granted there and then. Henderson asked me, in English, to produce my passport, which I did, and it

280

was taken off me and returned within a few minutes duly stamped with one all-embracing visa, both to leave Latvia and enter the Soviet Union via the Russian frontier town of Bigosova. It was also decided in conjunction with the officials that I leave Riga on the next train for Moscow, which would be the following day at four p.m.

We left the Prefectura and I was driven home. On the way I asked how it came about they'd come to Riga. Wilson said that actually they'd come to make arrangements for the evacuation of the British colony out of Latvia and the neighbouring states of Esthonia and Lithuania and that they would be staying on for a few days. I refrained from asking if they had known of my plight beforehand. Reaching home, Wilson said that I was not to worry, he'd be seeing me in Moscow, and that Henderson would be calling the following day to see me on to the train.

Arriving home, I told my mother the good news, explaining that it was through a mistake that my visa had been withheld, but now it was all right. That evening, when Dad came home, we sat quietly and talked of the future. I said that once in Moscow I would try and get them out of Latvia. They did not think it would be possible, but I said that one of the directors of my former Finnish firm, Sumer Limited, lived in Constantinople and that I would endeavour to get in touch with him to see if they could live in Constantinople. They both agreed that would be fine if I could arrange it. Then I said that if the postal service was normal between Riga and Moscow, I would write to them once a week and they could write to me. I pointed out that as sealed letters would be delayed by censorship, it would be best to write only on plain postcards, and only write to say how well things were going in Latvia. Should they be having any difficulties, they were to mention that 'the weather was bad', and I would understand and do something about it. They understood me.

Mother, as practical as ever, said, 'It will be cold in Moscow, you must get a good overcoat.' So I said that I would call in and see Mr Jakobson our family tailor and ask him if he could help me.

Early the next morning, I hurried off to see Elias Jakobson, owner of a large clothing business. He was an old friend of ours. When I had the cigarette factory, I used to make a special brand of cigarettes for him, imprinted with his name. When I reached the shop, he was serving behind the counter. 'Look, it has come to this, times have changed,' he sadly remarked. He explained that his business now no longer belonged to him but was in the hands of the works committee who had allowed him to stay on as a counter-hand. Most of his business was now making things for the Russians and their families who were arriving in Latvia, and it was for this reason they were allowed to obtain further stocks of textiles. I told him I was leaving for Moscow and would need a warm winter coat. He disappeared into a back room and came out bearing a beautifully-made padded black coat with a large beaver skin fur collar. 'I made this for myself,' he said, 'you take it, I don't think I'll be needing it now.' He absolutely refused to take the full value of the coat, so I paid him a nominal sum which was duly entered on my passport — in accordance with the newly-passed sales regulations. The coat was to give me good service throughout the time I was in Russia. As he was the same build as myself, it was a perfect fit. When I brought it home, my parents were cheered up by it.

The author in Riga, October 1940, before leaving for Moscow

Henderson called for me later that afternoon, and after saying goodbye to Dad and Mam we drove off to the station. Henderson saw me on to the train. I had practically a whole coach to myself, and the five or six Russian officers who shared the coach had separate compartments. It was about five p.m. as the train steamed out of the station. There seemed to be more goods wagons than passenger coaches to the train. At about midnight, we arrived at the frontier station of Bigosova and a porter appeared and motioned me to get out on to the platform. It was a miserable deserted station and consisted of a long wooden building dividing the two main tracks with wooden roofing jutting out over the platforms. My baggage and passport were collected from me, and I was by pantomime gestures, given to understand that I was to remain where I was until called for. I was not allowed to be present at the examination of my suitcases of which I had three. It was a wet, chilly October night, and I must have paced up and down smoking innumerable cigarettes for nearly two hours. There was no buffet and not even a waiting room. The lighting must have consisted of forty-watt bulbs it was so murky and dark. In the end, the porter approached and led me to the other platform where a second train was standing.

The coach I was conducted to was a big roomy, luxurious affair. My compartment had carpet and curtains; an upper bunk with clean sheets and blankets already prepared; and there was much gleaming solid brasswork evident. A small door at the side led to a sumptuously-appointed washroom with toilet. The woodwork was of richly-hued mahogany. I surmised that it was a luxury coach from the old Tsarist times, the furnishings and fittings being so obviously old-fashioned. A sliding door led into the corridor and soon the conductor appeared carrying my baggage. Having deposited my luggage, he went away and shortly returned with my passport and what was most welcome, a glass of hot pale tea with a slice of lemon floating on top. I had no money, but offered him a couple of packets of cigarettes which he accepted gratefully with a smile.

This coach, like the other, did not carry many passengers. The same officers, augmented by three or four more, were the only other travellers. They seemed to be picked from a special branch. Dressed similarly in smart uniforms and top boots, they stood about six foot, and must have weighed in the region of two hundred pounds. All were clean-shaven with close cropped hair. They made no attempt to speak to me as they passed the door of my compartment at intervals.

I was naturally very curious to see what Russia was like, but it was hopeless trying to peer through the double-glazed windows. There was only inky blackness outside which accentuated the reflection of the interior of my compartment like an impenetrable mirror. My mother had packed me a nice selection of sandwiches and after munching some of them, I turned in and went to sleep. This was not difficult. The comforting warmth of the coach and the steady rolling motion of the carriage, soon lulled me off into quite a deep sleep. It was eleven o'clock the next morning when the conductor woke me up with a welcome glass of tea and lemon, which was terrifically refreshing. It is amazing how dry and parched one's throat and mouth become when travelling all night in a train. I got up, washed, dressed myself and once again concentrated on having a look at the country through which I was travelling. So this is Russia! I thought as I gazed through the window.

The weather was grey and drizzly. For long periods we passed through thick pine forests, and when we emerged into the open there was nothing but vast expanses of uncultivated land with here and there an occasional

283

homestead to be seen. I never caught a glimpse of either cattle, sheep or horses. To me it looked a strange, forbidding, desolate sort of country. As the hours passed by, we did stop at a number of stations — weather-beaten wooden shacks, all unpainted and sadly in need of repair. There were no towns or even villages surrounding them. They looked as though they had been planted indiscriminately in the deserted countryside. Huddled in groups along the platforms were groups of peasants and working people. It was difficult to tell the men from the women, except the women had kerchiefs drawn tightly round their faces. They were all clad in dirty and greasy, padded three-quarter-length coats. They wore knee-length thick felt boots with rubber over-shoes. They seemed to wear all their wardrobe on their backs, their appearance was so fat and cumbersome. All had bundles tied up in cloth with bits of rope and straps. I did not observe one suitcase among them. As the train stopped, there was inevitably a free-for-all scramble to board the train and much shouting and pandemonium; none, however, approached the coach I was in — it was avoided like the plague! The same scene was repeated whenever we stopped at a station. The hours soon passed by and darkness fell at about four in the afternoon.

It must have been ten o'clock that night when the train finally steamed into Moscow's Baltic Station. At least this station was properly lit up and I peered anxiously through the window, wondering who would be there to meet me.

PART IV – THE SPY CALLED SWALLOW

The train stopped. It was hard to believe that I was at last in Moscow. Through the window I could see crowds of people swarming around the passengers alighting from the coaches at the further end of the train. The fact that there was an empty space in front of my coach, except for one of the NKVD officers who stood around, made the contrast very noticeable. Then, through the barrier opposite, two figures approached. To my surprise, I recognised one as Mr Bagshawe who I had met on a couple of occasions in Helsinki. He was the Secretary to the Naval Attaché in Moscow and sometimes came to Finland with the diplomatic bag on courier duty. The small sallow-faced man standing by his side was unknown to me.

'Hello, Murray, so you've arrived at last!' was his greeting as I alighted. 'This is Shura, my chauffeur. I've got the car outside. We'll drive home to my place.'

We were soon driving along in an old Hillman Minx that coughed and spluttered frequently and seemed to run in starts and jerks, but it was comfortable and roomy enough inside. Bagshawe was proud of it. He told me he had bought it for a hundred pounds from one of the newspaper correspondents who had had to leave Russia.

It did not take more than ten minutes to reach his place. We drew up to the gates of a fairly large house set in its own grounds surrounded by a high brick wall. Inside the gates stood a lodge out of which emerged a porter to open the gates.

'That's Vasily,' Bagshawe remarked. 'He's the porter, stoker, gardener and what-have-you for the place.'

When we got inside the house, he showed me round and pointed out that his flat consisted of three bedrooms, a large sitting room, dining room, and kitchen, and an adjoining bedroom which was occupied by the housekeeper, Rebecca, to whom he introduced me. She was a small Jewish woman of indeterminate age, sad-eyed with greying hair that had once been black. He said he also had a cook, Valentina, who lived out but came in daily to do the necessary shopping and prepare the meals. He introduced me to her the next morning. She was a fat, jolly woman, and I found out later, a very good cook indeed, whose culinary efforts though lost on Bagshawe, really roused the envy of our not-so-fortunate guests at the parties we gave.

He explained that the building was composed of several self-contained flats. There was another ground floor flat and this was occupied by the

Embassy archivist who lived there with his French wife. There were also two top floor flats, one of which was occupied by a Mr Scott and his Russian wife. Scott was the clerk to the Commercial Attaché. The other flat belonged to Colonel Greer who did not live in it but had all his personal furniture stored there. It was a lovely building and Bagshawe told me that it had been the former Finnish Embassy, and the name of the street we were in was called *Maly kharitonevsky*.

The first thing I did was to have a quick bath. After that I joined Bagshawe for a light supper of cold meat and pickles, with a couple of small glasses of Vodka. I was astonished at Bagshawe's capacity for it. He drank it as though it was water and seemed none the worse for it. During the meal he explained that there was a flat for me in a street called *Petrovka* which was some distance away. It was a tenement house and the other flats were occupied by Russian families and I could take it if I wished. My predecessor, who had been sent home for reasons of health, had formerly lived there, but should I be agreeable I could share this flat with him and also share the expenses which would turn out cheaper for me. I told Bagshawe that it was okay with me and that I'd prefer to share his place and would inform my chief accordingly.

At nine o'clock the next morning we drove to the Embassy. A large imposing building in the *Sofiyskaya naberezhnaya* which stood on the banks of a wide canal separating it from the massive walls of the Kremlin, above which could be seen the onion-shaped domes of innumerable churches. To me it looked like a scene from the Arabian Nights.

We drove through the gates of the drive leading to the Embassy entrance, armed sentries stood on both sides.

When we left our house, I'd noticed two cars, each containing two occupants in civilian clothes, standing opposite the house. One of the cars had immediately started up and tailed us as far as the Embassy where it pulled up at the side of the railings and joined a further line of cars standing there. Bagshawe's comment to my enquiry was, 'Oh, they are the YMCA, you'll soon get used to them following you around!' It appeared that the 'YMCA' was the humorous appellative bestowed upon the NKVD by the Embassy staff.

Inside the Embassy, I was first introduced to my future chief, Wing-Commander Hallawell, the Air Attaché, then to Captain Clanchy, Bagshawe's boss and afterwards to Colonel Greer, Military Attaché and his secretary, Jimes. The three services thus represented had their offices on the western side of the building.

286

Sir Stafford Cripps *Radio Times Hulton Picture Library*

After the introductions were over, my chief said it was time to keep the appointment he had made for me with the Ambassador, Sir Stafford Cripps. We went to his private study. In the room, already seated, were the two other attachés, Geoffrey Wilson, whom I'd met in Riga, and Mr Dunlop, senior secretary to the Embassy, as well as Mr James, the senior stenographer. After the introductory formalities were over, Sir Stafford, who was just like the pictures I'd seen of him, tall, thin, sharp-featured, wearing glasses, gave me a somewhat wintry smile and said, 'Well, it's nice to see you Murray. From what I can gather you seem to have had some difficulty in getting here. Perhaps you'd like to tell us about it. Take your time and tell us exactly what happened.'

They listened in silence as I recounted the incident of those nightmarish four months I had spent in Riga. When I had finished, Sir Stafford asked, 'Are you prepared to swear that the account you have given us is the truth, and sign a statement to that effect?'

'Certainly, Sir,' I answered.

He rose and came over to me. 'That is all, we shall prepare your statement for signature, but before you go, I should like to tell you that we have been aware that in the past, certain members of our staff have, from time to time, been intimidated by Soviet agents. You are the first one so far that has had the courage to come forward and report the fact. Thank you, Murray.'

The next day I was told to report to Sir Stafford, who handed me a typewritten copy of the statement I had made the previous day.

'Read it very carefully, Murray, and let me know if there is any point on which you disagree.' It was perfect, and I signed it there and then. He asked me if I was still worried about my parents and I answered, 'Very much so!'

'I have been thinking about them also,' he told me, and went on to explain that on behalf of the Government he was going to send a very strong protest to Vyshinsky, of the Soviet Foreign Ministry, about the treatment one of his staff had been subjected to by the Soviet Secret Police, pointing out that they had used the threat of taking action against his parents in order to force him to acquiesce to their demands. He surmised that following this, it was quite unlikely the Russians would take any steps to harm my parents, as they would certainly deny the charges the British Government brought against them, and would make sure nothing happened to my parents in order to prove their point. This seemed a reasonable assumption to me also. He asked me if I had any plans with regard to them. I said that I had business friends in Istanbul who would look after them if only I could make contact with Turkey and get them out of Russia.

'In that case,' he said, 'you can forward a letter by the next diplomatic bag going to Istanbul.'

At the end of my meeting with the Ambassador, he mentioned that he would very much like me to have tea with Lady Cripps and himself if I would care to come. I said I would be delighted. The next day I received an invitation signed by Lady Cripps.

It was quite an informal tea-party. Both his daughters, Peggy and Theresa, were present and they made me feel very much at home. Lady Cripps asked me if I would contribute to the Prisoners of War Fund she was organising and I said I would be only too pleased to, considering that I had very nearly been one myself. She asked me how that had come about, so I related my experiences in Norway. Sir Stafford also told me that Mr Lascelles was also now one of his secretaries in the Embassy which was news to me, as I had last seen him in Sweden and did not know he had come to Moscow.

April 28

Dear Mr. Murray,

I have just opened the box in the hall and found your note and your most welcome contribution to the Prisoners of War Parcels fund. We are very grateful for it, and it is good of you to promise us a contribution every month. Thank you very much indeed.

Yours sincerely

Theresa Cripps

A letter from Lady Theresa Cripps, wife of the British Ambassador, to the author on 28 April 1941

289

The next two days I spent in Bagshawe's flat sorting out my things and making myself at home so to speak. The arrangements I had made with Bagshawe suited me admirably and I was able to settle up with him for my share of the food store, wines and spirits, etc. that he already had in stock, which financially was of very great help to him.

I had already sent an open card to my parents telling them I had arrived safe and sound, that Russia and the people were marvellous and that I hoped they were keeping well.

The first task I undertook in my new appointment was to learn the combination of the Wing-Commander's safe. Under his watchful eye, I spent some time manipulating the combination until I was word perfect, as one might say. It took some effort on my part as I always was, and still am, pretty dim where remembering figures is concerned. Then we had a long talk about the scope of my duties, but the most important were the 'don'ts'!

We understood one another well, and I couldn't have wished for a better chief. Beyond saying that I typed out all his confidential reports and in conjunction with the other two services' secretaries did the deciphering and coding of messages to the respective service branches of the Foreign Office, I will say no more.

We three service departments — Naval, Military and Air Force, were pretty well occupied with work. Although it was all new to me, I quickly acquired the necessary knowledge, and I had the edge over my colleagues as I could both type pretty fast and take dictation in shorthand.

Captain Clanchy, as befitted the Chief of the Senior Service, kept up what appeared to me a quaint and pleasing custom, but my colleagues, Bagshawe and Jimes always made fun of it. Each morning before we

The author's Diplomatic Identity Card whilst working at the British Embassy, Moscow

commenced our duties, we would assemble in his office and he would take out a decanter of sherry from his cupboard with four glasses, hand a small wine glass to each of us, fill them up with sherry and we would drink a toast, 'To His Majesty, the King!' I always felt sorry for Bagshawe on these occasions — he could only stomach spirits and the sherry used to half choke him, but with his chief's eye fixed sternly upon him, he had to down it!

The second week after my arrival Bagshawe said it was time for us to throw a party so that I could be introduced to the rest of the 'Lower Deck' diplomatic circle, as he put it. As the social life in Moscow revolved round such parties, members of the British and American Embassies each gave parties in turn at the slightest excuse, it was the only means of relieving the tension of living in Moscow under constant and hostile supervision. Several members of the American Embassy turned up that evening among whom was Reinhardt, the cipher officer I had met in Riga. He asked me why I had been so long in getting to Moscow. I said it was due to visa difficulties, which surprised him, as he said he had had no trouble with his and reckoned it was because the Americans commanded more respect than we did.

Amongst others who turned up for the party were three very well known newspaper correspondents. Walter Durante, who I'd already met in Stockholm and who had come to Moscow hoping to obtain another interview with Stalin; Henry Shapiro who represented Associated Press, and Monsieur Champignon of Le Temps. He, in a way, was the odd man out and his quiet manner betokened the strain he was living under at the time. France having fallen to the Germans, it was a question of whether he represented the Petain Government or the Free French. Then he had also the problem of where his money was to come from and whether the Soviet government would allow him to remain in Russia. When members of the Press became *persona non grata* the time granted for departure from Russia was generally limited to hours, with no nonsense allowed. I really sympathised with his predicament. Although it was an Embassy instruction that we were not to fraternise with the Press you could never keep journalists out once they'd got wind of a party. On the whole, they were a good lot and as far as my experience went, they never tried anything on, either with regard to getting messages passed through the censorship or pumping me for inside information.

The party had just got under way when I was surprised to see three more guests turn up. My surprise was due to the fact that they were young Russian girls. Two of them seemed to be well known to two of our Embassy staff. They were introduced all round, and there was much laughing and gesticulating as none of them spoke English. It was the third girl that

291

attracted my attention however. Bagshawe explained to me that he had met her in the Hotel Metropole some weeks ago and having had already a party in mind had thought it a good idea to invite her along. During the introductions I found she could speak German and that her name was Nora. In contrast to the other girls who soon made themselves at home, she seemed very shy and reserved. The others were heavily made-up and drank and smoked a lot. She, on the other hand, wore no make-up at all and neither drank nor smoked. With her fair hair and complexion, large grey-green eyes and high cheek bones, she looked a typical Russian. She seemed much younger than the other two, about twenty-one, I surmised. I did not speak to her again after being introduced and when the three girls left shortly before midnight, I only felt curious as to how they came to be allowed to have contact with people like ourselves. Every report I had read on Russia, emphasised the fact that their civilians were neither allowed to mix or speak with foreigners unless supervised and that the secret police, who were everywhere and very much feared, made sure of this.

Nora – The Swallow

The party lasted until the late hours of the morning. I am not a teetotaller and will drink for company's sake, but I always drank very sparingly. When I first arrived in Latvia, I went to a party where I'd been given Vodka and then wine. I was violently sick and very ill for several days afterwards. It was a lesson to me in drinking that I never forgot. Vodka and wine do not mix and if you drink, it's better to stick to the one drink throughout the evening, and leave the hardened topers to drink spirits and follow them up with chasers. I spent most of the time talking to Champignon who also was not much of a spirit drinker and only drank wine. He seemed more knowledgeable than the others about life in Moscow and I was anxious to learn as much as I could. I asked if he knew the fair girl that had just left and he said he'd not seen her before at any of the parties and she was probably a new 'mozhno' girl. 'Mozhno girls,' he explained, meant 'permitted girls'; girls who were permitted by the secret police to fraternise with foreigners. Normally, as I have said, Russian citizens steered clear of foreigners. They were constantly exhorted through press and radio media to beware of foreigners who were all classed as agents, provocateurs and spies endangering the safety of the Soviet Union. The penalties for transgression were so swiftly and silently carried out and moreover, could bring such a wide circle of relations and friends under suspicion, that people were terrified even to speak to foreigners. Those that were involved with them in an official capacity even, never seemed to last long. The dapper Vladimir Barkoff, the Soviet Chief of Protocol whom I saw several times in the Embassy, was one of these. They ultimately disappeared at some time or other and any enquiries made met with vague and inconclusive replies. The mozhno girls, on the other hand, were not employed or paid by the State, they were just left to their own devices, but they had to give constant reports on their foreign contacts. These, too, as soon as they could serve no further useful purpose or in any way became embarrassing to the State, were silently disposed of and disappeared without any trace.

Champignon told me an amusing story about one of the former French diplomats who was having a steady affair with one of the mozhno girls. One day his car was stopped on a country road and he was approached by a couple of NKVD agents who had been tailing him. In the course of the ensuing conversation he was asked if he would like to work for the Soviet Union. When he indignantly refused, one of them produced a packet of photographs of intimate bedroom scenes portraying him in a series of very compromising positions with his Russian girl friend. These, he was informed, would be sent to the Embassy if he did not co-operate with them. He took one look at their photos, pulled out his wallet, and took out some photographs of his own. 'Phooey!' he said, 'that's nothing. Here! Look at these! Your people can't take photographs for nuts! Go on, take these, tell your bosses they can have them with my compliments!' He happened to be an expert photographer and had taken pictures of himself with the same girl in such an astounding variety of sexual postures, that even the Russians were astonished. After this they left him alone and the story caused immense amusement when it got around the diplomatic circles. The only sad part about the whole affair was that he never saw his girl friend again.

293

The weeks passed swiftly by as I gradually worked myself into the Embassy routine, but most annoyingly, I kept receiving telephone calls from Nora, the girl I met at the party, who was always asking me to go out with her. The fact that our telephone number was ex-directory and could not be obtained by people other than Embassy staff, was suspicious. Again, she always called when I was alone in the house — a fact she seemed to be aware of. When she rang I cut her off quickly as soon as I knew it was her, but she never took no for an answer.

The Christmas of 1940 arrived and the unusual procedure adopted by Sir Stafford Cripps for its celebration caused a few raised eyebrows in the Embassy. It also shed light on the character of the man. He invited the whole staff to a Christmas dinner held in the official Embassy reception hall. The invitation sent out stated that ordinary lounge suits should be worn to avoid embarrassment to those members who did not possess dinner jackets, and that seating arrangements would be decided by guests drawing lots instead of sitting at the table in accordance to precedence of rank. This gave the Embassy staff a chance of meeting each other socially on common ground.

The Christmas party was quite a success as far as I was concerned and Lady Cripps had done everything possible to make it so: we had turkey, goose and pork, with traditional Christmas pudding and mince pies, and plenty of beer, wine and spirits.

After Christmas a series of irritating incidents occurred. Bagshawe had gone out for the evening and I was alone in the house reading when the telephone rang.

'Who's speaking?' I asked.

'Is that Meester John? It's me, Nora. You remember me don't you?' came the reply in German.

I was angry at being disturbed and one thing I didn't want, was to start getting entangled with a Russian mozhno girl. I answered her back in the snappiest tone I could adopt.

'Yes I remember you, and this is Mr Murray speaking. What do you want?'

'I want to speak to you and...'

I cut her off short. 'But I don't want to speak to you, and I'm very busy! Goodbye!'

With that I hung up the receiver and went back to my book, feeling very satisfied that I'd nipped the unwelcome intrusion in the bud.

Half an hour later the 'phone rang again. I bet it's that damn girl again, I thought. Sure enough, I was right. I did not give her the chance to get properly started.

'Look here Miss Nora, will you please understand I do not wish to speak or hear from you at all! Is that understood?' and with that I banged the receiver down.

I was not disturbed again that night and I did not mention the matter to Bagshawe.

Two nights later however, when I was again alone in the house, the 'phone rang again. It was Nora.

'Can I meet you somewhere, Mr Murray? I'd like to talk to you.'

I was really angry this time. 'Miss Nora,' I spoke deliberately, 'I've told you before, I don't want to have anything to do with you. Please leave me alone and stop ringing me up!' With that I slammed the phone down.

I was not disturbed again until New Year's Eve which brought with it a dilemma that was to have an unexpected and shattering effect upon my stay in Russia.

Bagshawe had gone to a New Year's Eve party, I, having refused the invitation, remained alone in the flat. I'd just settled myself down comfortably when I was interrupted by the sound of the telephone ringing. I picked up the receiver — it was Nora! I shouted, 'Not at home!' and replaced the receiver. The bell rang again in a long incessant tone. Determined to put a stop to this situation once and for all, I picked up the receiver.

'Mr Murray, I must speak to you, I must, I must,' Nora's voice ended in a wail. I could almost see the tears as her voice ended in a sob.

'All right then come round, but I can't spare much time.'

There was a muffled sob and a click as she rang off. Within a matter of minutes the doorbell rang. I opened the door myself as Rebecca had long since gone to bed.

It was Nora and she gave me a nervous hesitant smile as I led her into the sitting room and told her to be seated. I had already made up my mind how to handle the situation and wasted no time. I adopted a bullying tone. 'Look here, Nora, you've been bothering me now for a long time. It's got to stop! You understand?' I spoke contemptuously. 'I know you are a mozhno girl sent to spy on me, but you'll get nothing out of me and I don't want to know you or have anything to do with you, so go back to your secret police and tell them I've said so. You ought to be ashamed of yourself — a young girl like you carrying on in this way! Now please go.'

295

It was a long-winded effort, but I'd got it off my chest at last. Naturally, I expected some sort of vehement denial, but the effect was totally unexpected. As I stood over her, she looked up at me. Her eyes widened like big grey-green saucers. Her lips began to quiver. In that instant her expression changed. I glimpsed the face of a young girl suddenly confronted with the realisation that the whole world was tumbling about her. She had the look of an animal beaten beyond endurance. With a long drawn out 'O–oh!' she put her hands to her face and sobbed as though her heart was breaking. I let her alone, waiting until the paroxysm should end, wondering meanwhile whether or not her grief was genuine. I could, however, not forget the look of utter hopelessness on her face just before she broke down. I stared at her — and as I looked down, I saw before me the face of a child, torn with unutterable grief and terror. For a fleeting moment I felt a strange feeling of pity and compassion for the girl in front of me. Again, her eyes had the look of a stricken animal that had been badly hurt — although she was looking at me, her eyes seemed to look beyond and through me. I felt strangely troubled. Leaving her, I went to the kitchen and made a strong pot of tea. I poured out a couple of cups, added milk, and sweetened them well and gave her one. She looked up at me dumbly.

'Here, have a nice cup of English tea, it will do you good,' I said in a coaxing tone. She took it and began to sip it mechanically.

'Now, tell me who you really are, and what your name is?'

My change of tone and manner began to bring her back to life and she gave me a timid smile.

'Go on,' I coaxed. 'Tell me everything about yourself. Where are your mother and father, and where do you live?'

'I have no mother. She is dead and my father is in prison.' She burst out crying again. I let her cry and waited patiently until her sobs had subsided, and repeated gently, 'Go on, tell me, don't be frightened, there is nothing to be afraid of.'

She began to talk, on and on she went and as her story unfolded I could not but help feeling a mounting wave of pity for the plight she was in.

Her full name it appeared was Nina Nora Vasilievna Korzhenko. She had been born in Zolotonosha, a suburb of Poltava in the Ukraine. Her mother had committed suicide when Nora was only seven years old. Her memory of her mother was that of a loving kindly woman who had treated her with all the affection and tenderness a mother could bestow upon an only child.

Her father was Major Vasily Korzhenko of the Soviet Security Force, the GPU, the precursor of the present day NKVD. He had a brother, her uncle

Konstantin who lived in Leningrad and had formerely been a colonel in the Tsarist Army. Her father and his brother often quarrelled but still had a great affection for one another. Her uncle was an eminent engineer and for that reason his life had been spared by the Bolsheviks, apart from the fact that his brother Vasily used his influence to get him out of the frequent troubles caused by Konstantin's outspoken criticism of the Bolsheviks.

It was during one of her father's interrogations of 'Enemies of the State' that he met the wife of a suspected German national and fell in love with her. The shock of his unfaithfulness had so preyed on the mind of Nora's mother that she poisoned herself and took her own life. Her father later married his new-found love Ursula and before long a son was born to them and called Felix, so she now had a step-brother. After this, Ursula's mother came to join them and the whole family moved to Moscow, Major Korzhenko having been promoted to a special appointment in the Foreign Ministry. Nora by this time had grown up and was studying for entrance to Moscow University, of which she was now a student.

All had been going well when, without warning her father was suddenly arrested and committed to the notorious Lubyanka prison.

Before the distraught family could get over this tragedy, her stepmother Ursula was also arrested in the middle of the night and exiled to Tashkent in Asiatic Russia. All this was at the time of the great purges in 1939 following Molotov's appointment as Foreign Secretary. In spite of these events, her grandmother managed to take care of little Felix and Nora herself continued with her studies for the University.

It was one morning in the April of 1940 that she observed an elderly man who turned out to be a Hungarian diplomat experiencing some difficulty in making himself understood in the Moscow main post office. He could only speak German other than Hungarian which the post office staff could not understand so Nora interpreted for him. He was very grateful and asked her if she would guide him around Moscow as he was a complete stranger. She did so.

Some days after this incident, as she sat alone in her study room preparing her paper for the next morning's lecture, there came a sudden knock on the door. Opening it she was startled to see two men in civilian clothes who brushed her aside as they walked in. They informed her that they were from the secret police and requested her to get ready and accompany them at once to their headquarters. She was too terrified to say or do anything but comply with their command. They drove her to the Hotel Metropole where, in an upstairs suite she was brought before a Major Kirilov, one of the heads of the

Soviet espionage departments. Bewildered and frightened, she listened as she was angrily accused of consorting with a foreigner who was an enemy of the state, the punishment for which would be severe. The Major then altered his tone and said he knew all about her and her family. If she really was a good citizeness of the Soviet and prepared to help her father who was still in prison and alive, she could prove it by working for his department against the enemies of Russia. The thought of at last being able to do something to help her father, about whom she had been unable to get any information whatsoever, made her only too anxious to accept the offer. She was then told that she would work under the pseudonym of 'The Swallow' and from thence onwards she was only to communicate with them under that name. After being given precise instructions as to her duties, which included permission to frequent the restaurant of the Hotel Metropole and contact foreign guests, she was made aware of the dire penalties that would be imposed upon her for betrayal or failure. Following this she was allowed to go home.

It was after this that one evening late in September she had met Bagshawe at the Metropole Hotel, and he had asked her to dance with him. During the course of that evening he mentioned to her that he would be shortly giving a party to celebrate the arrival of a new member of the British Embassy and he invited her to come to it.

This news she had passed on to Major Kirilov who had immediately summoned her to his presence.

She was showered with congratulations on her success. The Major then handed her a dossier. The first thing she saw was a photograph of myself with pages of written material which she was not allowed to read.

'This is the man you will meet at the party,' he said. 'He is not just a secretary but a dangerous British agent who is an armament and aerodynamics specialist. It will be your duty to contact him and use every means possible to gain his confidence. It is up to you. Do you understand?' He then warned her that under no circumstances was she to say or ask anything that would arouse my suspicions, as it would be for his department to take care of me once she had achieved her objective.

As she finished her narrative I looked closely at her. She reminded me more than ever of some poor animal that had been caught in a trap. Instinctively, I knew that basically what she had told me was the truth about herself. But I wanted to know more.

As she stopped she looked up at me. 'Well,' I remarked, 'go on.'

'But you would not meet me or even talk to me and the Major has said he will give me one more chance and if I fail, I will be put away. What shall I do? What is going to happen to my father now…?' Her voice tailed off into a hopeless cry.

I was in a dilemma. The proper course of action was for me to inform the Embassy of the incident. This, I figured, would result in two things. First, the girl before me would suffer; secondly, the Secret Police who it seemed were out to get me would resort to other means of pressurising me. As my parents were still in their power, they might even wreak their revenge on them, for the second rebuff that they had received at my expense.

The other alternative open to me was to play along with the girl and use her as a cat's paw in getting my parents out of Latvia, which was a chance I would have to take. I made a decision. I decided to tell her that I would meet her occasionally and if it came to demands for information, I would concoct trivia to keep her bosses happy for as long as it suited my purpose.

She had been watching me closely whilst I was turning all this over in my mind. I smiled at her, and said, 'Good. I will meet you sometimes Miss Korzhenko, but I am a very busy man and will not be able to see you often. So now, go home and report to your Major that you have at last made an appointment with me.'

'What do you mean?' she asked wonderingly.

'I'll tell you what I mean, you'll come here twice a week to give me Russian lessons, and you will come at eight o'clock until nine o'clock in the morning, because at that time everybody will be about in the house and it will look less suspicious than in the evenings when the flat is sometimes empty.'

As I finished, she did something that caused me no little embarrassment. She caught hold of my hands, drew them to her lips and kissed them. Tears ran down her cheeks as she murmured, 'Oh, thank you Mr Murray! Thank you.' I felt a bit of a hypocrite, but thought that anyway I was helping her as well, which was some consolation for making use of her.

Although throughout our conversation we spoke in German, she used the appellation Mister not Herr, so I said she was to call me John from now on. I then told her to listen very carefully to what I had to say. I spoke very slowly to make sure that she understood. I said I would trust her to be a faithful and honest friend, but as my life would depend on it, she, for her part, must trust me implicitly and I would try to help her. I impressed upon her that if the Embassy knew we were friends, it would be the end of everything, and that it was most important she kept me informed what Major Kirilov or any of his staff said, or instructed her to carry out, as this was the only way that I could make plans for her to keep her bosses satisfied with her work for them. She said she understood and swore that she would never betray our trust. By this time it was already the early hours of the morning so I told her she had better go and when she reported to Major Kirilov, she was only to say that we had a pleasant meeting and that she had finally persuaded me to employ her to teach me Russian.

It was a much happier girl that I escorted out from the gates of the house that early New Year's Day morning, and I smiled too, as after she had gone down the street, a waiting car standing outside the house pulled away from the kerb and followed her.

I knew Bagshawe would not return until the morning, for a party was a party to him, and as there was always unlimited booze I knew he would remain right until the bitter end.

I turned in and spent a restless few hours getting to sleep, my mind busy with niggling problems, doubtful as to whether I really could trust the girl who had just left. At all costs I had to keep the Embassy out of it, at this stage anyway.

Bagshawe came home at midday and I mentioned that I'd had a visitor the night before and that it was the Russian girl who had been at our party, and that she had promised to give me Russian lessons a couple of times a week. His only reaction was to turn to me with a twinkle in his eye and say, 'That'll keep you out of mischief, but be careful my lad, you know what she is!' and there the matter ended.

Three days later Nora 'phoned and said she would be coming to give me my first lesson.

The morning she arrived, I took the precaution of introducing her to the staff and we had breakfast together for the benefit of my first Russian lesson. After it was over, I escorted her to the gate and on the way, out of earshot of everyone, she told me what had transpired on reporting to her chief, Major Kirilov. He had been tremendously pleased and had congratulated her upon her success. He had told her she was to do everything to ripen our friendship and reiterated that under no circumstances was she to ask me any questions about my work, or say anything that would alarm me. She was to charge me well for the 'Russian lessons'. She had nothing else to do, but just that, when the time came, it would be he and his staff who would take me in hand. For the time being she was only to work hard to gain my trust and confidence in any manner possible, which shouldn't be difficult for a pretty girl like her.

I could only smile. The weeks, then months, went by. Occasionally on a Saturday or Sunday I would go out openly in the daytime for a walk with Nora and she would show me around Moscow, which has a charm of its own in winter. I was used to the cold. It was a dry, clean, fresh cold. We'd go on the Metro Underground, of which the Russians were very proud and rightly so, it was kept so clean and tidy. But my favourite spot was the Sokolniki Park which was an ideal place for freedom of conversation. It had one advantage, one could walk there and if we were followed, our followers were easily discernible. Nora had by now lost that frightened appearance and was beginning to look quite bright and cheery. It was on one of these occasions that I told her, should she by any chance have any trouble at any time and could not come to my home, she was to telephone me or get a message to me simply saying she would see me in the Park and I would meet her here in the Sokolniki, not that I thought there would be any trouble for her. After some weeks had elapsed, her Russian masters got impatient and began to press her to make arrangements for me to meet one of their staff. I fobbed this off with an explanation that I was being watched by my own Embassy. To sweeten the pill of disappointment I gave her certain 'information' to pass on. I compiled this information from a detailed study I made of the Russian newspapers we were supplied within the Embassy, together with items that were openly broadcast on the radio from England. I embroidered this information with highly complimentary bits about the size and power of the Soviet air force that was being talked about among the diplomatic staff. As I strung it out and Nora passed it on, she got gratified acclaims of approval from the NKVD. I spent a great deal of time and ingenuity in formulating these so-called reports.

One night as I sat up late doing my Russian homework, I decided to go into the kitchen for a glass of milk. As it was so quiet I became aware of a strange shuffling noise coming from Rebecca's room which adjoined the kitchen. Now Rebecca was a strange woman. She would carry out her duties silently and a 'good-morning' and a 'good-night' was the most one would get from her, although she spoke English like a native. This shuffling noise disturbed me; even when I went back to read it was annoyingly audible. As it was getting on my nerves, I went back to the kitchen, deciding to peep through the keyhole of her door to see if it was anything serious. As I looked I could make out Rebecca trudging round and round the small table in her room. Her head was sunk on her breast, her hands tightly clasped behind her. She did not walk – she just shuffled along; her eyes downcast, staring at the floor. I went back to my room wondering.

The next morning when talking to Bagshawe, 1 said I'd heard a strange shuffling noise coming from the kitchen. He replied, 'Oh, that's Rebecca. You needn't let that worry you,' and went on to give me the history of Rebecca as he knew it. She had been brought to England from Russia by her aunt during the Bolshevik Revolution, she grew up there and later worked in a bank in London. Misled by the glowing reports advertised by the Soviet Intourist Bureau, she decided, as she was now a British citizen, it would be safe for her to travel to Russia and meet all the relatives she had never seen. She arrived in Russia during the early thirties, and went to Minsk. Her relatives, frightened by her arrival, disowned her. She was arrested by the Secret Police, her passport and papers confiscated, and sentenced without trial to five years' imprisonment. In vain she protested that she was a British subject. They said that she was a Russian and as such, subject to Soviet law. She served her time — God knows how she survived, but survive she did. After her release, she managed to contact the British Embassy who tried to help her. But, as according to Soviet law, she was still a Soviet citizen, the most her Embassy could do was to persuade the authorities to allow her to work for them, and so she was given the job of housekeeper in *Maly kharitonevsky*. Bagshawe said that whenever she was upset, her mind reverted to her prison experiences, and she would walk round and round the table in her room as she used to do for exercise during her term of imprisonment. I was deeply moved by this story, and put myself out to be extra kind to her.

At this time there was one thing that did much to alleviate the apprehension I felt over the safety of my parents. Up to the time of meeting Nora, I had regularly written them a postcard, as agreed, every fortnight. I never had a reply. Later I was to learn that they did in fact receive my cards and replied immediately, but their replies never came through. But it was not long after taking Nora on as my Russian teacher I began to receive postcards regularly from Riga addressed to the Embassy saying that all was well. This was a great relief, but it also confirmed my suspicion that the NKVD were adept in the use of psychology to gain their objectives. Why they were still so interested in recruiting my services I could not fathom. I could not understand how they came to classify me as a dangerous agent. I was, however, glad that I'd befriended Nora even if I did not trust her entirely. I felt that I could handle the situation and my only fear, which was a valid one, was the Embassy. I did not want them on my back at this stage, because they would certainly not understand or condone my actions and it was for this reason I made sure that my acquaintance with Nora could not be misconstrued. She herself must have often been puzzled by the brusqueness of my manner at times.

I was very curious to see the Hotel Metropole, which I now knew to be one of the centres of Russian espionage and got Bagshawe to accompany me

302

there on several occasions. He was quite happy to take me and it broke the monotony of some of our evenings. I'd treat him to a bottle of Vodka and generally had half a bottle of Russian wine myself, which I found extremely good. It was quite an impressive building, situated on the corner of Sverdlov Square, based on an imposing red granite podium which accentuated the simple smooth white plastered walls of its upper four storeys. It had actually been designed by the British architect, W. Walcott in 1899.

The Hotel Metropole, Moscow. The first floor suite housed the Soviet Espionage Headquarters

The restaurant occupied the ground floor of the building. It was sumptuously furnished with old-fashioned chairs and tables, crimson velvet curtains, crystal chandeliers and much ornate gilded plaster work. Near the centre, set on a marble terraced pedestal was a huge glass tank containing live fish, mostly carp, from which the customers could select the one they wanted to eat. I came to the conclusion that the Metropole was a relic from by-gone days, preserved in its entirety, to impress visitors who came to Moscow.

On the occasion of our first visit we were greeted by the Maitrê d'Hôtel himself, a tall stately gentleman in his early fifties. He was clean-shaven with a pallid complexion but had rather warm-looking, deep brown eyes. His features were heavy and his thinning hair was tinged with grey. He ushered

303

us to a small table at the side which gave us a good view of the restaurant. After he had taken our order and passed it on to one of the waiters he disappeared. Some distance away on the opposite side of the restaurant I had noticed a small table backed by red velvet curtains and half screened by fronds of palms. There was no one sitting there when we came in, but shortly after our drinks arrived it was occupied unobtrusively by two men who just sat there drinking from a carafe of Vodka and smoking innumerable cigarettes. We were watched. The same thing happened on all our subsequent visits, the same tables, the same people. It was an experience, no matter how many times it occurred, which always aroused a feeling of expectancy. In knowing you were being watched, you waited for something to happen. I got to know the name of the Maitrê d'Hôtel, it was Gabaridze. He was a Georgian who spoke several languages and his English was very good. I complimented him upon it, remarking that he must have been in England to speak it so well. He told me that many years before, he had lived in London and worked in the kitchens of the Savoy Hotel.

When I remarked slyly that he must find his present work very boring, he smiled. We understood one another well! Apart from the few foreign diplomats and business men the place was always filled with Russians. These were men from the far off regions of Russia, factory executives, and commissars, to whom the visit was part of their perks. They ate the plentiful supply of food with gusto and seemed really to enjoy themselves. There were, I noticed, very few women present.

One day about the middle of March I received an unexpected chit from Sir Stafford Cripps requesting me to report to his office the following morning at ten a.m. It was with some misgiving I presented myself the next day, the thought uppermost in my mind being that I was due for a reprimand for associating with a Russian. But it was quite otherwise. After telling me to be seated, Sir Stafford handed me a typescript. 'I thought you might like to read it, Murray. It's Vyshinsky's reply to our protest.'

The gist of the document I read was that the allegations made were totally untrue and unjustified, and were without foundation. The Soviet Government dismissed the charges as absolute fabrication! There was one short paragraph at the end which I well remember, it ran, 'Mr Murray might have been approached, without our knowledge by members of our tobacco industry with an offer of employment as a tobacco specialist, for which he would have in any case been most unsuitable.' Signed A. Vyshinsky, Minister for Internal Affairs.

It was so ridiculous that I could only shrug my shoulders as I handed it back to him.

'There's nothing to worry about, Murray,' he said, 'but I would strongly advise you to write to your parents now and tell them to apply for an exit visa to leave Latvia and Russia!'

It was sound advice and after leaving him, I wrote to my parents at once.

Within a week I received a telegram from my parents saying they had received their exit visa to leave and were already on their way to Moscow. I was overjoyed at the news.

When Nora came that morning to give me my usual Russian lesson, I told her that my parents were arriving from Riga and I would not be taking any more lessons for the next two weeks. She was a bit downcast at this, but brightened up when I told her I'd be definitely continuing them later. I added she could report this to her superiors as it would show she still had my confidence.

I felt really happy and tremendously relieved when the next day I was once more re-united with my parents. They stayed for two weeks. Though I tried to get permission for them to remain in Moscow it was categorically refused. They were precious days. Only the thought that they had to leave and we would be parted once again cast a shadow of sadness over everything. I tried to make them as happy as possible. Rebecca could not do enough for my mother to make her comfortable and my mother in turn stripped her wardrobe of clothes, which she made Rebecca take. Poor Rebecca, she had so very little and my parents had been deeply touched when I recounted her history to them.

One of the places I took them to was the Bolshoi Theatre to see the ballet, *Eugene Onegin*. The ballet was always a great favourite of mine. It was the only time I experienced complete relaxation. I would sit through a performance with half-closed eyes, drinking in the music, hypnotised by the floating dancers before me — a veritable wonderland of sweet music and muted beauty. I saw the now aged Ulanova and also the famous Galina; they danced superbly. The Russians really appreciated their artists, and rightly so. In contrast, Russian films were really pathetic in their childishness. One I saw was about a saboteur who damaged the factory plant and put the blame on the heroine's lover. The heroine had then unmasked the saboteurs, the hero was reinstated and he, not content with getting production back to normal, had actually increased production. The workers then all cheered him and the scene ended with the lovers giving each other an embrace and kiss of such unbelievable chastity, that an American producer would have wept on the spot!

Another I saw was of a poor young peasant who could neither read nor write, when along came a buxom down-to-earth young teacher who soon put him to rights, whereby he was able to become such a capable engineer that all production norms rose to incredible heights — the final scene being the same as the previous film. I did not bother to see any more films, and did not take my parents to see any either. It would have spoilt their wonder and appreciation of the ballet they had seen.

The time however was passing very quickly and my parents seemed happy enough, but there was one piece of news I kept from them, though it was hard to contain my grief. I had received a letter from my cousins in London saying that following a recent air-raid my brother, Nicholas, was missing and presumed dead, as all efforts to trace him had been of no avail. It was a shock to me, but I could only grieve in silence, my main concern being to see that my parents remained troublefree.

The time for them to leave came too soon. It was sad. The only consolation was that we were all well and in good health and so far things had run smoothly. I saw them off and they promised to cable me from Istanbul as soon as they arrived. Three days later I received a telegram to say they had arrived safely and a letter would follow. The letter arrived shortly afterwards and I felt that a great weight had been lifted from my mind. I also felt the emptiness of being once again alone.

It was on a Friday when their letter came and that evening as I sat alone reviewing the events of the past few weeks, the telephone rang. I picked up the receiver.

'John, it's me, Nora. Can I see you please, it's most important.'

'All right, come over but I can't see you for very long,' I said.

I was a bit annoyed. I'd wanted an early night, but I knew that it must be something important Nora wanted to tell me about, because I'd impressed upon her the danger of calling me up on the phone too often.

Within a short while there was a knock on the door. It was Nora. I led her into the house.

'Well, what's it all about?' I asked.

She sat perched uncomfortably upon the edge of her chair and looked up at me apprehensively.

'It's Major Kirilov,' she began somewhat hesitantly.

'Go on, what about Major Kirilov, what's he done now?' I began jokingly. But her face was quite serious.

306

'He's ordered me to bring you to the Hotel Metropole tomorrow night for dinner, and when you are there I am to introduce you to two of his friends who will be waiting for us.' She blurted it out all at once as though glad to get it over with.

'So, we'll tell your Major Kirilov that I'm not coming to any dinner party and what's more I don't want to see him or any of his friends either!' I spoke very emphatically. There was a pause.

Then Nora, still looking at me apprehensively, said in a pleading tone, 'Perhaps, John, you could just see them, just for once, don't you think—' I cut her off.

'No! Nora, I'm sorry but it can't be done. Don't worry, we'll find some other way of pacifying your Major.'

She gave a faint smile, said, 'Oh well,' and left.

Sunday evening came and I was again interrupted by the telephone ringing. It was as I expected, Nora. This time I did not wait, as I was alone in the house, I invited her round.

I could not but help noticing that she looked pale and tired when she came. She looked listless and after greeting me, added in a flat voice, 'I'm going to Leningrad.'

'Going to Leningrad? Why? When?' I asked, quite astonished at this sudden news.

'Tonight, the train leaves in two hours. I'm going to see my Uncle Konstantin.'

'Then don't stay too long, there's my Russian lessons, I'll miss them,' I countered, but there was no answering smile. She did not remain long and seemed very uneasy, but before she left I pressed her to take a little extra money for the lessons I'd had and as an afterthought, took off the little silver wrist-watch I was wearing and gave it to her, knowing that she had always admired it. I felt amply rewarded when I saw how her face lit up at this unexpected gift.

When she had gone, I thought a lot about this young girl who had so innocently become embroiled in espionage, it was a sad thing to my mind.

Some three weeks elapsed, and I did not hear from Nora. Her visit was only to be a short one she had said. I had a presentiment that something had gone wrong somewhere and had begun to feel worried as I felt responsible for her. Further, I realised that I was missing her. Imagine my surprise one day when I was given a note that had been left at the gate for me.

It was from Nora. Vasily, the porter who gave me the letter, explained that a poorly-dressed little old woman had handed it to him saying that it was to be given to no one but 'Mister John'. Although he was supposed to let his superior know of anything unusual happening, he assured me that he had not reported it. Funnily enough, I believed him, and I think he did speak the truth.

The note from Nora was short. It was written in German and gave me her address. She simply said she was staying there, but was very ill and was so sorry to trouble me, but the people with whom she was staying had very little of anything themselves in the way of food and she would have to leave soon.

It was a pathetic little note and I read between the lines. Now the Staff of the Moscow Embassy, in view of its unique situation and the food shortages in Russia, had an arrangement whereby wines and spirits and canned beers and provisions could be purchased in bulk, duty free, from England, and transported to Moscow under a special diplomatic dispensation once a year. These supplies were not only for personal use, but also to enable the staff to undertake their obligations as regards social get-togethers with other Embassy and Consular staff. This was a form of liaison quite important for Foreign Office personnel living abroad. By a lucky chance, the last orders that were to be permitted for many years were just being made up when I arrived in Moscow, so with Bagshawe I was able to stock up with a considerable amount of provisions. From our stores I made up a parcel of tinned provisions, soups, meats, cereals. I also enclosed an envelope with several hundred roubles and a note saying 'Get well quick, John.' I got hold of Valentina, gave her the address and asked her to deliver the parcel to Nora, who I'd heard was ill. I blurted out that if she wished she could also report the matter to the NKVD — the matter meant nothing to me, as Nora was only my teacher and I would do as much for anyone who was ill and in trouble. Do you know, women are women the world over? She gave me a kind of mysterious smile and looked straight at me.

'Don't worry, Mr Murray, it will be all right.'

I left it at that. Valentina delivered the parcel and returned in a very serious mood. 'Your Nora is very ill. She has inflammation of the lungs. She cried when I gave her your parcel, but she is very, very grateful to you.'

I thanked her. She still gave me that pitying half-smile.

One day soon after this incident my chief called me into his office and told me that instructions had been received from the Foreign Office that the Embassy was to reduce its staff to essential personnel only and all the redundant staff together with the womenfolk were to be sent back to England. Amongst those to go were all those living at *Maly kharitonevsky* except myself. Sir Stafford had decided that I should move into one of the vacant furnished cottages that were situated in the rear garden of the Embassy grounds itself. This suited me, but I asked about the staff we employed. The outcome was that both Rebecca and Vasily the porter should remain as caretakers, and Shura the chauffeur should be paid off as I had no car and in any case would not require one. With regards to Valentina the cook, she could still be employed as such at my new place, should she so desire.

When I saw Bagshawe later that day his first words were, 'You've heard the news, John?' I nodded. 'Do you know,' he continued, 'I'm glad I'm going. It'll be good to get back home again!'

I told him about the plans that had been made for me regarding my new home.

'You'll be better off there. This is an unlucky place,' he said.

'Never mind,' I said. 'I'll get the lads together and we'll give you one hell of a party at my place, so you'll have a real good send off.' At the idea of the party to be held in my new home Bagshawe began right away to prepare the invitations.

We called Valentina in and told her about the new state of affairs and I asked her if she would like to continue at my new place. She was not only delighted, but grateful. It was arranged that I should still eat at *Maly kharitonevsky* for the next couple of days until Bagshawe left. I told her that her first job with me would be to prepare for the best party she'd ever organised, for Mr Bagshawe who was leaving.

It was a Friday and Bagshawe was going on the following Monday so our party was scheduled for Sunday evening. As I was leaving the house after lunch, Vasily handed me a note. It was from Nora. It simply said, 'Tomorrow at noon in the park.' Throughout the time since receiving the first note some three weeks ago, I had sent several parcels of food, with money, to Nora through Valentina who had told me she was gradually getting better. I never expected a written reply as it was quite possible that Nora could not trust Valentina. Receiving this note now, I knew something had happened to Nora. Luckily Saturday was my day off.

Making use of the large crowds to shake off any followers I dodged in and out and slipped into the *Krasny dvor* underground station and boarded a train to Sokolniki Park.

It was not long before I saw Nora, she looked awful and I was shocked to see how pale and thin she was.

'Hello, Nora, having trouble?' I tried to speak lightly.

She said nothing, opening her handbag she took out her passport and handed it to me.

I examined it wonderingly. Underneath her photo, across the place of residence, a thick black line had been drawn. To a Russian, this meant that the owner was no longer entitled to reside in Moscow, and further, should the owner be picked up by the Militia he or she would be liable to instant arrest followed by deportation from Moscow to a place of exile.

I handed it back, all I could think of was to ask how this all came about. I could see she was still pretty weak, so we found a deserted bench and sat down.

She told me her story in a listless, faraway voice as though nothing really mattered any more.

Before she had come to see me on the night she left for Leningrad, she already knew all was lost. She'd had to report to Major Kirilov my adamant refusal to meet himself and his colleagues. His reaction had been one of violent rage. He had stormed and raved at her that she was a traitor and an agent of the capitalist dogs. That she was no longer to be trusted and had let the wicked and dangerous Englishman she was supposed to have watched make fools of them all. At this point she had protested saying that I was not the wicked man he thought I was, and that on the contrary I was a kindly person who had a great affection for the Russian people. This only increased his outburst of rage, and he had turned on her and accused her of falling in love with me instead of doing her duty. He said that it was no good her protesting, they had been watching her all the time. With that he ordered her to give him her passport, cancelled it, and then flung it back at her saying, 'See if your damned Englishman can help you now!' He then shouted at her to get out and leave Moscow immediately, warning her that if she did not do so, or attempted to see me again, she would be arrested and pay the full penalty as a traitor to her country.

In spite of the threat she decided she would see me before she left for Leningrad.

'Why didn't you tell me all this before?' I asked her, remembering how strange she had acted the last time I saw her.

'Because I knew how worried you were about your parents coming and I did not want to add further to your troubles,' she replied.

She then went on to tell me how after arriving in Leningrad she had gone to her uncle's flat, but for his own and her aunt's safety, he had refused to let her stay more than a couple of days. She then contacted a former friend of her father's, a woman whom she knew as Nina. Nina had pretended to be very kind to her, they had exchanged confidences and she had told Nina about her troubles and friendship with me.

310

Within a matter of twenty-four hours she was picked up by the Leningrad secret police for interrogation. Her so-called friend Nina had proved to be an informer!

She was kept in the cells all that night under constant observation and questioning. In a last desperate effort to clear herself she revealed to them that actually she was a Soviet agent working for the special branch of security under the *nom-de-plume* of 'The Swallow'. They asked her why she had not mentioned this before, and she told them she could not for security reasons. Shortly afterwards she was released and told she must leave Leningrad and return to Moscow. When she arrived in Moscow, she had nowhere to go and, frightened of being picked up again before deciding how she could contact me, had taken refuge in a cemetery. That night, the cold and dampness of the graveyard had made her very ill. Delirious, she had been found by a kindly old woman whose custom was to search the deserted cemetery at dusk for anything that could be used for fuel. She had managed to get her home and nurse her. It was this brave old lady who had brought me the first note and the second. The illness had developed into pneumonia, but the old lady had continued to nurse and look after her even though she had very little herself. The food and money I had sent saved her life and for this she was very grateful. Two days ago however the old lady informed her that the house porter had reported her to the police who were now enquiring about the unregistered guest she was sheltering.

She realised then that the net was tightening around her and how hopeless her situation was, that it would only be a matter of hours before she would again be arrested. Her one thought was to see me once more, if only to thank me for the kindness I had shown her.

It would be hard to describe the thoughts and feelings I experienced as I listened to this hurried narrative. She had sat all the while with her hands clasped upon her lap. I put my hands over hers, they were ice-cold. Leaning forward I said, very softly, 'Nora, tell me, is it true what Major Kirilov said? Do you really love me?' She hung her head and was silent. Only as the hot tears began to fall upon the back of my hands clasped around hers did I realise she was crying.

For me, that was enough! I stood up. In my agitation I paced up and down trying to gather my thoughts as to what course of action I should take. The biggest shock was the fact that this girl was actually in love with me. It seemed so unbelievable and was something I'd not even dreamed of as possible. The whole situation was so absurd, there was nobody I could turn to for advice. I knew I'd be out on my neck if anybody in the Embassy knew of my predicament for, already whilst listening to her story, the full horrors of her plight had become evident to me and I knew it was partly my fault. Another thing, although our relationship had been 'strictly business' as far as I was concerned, I suddenly realised how I had missed her and the strange empty feeling I experienced whilst she had been away.

Without giving the matter any further thought, I made an instant decision. I told her about my new accommodation arrangements and explained to her how one could reach the cottage where I now lived. It meant passing the guards at the main gates to the Embassy. She was to say Mr Murray had sent her if questioned and ask for Mr Velukin. With that, I drew from my pocket the spare key to the cottage, took both her hands in mine and pressed the key into them.

'Nora,' I said, 'this is the key to my house. Go there and wait until I come home.'

I did not wait for her reply, but turned quickly on my heels and strode away without looking back. The matter was now out of my hands, if she was there when I returned, I knew that it would be Fate that had decreed it so. There was nothing more I could do, to have accompanied her myself would have been fatal once my shadows picked me up again.

I made my way to Bagshawe's place first, as I had still to arrange quite a number of things, which included extra staff for my party the next evening. Two hours later, Shura was driving me back to the Embassy. When I entered my cottage it was dark and silent. I went to the sitting room and switched on the light. From an armchair in the far corner, a puffed, tear-stained face looked up at me — it was Nora. She sprang to her feet and put her arms around me, 'John, Oh John,' she murmured as I held her tight. She was warm and soft and clinging. I tasted the salt of her tear-stained face. We made love that night. Nora was the first woman to whom I had ever made love. She was twenty-one — I was thirty-three. All through the years up to that moment I had imagined what love would be like, from the guilty stage of early adolescence to my older, more reflective years. But I had had very little to do with girls and I was never popular with them, being of a far too serious disposition and somewhat old-fashioned in my ways.

That night was one I shall never forget. Nora gave me everything that a woman could give a man and I was intoxicated by the release and power of the passions which had remained pent-up for all those years. It was not only the physical ecstasy of being one with her, it was the aftermath that was so wonderful — that feeling of unutterable sweetness and tenderness that permeated our whole beings. As I looked upon her lying at my side, I sensed the indescribable happiness that enveloped us both and vowed within myself that should anyone dare to lay hands on Nora, I'd tear them apart with my bare hands, for she was now of me as I was of her, with our very lifestreams already mingling and coursing through each other's veins.

Just before we finally fell asleep, troubled as I was by conflicting thoughts on the dangerous consequences of bringing Nora inside the Embassy grounds, it occurred to me to ask her why she had sought refuge in the cemetery. It was a trivial matter, but I had to know everything now my mind was made up. She then told me the story, a story so incredible that it could only happen in a place like Russia. It would take far too long to give the full narrative, but the gist of her story was as follows.

As she had hurried down a small dark side street after leaving the station on her return from Leningrad, she heard footsteps behind her. Glancing round she saw an NKVD officer. He called on her to stop, and grasped her arm. She tried to struggle free.

'Don't be afraid Nora Vasilievna,' he said. 'I am a friend, I knew your father, Vasily Savich. Come with me, I must talk to you.'

The tone of his voice reassured her and they walked some distance together in silence, she wondering all the time about the meaning of this strange encounter. He led her into a 'traktir', the Russian equivalent to our pubs, where one could get a drink — they soon had a small table to themselves, the other customers melted away on seeing the NKVD officer.

Her companion ordered a carafe of Vodka and though she drank very little, he drank continually, filling the small glass and emptying it in great gulps. In between he spoke.

'Norachka, you don't know me do you?'

She shook her head.

'That is well, it is better so,' he said and continued, 'your father Vasily Savich and I were great friends, when you were a baby I often dangled you upon my knee. Your father was a good man and a brave one, a true patriot. When he was arrested I was shocked, I knew he was innocent, but that is how it goes in Russia today.'

He paused to fill himself another glass of Vodka and continued. 'Listen carefully Norachka, you are in great danger. An order has been issued that you are to be arrested as soon as you are found and executed immediately, it is my department that deals with such orders. Believe me Norachka, I have to deal with many such. Up until now I have been able to protect you by keeping this order back, but I can do so no longer!'

313

She had listened not knowing what to say and he continued, 'It was me who handled the enquiry from Leningrad and I've been waiting around for your return. It is only God's will that I have seen you today. There is so little time left, yes, so very, very little time left.' He looked at his watch.

'Norachka, tonight I leave for the front, my train goes in one hour's time.'

'What front?' she had asked. 'There is no war.'

'Ah, Norachka, you do not know of what is happening. Shortly, maybe in a month's time we shall be at war with the German dogs who seek to invade our Russia, but we will destroy them, have no fear, but there will be hard times, such hard times as none can imagine.

'Yes, very hard times, and I...' he shook his head from side to side. 'I will not return alive, I feel it in my bones. God knows what will happen to my daughter.

'Yes Norachka, I have a daughter, a young and beautiful girl just like you. Perhaps God will be good and provide a protector for her too when I am gone; who knows? Now, Norachka, I can do no more for you. You must go. Go far away from Moscow and keep away from the big towns, anywhere, but you must go.'

He stood up and thrust a handful of notes into her hand. 'Here, take this my child, and God bless you and guard you! Above all, do not confide in anyone ever again, there are informers everywhere!'

With that he saw her to the door and returned to his table where she noticed the empty carafe of Vodka had been replaced with a full one.

She had then wandered through the streets avoiding the crowded places, gradually working her way from the centre of the city to its outskirts. She felt tired and confused. There was no place she could go to and her fear of being arrested gradually increased to terror. Above all, she wanted to be alone, to think quietly what to do next. Although it was cold she felt hot and giddy and her limbs began to feel dead. She came to a churchyard, the gates long since gone and the stillness seemed so inviting to her now weakening body. She went through the portals and staggered among the graves and finally knew no more until she opened her eyes and found herself lying in a strange bed with the anxious-faced old lady bending over her.

As she finished her story she shivered and began to tremble.

'There, there, Nora, it's all right, don't be frightened, no one will touch you now!' I said, and held her tightly in my arm meanwhile caressing her face with my free hand.

She murmured something, and fell asleep. I was satisfied. Now, I knew what to do! I had done the right thing in bringing her to my home.

314

There was no doubt in my mind that it was going to be a very tough job protecting her. But Nora's narrative, coupled with what I had learned from her about Major Kirilov, led me to the conclusion that his department, being a very special one, shunned publicity and acted with such secrecy that not even the ordinary police were taken into their confidence. She would have certainly been arrested long ago if this had not been the case, and it was this that gave me hope. From now on her future was my responsibility.

In the early hours of that late May morning of 1941 I awoke and with the approaching cold grey dawn, the full realisation of our predicament became depressingly apparent.

Nora lay beside me, quietly breathing and fast asleep. I looked upon her face, so beautiful and sweet in its relaxation. My determination hardened; somehow, some way, I would marry her and get her out of Russia to safety. Nothing else mattered. I began cold-bloodedly to review the situation. The NKVD had now no further use for Nora — she was a discredited agent. Furthermore, she had betrayed their trust and vengeance would be swift and merciless if they could lay hands on her. For the time being, whilst in the Embassy grounds, she was safe, and they could not touch her. For me to appeal to the Embassy would be hopeless. I had brought her to my house without approval or permission. I would be shipped off home immediately and then, God knows what would happen to Nora. It did not bear thinking of. I'd got Bagshawe's party on that day. How could I explain Nora's presence?

The only staff I had was Valentina. She was commencing her duties with me as from that day but her hours of work were from nine a.m. until three p.m., after which she would return home, so for the party at least, a waitress would be needed to serve the food and drinks, and to tidy up — this would provide a legitimate excuse for having Nora — she would be the waitress! No one else knew of her existence except Bagshawe and Valentina. Valentina, I knew would be surprised to see Nora. I also knew she would have to report Nora's presence at my place, but that could not be helped. All I and Nora could do, would be to wait and see what transpired, and hope for the best. When Nora awoke, I explained my idea to her.

Her first reaction was, 'But I've no clothes! Only the black dress I've been wearing!'

'Don't worry,' I said. 'You look beautiful as you are, but I'll go over to see Rebecca at *Maly kharitonevsky* and get you a nice little pinafore to wear,' and as I gave her a kiss, added, 'And you'll be the world's most wonderful waitress!'

Valentina arrived and got the shock of her life when she saw Nora, but I explained in quite a matter-of-fact manner that I'd brought her in to help at the party. I went to Bagshawe's place and told him his party was going to be a real good one, and also mentioned that I had managed to find Nora who was going to give me a hand with the serving. He thought it was a fine idea. I saw Rebecca, who willingly lent me one of her aprons, I then returned home.

The evening was a huge success. Most of the junior members came from our Embassy staff. Bagshawe's chief, Captain Clanchy did not come, neither did my chief, but Colonel Greer representing the Services, and his secretary Jimes came. Quite a number of our friends from the American Embassy arrived, including Reinhardt. From the other Consulates, the Greeks, Turks and Persians came, and of course the newspaper men who could never be kept out of anything. Besides these there was a fair contingent of staff from our late Legations in Czechoslovakia, Hungary and Yugoslavia who had been unable to get home when the Germans invaded those countries and had found temporary asylum in Moscow.

For the party I had laid on plenty of drinks, several wines, whisky, gin and Vodka. The food Valentina had prepared consisted of hundreds of open sandwiches, Swedish Smorgasbord fashion, of every variety of meats, cheeses and fish, all beautifully garnished. Fresh fruit, of course, was not available, but we had a large variety of tinned fruits. The *pièce de résistance* at the end of the evening was, of course, ice-cream served with champagne, which was a Russian fashion. Valentina was proud of her ice-cream which she made from quarts of fresh cream in a hand-operated freezer, which used to be lent out and around the Embassy for party-givers on such occasions. All enjoyed themselves, and a real friendly atmosphere pervaded. I was both congratulated and chipped about the new waitress I'd found. Jimes, who though married, always had an eye for a pretty face and legs, was most attentive to Nora, who carried out her duties as quietly and efficiently as a real waitress. The party finally came to an end at about two a.m. Normally it would have gone on much longer, but as many of the guests were leaving Moscow in only about another eight hours, it helped to bring the party to a close. All I wanted, was to be alone with Nora. I was so frightened that our hours of happiness might be short.

But it had been a good party and I was so pleased that I'd been able to give Bagshawe a good send-off as I'd promised. In a way I was sorry to see him go because I knew that at heart he was one of the best.

The days that followed were ones of bliss. But I had to work hard and late; things were happening. The messages we decoded from London were full of portent and they made me think. Of course, we did not discuss them even among ourselves. You just carried on doing your job regardless. Nora was happy and content to stay in the house. We would walk round the garden during the now warm nights. I'd warned her never to leave the Embassy garden, and this she understood.

I could not help feeling a little apprehensive sometimes, and it was Velukin, the Russian messenger, who gave me the first hint of what was happening. I often had brief chats with Velukin who told me he was married with a wife and two children. He told me he hated the job he was doing and felt very insecure. I understood. His masters, the NKVD were an unpredictable lot. He also sensed I understood his position. I always gave him a cheery greeting when I encountered him of a morning, and occasionally would give him a knowing wink, which made him smile. Three days after Bagshawe's departure, he approached me and said in a low tone, 'Mr Murray, you have a citizeness, Korzhenko, staying in your house. It's not good. Send her away or THEY will make a lot of trouble for you.'

'No! I like Russia, but I love my Russian girl and I am going to marry her and make her my wife, and you can tell that to THEM,' I said heatedly. He just shrugged his shoulders.

'It's so difficult — I only wanted to warn you.'

So, this is the first round of the battle I'm going to have on my hands, I thought.

Nora seemed very downcast that evening, and she told me she didn't know why. 'But you shouldn't be sad,' I said, 'I'm going to marry you and take you back to England.' It was the first time I had mentioned my intentions. She looked at me and laughed.

'But that's impossible, you know it is.'

'No, nothing is impossible if we truly love one another. Shall I read you the cards?' I added.

'What do you mean?' she asked.

I produced an old pack of playing cards from one of the drawers in the dresser, and whilst shuffling them explained to her that my mother was Irish and like the gypsies, the Irish had strange powers.

Now I'd watched my mother many times when I was a boy tell neighbours their fortunes — they were always women who'd had some trouble or other, or who were beset with fears of some sort. My mother would firmly state she was not a fortune-teller, but could only read and interpret the cards that they blindly selected from the pack. She would lay them face down on the table and they would select a given number from

317

them. Needless to say, my mother was very shrewd besides being wise, and somehow the portents always fitted in with the events that later transpired.

Did I believe in such powers myself? I do not know. I am one of those persons who strongly disclaims any supposition to be superstitious. Nevertheless, I always threw salt over my left shoulder if I spilt any, if you know what I mean.

Nora looked at me wonderingly and I saw the gradual excitement of anticipation light up in her eyes. I began by selecting sixteen cards – the four queens, the four jacks, the four aces and the four deuces. I did not show them to her but simply laid them face downwards on the table and shuffled them around. She watched me intently. 'Now, don't think about anything at all, just pick out four cards and give them to me without looking at them!'

She selected four cards at random and handed them to me. Even I did not know what to expect. Slowly, one by one, I turned the cards over and placed them face upwards on the table in front of me, pushed the remainder to one side and turned them face upwards also.

By an amazing coincidence, she had selected the very cards I was hoping for. They were the Queen of Hearts, the Jack of Spades, the two of Hearts and the Ace of Clubs.

'Look,' I said, 'from all the cards on the table, you have picked the Queen of Hearts. That is your card. You are all heart, throughout your life whatever you do, or wherever you go you will be dominated by the heart. There is nothing but good in the heart and it will protect you from all evil. Had you picked the Queen of Diamonds that would have told me you were hard, unrelenting and avaricious, with no thought but of yourself. The Club would have told me you were of a restless dissatisfied character, for ever bemoaning your lot, and if you had picked the Queen of Spades, that would have meant that you were evil and mean and would bring nothing but harm to all those around you. In fact,' I continued, 'if you had picked up anything other than the Queen of Hearts, I would have run away and left you as quick as I could!'

'But the other cards. What about them?'

I could see she was impressed and longing for me to continue.

'See, here we have the Jack of Spades. This is the man that Fate has chosen for your partner. He is young and dark, he should have been Hearts, but really he is Hearts, and it is only the evils of darkness that surround him and cast the shadows over his card that appear as darkness, but in any case, this young man is bound to you, for the next card is the two of Hearts which means the first two cards you have picked will be joined in love and happiness, two hearts on one card!' I nodded impressively.

'Is it you?' she whispered.

'Why, of course it's me!' I answered. 'It's all here, in the cards you've picked yourself. They don't lie! But see, now we have the last card — it's the Ace of Clubs. The Clubs among other things represent your home or dwelling. It means a new home for you; the white space that surrounds the Club denotes the sea. Surely it is a home far away, beyond the seas and surrounded by the seas. Why, that must be England!'

She looked at me in awed silence. I felt elated.

'Tell me more,' she commanded.

'I've not finished yet,' I said, as I gathered all the cards together and shuffled them. 'Here, you shuffle them now,' I said. After she had finished I took them and counted out four packs of thirteen each, laying them out face downwards.

'In one of these packs, my Queen, your card will appear and all the cards that surround it, will be the ones that will tell me your future!'

I could feel the mounting curiosity and excitement I had aroused, and I began to feel infected with it myself. I examined the first pack for Nora's card, then the second pack, and then the third pack. With a flourish I picked up the fourth pack and began to lay the cards down face upwards in the shape of a cross. Then an incredible thing happened, which even I took for an omen. The Ace of Hearts appeared in the centre of the cross, with the Queen of Hearts appearing to the left and the Jack of Spades to the right of it. Above the Ace of Hearts came the two of Hearts. A mixture of cards formed the rest of the cross.

'There you are!' I cried. 'Look, everything is confirmed. There's you, there's me, there's the Ace of Hearts — the greatest of all Love cards and the two of Hearts above us, which means we two shall be joined together!'

I grabbed Nora and we danced round the table like a couple of excited kids. After dancing around for a couple of minutes, Nora wanted to know what the rest of the cards had to say. I explained that the Ace of Clubs which had turned up, really meant that she would cross water to a new home, especially as it was backed by the two of Clubs which confirmed the presence of two homes divided by a space which meant water. There were Hearts and Diamonds which I said denoted surprises, presents, and all things nice. There were the black cards, especially the Spades, which I said were the cards of ill-omen of the trials, sufferings, sorrows, and tears to come. She looked apprehensive at this, but I told her I had to read all the cards for her, the good with the bad, if I was to be truthful.

319

She was not to worry because the very centre was subordinated to the Ace of Hearts which finally triumphed over everything, through the love, happiness, and warmth of heart that bound us together. This had all taken time, and by the end of it Nora's sadness had vanished. That night as we lay together, I felt teardrops running down her cheek onto mine. She was fast asleep, dreaming. Whether they were tears of joy or of sadness, I did not know, but I held her gently but firmly more close to me.

The next morning, Nora was bright and sunny again and I felt cheerful as I went into the Embassy for duty, glad indeed that my ploy of the evening before had worked. But a shock awaited me when I started my duties that morning. I was summoned into the presence of Mr John Dunlop, the Embassy Secretary.

There was no beating about the bush: 'I hear you have a Russian woman in your employ as housekeeper, Murray?'

'That's right,' I said.

'But it is not all right. You know that no staff is permitted to be employed here without the sanction of the Burobin,* and I have just received a notification from them about this matter. Will you please see that she leaves immediately!'

I protested that I had to give her time to leave and he said she must go as soon as possible.

I did not tell Nora, as I was determined to keep her on. A week passed and I was again summoned to Dunlop.

'The Burobin inform me that your housekeeper is still on the Embassy premises. Really, Murray, you must do something about it!'

I told him that I had not forgotten his instructions, but the difficulty was that she was in trouble with the Soviet authorities and I dare not let her go until I had at least made some preparations for her safety, which just at the moment was difficult owing to the volume of work which had increased so enormously lately. He understood what I meant. We were really quite good friends. The point was, he was in authority. In the end it was agreed I should do what I could, as soon as I could, to resolve the matter. I did not tell Nora about this either. The work was growing — we were already working late in the evenings, busy decoding the stream of messages from the Service Departments that multiplied in number each day. The only heartening thing about them was that they also told of decreasing air activity over England and consequently lower casualties and damage to our armament production. It

* Burobin: The state bureau for supplying domestic staff to foreign embassies and consulates.

was already well into June and in the early summer mornings, rising early, Nora and I often peered through the curtains to watch Sir Stafford Cripps taking his morning exercise, striding quickly with his long legs. Nora told me that she thought our Ambassador looked a very stern and severe man indeed. I told her it was not so, that he was actually a very kind and human man, who was what I would consider a real socialist.

To keep Nora occupied I had managed to get some books and plenty of writing materials for her, thus she was able to continue her studies on her own — in between looking, or perhaps I should say, loving me and looking after the cottage, there being no hope of her visiting her University. I still employed Valentina, but she and Nora did not get on together; Nora had her own private room and she always retired to that when Valentina arrived. I had to keep Valentina on because she did the shopping, but my chief reason was I did not want to give the NKVD a handle to start something by dismissing her.

PART V – WAR COMES TO THE SOVIET UNION

On the night of 21 June, 1941, Nora and I went to bed earlier than usual as I was exceptionally tired and we soon fell asleep in each other's arms. We seemed no sooner to have fallen asleep when we were awakened by the long drawn-out howl of what seemed to us, a wolf. Then another, and another, and then several creatures took up the howling. It sounded spine-chilling in those early hours of the morning. We got up; I looked at the clock, it was two-thirty a.m. It seemed almost a portent of what was to come. I knew what it was. When I had first come to the cottage, Velukin had asked me how I liked it. I'd told him jokingly, 'fine', now that I had a back wall to nip over when I wanted to dodge my unwelcome shadowers. He had instantly become alarmed.

'Never, never do that, Mr Murray. The walls at the back of the Embassy are patrolled by security personnel with huge, fierce wolf-hounds. They would tear you to pieces instantly!'

I had never ever caught a glimpse of them or heard them, but this night of blood-curdling howling confirmed their presence. The noise subsided. What had started the wolf-hounds off I was never able to discover, but it was very disturbing and neither Nora nor I could sleep, so she made some coffee and we sat silently, both waiting for we knew not what. Sure enough, before the hour had passed, the wail of an air-raid siren sounded.

'That's an air-raid warning,' I told Nora. 'Stay here while I go and see what it's all about.' I rushed out into the garden and made for the main Embassy building. I met one of the Chancellery servants shepherding Sir Stafford's personal staff — the butler and maids — through a door on the side of the building, leading to the cellars.

'What's up?' I asked him.

'The Germans are attacking Russia!' he said, dramatically. 'You'd better get inside.'

I rushed back to the cottage to tell Nora the news. She took it quite calmly and flatly refused to join the others, saying she would stay in the cottage and wait for me. I went to my office in the main building to await the arrival of my chief. It was not long before all the Service Attachés arrived. Everyone knew the Germans were about to attack Russia, but we had no details as to when and were awaiting instructions from London. The 'All Clear' sounded and later, in the early hours of that morning, military music began blaring through all the public loudspeakers in Moscow. Then came the first official announcement over radio and loudspeakers, made by Molotov, denouncing the treachery of Hitler and the fascist bandits, and then telling us what the glorious armies of the Soviet would do to them. But as the day wore on, the most important thing to us was Churchill's speech offering the hand of friendship and help to the Soviet Union. This was wonderful news, and when I got home and explained to Nora what was happening, I said that surely now the NKVD would not persecute her, as we were now all friends.

The days, then weeks passed swiftly by. It was a case of eat, sleep and work in one continuous routine. The question of Nora's presence in my cottage seemed to have been forgotten, and though our relationship with the Soviet was that of allies, I would still not allow Nora to leave the Embassy grounds. In the Embassy itself there was nothing but feverish activity. The arrival of the 'hush-hush' visitors, Churchill, Lord Beaverbrook and their staff, was chewed over with bated breath by the lower echelons of the Embassy personnel who were actually given very little official information. Nevertheless, we knew what was going on. One day Sir Stafford sent me to the Kremlin with a personal note for Molotov. I felt quite thrilled at the thought of going inside the Kremlin, which was not very far from the Embassy and could easily be seen across the Moscow Canal, which ran parallel with the *Sofiyskaya naberezhnaya*. I was driven there in the Ambassador's Rolls Royce — the first time I had ever ridden in one. Although it was very ancient and the bodywork well-worn, it was like riding on an air-cushion. It must, however, have been twenty years old. Much to my disappointment, we were not allowed beyond the portals. A smart uniformed officer came out and after I had verified that he was the proper person to receive the document, we returned to the Embassy.

In August 1941, the Thirtieth Military Mission, headed by Lieut-General Sir Noel Mason-MacFarlane arrived. With him were Vice-Admiral Miles, Air Vice-Marshal Collier, Group Captain Bird, and a Colonel Exham — a brass-hat who represented the CIGS (Chief of the Imperial General Staff), each with their various staffs. The main body of the Mission was meanwhile being established in the ice-free northern part of Murmansk and the White Sea port of Archangel that was more or less frozen in during the winter.

After several weeks had elapsed and the Mission was really getting under way, Sir Stafford Cripps called me in and informed me that although I would still be serving the Foreign Office, I was to be seconded personally to Lieut-General MacFarlane. I was very pleased about this, and had, in fact, been making myself as useful as I could in many small ways to members of the

Lieut. General Sir Noel Mason-MacFarlane

Mission staff. Macfarlane was, to me, not only a high-ranking soldier, but he was what I called 'a man's man' in every way. There was no stuck-uppiness about him in his dealings with the ordinary staff. He looked and acted every inch like a soldier. He stood well over six foot and was as broad as an ox. He called me in after my interview with Sir Stafford and told me I was to write up his War Diary. This was extremely confidential, and there would be one original which he would send to London, and one copy which would be retained by Sir Stafford. This was to be one of my special duties and under no circumstances was to be discussed. I found him a very considerate chief. The diary write-up was one of the jobs previously done by Colonel Exham who had been seconded to MacFarlane by the War Office.

There is one anecdote that I would like to relate concerning my new chief. It always makes me smile when I recollect it, especially as it gives some idea of what the Russians at that time thought to be right and proper.

Sir Noel, as a true Scot, always wore his kilt and sporran. A discreet intimation was one day passed on from the Kremlin that the Russians thought it was not very becoming for a man to be seen wearing a skirt as it offended the moral ethics of the Russian people. For the rest of his stay, he wore the regulation army trousers.

The Germans through their conquest of Norway had been able to establish air bases at its most northerly tip and Murmansk was already suffering from the attentions of the Luftwaffe, to which the Russians had no answer. Although we were in a very tight position ourselves it was nevertheless decided to sacrifice an air squadron from our own meagre forces to help the Russians. As there were no air bases in Murmansk, Group Captain Bird was sent there to work with the Russians on the details for building one. The place was mapped out and the Russians said they would have it ready within two months. Group Captain Bird returned from his trip, tired, unshaven, and a visibly shaken man. He gave me his notes and asked me to type out his report in time to catch the courier plane leaving for England the next day. I worked all night on the report, and had it ready for him by six in the morning. He was so grateful; he did not know how to thank me enough, especially as he received a commendation from the Chief of Air Staff. Bird told me confidentially he did not think the Russians would be able to do the job, especially in the time stipulated. He said the Russians had absolutely no equipment of any kind to do it with and their only labour force was comprised of thousands of ill-nourished, under-fed political prisoners and the site they had picked was all forest.

But the RAF 171 Wing of Hurricanes arrived on schedule and an air base, of a sort, was already completed by that time. Bird later told me that the trees had been hacked down by hand. Prisoners in their thousands had been put to work on it and those that fell from sheer exhaustion and or died were simply left where they fell and pounded underfoot with the ice and snow that formed the runways. 171 Wing did their job and earned the grudging admiration of the Russians, who were very sparse in praise of anything we did for them. After a while, the planes were taken over by the Russians themselves.

We were meanwhile receiving a stream of reports from Intelligence in London, detailing the appalling losses the Russians were suffering and the extent of the German advances. We were supplying the Russians, too, with reports from our Intelligence Service on dispositions and movements of the enemy. But they would not reciprocate by giving us information from their side. A tight silence was maintained by the Russians. MacFarlane tried by every means possible to visit the battle fronts, but he was sidestepped and blocked at every turn. Later, much later, he was allowed to visit one battlefront but it was not one of the important ones.

The naval side of the Mission had a much better reception from the Russians. This was evident to me later, when I was in Archangel.

Shortly after the Murmansk report, I was asked by Vice-Admiral Miles if I would do the report of one of his submarine commanders who had acted as an observer on one of the Russian submarines during an action in the Black Sea. It was another all-night rush job for me which I completed satisfactorily. I do not think I will be breaking any Security Act when I mention that the report praised the high standards of efficiency and discipline among the Russian crew; even when the submarine, following a successful action, was constantly depth-charged and damaged, they still maintained their high morale. He also found them friendly, though guardedly so.

By this time, it was already August. A new 'Hush' machine had arrived from England — it was a 'Code Scrambler'. This chattered away frantically, churning out messages at a fantastic rate. Certain of the messages, however, we still had to decode manually. It appeared there were only two other machines like it in the whole world — one in London and the other in Washington. With it came an Army Signals Corps Group headed by a Captain, who was soon installed in our cipher room. It was then that my chief summoned me and explained that the Mission with the arrival of the Signals' personnel were having accommodation problems. He wanted to know if I would give up the cottage in the Embassy gardens and return to Bagshawe's old place. If I consented to do this, it would be possible to quarter the Signals staff in my cottage, which would be more convenient for them as the Scrambler had to function day and night. I agreed, and transport was provided for all my things. Nora, of course, came with me and, like me, was quite pleased about the change. She would be seeing Rebecca again with whom she had been quite friendly and so would have someone to talk to.

All the senior staff of the Mission had been quartered in the former Yugoslav Embassy, where they were well looked after by the Russians who had turned it into a kind of hotel. I had occasion to visit there on quite a number of times in the course of my duties. It was run by Gabaridze, the Maitrê d'Hôtel from the Metropole Hotel. It was he who arranged the menus and I had many sumptuous meals there. The thing I enjoyed most was the Caviar and real black Russian bread. Very few of the Mission cared about Caviar and there were always four huge bowls of it containing about two pounds each on the dining table at lunch-time. I used to waffle about a quarter of a pound of it at each sitting. My mouth always waters when I think of it. The Russians also supplied a fleet of the large black 'Zis' cars with chauffeurs to provide transport to and from the Embassy for our staff.

After Nora and I were comfortably installed in *Maly kharitonevsky*, Vice-Admiral Miles asked me if I could put up one of his staff, a young naval writer who had had a bad time coming over from England. It appeared that his mate had been killed right next to him on the ship bringing him over. Group Captain Bird also asked me if I could put up one of his Flight Sergeants. This youngster had arrived in Moscow to a tumultuous reception from the Russian populace as he appeared with his head, face, and hands swathed in bandages. They thought he had been wounded by the Germans. In actual fact, on arrival in Archangel he had been badly bitten by mosquitos with resultant blood poisoning! Then Sir Noel asked me if I could put up his Quartermaster Sergeant. Having plenty of room in the house, and the adjoining archivist's flat being empty, I took them all in, and this made good company for everyone.

Not long after this, we had our first air raid in Moscow. It is a night I shall never forget for quite a number of reasons.

I was on duty. It was about ten-thirty p.m. I was in the Cipher Room with three of the Signals staff busy decoding. The Captain in charge lay stretched out on a couch in the corner fast asleep, having just finished a long spell on duty. A terrific explosion shook the building. We heard the roar of a bomber passing overhead. Following the explosion there was a heavy dull thud in the distance.

One of the signallers said quietly, 'That's Jerry; he's passing overhead. There's generally a stick of five — that's two gone — I hope to Christ the next will miss us!'

There was another shaking thud, this time from a distance. We sat quite still waiting for the explosion, when it came it was in the distance.

'They've missed us!' the signaller said. But even as he spoke there came the sound of a whole series of light thuds. Just then the Captain woke up and groggily got to his feet.

'Air raid, eh? Carry on. I'll go and look around.' With that he unbolted the French windows that led out into the garden and disappeared. We continued working. After a while he reappeared with an armful of incendiary bombs. They were aluminium clad cylinders, about fifteen inches high; he'd got six of them. He staggered over to our table and stood them up in a row, saying, 'Here's a present from Germany,' went back to the couch, fell on it, and was fast asleep again.

We eyed the incendiaries warily, but carried on with our job. None of us dared touch them, because we did not know anything about them. In the meantime, we heard a lot of shouting and banging going on in the building. We carried on until our scrambler stopped, and then I decided to go out and have a look. In the main hall were two huge supporting pillars. Hugging one of them closely with outstretched arms, was one of our Chancellery servants. He was a Cockney.

'What on earth are you doing?' I asked.

'Well, it's like this 'ere. If a bomb drops that-a-way, I slides round 'ere. If it falls this-a-way, I slides round the other side, see?'

I couldn't help laughing, as I made my way to the front door. On the steps outside sat the General and several of the Mission staff — they were all begrimed with soot. It appeared that the Embassy had been hit with incendiaries and they'd all been on the roof putting the fires out. There was also a thick pall of dust hanging in the air which was making everyone cough — the Kremlin Walls just beyond the canal, facing the Embassy had been hit, so filling the air with the centuries-old dust from the brickwork. I was told the bomber had passed overhead letting loose a stick of bombs, one of which had blown up a building to the rear of the Embassy. One had fallen by the front gates but had not exploded — a bomb-disposal squad were working on it. A third had hit and gone right through the canal bridge without exploding. A fourth had fallen by the Kremlin Wall and also had not exploded, and we had sent a couple of our bomb-disposal experts to deal with that. The fifth bomb had actually landed on the Kremlin Wall and had exploded. Hence the heavy pall of dust and smoke which now enveloped the Embassy.

Sir Stafford Cripps' butler now appeared on the scene and the General sent him to get something for them to drink. He appeared shortly with several bottles of Sir Stafford's best wine. He was so nervous, he had forgotten to open the bottles or bring glasses. The General just took them off him, knocked the top of the bottles off on the stone steps and poured the wine into the cupped hands of his colleagues, got one of them to do the same for him and that's how they refreshed themselves. After picking up all the news, I mentioned we'd got some incendiaries on our desk in the cipher room and then went back to work and tell the others what had happened. Shortly afterwards, one of the bomb disposal chaps came in and took the incendiaries away. He said that there was no need to have been frightened as they had already been expertly defused. The Captain still lay fast asleep, quite unconscious of what had been happening around him. I wish he'd told us that he had rendered them harmless before passing out. It would have saved us a lot of worry. The expert told us that two of our bomb-disposal chaps who had gone over to the Kremlin to help the Russians to deal with their bomb had returned scared out of their wits. They had found the Russians sitting astride a thousand-pounder stolidly pounding away with a cold chisel and hammer at the bomb in an attempt to defuse it. It appeared they had very little equipment. They would not let our chaps touch it and finally completed the job, only taking their advice on its mechanism.

At midnight, I was relieved by my colleague, Jimes, and was driven home, glad to get back. I rushed into the house expecting to be greeted by Nora who always waited up for my return. Not seeing her I rushed into the bedroom calling her name. The bedroom was empty and there was no answer to my call! I had a sudden feeling of apprehension as I dashed around the rooms searching for her. I woke up the young Air Force Sergeant and my two other guests in turn. They had come back to the house at various hours during the evening, but none of them had remembered seeing her. I felt my fears rising. At that moment the telephone bell rang. I rushed to the phone wondering who'd be ringing at such a late hour. It was Jimes.

'Listen, John, I've some strange news for you. I've just had a telephone call put through to me. It was from your Nora. She sounded terrified. All she could say was that she was being held at the sixty-sixth Police Uchastok (the district precinct). Tell John, she said and then the line went dead.'

As I listened, I felt a dreadful feeling of sickness overtaking me, my legs wobbled. I could only gasp. Dimly I heard Jimes' voice continuing, 'Sorry, old chap, it looks as if our old friends the YMCA have got your Nora. If there's anything I can do, let me know, John.'

I could only mutter, 'The bastards. I'll murder them!'

329

At that moment I did not know what to do. I was stunned and sick. I went to the cupboard and got a bottle of whisky, opened it and gulped down a couple of swigs, and began to think.

Vasily! Surely he must know something about it. Without more ado I dashed over to the porter's lodge. Vasily was seated at a table with three of the shuttle-service chauffeurs. He looked startled as I rushed up to him shouting, 'Why didn't you tell me about Nora? What's happened to her?' I grabbed him by the shoulder shaking him. He seemed very confused.

'But, Mr Murray, I know nothing, really I don't. All I know is that this evening two men called at the gates and asked to see her. I didn't let them in but called Nora to them. She spoke with them and then they went away. I don't know what they talked about, and Nora afterwards came back and went out herself. I don't know anything more,' he concluded plaintively.

I turned to the chauffeurs, waving my bottle of whisky in the air, 'Come,' I shouted. 'Who'll drive me to the sixty-sixth Police Uchastok? The police there have arrested my wife. I'm going to get her out!' I looked round. Their faces had a sullen, set expression. I knew it was hopeless. All these men were handpicked by the NKVD. They were definitely not going to get entangled with their masters! I groaned in despair. I'd no idea where the Police Headquarters were, and knew that there was no way of finding it, and time was precious.

Then, all of a sudden, several things happened at once. The sirens started again and at the same time a tremendous barrage of anti-aircraft started up. The very building seemed to dance. I had never heard such intensity of gun-fire before. The London barrages that I was to hear later, had nothing on this. It flashed through my mind how the Russians had demanded more antiaircraft guns from our Military Mission, and here was a barrage going on that would have put any air defence to shame. It was fantastic! Then the door burst open and in stepped another chauffeur. He was huge — a bear of a man, with a big smile on his broad Russian features. He had had to bend down to enter the doorway. He looked askance at us all. Without giving him time to say anything, I turned to him, and still waving my bottle of whisky in the air, implored of him — 'Will you drive me to the sixty-sixth Uchastok? My wife is there. They have arrested her. She is my Russian wife. I love her. Do you understand? I'm British. I'm from the Embassy!'

He gave me a searching glance, there was a pause, then he said in a deep voice, '*Da, da, ya pomogu!*' (Yes, yes, I'll help!) He turned round to the others, the smile gone, his lips curled into a sneer and said something very quickly which I could not catch. Then turning to me said simply, 'Come.' Before we went out I proffered him the bottle.

'Here,' I said. 'Have a drink of this.'

He took a couple of gulps, and his face lit up in a most beauteous smile. He'd such a terrific homely face, it was like a ray of sunshine coming suddenly into my life. He offered the bottle back to me with one hand and thumped his massive chest with the other and boomed, 'By God! That's some drink!'

'Keep it!' I said, 'and put it in your pocket.'

This time he treated the rest of them to a triumphant smile, pocketed the bottle, and went out. The barrage was still on. Lumps of metal were sizzling all around us from the exploding shells. Several windows had already been broken. They were lethal, but by some unexplained miracle, we were not hit. As we drove to the police station, I told him how I had fallen in love with a beautiful Russian girl who loved me, and how the NKVD for no reason at all were persecuting her. I asked wasn't it a shame? Here was me helping Russia, when I could be doing better things, and all the NKVD could do was to make my life a misery. He was of course under the NKVD himself, but I had long ago learnt that there were Russians and Russians, and what I called the real Russians were the most kind-hearted and sensitive people one could ever come across.

We arrived at the police station and I dashed in, followed by the chauffeur, and strode straight to the room marked Chief of the District Police. The chief, a podgy pasty-faced individual was sitting at a table covered with forms and documents. He glanced up with a look of surprise on his face as I walked up to his desk, showing him my passport.

'I'm John Murray, an Englishman from the British Embassy. You have my wife, Nora Korzhenko, here. I've come to take her away.'

He ignored my proffered passport and stared at me with a deliberately insulting sneer. 'Get out of my office. I don't know what you're talking about. There is no Korzhenko here. Go!'

That was enough for me. 'Who do you think you're talking to, you lying son of a bitch, you lying...' and I let loose all the Russian swear words and invectives I knew. I'd never used swear words before and never have since, but this was the one time I was in a white-hot rage. 'You — you, devil. How dare you lie to me?' and as I swore I leant over his table and drew my arm back to give him a back-handed swipe that would have blasted him into eternity. He shrank back. Two policemen rushed into the room and stood on either side of him awaiting instructions. At the same time I was gripped by the shoulder and spun aside. It was the chauffeur.

'Softly, softly, *gospodin*, stay, stay,' he boomed at me. I wriggled away and went back to the desk and thumped it with my fist.

'Don't you ever dare lie to me, you dog!' I shouted. His face assumed a puce colour, he was so taken aback, he did not know what to say. The police in Moscow are always used to dealing with abject, cringing wretches who are in fear and terror of them, and it must have shaken him to have someone address him in the way I did.

He lifted up a hand placatingly, 'Wait a minute. I'll try and find something out for you.'

With that, followed by his henchmen, he retired to a back room. Some twenty minutes passed and still he did not reappear. I was stamping up and down, smoking one cigarette after another. My chauffeur just stood placidly there, occasionally shaking his head and also smoking the meanwhile.

I was just reaching that boiling point when I thought I'd start smashing things up, when two comical looking individuals scuttled in; with their absurdly long black overcoats and pointed shoes sticking out from underneath, their trilby hats squashed well down over their ears, there was no mistaking who they were. They went straight through to the back room. Another fifteen minutes passed and the inspector came back into the room. He was most apologetic. Yes, citizeness Korzhenko was in the building but she had to be kept to have her documents put in order, and if I would go away quietly, she would be sent home in the morning. But I wasn't having that at any price. Now that I knew she was definitely in the building, I was determined to get her away. As far as I was concerned there would be no let-up.

I launched into another paroxysm of invective and as the two NKVD men sidled to the door to see what was going on, I took off my coat, flung it among all the papers on the desk, and stated that I was not going away without her. Furthermore, I said that if I had any more nonsense from him, I would go back to my Embassy and ring up Gospodin Stalin personally and complain of their treatment of me.

As I was saying all this, the towering figure of the chauffeur came up beside me and nodding his massive head kept on booming out interjections, such as 'Yes, listen to him, he's a Minister of the Great Britain! Yes, he's got much power! Be careful what you say to him!'

332

The things he was saying were so ludicrous that under any other circumstances I would have laughed my head off, but his manner made him look like Jupiter admonishing his lesser gods.

The inspector's face had by this time turned an ashen-grey colour. Then he motioned to the two NKVD men to go into the back room and they went into another pow-wow. Meanwhile I was again pacing up and down smoking cigarette after cigarette, boiling up internally, fit to burst.

I'd nearly reached the end of my tether, what with fear and anger, when the side doors opened. There stood Nora blinking in the unaccustomed light, held by the arm on one side by a tough looking policewoman. Nora's face was bruised and puffed; her eyelids were swollen with crying. As soon as she made me out standing there, she tore herself away and rushed into my arms.

'Oh, John—' was all she could say, and leant her head on my shoulders, her body trembling and heaving as she sobbed. The surprised look of disbelief that suddenly flashed across her face when she first recognised me was one that I will never forget. The inspector and the two stooges had meanwhile silently entered. I looked enquiringly over Nora's head, thinking there would be some sort of document to sign.

'Go, go, go now; go right away!' He gestured with his hand.

We turned and left, the chauffeur leading and I following with my arms round Nora. At the door I stopped and looking back spat out, 'Tell your people if they ever lay hands on my wife again, I'll kill them!' and I meant every word I said.

We got back to the house. I slipped another bottle of whisky from my precious store into Ivan Ivanovitch's hands and thanked him for his help. He patted me on the shoulder, 'I was glad to help, be careful, and God bless you both.' Such was the heart of this Russian.

Back in the warmth and security of our home, Nora told me what had happened. Vasily had come that evening to tell her two strangers were at the gate and they had some news for her concerning her passport. She had gone to the gate and they had told her in a friendly manner that owing to the new regulations, all Russians had to register for food ration cards, and she would get hers if she went to the district police station despite the fact her passport was not in order, that this in fact would be restored to her, now she was living with Russia's Allies.

Overjoyed, she had later set out to go to the police station. When she had reached the end of the street, a black car had drawn up alongside her. The same two men had sprung out and bundled her into the car. They drove to the station where she was put into a room and told she was under arrest. At that moment the air raid sirens began to wail and the anti-aircraft guns began to go off. There was instant confusion. Seeing the telephone, she dialled the Embassy and was put through to Jimes. She managed to speak a few words when the door opened and a policewoman rushed in and tore the telephone from her. She was then stripped and searched. Her ring and wrist-watch were taken from her and her passport was doubly cancelled with another black streak. When she tried to speak, she was struck across the face and told to shut up, and that as soon as the raid was over she would be transported to the Lubyanka prison. This was Russia's most notorious prison for political offenders; few who passed through its doors ever came out alive.

She had then been taken down the steps to a cell where the only other occupant was a prostitute. There was no light and they had to keep moving about because of the rats that kept scuttling around. She had lost track of time and had given up hope of ever seeing me again. When the policewoman had unlocked the cell door and ordered her to accompany her, she had thought this was the end. When she came to the part of telling me how she felt when she recognised me standing in that room, she broke down and could say no more. I comforted her as best as I could and reminded her softly what the cards had foretold. 'See,' I said, 'they never lie!' I couldn't think of anything more to say. It took Nora a couple of days to get over the shock. That night I hugged her closer than ever, vowing I'd never let her go.

Next morning I made a point of going to the Yugoslav house and getting Gabaridze on my side. I knew the chauffeur would be in for big trouble and I wanted to do everything I could to shield him. I told Gabaridze the story and said I hoped no harm would come to Ivan Ivanovitch for helping me, that he was a true Russian with the kind of heart that I so admired.

'Real Russians like that are the backbone of your country, and it makes me proud to help such people. While there are such brave men in Russia, there is no fear of the Germans being able to conquer them!' Then I added, 'I'm sure even the NKVD would not harm such a man, so brave and filled with true human kindness!'

Gabaridze took it all in. I'd guessed he was quite an important man himself in the NKVD.

He told me they were sad times these days. Not long ago his wife had died and he had not even been able to get permission for leave to go home and arrange the funeral. His only son was a soldier at the front and the bad news, which he knew about — the Russian defeats which the Russian public was kept ignorant of, made him greatly fear for the safety of his son. I commiserated with him.

I was glad to see Ivan Ivanovitch still doing service as a chauffeur. He avoided me and I knew that he'd been put on the rack, from his pale appearance and sober manner. The main point however was that he had not 'disappeared'.

Some time after this event I fell ill. It all began with a temperature, headache, and vomiting, then diarrhoea. At first I thought I was from overwork and catching a chill through the long nights of duty. Eventually, I had to stay at home, unable to carry on any longer. Jimes came to see me and said he would report my sickness to the Embassy. He said everything was now chaotic there. I reassured him I would soon get well. But I didn't. Things got worse and worse. Nora did everything for me — washed and bathed me, but the illness was so severe and took such a rapid turn that Nora became frightened. With the diarrhoea I was now passing flesh and blood from my intestines and lost weight alarmingly. I told Nora that I thought I was dying. My one worry was what would happen to her. One afternoon while I was in a semi-coma, she slipped out of the house without telling me, and went to search for an old family doctor who'd once served in the Kremlin. She managed by some means or other to find him and explained what had happened to me. He told her to go home and he would call. He came that very evening. A little white-haired fellow whose face was lined with care. He examined me. The first thing he asked for was a glass of warm water in which he put some crystals. I asked him what they were; he said *angliysky sol* (which meant Epsom Salts). Well, I thought, this is the end, Epsom Salts! Why, I'd nothing more to pass through me except my intestines. But he was firm. I had to drink the Salts and then lots of boiled water. You can imagine what happened to me!

He went away and returned some hours later with a small conical sealed glass in which was some yellow liquid. He broke off the top and poured it into a tumbler and made me drink it, gave Nora a couple of tablets to give to me sometime later, and then said he had to leave. He told Nora that that was all he could do. I had a virulent type of dysentry and he had given me a bacterial solution to combat it. Whether I recovered was in the hands of God. If I was to feel better later, she was to feed me at first on nothing but the water from boiled rice and later the whites only of lightly boiled eggs, until my stomach healed. He said she was not to worry too much as I was a healthy and strong young man and should get over it. I really thought that my days were numbered. But gradually, through Nora's care and devotion, I began to pull round. That doctor had saved my life. Nora would not let anyone but herself prepare my food. Two and a half weeks later, I was on my feet again, a little thin and wobbly, but increasing rapidly in strength.

It was on 15 September, 1941, that I resumed my duties at the Embassy. Things were pretty grim, the Germans had broken the Russian Lines and were preparing for their advance on Moscow. Irrespective we still worked on. The difficulties of the Embassy were further complicated by the arrival at the end of September, of a Trades Union delegation headed by Sir Walter Citrine. Shortly after their arrival I was summoned to Mr Dunlop's office. He informed me that the whole of the Embassy and Mission staff were to be evacuated temporarily to Kuibyshev, and my flat and belongings had to be left in charge of the servants I designated for this purpose. I filled out the form there and then in his office, naming Nora Korzhenko, Rebecca and Vasily as the custodians. He accepted it without a word.

When I returned home that evening to Nora, I explained what was happening and pointed out it would be too dangerous for her to go with me as once outside the house I could not protect her, but as long as she stayed and was regarded officially as the person responsible for my property, no one could touch her. I said it was bound to be only a temporary evacuation as I was firmly convinced in spite of what everyone said, that Moscow would not be taken. It was a hard decision, but she agreed that it was the right one. The next day, 9 October, the Embassy staff got official notice of the evacuation. General MacFarlane said I was to be issued with an Army uniform to wear. So I was given a battledress. It was too big, but Nora worked on it to make it a better fit. It was quite damp with tears when I tried it on. The next day was simply pandemonium getting everything ready at the Embassy. I went back home in the afternoon and was told to await the Army lorry that was to take me to the station.

I learned that General MacFarlane had also to leave Moscow in spite of protesting vigorously that he preferred to remain. Several members of the American Embassy staff, however, were permitted to remain — America at that time still being a neutral country, and as during the Norwegian invasion, would look after British interests. Finding out that my old acquaintance, Reinhardt, would be one of those staying, I contacted him and asked him to keep an eye on Nora for me and help her all he could as she was more to me than just my housekeeper. This he promised to do — a promise that he fulfilled as I was later to learn. Nora, of course, was very sad and tearful as the time approached for me to leave. Now I still had the small figurine of my Madonna, I had carried it around with me wherever I'd been, in Finland during the Finno—Russian war; in Sweden; in Norway, during my escape, and I had brought it with me to Moscow. It had always been a kind of mascot to me.

I gave it to Nora and said as long as she kept it with her, no harm could befall her. The lorry, an open truck, arrived about seven that evening. The young naval rating and I climbed into it. A last tearful farewell to Nora and a goodbye to Rebecca and Vasily, and off we went to the Embassy. There the Cipher Scrambler was loaded on to it, a rifle with no ammunition was handed to each of us and our truck set off for the station. Arriving at the station, which was jammed at the entrance with troops and lorries in ever-increasing numbers, we were told our train was not ready and that we were to park at a spot some distance away from the station in order to avoid getting entangled with the mounting traffic. We found the place and settled down to wait. It was now about ten. The night was dark and damp, drizzle and sleet were falling. We stomped up and down in the open truck to keep warm. An unending stream of lorries of all types were passing us. Some were filled with troops, mostly young men with weather-tanned faces. They were warmly clad in greatcoats or three-quarter padded tunics, with the usual thick round helmet hats that could be let down to provide ear and neck mufflers. They looked in superb physical condition, well-fed and well-built.

In contrast, some lorries were filled with civilians, mostly women, shawls on their heads, clad in heavy drab coats, women with grim determined faces, only a few men but quite a number of young teenagers full of chatter and restless movement. They were the same type of youngsters that I had noted during the air raids. They would be on the roof-tops during an attack, dancing up and down, skipping across from roof-top to roof-top, shouting and gesticulating to one another, quite oblivious of the danger, and enjoying every moment.

Such was the cavalcade that passed us on their way to the Moscow front. After three hours, we received notice to return to the Kazan Station, and I soon found myself in the welcome warmth of one of the carriages, sharing a compartment with the young naval rating, Jimes and two of the army personnel. After a further delay of about an hour owing to another air raid, our train steamed slowly out of the station, destination Kuibyshev. That journey of some five hundred miles, normally a twenty-four hour trip, took five days. There were constant stoppages en route. Some to arrange food for our hungry party, which had left Moscow without loading the provisions that had been stacked up in the Embassy main hall specially for this purpose. Everybody blamed everybody else. The young naval rating remarked, 'It's just like the Pongos!' A remark that nearly caused a fight in our compartment, but after all, the military personnel of the Mission were responsible.

The Russians fed us from their meagre food supplies. It consisted mostly of rye bread and cabbage soup of an indeterminate colour. Luckily for Sir Stafford and some of his very senior staff, the American Ambassador and those of his staff travelling with him shared their food with them, they having had the foresight to see that they were well-provided with rations before they started. The Trades Union delegation also travelled with us, having hardly had any time to confer with their Russian counterparts. In any case, their arrival had served the purpose of window-dressing which was most essential.

The most outstanding event I can recall from that journey was a scene at one of the marshalling yards through which we passed. I looked through the window and saw a stationary string of goods wagons, some open, others vans with partly opened doors. The open wagons were piled with machinery, transmission shafts and wheels, machine frames, huge electric motors; and sitting among them were women workers in their thickly padded jackets with shawls over their heads, all dappled with snow, and huddled together for warmth. Their faces were a grey putty colour, their eyes sunken deep in their sockets. They showed no sign of interest in our train passing them by. There was no animation or movement among them. They could have been frozen corpses for all I knew.

Eventually we arrived at Kuibyshev and were mostly quartered in one of the newest co-operative buildings. It was quite large. We slept and worked in this building which was situated on a main road that led down to the Volga. The river was of immense breadth and the opposite bank seemed to fade into the mist. It was a bright, sunny, cold day when I first set eyes on the River Volga and it made a wonderful picture, with huge ships in full sail and barges ploughing through its waters, which were still unfrozen.

Work was still hectic and as the news we were handling grew in seriousness, my mind often went back to Nora and how I could get in touch with her. But communication was impossible. Moscow was virtually surrounded by that time. I had only been in Kuibyshev two weeks when I got the shock of my life. Air Vice-Marshal Collier called me in to his office and told me the Mission had decided to send me home for reasons of health! I had recovered from the bout of dysentery and was feeling fine in myself, although outwardly I may have shown some effects of the illness. The arrangements were made; I was to fly to Archangel with the Trades Union delegation and certain of the Military Mission personnel, and a visiting journalist, Mrs Huxley.

338

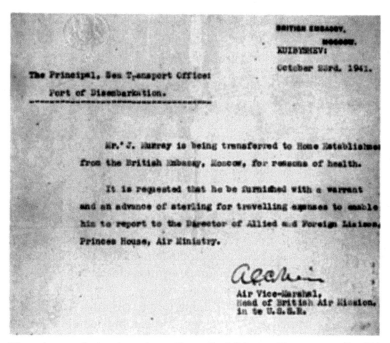

The order transferring the author to Home Establishment 'For reasons of health'
following the discovery of his liaison with Nora

Our flight was fixed for the following day, 23 October, 1941, at the ungodly hour of four a.m. The plane was a converted Russian two-engined bomber. The machine gun under the roof blister had been removed. There was a long table in the centre of the plane, with a continuous bench seating all round the interior. The pilot and radio-navigator sat in the front nose of the plane. All the luggage was loaded and also four small wooden cases that had seals upon them. They were about three feet long by one foot square, made of thick timber. It took two men to lift one, they were that heavy. The Embassy Secretary who was seeing me off, told me that they contained about three-and-a-half million pounds worth of platinum that Stalin was sending to England with the Trades Union delegation as a gift from Russia for our aircraft engine industry.

It was quite dark when we flew off. The plane flew quite steadily and I could get up and walk about and peer over the heads of the pilot and navigator through the nose of the plane. After four hours of flying we reached Gorky where a Russian delegation of Trades Union officials with an interpreter awaited us at the airfield to drive us into the town itself. The

Mission personnel stayed behind, but the journalist, Mrs Huxley, and myself went with the Trades Union. First we had a good solid breakfast, and afterwards were taken to the Gorky Motor Works where we were shown the Russian war effort. It was only a quick, cursory look around and afterwards we were soon gathered together to be taken back to the plane.

It was then discovered that one of the Trades Union delegates was missing. This caused a great deal of upset among the Russians and their interpreter was so upset she could hardly speak. So I did the interpreting. We found the missing chap, all innocence, toddling down a road to look at a church building. Neither he nor the rest of the delegates could understand the fuss. They were so naïve and ignorant of how life was conducted in Russia, that to me it was unbelievable! They still had the starry-eyed belief that it was a free, democratic country, where people could live normal uninterrupted lives. I think they even believed they were dealing with genuine Trade Unionist counterparts. They did not realise that if anything had happened to one of our party, the whole of our so-called Trades Union hosts and the interpreter, could have been liquidated without even a trial.

I had to do a great deal of explaining to the Russians to convince them that it had been a harmless and innocent mistake, but some members of the Trades Union still thought it a huge joke.

Finally, we were all shepherded on to the plane again, which had in the meantime been refuelled. It was about noon when we took off on the last lap of our non-stop flight to Archangel. We flew for seven hours on this lap, flying just a few hundred feet off the ground. We seemed to be flying for hour after hour through a lane in the midst of a vast unending forest. In actual fact, we were following the railway cutting of the line Moscow-Vologda-Archangel and had to fly low to avoid enemy planes.

It was about seven p.m. that same day when we landed on the ice-covered airfield at Archangel. It was the darkest, coldest, most unfriendly place I had ever arrived at. As soon as all the baggage was off the plane several cars drove up and we were surrounded by a very friendly group of Russian Trade delegates who said that a special official evening supper had been prepared for our party. Just as I was about to step into a car, a little short busy-looking member of our own Trades Union delegation told me that I was not included in the invitation as it was only meant for them. The Military Mission staff had already gone with some of the others — I think the upset in Gorky had something to do with this because I had been somewhat outspoken at the time. The Russians looked a bit puzzled when I did not go with them, but I didn't enlighten them. They all drove off and I stood for a while taking in the scene.

There was nothing in sight except our lone plane standing on the snow-covered airfield. The airport was just a large low-roofed building made of wood consisting of one huge hall, surrounded by a few small offices and a Radio room. A couple of uniformed officers were eyeing me speculatively. I went up to them, showed them my passport and explained that I wanted transport to the town of Archangel where I would be staying at the Intourist House. Within a short time they produced for me a horse-driven sleigh and soon I was bounding along over the ice and snow with a big warm fur rug wrapped tightly round me and only the tip of my nose exposed to the wind. Over and over again the thought went through my mind, 'What the hell am I doing here, in this Godforsaken dump?' Nora was constantly in my mind. I felt I was being drawn along a path to which I had no affinity. I couldn't think clearly. I was aware only of a hopeless, helpless sense of tiredness creeping over me. After what seemed ages of sliding, with occasional back-breaking jolts over a desolate wilderness of ice and snow, we gradually approached lanes of small timber buildings, in between which ran a road of packed snow that gradually led to the Intourist building.

Imagine my surprise when, before entering the building, I noticed the four wooden boxes of platinum stacked against the wall outside. I paid off the driver and gave him a packet of cigarettes which I rightly guessed meant more than the money to him. I went to the desk and asked if there were any messages for me. It appeared I was expected; a message had been left for me and a room reserved on the first floor. The message was a note from Lieut. Fisher, RN, who'd first of all been with the Mission in Moscow, and later sent up to Archangel. He was an ASDIC (Anti-submarine devices) expert and the Russians needed his expertise up here against the submarine and acoustic mines menace. He wrote he would be seeing me later on in the evening and that I was not to turn in until he arrived.

I took my things and went up to my room, passing a grim-faced woman seated in the corridor. She was the 'watcher', and as I later found out, seemed to be on duty twenty-four hours a day. She was about forty-five years of age, buxom, dressed in black, with greying hair tightly swept back and formed into a top-knot bun, which all added to her formidable appearance. When I spoke to her in Russian, asking the way to the wash-room, I found I was quite mistaken about her. She brightened up at once and her features assumed quite a homely expression. I had a quick wash under a tap of running cold water which was very refreshing, and then went downstairs to the restaurant.

341

The place was full, mostly of Officers and Captains from the various ships lying in Archangel. There was also a sprinkling of some of the Military Mission's Ordnance Corps soldiers, a couple of whom I recognised had been in Moscow at the time of the first arrival of the Mission personnel.

My biggest surprise, however, was to see Gabaridze striding forward to greet me. It was like meeting an old friend. He told me the Yugoslav house had been closed down with the evacuation of Moscow, and he had been sent up to organise a special hotel and club for all the foreign crews of the ships that were beginning to come in. He would also be running the Intourist House, which was used mainly for the Russian officers and officials from the labour camps in the vicinity. He immediately set about getting me a decent meal. When that was over, I got up and went outside to stretch my legs. Still lying outside on the pavement were the neglected cases of platinum. I was shocked and went back into the restaurant and asked two of our Ordnance Corps lads if they would take the cases up to my room. After much puffing and blowing they managed it, asking me if it was lead I'd got in them. Laughingly I said yes, something like that but not quite.

Lieut. Fisher arrived about eleven-thirty that night. He said they had been extremely busy as there was a Destroyer which was due to sail with a crowd of Trades Union blokes. He told me there was a hell of a shemozzle going on downstairs over some boxes that were missing. I smiled, and pulled away the bedspread which I'd used to cover the cases of platinum.

'This is what they're looking for,' I said. 'There's about three- and-a-half million pounds worth of platinum there, which I found lying on the pavement outside unattended!' and then told him the story. 'You'd better nip down and tell 'em it's here!' which he promptly did. Within a matter of seconds, one of the Trades Union members burst into my room demanding to know what right I'd had to touch the stuff. He really went on alarmingly. I thought he was going to have me clapped in irons on the spot. By this time there was a crowd round the door. I cut him short.

'Shut up!' I said. 'Everyone knows me. I'm from the British Embassy. Do *you* want to make a case of this or do you want me to make a case of it? This stuff was lying abandoned on the pavement outside for hours. You can thank your lucky stars it was I who turned up.'

That was that. Lieut. Fisher, whose Christian name was Sasha, stayed with me for a couple of hours swapping yarns and before he went told me he would call in the morning to take me to Norwegian House where I was to report to Group Captain Bird who had been appointed Officer in Charge of the Air Mission to Northern Russia. This was unexpected good news as I was very pleased to have the opportunity of meeting him again.

Sasha, by the way, spoke perfect Russian and held quite a high position in the Naval Mission to whom he was extremely useful. He told me that although he and his father were British, he had, like his father, been born in Russia where they had come under the dual nationality law, under which anyone born in Russia was regarded politically as a Soviet Citizen. At the time of the Revolution, the family had been separated and his father had been conscripted by the Bolsheviks as part of their labour force who mended roads. His mother, with little Sasha (he was then only four or five years of age), had undergone untold hardships in their search for him. They had wandered far and wide until by one of those incredible strokes of fortune, they came upon him working by the roadside with a labour gang. Managing to stifle their excitement at the mutual recognition, they had bided their time and one night he joined up with them. They fled south to the Crimea and managed to get away with other refugees, landing eventually in England. He could still remember the terrible experiences they had undergone during those days of flight.

The next morning I saw the Group Captain who told me he was not sending me off, as the destroyer, on which I was supposed to travel, had in fact already left, but would arrange passage for me on one of the ships in the next convoy. As he was very short-handed, he hoped I would be able to help him out. I was glad of the respite, for the fate of Nora was still uppermost in my mind.

My first big job was to make a verbatim report of a Court of Inquiry that was to be held. As I was, amongst other things, the only shorthand-typist available, I could not refuse. Besides which it was pointed out I would receive a special remuneration from the Admiralty for the work. I did this job satisfactorily and was commended by the Mission heads. It dealt with the mysterious and unaccountable disappearance of a Foreign Office diplomatic bag that had been unloaded from one of the ships; a serious matter, and it remained one of the minor unsolved mysteries of the war. Later on, Group Captain Bird told me, very apologetically, that owing to the fact that I was still attached to the Mission, a special payment could not be sanctioned. I told him not to worry. He was of course anxious to hear all the news I had about Moscow and Kuibyshev. I mentioned the Trades Union incident and we had a good laugh over it. Further, I told him of a private conversation I had had with Sir Walter Citrine on the plane whilst we were flying to Archangel. I had asked Sir Walter what he thought of the chances of Russian survival now that the Germans had reached Moscow and he had answered that he saw no hope for the Russians and that in his opinion they were finished.

I had answered that nobody in official quarters seemed to have a true knowledge of Russia and the Russians and that in my opinion no one was aware of their true strength, and that they would not only defend Moscow, but also eventually defeat the Germans. But he said he knew more than I of the true position and was afraid that this was the end for Russia. Group Captain Bird reckoned I was right but said there was still a long way to go.

Archangel was a terrible dump in my opinion, especially in the winter months when everything froze solid and the cold was intense. From what I could see the whole town appeared to have been built on a raft of logs. The pathways to the buildings, the roads and sidewalks were composed of rough hewn logs. During the spring, summer and autumn months Archangel was one huge swamp. From the paths and roads to the houses one walked on wooden platforms over the morass underneath. Woe betide anyone who fell overboard. The hordes of mosquitos were fantastic and quite virulent as I was later to learn. But winter froze everything into one solid mass, as soon as the snows came. Archangel itself was on the mouth of the river Dvina that flowed upwards, from the south to the north into the White Sea. Its one main road ran parallel with the river mouth and was divided from the sea by a series of low, squat, white stone buildings. The walls of these were of incredible thickness, some two to three feet broad. It was also at this time that I saw the reindeer driven sleighs. The reindeers were in superb condition, a tribute to the care and love bestowed upon them by their owners. The sight of them trotting so pertly down the snow-covered roads and the tinkle of the bells that adorned their harness always gave an unexpected fairyland touch to the winter scene.

There was another aspect to Archangel and its surrounding districts. It had been used as a place of banishment even in Tsarist times. Most of its inhabitants were either exiles or descendants of exiles. Once there, the possibility of escape was minimal. There was only one railway running from it and that was always tightly controlled and the same applied to the ports on the White Sea coast. The surrounding impenetrable forests and swamps were of such vast depth that anyone managing to run away would probably perish. There was, however a kind of free community, that is, exiles among whom were professional people, like doctors, dentists and teachers who lived and formed a mutual aid group that were allowed to exist, but not leave Archangel. They married, bore children, and plied their various professions where and how possible. The officers of the NKVD who watched over them were themselves mostly men who had fallen into disfavour at some time or other and had been relegated to duty there as some kind of punishment.

After my arrival I was kept very busy, which was just as well, as I was in a state of despair and almost crazy with anxiety about Nora. One consolation I found very gratifying: Group Captain Bird's appreciation of my help. As I was on call for all three services on a variety of tasks my time was fully occupied.

In the course of my duties I had occasion to visit one of our ships lying at Molotovsk, one of the new ports constructed in the White Sea, and having some time to spare, wandered through the high stacked blocks of timber to the edge of a broad highway that had been trampled out in the snow. Suddenly to the left of my vision I saw the vanguard of a long line of human beings marching eight or ten abreast guarded on either side by immensely tall heavily-built soldiers, armed with rifles and revolvers strapped round their thick grey long coats. Others had huge wolf-hounds, a pair to each man, straining at their leashes as they marched along. The column seemed to have suddenly erupted from the snow-covered background and it seemed without end. The guards completely ignored me as they occasionally bawled and cursed the prisoners to get a move on. I was a bit anxious but held rooted to the spot as I watched this strange sight.

Instinctively counting, I reckoned there were about 2,000 of them. I was amazed that the guards disregarded me, but it gradually dawned upon me that, dressed as I was in a Russian fur cap, with my fur collared coat of black cloth and leather knee boots, I looked to them like one of the dreaded Commissars from Moscow checking on their behaviour. It was a dark, gloomy winter day, the cold intense and deadening, all around was an unending expanse of snow and ice, with the fringes of a black impenetrable forest in the background. The prisoners I saw were past looking like human beings. Dressed in ragged and patched-up quilted jackets, greasy and stained, held together by bits of string, rope and straps, with legs and feet covered in formless felt knee-boots patched and wrapped round with dirty strips of cloth, they presented a dreadful sight as they shuffled along with stumbling, leaden steps, seemingly unaware of the shouts directed at them.

To me, it was what could be seen of their muffled faces that was so terrible and nightmarish. From under a fantastic array of fur and cloth headgear they appeared as skull-like faces over which layers of grey yellowish skin had been stretched. From out of deep set eye sockets stared glazed, unseeing eyes, with an unforgettable look of hopeless despair. Their heads bobbed up and down with each shuffling step they took, as though it

345

was a supreme effort even to move. Although these were men and women together they were practically quite undistinguishable.

After the column had passed, curious to see where they had come from, I walked in the direction from which they had appeared.

I soon came upon what appeared in the distance to be a wooden lighthouse, it was a watch-tower and on my right, parallel with the highway, I became aware of a steep ditchway that was so deep, the high wooden palisade topped with barbed wire that ran with it was not even discernible from the roadway. Far behind, I could make out endless rows of long wooden huts half buried under the snow. I could detect no movement among them. So desolate and silent was the scene that it was almost as though I had stumbled across some long-dead outpost of the arctic.

I veered away from the scene and quite unexpectedly came upon a shipyard. It was derelict. Something that had been started, left unfinished and neglected. The snow-capped skeletons of wooden stocks seemed incongruous in such a place so I made a quick investigation. Strewn here and there along their length were the hulls of five submarines in various stages of abandoned construction, some almost buried in the snow. The whole lot intermingled with steel plates and wheels long since eaten away with rust. Such an installation did not make sense to me. I wondered what the Russians had been thinking of to set up a naval shipyard in such a desolate area, so far from communications and engineering facilities. It puzzled me at the time. I made some cautious enquiries among the few Russian friends I had made in Archangel. From them it appeared that two years previously, early in 1939, German specialists had arrived from Germany to set up the shipyard. What for, no one knew, except that prison labour had been employed. These specialists I was told, had all packed up and hurriedly gone home two months before the outbreak of war.

Most of the Russian officials with whom we had to deal were quite uncooperative and contrary, and even though we were helping them, they remained suspicious and were always putting difficulties in our way, apart from keeping us well-watched. For instance, when the tanks and guns were unloaded from our ships, the Russians took over at once and our people were not even allowed to touch them. We were not even permitted to set up a hospital for the sick and wounded that arrived with the convoys, which was also a source of friction. The officials we had to deal with were hand-picked men who would never take any decisions unless directed from the very top, which meant their superiors in Moscow.

Some of the Russians, however, were what I call human and one could get on well with them in a guarded sort of way. Gabaridze was one. When I had first arrived he got the small five man orchestra to strike up the popular old First World War marching song, 'It's a long way to Tipperary' as a kind of welcome for me, much to the astonishment of some of our men in the restaurant at the time, who joined in the chorus. It was a terrific hit with the Russians. Later I asked if they would play a real Russian song for me and he chose a piece called 'Suliko', a haunting Caucasian folk melody about a lover who had been turned into a nightingale. It was such a sweet song that I got him to get the orchestra to play it several times for me.

There was a little wizened old man that used to sit drinking alone in the restaurant. I had noticed him several times. One evening I went over to his table and bought him a drink. He was so delighted his gratitude was quite moving; I'd noticed he seemed very sad and dejected. In the course of our conversation he told me a very tragic story. He was Captain of an Esthonian ship bringing the first load of tanks to Russia. Previously he had been on the Atlantic run braving all the perils of the sea. His ship, having been in an English port at the time of the outbreak of the war, had been commandeered for war service. He and his crew, some with their wives, had been quite content to serve under the British flag on the Atlantic war run. They had then been frightened and upset about this, but had been reassured all would be well sailing under the British flag.

Once they had docked and unloaded in Archangel, however, the Russians had put the ship under arrest, claiming it was Soviet property. The Captain and his crew were then hauled before the Russian Authorities (NKVD) and told they must consider themselves as Russian citizens and would not be allowed to leave Russia. Without the Captain explaining, I could well imagine the terror and anxiety this aroused in them. Up till now, they were, however, allowed to live on their boat which was docked further down in a place called Ekonomiya where our Military Mission personnel were stationed and, beyond infrequent calls from a 'politico' officer, were allowed to come and go freely in Archangel. This was no doubt due to pressure exerted by our Military Mission. The main point of his story — they did not mind leaving the ship that had been their livelihood for so many years, if only they could be allowed to get back to England where they had already got homes and even wives. They were not informed of what was happening, did not know what was being done about their case, and were just living from day to day in an atmosphere of terror and uncertainty. I listened with growing indignation. I could feel for them in their predicament. Like cattle they were being shunted around, waiting for the slaughter, and as I later met some of the crew and their women folk who had travelled with them, I realised how simple and trusting these people were.

I asked him if they had ever made an official protest. They had not. English was a foreign language to them, although they all spoke it in a broken fashion. He looked so pleadingly at me when he asked if I could help in any way, that I gave the matter some thought. I said that at least their plight should be put down in black and white and handed to the Ministry of Transport representative of the Mission. I decided I would write a petition for them which all could sign, simply stating they had been in the past faithful servants of His Majesty's Government, wanted to continue being so, their situation at present was such and such and they wanted nothing more than to be shipped back to England by any means possible. I carefully translated this to the whole of the crew whom I met later. They signed it, as though it was a passport to Heaven. Poor devils. It at least gave them some sort of hope. I never found out what eventually happened to them. I know their Captain handed it in for them and the copies I made for them, which they also signed, were regarded as treasured possessions among themselves.

I knew it had been handed in because I received a severe reprimand with an injunction not to meddle in affairs that did not concern me. This came through my Chief. It was. official, but it was kind of half-hearted, because when I related their story to my Chief, he understood the situation.

The weeks had gone by like lightning, Group Captain Bird could not hang on to me any longer, orders were orders. The next homeward bound convoy was leaving on 25 November, 1941. The ship I was to sail on was the *Temple Arch* which was docked at Molotovsk, a port some eight to ten miles from Archangel. This news made me very downhearted for Nora was never far from my mind. On the night of the 12th November, as I went wearily to my room, the old Russian war-horse guarding the corridor relaxed her features to give me the faintest suspicion of a smile. I was really taken aback for she was always so grim-visaged, and when Russians smile their whole features change. There is nothing so warm as a Russian smile. Maybe it's the climate that does it. It set me thinking. There was a telephone hanging on the wall in the corridor. I often wondered whether it was in working order. I decided one night to ask the porteress if she could get me Moscow on the line, and gave her my house number. I explained I had a little Russian devushka (girl) with whom I was deeply in love and as I was soon to leave Archangel, I wanted to say good-bye. I told her this and looked terribly sad, for I felt sad. Her face lit up into a full smile. Certainly she would try for me she said. What an awful thing to happen to anybody!

She took the phone and said something to the exchange operator and then I heard her repeat my telephone number. There was a short pause, then she thrust the receiver into my hands and said, '*Vot!*' Clear and distinct, Nora's voice came over the 'phone, '*Kto tam?*' (Who's there?')

'Nora!' I said. 'It's john.' I almost felt her swaying.

'Oh, John. Where are you?'

'I'm here, in Archangel, speaking from the Intourist. I have received orders to leave for England. I am leaving in twelve days' time, but I'll come back for you, Nora. Wait for me. I promise I'll come back for you.'

'John, John, I love you so. I'll come to Archangel,' she gasped.

I was alarmed. 'Don't try, Nora. It's dangerous. Everywhere the lines are under fire.'

'I'm coming—!'

The line suddenly went dead. I handed the receiver back to the porteress. She rattled it and spoke a few words into the mouthpiece then turned to me and said, 'The line's been cut,' shaking her head mournfully. I was surprised that we had got through at all. It seemed a miracle to me, especially as I knew the railway from Moscow to Archangel had been repeatedly cut by enemy action near Vologda.

Actually, I never gave another thought to the possibility of Nora carrying out her intention to come. First, once she left the house she would be picked up by the Police. Secondly, the only method of travel was by train and the line was insecure owing to the German advance, and thirdly, only such persons as were permitted by the NKVD were allowed to board the trains, which were constantly searched and checked throughout every journey. At this time, only military personnel were using them and they, of course, could not run to a definite schedule.

I tried many times to get through to Moscow again, but all to no avail. My hours of duty were still long and arduous. We were so terribly short staffed and there were still constant bickerings with the Russians who interfered with our men on the unloading of the armaments for Russia. All this led to a lot of unnecessary friction and suspicion. The only members of the Mission who achieved any sort of friendly relationship were our Naval personnel, some of whom were even allowed to sail on their ships. The biggest shock our naval officers got on such trips was the Soviet employment of women naval officers – captains, engineers, the lot! It took ages for the Senior Service to get over the shock of women's encroachment into a man's world. A bigger

349

shock still was their efficiency. Alas, our people knew so very little of the real Russia!

At last the dreaded day when I was to leave Russia arrived. On 25 November, 1941, I boarded *Temple Arch*, but not without first a close scrutiny and thorough search of my belongings by the Russian Police and frontier controllers. I felt utterly weary and dispirited and must have looked it because the Captain invited me to have a drink with him. I told him the cause of my despondency was a Russian girl I'd had to leave behind and that she was in danger and I did not know what to do. Of course I could not tell him the whole story, but he was very sympathetic and tried to cheer me up. Some of the crew were on the quayside having a game of football, a final opportunity to stretch their legs on terra firma for we were due to sail at dawn. I went on deck and leant on the rail to watch them. It was about three p.m. Six powerful overhead lamps lit up the scene. Dusk was already approaching. The lamps, by the way, were to enable the Russians to keep the ship under observation until it left. Already the ground was covered with a thick carpet of snow and it was still falling, but our lads were thoroughly enjoying their game. I'd been watching them for a few minutes when in the distance I noticed a figure weaving and stumbling in the snow, approaching our ship. At first I thought it was some poor devil who had escaped the chain-gang. Not an infrequent event, sometimes a prisoner did break loose, the sight of a slop basin being emptied from a ship's side being too much for the half-starved creatures. Men had been known to scramble to a ship to gather up the waste food that was emptied overboard. They were generally clubbed before they could achieve their purpose. As the figure approached nearer, the whole universe seemed to sway round me. I could hardly believe my eyes. It was Nora! She had seen me and was crying, 'John, John!' I was over that deck in a flash and fairly leapt down the gangway, nearly knocking the Russian guard over as I sprinted to meet Nora. How can I describe that moment when we fell into each other's arms; even I cried from the shock. I could hardly believe it was real.

Ignoring the menacing action of the guard with an *'Idi k chortn'* (Go to the devil!) I led her up the gangway into the ship. There was pandemonium as the game of football stopped and the crew came up and stood around us — all I could say was 'Nora, Nora,' over and again. The Captain came up and shepherded us into his cabin and ordered the steward to bring tea instantly. Nora was half-frozen and shaking like a leaf. I turned to the Captain and said, 'This is Nora – the girl I have been telling you about. How she's got here, God only knows.'

350

The Captain finally soothed us both down into a semblance of sanity and we began to take stock of the situation. I'd already made up my mind what was to be done. We were on a British ship, the Captain could marry us and we'd sail for England together. I saw no obstacles in the way. But the Captain, poor fellow, suffered with us as he pointed out that we were still in Russia and he had no power to do what I begged. He would not only have to get permission from the Russians but our own authorities. As we were going over this problem the door burst open and in strode a couple of NKVD officers. Their commands were peremptory. Nora must leave the ship instantly. She was an unauthorised person. I asked Nora if she had any documents on her. She had! It was a most imposing official-looking document indeed. It was a foolscap sheet, headed with the emblem of the United States Embassy to which was attached a magnificent beribboned seal with the American Eagle. Her photograph was also stamped on it, and it enjoined all aid to be given to Citizeness, Nora Nina Korzhenko, in carrying out her duties to deliver the personal effects of British Embassy official, John Murray, to Archangel.

The officers were quite awed by this but stuck to their orders that she must leave the ship and this forbidden territory and go back to Archangel and they would personally see her safely there. We could do nothing. There was a very tearful farewell and we parted once again. I was at my wits' end, bitter, disappointed, and still feeling the effects of the shock of our meeting — everything seemed unreal, I thought it was a dream. I was for leaving the ship immediately and going back to Archangel, but the Captain said my official embarkation orders were still with him and it would be more than his life was worth to allow me to disobey them. He pointed to a small hut on the quayside.

'There's a telephone connected to the Mission in there, ring them up for instructions.'

I did so and was lucky to be able to get Group Captain Bird first time. I quickly explained my position. 'Stay where you are, Murray. I'll send someone over right away to bring you off!' He could have said otherwise, but he was now repaying me for all I'd done for him. I felt grateful.

Within an hour Sasha Fisher drove up in a car and handed me a document officially recalling me from the ship. Saying farewell and wishing the Captain and crew a speedy and safe voyage I drove away with Sasha to our headquarters at Norwegian House. When I arrived there, Group Captain Bird, after listening to my profuse thanks, gave me an odd quizzical smile.

'Well, John, what are you going to do now? I can't keep you here for ever.' I told him that to me Nora was more than my housekeeper. I had fallen

in love with her long ago, and it had been and was my intention to marry her
and get her out of the country at the first available opportunity.

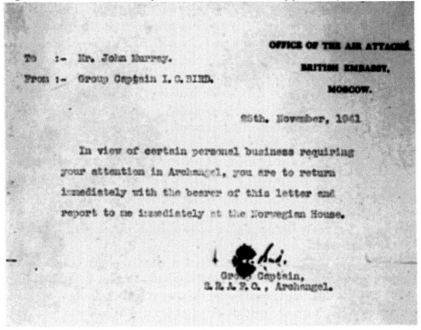

To   :- Mr. John Murray.

From   :- Group Captain I. G. BIRD.

OFFICE OF THE AIR ATTACHÉ.

BRITISH EMBASSY,

MOSCOW.

25th. November, 1941

In view of certain personal business requiring
your attention in Archangel, you are to return
immediately with the bearer of this letter and
report to me immediately at the Norwegian House.

Group Captain,
S. R. A. F. O. , Archangel.

The order recalling the author from aboard the S.S. *Temple Arch*

'Well, the best of luck, John. You've certainly got a job on your hands.'

He was of course glad of the excuse to have me back, but there was still
something I could not understand.

Sasha drove me back to the Intourist Hotel. On the way he explained that
he had met Nora when she had arrived, and had put her in my room. He had
known who she was from what I had told him of her. He had reported her
arrival the day before to Group Captain Bird as she had brought along with
her from Moscow a whole cartload of my effects. The Group Captain had
told him to tell her I had already embarked on my ship for home, the news
had shattered her.

When we arrived, I dashed straight up to my room. Nora lay on the bed
sobbing. For some minutes she could hardly realise it was I who had come,
and kept touching me to see if I was real. I told her my Chief had recalled me
at the last moment, just before sailing. Again it would be hard even to
attempt to describe the joy at our reunion. We spent practically the whole of

that night talking, questioning and counter-questioning. Bit by bit I got the whole story out of her.

She explained that Sir Noel Mason MacFarlane and Air Vice-Marshal Collier had returned to Moscow from Kuibyshev and following some vicious air attacks on Moscow the two of them had decided to make a spot check upon my former place in *Maly kharitonevsky* to see if everything was all right. Probably they had also received a hint from Dunlop, the Embassy Secretary, that my housekeeper was an undesirable (from the Russian point of view).

Now MacFarlane, though a rough and ready soldier of stern appearance, was in fact a very warm-hearted man, and Nora, sensing this had told them the whole story of our relationship and her past. It must have been a shock to both he and the Air Vice-Marshal, but the pathos of her story must have touched him deeply and he assured her of his protection. Collier, however, was furious and when he later arrived in Kuibyshev issued the command for me to be sent home under the guise of ill health, without giving me any explanations of what had transpired. By that merest chance of getting through to Nora by 'phone from Archangel, a whole sequence of events followed. Nora, frantic and out of her mind, remembered my instructions as to what to do in an emergency and decided to contact Reinhardt at the American Embassy. Reinhardt did not hesitate to help her. Nora's only desire was to get to Archangel, no matter what the cost, to see me if only for once more. It drove her on to achieve the impossible. Reinhardt supplied her with an American protective pass that even the Russians dared not ignore. He also gave her the necessary money and even had the Embassy car drive her to the station, all official and business-like. It was only her supreme courage and audacity, spurred on by love, that carried her through in those dark and dangerous days.

When she had arrived at the Intourist Hotel in Archangel, she met Sasha Fisher who told her I was already aboard the *Temple Arch*. She was heartbroken as well as exhausted. Later, driven by hunger, she was compelled to go down to the restaurant for some food. Imagine the mutual shock and surprise when she came face to face with Gabaridze. He already knew my story and was kind to Nora. Whether accidentally or on purpose, he sat her at the table occupied by my friend the Esthonian Captain. The kindly old Captain, watching her eat with tears falling down her face all the time, asked her what was wrong. Nora, now realising all was lost and not caring what might happen, poured out the whole story to him. He understood the situation immediately. He let her finish and said, 'Why, you must be John's Nora. He told me all about you! He has not gone yet. His ship is due to leave the day after tomorrow. He is still in Russia!' He then gave her minute details of how to get to my ship. How, that it lay in a strictly forbidden area and special permits would be needed for all the Security Stations guarding the way. He told her what to avoid and all the snags, and finally warned her how dangerous it would be. They decided that it would be best for her to attempt to reach my ship in the morning. She succeeded, thanks to this brave old seaman.

I now looked around our room. There were two large suitcases and fifteen bundles of various sizes. Bundles wrapped in sheets and blankets, carefully sewn up. It was staggering. These were some of my effects that Nora had packed and brought with her. I could not imagine how she had managed to bring so much. Nora told me that Rebecca had helped her to gather and sew up the bundles. There were clothes, tinned conserves and most extraordinary of all, my glassware consisting of brandy, wine, liqueur, hock and champagne glasses that I'd used for entertaining. Some three hundred pieces in all, carefully wrapped in toilet paper. To me, they were of little value. I had bought them off Bagshawe before he left. They looked beautiful but in fact were all Woolworth's stuff that he'd had sent over from England years ago. The average price had been half-a-crown a set of one dozen. She'd managed to see that not one had been broken on the journey. Even today I still marvel how she was able to bring this stuff at such a time.

As we went on talking we came to the inevitable question of what to do next. I was determined not to lose her again and was still frightened of the long arm of the NKVD. One thing I was determined on, by hook or by crook we would get married. To Nora the idea still seemed an impossibility, but we agreed that the next day we would make enquiries as to how this could be done. It was already the early hours of a new day. We slept in each other's arms, once again confident we would be able to win through and the little Madonna that Nora unpacked seemed to shed peace on our slumbers. The morning came all too soon, but we were buoyed up by our excitement. The first thing I did was to telephone the Group Captain for time off to attend to my affairs (meaning Nora). He gave me a free hand. Next, I introduced Nora to our 'watchdog' — the lady who sat on the chair that commanded a view of the corridor on that floor. We told her we wanted to get married and asked her how we should go about it. She actually beamed — this was a unique romance for her hotel. She explained that we should go to the Marriage Bureau Registry at the municipal building, gave us directions, and wished us well.

Breakfast over, supervised by Gabaridze to whom we mentioned our project and to which he, too, wished us well, we set out. The marriage registrar, who was a woman, was quite astounded at our request. Nothing like this had ever happened before in Archangel. She would love to marry us she said, but she did not know what regulation applied to a Soviet citizeness marrying a foreigner and advised us to see the Chief of Police for the Archangel District, giving us instructions of where to go. So off we marched to the Chief of Police, a Major Dritz. He, too, was astounded, but told us he could not do anything himself because it was a matter for the Chief of the NKVD. He would give us the necessary permit and recommendation to go to the NKVD building where we were to ask for Major Sokolov who was responsible for the security for all Archangel.

We went to him after being passed from one guard to another. He was very abrupt and guarded when we explained our intentions and begged his help. He told us he could not give an answer, but we were to call back in two days' time. I knew then that it was a case of his getting instructions from Moscow, and I determined there and then that the only weapon we had, was to spread around to every Russian official person with whom I had contact, and my job entailed many such contacts, that Nora and I were truly in love and would surely get the blessing of the Soviet authorities seeing that I was working so hard in the Military Mission bringing aid to Russia. All this, of course, would be reported to the 'right quarters' and open them up to public censorship should they refuse our request. In a way it worked: all Archangel seemed to be buzzing with the gossip of this most extraordinary romance. Quite a number of people came into the Intourist restaurant, just to look at us during meal times and would greet us with sympathetic nods.

Meanwhile, unbeknown to me at the time, Group Captain Bird had reported my situation direct to Sir Noel Mason MacFarlane and he had contacted Sir Stafford Cripps and they were both subsequently to plead my case personally with Stalin himself several times, much to Stalin's annoyance over such a triviality while the war was on. They were rebuffed each time as I later found out. When we went to Sokolov we were further put off and more brusquely than ever. I was frightened and forbade Nora ever to leave our hotel room whilst I was away on duty. Sometimes I took her to work with me to the Military Mission's mess room to wait for me, but this was later forbidden. This added to my anxieties. Nora received a summons some days after to call at the NKVD office alone, but I accompanied her and after a bit of a row was allowed in with her to see Major Sokolov. He told us that the Moscow authorities had demanded that Nora return immediately to Moscow as she had no legal Russian documents. If she went she would be granted them and probably would afterwards be permitted to marry me. It all seemed so vague and I demanded that the documents be sent to Archangel instead. He began to get really nasty and said those were the instructions and if she did not carry them out she would be arrested on the spot and be dealt with accordingly. Once again I felt that terrible fear for Nora's safety.

Nora came back with me to the hotel. I gave Group Captain Bird an account of our interview. He said nothing but called in Sasha and they went to see Major Sokolov to sort things out on my behalf. They returned some two hours later but gave me no account of what had transpired at their meeting, except gravely to inform me that it definitely would be necessary for Nora to leave for Moscow, Sokolov assuring them that Nora would not be molested in any way and she would get her necessary documents. Nora and I talked it over with my chief. There was nothing we could do. I was depressed, and suggested that I be allowed to travel with her. My chief said no, as I was still under embarkation orders, but he then informed me that he had been in touch with Sir Noel who had informed him that both Sir Stafford Cripps and himself were again speaking with Stalin about us. This was good news to us, and we agreed that Nora should leave.

Sasha and I saw Nora on to the train. It was another sad and tearful parting full of mingled fears and hopes.

Over a week went by and still no news from Nora came through. We had arranged that on her arrival in Moscow she would let me know of her safe arrival via the Embassy. I managed to get calls through the Mission 'phone both to the Embassy and Rebecca at *Maly kharitonevsky* to ask if she had arrived. That answer was that they had neither seen nor heard from her. In spite of Sokolov's guards I made my way to him and threatened that I'd shoot him if I found out that anything had happened to Nora; I was in such a frantic rage. He protested that everything would be all right. I got home and gradually cooled down and began to think what I could do next. The man who was the cause of the trouble was the head of the NKVD, Beria. I decided to send him a cable and compiled a long telegram in Russian, stating who I was and the fact that I was helping the Soviets by my service with the British Mission that was bringing aid to Russia and all I begged of him was to use his power to allow me to marry the Russian girl I loved, and I would be deeply grateful for all the help he could give me.

It was a very long telegram and the woman in the Post Office looked shocked when I handed it in. I asked her if it would reach Beria; she said certainly as no one would care to intercept a telegram addressed to him

Joseph Stalin *Hulton Picture Library*

personally. Within seven days we got the message through from the Embassy that Nora had reported to them. She had been granted her documents and was on her way back to Archangel and the question of permission to marry would be decided by the NKVD in Archangel.

This was the most heartening news I could ever have received and I counted every minute until her arrival. As the trains from Moscow ran indeterminately, sometimes once every five days or ten days dependent on the fighting in the area, I kept a check on the railway activity and was able, with Sasha, to be at the station when the train bringing her arrived on 20 January, 1942. What can I say about the happiness of our reunion — no words of mine can do justice to the joy and happiness we felt. We got back to the Intourist Hotel and there was all the excitement of our own people and even the Russian staff of the hotel and others who were amazed at Nora's return. Everyone had thought that I would never see her again. Nora gave me an account of what had happened after the train had steamed out of Archangel.

The first three days of the journey had been uneventful. At midnight on the fourth day, two armed NKVD officers had entered her compartment and ordered her to pack her things and be ready to leave the train at the next stop. What station it was, she did not know. She was escorted off and marched to a building, put in an empty room and her escort left her there without any explanation, locking the door behind them as they left. She was terrified, not knowing what was going to happen. She was kept there for four days and nights, but was given food and only allowed out to the adjacent toilet room. No word was spoken to her and whenever she attempted to speak was sternly ordered to shut up. She could hear no movement of trains or vehicles. There was nothing but silence. The fourth day a train steamed into the station. The door of her room was opened and an officer walked in and told her to get her things and board the train which would take her to Moscow. She arrived without any incident and went straight to *Maly kharitonevsky*.

From there she telephoned Sir Noel who came to see her and told her to have courage as he was doing all he could for her. She later reported to the District Police Officer as she had been instructed to do by Major Sokolov before she left Archangel. With some trepidation, not knowing what would happen, she once again entered the Police Headquarters from where I had rescued her during that memorable night of the air raids. She was surprised at the reception she got. Although not cordial it was not altogether unfriendly. She was given a new set of Russian identity documents, passport, and informed that she was now a free citizeness of the Soviet Union and should be thankful her civil rights had been restored to her. After reporting to Sir

Noel she once again was escorted and put on the train for Archangel. It almost seemed like a dream.

We got another surprise of tremendous importance two days later. At the ungodly hour of midnight we were summoned by a police officer to accompany him to the Chief of Police Office to see Major Dritz. With our hearts in our mouths, not knowing what was to happen next, we came face to face. He greeted us with a smile and apologised for bringing us in so late, but he had good news for us and was sure that we'd agree he had done the right thing. Instructions had just been received that our permit to get married had been granted! After all we had gone through it seemed as though miracles were happening. We embraced one another and danced round Major Dritz's room like a couple of demented persons and the Major just sat at his desk and laughed. 'Now,' he broke in, 'when *do* you want to get married?' If the marriage office had been open we'd have flown there right away. 'Can we get married in the morning?' we asked. 'Certainly! Now go — I've a lot of work to do!' We shook hands and returned to our hotel as if in a dream. What a night!

The morning seemed as if it would never come, but when it did Nora rushed round telling everybody we were going to get married, and I got on the phone to Group Captain Bird and told him the news. He was full of congratulations. The Intourist was in an uproar. The Russians could hardly believe it. The first to congratulate us was Gabaridze who said he'd make a wedding party that very night for us and all our guests. All he could do was to shake his massive head repeating '*Vot, vot, vot!*' Nora and I went to the Zags Bureau, the State Registry Office for Marriages, at its ten o'clock opening time. We were ushered into a medium-sized room with just a desk at which was seated the marriage official, a woman, whom I would say was in her forties. Very pleasing and very businesslike. On both sides of the desk stood two pedestals, one adorned with the bust of Karl Marx and the other with the bust of Lenin. A huge picture of Stalin imposed on the Red Flag adorned the background. I left all the talking to Nora. We were both handed a much-thumbed card on which was a list of various diseases starting with tuberculosis, insanity, venereal disease. We had to affirm that neither we nor our families suffered from any of these.

Then the marriage code was read out to us, the gist of which was that we would be faithful and helpful to one another at all times and be good and lawful citizens. Then Nora was asked what name she would adopt for her marriage — her husband's or still retain her own. At once Nora said mine. But it was pointed out that it was quite unusual now to adopt the husband's name and she was quite free to keep her own name. But Nora insisted on her decision.

Page 14 of the author's passport showing the stamp of the official Soviet Marriage Bureau, denoting his marriage in the Soviet Union.

Then a Register was handed over to us to sign. A clerk, who was also a woman but much younger, came in, took the Register into another office where a marriage certificate was prepared, and brought it back for the marriage official to stamp and sign. Even our passports were asked for as they too had to be stamped with the record of our marriage. We were then handed the duly completed marriage certificate, shaken by the hand in turn and pronounced as lawful man and wife.

We went out in a daze. Everything seemed to be happening.

Gabaridze's party for us that night was a thing to remember. I invited as many members of the Mission as I could – the Navy, Air Force and Army were all well represented and from the Russian side quite a number of NKVD officers including one of the Governors and his wife, in charge of one of the prison camps. They were frequenters of the Intourist whom I had met before. This Governor had been a high-ranking NKVD officer in Moscow, but as a sign of displeasure had been demoted to this job in Archangel. As the Intourist was the only social centre in this God-forsaken part of Russia, he and his wife found relief in coming to it from the inhumane and distasteful, as well as dangerous job he had been forced to take. It is not my intention to relate the many stories he told me concerning the actions he was unwillingly forced to take in the execution of his duties. Even the most broad-minded would not believe them.

Gabaridze even produced Russian Champagne for the unending round of toasts that were drunk. The orchestra played for us incessantly. Our old

Esthonian sea captain with many of his crew, including the women, were there. The party was a huge success. There was an atmosphere of friendliness and goodwill all round and I was subjected to much leg-pulling and good-humoured marital advice. Everyone seemed glad of the opportunity to forget their fears and sorrows for at least one evening, and this applied to the Russians too. We had plenty to drink in the way of Vodka. Our Mission lads, unaccustomed to the potency of it, drank a lot without feeling its effects in the warm and crowded restaurant. It was only when they got out into the open cold air that its full effects became evident. They would be walking back when suddenly, after staggering along for a bit, they would keel over and flop into the mounds of snow on the side-walks, and a busy time was had by organising search parties to dig them out before they froze.

All in all it was a happy and enjoyable party, but I could not help feeling a tinge of guilt about being so happy, when all around us there was such an element of deepest misery and despair. My marriage was reported to our Embassy in Moscow and diplomatic action was put in motion to effect Nora's departure with me as my lawful wife. Two weeks later, Group Captain Bird called me into his office for a personal talk. His face had a very serious look. He told me that the Embassy's request had been rejected out of hand. I would be allowed to leave Russia any time, but Nora could only leave when the war was over, as in spite of our marriage she was, by Soviet Law, still a Russian subject and as such could not claim British Nationality whilst on Russian soil and as there was no agreement in existence between our two countries that could deal with the case, there was absolutely nothing that could be done.

The only solution to this problem would be a decree to be passed by the Supreme Soviet giving Soviet subjects the right to renounce their nationality if they could first prove that the country of their adoption would accept them. Such a decree was not in existence. As all this depended upon such a decree being passed by the Supreme Soviet, it was pointed out that such trivia could not even be entertained by the Soviet Government who had more urgent priorities to consider.

When I heard this my heart sank. The Group Captain then went on to say that in view of this state of affairs, for security reasons laid down by the Foreign Office I would either have to leave the country, in which case I would be transferred to the British Legation in Istanbul, or, I would have to face dismissal from the service. As I realised the full portent of what he said, I felt really depressed. Up to this time, my hopes had been buoyed by the permission we had received to get married. This news however was a bombshell! But I was determined. I would not leave Archangel without my wife, and I told him so. He asked me to think it over very carefully and let him know the next day. When I arrived at the hotel I told Nora the news. She looked at me dumbly. I could read the anguish in her face. I clasped her tightly, 'Don't worry, Nora. I'll never leave you!' The following day, 5 February, 1942, I told Group Captain Bird of my decision.

I typed out my own Notice of Termination of Employment at his dictation, which he signed. It read:

'You are hereby notified that your appointment as clerk to the Attaché, Moscow, will terminate one month from today's date.' It was dated 5 February, 1942. I carried on with my duties throughout the month of my notice, and as there was so much to be done, I was heavily occupied.

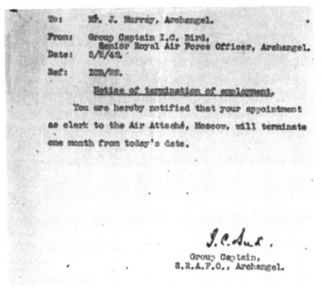

Notice of the author's termination of employment after his marriage because of security reasons

As my term of notice drew to an end, I began to give some thought to the serious position Nora and I were in. One thing, my rouble allowance would stop and I would need roubles for us both if we were staying on in Archangel indefinitely. For one English pound which I could only exchange officially through a Russian Bank, I would get three-and-a-half roubles. I had already enquired the cost of staying in the Intourist, the only hotel in Archangel, and the price was seventy-five roubles per day for full board for each of us! As far as I knew, I had only a matter of £1500 in the bank in England. I never was any good at figures, but even I realised that our position was bordering on disaster, and I did not want to add to Nora's worries if I could help it. Turning things over in my mind, I realised that in a country like Russia everything, including one's existence depended upon one man, and one man alone – Stalin, and that was the only course left open to us – to appeal to him direct. I discussed with Nora, who being Russian, understood what I was getting at. Eventually we decided on sending him two telegrams, one from her and one from myself. To my question, would he receive it, she assured me that, as in the case of the telegrams I had sent to Beria, no one would dare interrupt or interfere with a communication addressed personally to Stalin, not even Beria. That it would be handed to him, she knew that for sure. We set about composing the two telegrams. That from Nora read:

'Gospodin Stalin. I am a loyal Russian Subject and have married John Murray of the British Embassy whom I love very dearly. I plead with you Gospodin Stalin to allow me to travel to England with him as he is being sent back to his country.'

The one from me read:

'Gospodin Stalin. I have done all I can to help Russia. You, Gospodin Stalin, are the only person in the whole wide world that can help me now for I must return to my own country and I wish to take my Russian wife whom I truly love with me. I beg your help to enable me to do this, Gospodin Stalin.'

Nora made the telegrams out in her bold Russian handwriting and we set off, hand in hand, to the Archangel Post Office. The woman counter-hand's face was a picture as she counted the large number of words and digested the contents of the telegrams. Those telegrams I knew would pass through many hands before they reached Stalin, but receive them he would. A load seemed to be lifted off our minds as we returned home. There was nothing more we could do but hope.

The telegrams were sent off on 1 March, 1942. If Stalin really wanted to do anything, I knew our dossiers would be called for from the NKVD. Apart from Nora's espionage career, there was nothing that could be held against us. I, in particular, had been careful to maintain a friendly personal attitude towards all the Russians I had met knowing full well all would be recorded somewhere or other. My term of office ultimately came to an end, although I did not carry on with the confidential stuff, in order to comply with the security code, I gave a hand wherever possible in the Mission and in order to

363

save on the bit of money I possessed, had my meals in the Mission mess, a kind of unwritten arrangement accepted by all.

Nora throughout this period was kept quite busy which was as well for me, as it was imperative she should have something to take her mind off our precarious predicament. Her demeanour by now had undergone a complete change, she was smiling, cheerful, with a friendly word for everyone. She was well liked. Gone once more was that fear and hunted expression from her features.

Into the Intourist Hotel batches of Poles had begun to arrive. They were quartered in tens to twenty persons per room and the hotel was full of them. In charge were two Polish ex-officers — Pan Gruya and Pan Loga. The Poles were coming in from various labour camps throughout the Siberian and Archangel areas. They were being freed to join the Polish forces. There were women among them as well as men. Their condition was pitiful. A train was being organised by the Russians to take them on their long journey to Persia from whence they would be shipped to England. The two Pans' work was enormous. The Russians were only grudgingly setting the Poles free. From their point of view they were only useless cattle. Nora worked with them to prepare their bits of belongings and advise on the necessities for the long journey that lay before them. All this kept her busy and I was thankful for it.

When 'the shoe began to pinch' moneywise, I was able to sell my stainless steel wrist-watch that I'd brought from Sweden (bought there for £35) to one of the Russian officers who'd long admired it and could never take his eyes off it when we met. When I offered to sell it to him, he was tremendously grateful. Few Russians had watches at that time and those Russians who had looked ridiculous — their watches were like big alarm clocks strapped to their wrists. We did not even discuss price. He just took the watch off me and handled it as though it were some precious jewel. Then he put his hand into his tunic pocket and brought out a fistful of rouble notes that I pocketed without even counting. When I showed them to Nora there were three thousand roubles in that handful! Following this, Nora, who had become friendly with the wife of the Commandant of the Archangel labour camp sold my glassware to her for five thousand roubles! She had often seen them and admired them whenever she came, ever curious, to our room for a chat with Nora and I was quite willing for her to have them. Nora found that she could dispose of other oddments, too, especially some of the clothes I had which were of no use to me. Poor girl, she herself had no clothes of her own beyond one dress and a set of underwear — because in those days clothes were not available; even if I gave her money she would not have been able to buy any. She wore my underwear of which I had a fair stock and one of my tweed suits and seemed quite content.

There was one other thing that happened. When Nora and I finally got permission for our marriage, she had sent a telegram to Tashkent, to the last address she had heard from her exiled stepmother, mother, who had now been joined by her step-grandmother and little Felix her stepbrother. Nora received a short reply saying a letter to us was on the way — about three weeks later the letter arrived. In it her stepmother said they were as well as could be expected. She had been able to find work helping on a farm, but her mother was ailing and little Felix was weak through lack of proper food, and if Nora could only send a few hundred roubles to her, she could purchase a goat to obtain milk for the boy. Nora and I decided that we would send what we could from our meagre store and eventually sent two lots of money by telegraph. One was for five hundred and the other for one thousand roubles. As the Polish repatriation train would be passing near Tashkent, Nora began to sew up a couple of parcels with what was left of our tinned goods from Moscow and clothes from my wardrobe and also a primus-cooker that I had managed to obtain. The Polish people promised they would see that her stepmother got them. She never did. Why, I do not know.

Just about the middle of April, Gabaridze came to our room, his face twitching — he looked to be in great distress. As we invited him to sit, he broke down and cried. He had just received a notification that his only son had been killed at the front. Nora and I wept with him. His anguish was terrible. There are situations when one feels really helpless. I went downstairs to get a drink for the want of something better to do. Gabaridze I left, his head on Nora's breast weeping, while she stroked his thin greying hair, murmuring her sympathy in Russian. When I returned some time later he had gone. From that day the light left his eyes and he carried on with his duties like an automaton, there was only a twitchy grimace left on his face to replace the warm soft smile he used to have.

On 17 April, 1942, in the early hours of the morning (it was two a.m.) there was a loud knock on our door. When we opened it, an NKVD officer stood outside.

'Citizeness Korzhenko, you are to come with me to Headquarters, Major Sokolov will speak to you!'

Terrified, we both got up and though the officer insisted that only Nora went, I accompanied them. We arrived at Major Sokolov's headquarters and Nora was conducted to his room. I had to stay outside. A great fear welled up inside me. I waited for what seemed ages. Then I saw Nora being escorted from the corridor. She walked as if in a dream and her face had a stunned look.

'Let us go home,' she said.

I knew something of very great importance must have transpired, but she seemed to be in such a pitch of suppressed excitement, I thought it best not to question her but let her tell me in her own good time. The thing that mattered to me at the moment was that she'd come out safe and sound, and my relief at that was enough. When we got back to our room, she suddenly hugged me and cried, 'I'm free!' She then went on to tell me what had happened.

The Soviet Marriage Certificate given to Nora on 5 March 1942 which enabled her to acquire a British Passport

When she was conducted to Major Sokolov's room, there was another officer standing beside his desk. He introduced her to him and explained that this officer had just arrived from Moscow on a special mission from Comrade Stalin. The Supreme Soviet had passed a special decree whereby, providing the country of her husband would officially accept her into their country as the lawful wedded wife of her husband, she would be permitted under this decree to renounce her Soviet citizenship and leave Russia. If this was her final wish, she was to report to Major Dritz, the Chief of the Police, who would arrange the necessary documents for her to sign and issue her with a visa to leave the country. When she had finished, I could well understand the reason for her looking so stunned.

I contacted Group Captain Bird at the first opportunity to tell him the news and he called us to his office.

After congratulating us, he went to his desk, unlocked one of the drawers, took out a British Passport and gave it to Nora. She looked at it with a kind of holy awe, kissed it, and suddenly flung her arms round the startled Captain and kissed him too, tears of happiness running down her cheeks all the while.

We then went on to Major Dritz at the Police Headquarters. Again I was not allowed at the interview, but the Major finally came out with Nora and, shaking my hands, wished me the best of luck and every happiness. Nora explained later what had happened. She was told Stalin himself had given personal consideration to her case. The document for renunciation of her Soviet citizenship was there for her to sign providing her husband's country accepted her. She signed the paper after handing her British Passport over to him. It was stamped and signed with an exit visa valid for three months. She was told that the authorities were sorry for the difficulties she had experienced, but they had only been carrying out their duties. She was never to forget that she was a Russian, and not to bring disgrace to the country of her birth.

After this, events began to move rapidly and Group Captain Bird informed me that the Mission were preparing an outward-bound convoy and Nora and I would shortly receive embarkation papers to board one of the ships that would be sailing in it. Later I went down to Molotovsk to have a look and watch the giant Russian icebreaker, *Stalin*, crashing through the thick ice that carpeted the White Sea in order to make a lane for the ships to pass through. This was a remarkable sight. The *Stalin* was a huge black ship, broad of beam, with an unusually blunt bow. It would move slowly forward and then come crashing down on the ice beneath. This would break and shatter the ice with a sound like big guns booming, to the accompaniment of loud sharp cracking noises. Backwards and forwards it would move all the time until long black streaks of water could be seen. The ship chosen for us was the SS *Empire Stevenson*, we were to board her as soon as she was ready —

S.S. *Empire Stevenson. Photograph by courtesy of Messrs, Wm. Brown Atkinson & Co. Ltd., Hull*

approximately some two days before the convoy was due to start. As Group Captain Bird said, 'Better get aboard before the Russians change their minds.'

367

PART VI – THE CONVOYS OF DEATH

By this time both Nora and I were in a state of physical and mental exhaustion. Every knock at our door had made us jump, and knowing how things could change without cause or explanation, we were both tense with the uncertainty of our situation — things seemed too good to last.

We boarded the SS *Empire Stevenson* on 21 April, 1942. For security purposes Nora was signed on in the official ship's log book as 'stewardess' and I as 'assistant steward' and we were given the steward's cabin which, though small, was quite comfortable.

As soon as we embarked we were followed by the Russian passport and customs control officers to examine our, by now, very meagre possessions. The former did their duty of stamping our passports quickly and silently. In my baggage I had about thirty figurines carved from mammoth bones dug up in the Siberian wastes and fashioned by prisoners in the labour camps. They were beautiful and delicate works of art — reindeer, hunters, and various animals. I had been able to

A page from the Log Book of S.S. *Empire Stevenson* where Nora and the author were signed on as a Stewardess and Asst. Steward respectively to cover their identities

procure them in return for tins of conserves from various needy looking individuals that one would occasionally see standing about the streets of Archangel, just dumbly offering their figurines from upturned hands. The big burly customs man, looking twice as big in a shaggy sheepskin coat, called me into our cabin. 'Uh! What are these?' he said. All I could think of to say whilst shrugging my shoulders was, 'Presents.' Without a word he crushed them in his hands. I could say or do nothing, except silently wish that one day his turn would come. Knowing Russia, it probably did.

We spent the next two days getting acquainted with the crew and the ship, which was a six-thousand ton merchant ship. She was loaded with timber. Even the upper decks were stacked with it. From then on, until we sailed, we were not allowed to go off the ship. The steward's cabin was situated near the stern of the ship, just behind the twelve-pounder. The adjoining cabin had been converted into a powder magazine for the gun and the rear wall of our cabin stacked with depth charges.

The date of sailing arrived – 27 April, 1942. In the distance the other ships from various quaysides in the White Sea began to converge to take sailing orders. It was a bit cramped in the beginning as there was only a limited area of water freed from the ice. Slowly we steamed out as our turn came. We were the last in the line. No waving friends to see us off. Only the silent figures of the Russian port guards could be seen against the grim receding coastline. The first day of the journey was uncanny. We were actually on our way to England. Everything seemed like a dream. We could not talk in anything but awed whispers to each other.

The convoy we sailed in was the QP 10 and consisted of sixteen ships. We were due to cross with the convoy PQ14* from England at a point in the Arctic Circle near Bear Island. The convoy consisted of twenty-four ships which were bringing arms and munitions to Russia.

When the two convoys did meet they were attacked by German destroyers, submarines and aircraft, and four of our ships in the convoy were sent to the bottom. But our ship was not among them. It happened like this.

Our ship had been steaming along following the others for about four hours when there was a heavy jolt, and the whole ship began to shake from the vibration of the propeller shaft revolving at a tremendous speed as though the engines had suddenly gone wild. The engines were cut off as we all rushed to the side of the ship and men came tumbling up from the hatches. It

* The PQ convoys were those sailing to Russia.
The QP convoys were those returning home from Russia.

was soon ascertained that our propeller had been broken. By some mischance the propeller had fouled a submerged block of ice. The ice in those parts was of quite unbelievable toughness. When you consider the winter temperature is an unending ten to twenty and more degrees below zero, day in and day out, without any let-up for nearly six months on end, it is no wonder that it was so. The sea anchors were dropped and we remained stationary, the rest of our convoy sailed on without us. More than four weeks were to elapse before we could move again.

After a couple of days we were boarded by Royal Naval divers who were to check the damage. It was confirmed that the blades of the screw had been broken off and we heard that a new screw was to be flown over from England. As the weeks went by, one could feel a mounting tension all round. The crew were kept busy round the clock, working in shifts. Lowered overboard with poles and stanchions they would push the ice-floes away from the ship to prevent us getting iced in. A constant watch had to be kept on this ice. Meanwhile I was co-opted for gunnery practice. We would spend hours training on the twelve-pounder which was mounted on the stern of the ship. This took some of the boredom away and provided a modicum of physical exercise of which I was glad.

As Nora was the only woman aboard the ship, she thrived on the admiration and kindnesses of the crew. One unfortunate incident occurred some two weeks after our propeller broke. One must take into account that under normal circumstances the crew would have been by now safely home with their relatives and friends if things had gone all right. The air was still bleak and ice cold. The men doing most of the hard work of keeping the ice away were the stokers who were often exposed to the raw weather conditions.

One day our cabin door was suddenly opened and the steward popped his head in and shouted, 'Lock your door!' I locked the door and then went to the window. About seven or eight of the crew were milling round, dancing and shouting on the deck. They were calling in no uncertain language for the Chief Engineer to come out. Apparently they were stone drunk and after somebody's blood. This pandemonium went on for some time, then the hatch at the end of our cabin, which led to the stewards' galley opened and our steward's face appeared. He looked pretty shaken. He told us that some of the stokers had broken into the stores and got at the emergency rum ration. They were completely drunk and anything might happen. All the Officers and the Captain had locked themselves in.

He was pretty scared. We watched through the window again, and as we looked we saw one big chap walk, or stagger to be correct, straight over the ship's side. He gave a terrific yell as he fell. Instantly, everything was quiet as everyone rushed to the ship's side to peer over — even we rushed out. Normally the ship would have been clear of ice so we expected him to have gone under, the chances of survival in water of such freezing temperature being minimal. To everyone's surprise, he was lying spread-eagled, quite motionless, on a huge ice-floe that had, unnoticed, floated back and now lay against the ship's side. Everyone was sober now and immediate steps were taken to rescue him. They detected faint signs of life when they got him aboard and laid him down in the steward's cabin.

The wireless telegraphist put a call through for medical aid to the Mission Station. I heard afterwards that the Russians had a tremendous row with the Military Mission about the breaking of the radio silence by our telegraphist. Four or five hours later we discerned a black object moving against the whiteness of the distant horizon. It was a reindeer-drawn sleigh. The sleigh came within about a quarter of a mile of the ship and then two bulky figures stepped out, moving from one floe to the other until they came to the clear stretch of water round our ship, from where one of our boats picked them up. When they climbed over the ship's side, I recognised one of them as a Vet Doctor from Archangel.

Her examination of the patient consisted of tapping round his skull with the tips of her fingers. Then taking a pair of scissors from the small cloth bundle she carried, she cut a 'lane' through his hair from forehead to crown, looked at the wound thus bared and gave instructions for the patient to be held firmly and securely while she took out a swab of lint which she soaked with spirit and then swabbed onto the wound. Even though the man remained unconscious with eyes closed, he groaned and struggled, and as he was about sixteen stone they had a job to keep him still. The Doctor then stitched what she could of the gaping wound, and bound his head with lint and bandages that we supplied. Her task finished, she had worked with a kind of set expression all the time, she gave the man two hearty cuffs, one on each side of the face and growled in Russian, 'Phew! To think I have to risk my life for a drunken pig like this!' and then something else which I won't translate.

The Captain and those of the crew around were startled at this behaviour, and I had to diplomatically explain that it was part of the treatment to bring the patient back to consciousness, and that she had said he would soon be all right. Luckily the stoker was up and about the next day as large as life, though a shade more subdued in his manner. Ever since this affair I have had a great deal of admiration and respect for the toughness of the Geordies.

During the weeks that followed, we got confused with days and dates. We seemed to be living in a state of suspended animation with no knowledge of what was going on around us. Eventually our new propeller arrived from England. It had been flown over specially and was delivered to us on about 12 May, 1942. There was, however, still a job to be done before it could be fitted. The remains of the old propeller had to be removed. What had at first been considered a routine task, proved more formidable than our Naval divers had anticipated. I gathered it was so tightly jammed because of the cold that it was impossible to unjam the shaft — apart from the fact that the intense cold of the water only allowed them to submerge for a short time. The Russians, not being at all happy about having a sitting target stuck helpless in the White Sea, offered their assistance, which was accepted.

They sent a couple of their own divers to our ship and after examining the shaft reported that although it might seem impossible, they could do the job by dynamiting the propeller collar off the shaft. It was a technique our chaps were not accustomed to, but the Russians said it would not be the first time they had undertaken this kind of work. The trouble was, we were carrying a load of depth charges and powder for the gun, and as the means of unloading them were not available, they were afraid the explosion might spark them off too. The whole matter was gone into with the Mission and the Russians in Archangel. It became very pressing as the ship was urgently needed. Then it was referred to the Admiralty and Ministry of Transport in London by our Mission for a decision. It took them ten days to decide to let the Russians try it their way. Another homeward bound convoy was already being assembled – the QP 13 and they wanted, if possible, to include us in it.

On about 17 May, 1942, the two Russian divers once more came aboard. There was no doubt, the propeller casing was jammed firmly on the ship's shaft. They worked for about twelve minutes at a time under the water. When they surfaced and came back on the ship, their hands and face looked almost black to me, so deep was the shade of purple. It must have been a cold job. They were, however, fortified by generous tots of British Naval rum that our divers had brought with them. As they smacked their lips it sounded like small arms fire! They were on the job about three hours, including the many necessary breaks. As soon as they were ready to detonate the charge, everybody was ordered to the uttermost tip of the ship's bows, our depth charges having meanwhile been moved from their position at the stern of the ship to a safer place further midships behind the timber stacks.

I think everyone was anticipating a spectacular explosion. But when the charge was detonated all that was heard or felt was a dull thump with the ship swaying ever so slightly. One of the divers descended immediately and soon came up to report that the operation had been successful. Within a few hours, the new propeller had been lowered overboard and fixed into position. After several hours of testing, the Chief Engineer was satisfied enough to report that we could sail again at any time. Everyone felt cheerful at this news, and more so when next morning we awoke to find our ship surrounded by about twenty other ships, with their heliographs signalling away like mad to one another. We knew that once again we would shortly be sailing.

We watched fascinated as the ships slowly took up position. Our own engines began to hum with a steady throb and soon the whole fleet was moving in a northerly direction, our ship sharing the rear end of the formation with three other ships. It was on 21 May, 1942, as our convoy, the homeward bound QP 13, which together with those from Murmansk was to consist of thirty-five ships, began their voyage. We were escorted through the White Sea by two Russian destroyers that moved constantly round our group. By the next day we were out of the White Sea and joined by the other ships from Murmansk with several English destroyers as escorts, and two submarines, one of which was pointed out to me as the *Trident*. The Russian escort then turned back.

The sky was blue, the warm sun shone brightly and the sea was perfectly calm. In a few days we would cross with the Russia-bound PQ 16 which had left Iceland on the same date as ourselves with a similar total of thirty-five ships. They had the protection of several heavy cruisers, a number of destroyers, anti-aircraft ships, armed trawlers, corvettes, and submarines. Soon we would meet them and they would escort us on to Iceland. Meanwhile, as Nora and I leaned over the ship's rail, we could not help feeling proud and reassured at the sight of our own flotilla of ships, albeit they were merchantmen. They stretched far and wide before us and we ploughed on so steadily and in perfect formation that it looked as though nothing could stop us.

One day the ships all around us began exchanging signals rapidly with their heliographs and the word quickly spread that something was amiss. I was called to join the gun crew. We could see a destroyer racing round our convoy darting in and out of the ships: the submarines that had been riding on the surface with us dived. After a few minutes of anxious waiting, a black speck in the sky behind us became visible and revealed itself as a gigantic German Dornier flying boat, with a fantastic wing-span on which could be seen the twelve engines that powered its flight. As we were on the tail-end of the convoy we got a good view of her as she came closer and could even discern figures moving about on her flight deck. The destroyers let fly with their pom-poms, but she kept out of range. We could do nothing with our gun because we couldn't get the elevation. The First Officer instructed me to get Nora to put on her lifebelt as he reckoned the flying boat's job was not to attack us but to signal the submarine pack of our position and we could expect action at any moment. Sure enough, the signals were flashing again and we began to drop our depth charges. One-two-three-four-five and over one would go, a gigantic boiling spout of water would spume into the air behind us and the ship would shake and shudder as though it was falling to pieces.

The sea all around would seem like one vast multi-spouting cauldron as the other ships did the same. We could tell that our course was being changed by the white trail of foam from the paravanes which revolved on leads from the stern of each ship. These paravanes were quite important because they acted as guides, starting from the leading ship to those following on behind in the line; their effectiveness was especially important at night when the churning foam took on an almost phosphorescent glow which could be easily discerned in the darkness.

To the officers, 'Wait for it, the fireworks can start any time now!' we sailed on, the Dornier having been left behind. It was now dusk. I looked at Nora strolling round the deck near by, quite calm, cool, and totally unconcerned with all the bustle around her. She was wearing the life jacket, which she had only put on after strong insistence from me. It made her look too fat she said. I muttered a silent prayer to myself. We slept in our clothes that night and every night afterwards, dozing fitfully whenever we could. One night we became aware that the steady throbbing of the ship's engines had stopped. We got up and went on deck. We could not see a thing. Even the deck rail was indiscernible. We were shrouded in a thick blanket of fog. It was quite eerie. We made our way to the officers' mess room which was deserted, and waited a while. The steward was the first to appear with mugs of hot coffee. We refused the offer of food. Later one of the officers joined us and from him I gathered what had happened.

It appeared that the fog came so suddenly and thickly it had been impossible to make out any signals from the other ships. We had also lost sight of the paravane trail. To make matters worse, the Captain had fallen ill and was unconscious in his cabin. Only the steward, the First Officer and the Chief Engineer were allowed to see him. They had decided to stop the ship's engines for fear of being detected by lurking submarines. It was not known how long the fog bank would last, so we were drifting along helplessly, hoping for the best. Such was our plight and it continued for several days. When the fog did eventually lift, we emerged once again into bright sunlight, to find ourselves quite alone with not another ship in sight. I recalled the words of *The Ancient Mariner*, 'Like a painted ship, upon a painted ocean'. It felt just like that! The engines were started up again and we began to move. I went along to the navigation room. Our officers were busily engaged plotting out our position and movement from the charts on the table. They looked very serious and puzzled. Another anxious day and night went by as we forged steadily onwards. Once we were called to action stations as the look-out picked up a black speck in the sky which turned out to be the Dornier again. It circled round at a respectable distance and after some time flew off. Again we waited, keeping a close watch for the expected submarine attack and tell-tale tracks of torpedoes. We zig-zagged on for several hours, the tension mounting with each passing hour. We ran into a fine mist which suddenly turned into thick impenetrable fog and again our engines were stopped. Once more the fog suddenly lifted to reveal we were alone with not a ship in sight. Again we set off on a course that even our officers were not sure about.

After a couple of days we were again picked up by the damned Dornier which fluttered round us like a huge black bird of ill-omen. Once again came the call 'to action stations' and there were many hurried consultations in the chart room, the Captain still being very ill. How I silently prayed! Nora, meanwhile, seemingly unperturbed, was busy with furrowed brows studying English to which she devoted much of her time with patience and diligence. Yet again, as though in answer to my prayers, we were suddenly enshrouded in a thick blanket of silencing fog. The engines stopped once more and again we drifted helplessly. The days since we had left Archangel had now turned into weeks; we had lost all track of time. It was terrifying trying to peer through the fog, yet we dare not relax our vigilance. How long we remained sightless in this bank of fog I do not remember. The awful memory of its lifting was to haunt me throughout my life in recurrent nightmares whenever I came under stress.

While standing at the ship's rail leaning over, trying to penetrate the fog that surrounded us, I became aware of several figures on either side of me, quite still and silent, elbows apart, resting on the rails, occasionally they would spit reflectively into the waters below. They were some of the stokers who had come up for a breather. They too stared into the thick mist. There were two on either side of me with sweat rags bound round their foreheads which gave them a most peculiar appearance. By now the fog was getting

375

lighter and it would swirl in patches round these silent staring figures beside me. Their features would seem to recede and then come forward at me as though they were ghosts constantly disappearing and then re-appearing. I felt a sudden feeling of disembodiment, as though it was not me but someone else, looking down upon the strange mist-filled scene. It was then that looking over the side I became aware we were cutting into a floating island of dead fish of all shapes and sizes, floating motionless, white bellies upwards — to my horror I could discern here and there among them, the half submerged floating corpses of men — the waves washing over their white faces, jaws agape; their hair awash around their heads as they bobbed up and down. I motioned my companions and pointed out to them the horrible sight below us. They said nothing – just nodded their heads and turned away to recommence their duties. It all happened so quickly, we were once again in the bright sunlight surging forward with ever-increasing power over a sea that was calm, deep green and beautiful. Still feeling dazed and somewhat detached I returned to our cabin. As the long watchful day ended and whilst Nora lay fast asleep in the stillness of the night, I looked down upon her calm untroubled face and scribbled the following lines upon a scrap of paper:

I am alone, quite alone,
And all things touch me not,
For I am as nothing,
In utter nothingness,
Where time, endless, boundless time,
That has no beginning or end,
Fetters my restless soul
To the void of spaceless destiny.

4th July, 1942, somewhere in the Arctic Sea

It just about described my feelings at the time, for it seemed my life was set upon a course already charted by fate and the extraordinary events that had taken place and those to come were a prescribed destiny.

During this period we had been very short of food, having been unable to re-provision before joining the second convoy. We had bread, tea, tinned milk, sugar, coffee and cocoa. The rest of the meals were made up of a concoction of various ingredients including oatmeal. We had no meats or vegetables, but the worst shortage was lack of tobacco and cigarettes. This was something the men felt very keenly about as their nerves were on edge.

When the steward came to me and asked if I happened to have any more of my own left, which I had not, he explained his dilemma. I asked him if by any chance he happened to have such a thing as snuff in his stores. To my surprise he said he had about sixteen pounds of it. I told him that as good snuff is composed of over seventy per cent tobacco dust, he could use it with the used tea leaves, which after being dried could be mixed with the snuff and used as tobacco for rolling cigarettes. As there were plenty of cigarette papers in store it proved quite successful in bringing some relief to the situation and was better than nothing.

We sailed on for another couple of days without anything more untoward happening. The ship's officers were anxiously poring over their charts, convinced we were somewhere near Iceland by this time, when the shout came, 'Land, Ahoy!' I could not see any land, but they could. A corvette also speedily came into view and after a lot of signalling, we followed the corvette which led us along a high rocky coastline into an inlet. This was Seydisfjord on the east coast of Iceland, some five hundred miles from Reykjavik on the west coast of Iceland, which should have been our destination. A boom across the mouth was lifted and we sailed into the fjord, where three destroyers were lined up, their funnels smoking, showing that they were at action stations. As we steamed in between the steep sides of the fjord I noticed a small town, or I should say, village, at the end of it running down to the jetty at which we would land.

As we got nearer, I discerned a little picturesque church, painted white, with a bright red roof and green spire standing at the end of the village high on the rocky slope. I vowed to myself that as soon as I got ashore the first thing I would do would be to get to that church and offer a silent prayer to God for bringing us safely through. We docked, and leaving the ship's officers to do their job, asked the Naval Embarkation Officer for permission to go ashore with Nora. This was granted. Waiting on the quay was a YMCA representative by the name of Ernie Corkhill who ran the Forces' canteen there. He made us extremely welcome and looked after Nora while I made my way to the church. It was an uphill climb. The doors of this little chapel were open and I heard the strains of an organ playing as I entered. What the organist was playing I do not know, but it was the sweetest sound in the world. Silently I entered and went down on my knees, covering my face with my hands in deep meditative thanks to God for the mercy He had shown. I stayed a few minutes and then made my way down to the YMCA canteen. Nora had already eaten.

Ernie cooked me a couple of eggs and several rashers of bacon, which I washed down with a big mug of tea. The meal tasted great. Nora badly needed some clothes by now, she had been wearing mine since we left Archangel. I had no money, only a cheque book. Ernie insisted that I was not to bother — he would see me and settle up in England if I would let him know my address. He took Nora to a ladies outfitters where she got a dress and other things and we returned to the ship, which was to leave for Reykjavik the next morning, 9 July 1942, in the company of an armed trawler for part of the way.

The journey to Reykjavik was uneventful. We had a clear, smooth passage, hugging the rocky coastline all the way. On the night of 11 July, 1942, we docked alongside some badly battered ships in the harbour. Nora and I were greeted very warmly by Wing-Commander Leeroy Brown, a veteran Canadian Pilot from the First World War. He was the RAF embarkation officer and did everything possible to make us feel at home. He became one of my greatest friends. We were provided with a room in a neat, clean little hotel and had meals in the RAF Officers' mess. To all we were a source of wonder as the news of the *Empire Stevenson's* adventurous journey became known. I cannot remember much of Iceland and would dearly like to see it properly sometime. The thing that really caught Nora's interest was the quaint old-fashioned attire of the Icelandic women in their national costume which had been very evident in Seydisfjord.

On 12 July 1942, Wing-Commander Leeroy Brown informed me that he had arranged a transfer for Nora and myself to an American troopship, the USS *Siboney* which he reckoned would get us home quicker, as the *Empire Stevenson* had to be delayed for overhaul and re-fuelling. It was then that I heard from him of the terrible and tragic sequence of events that had been taking place whilst our own ship had been blindly zig-zagging its course alone across the Arctic Ocean. Cut off as we were from any means of communication, owing to the strict necessity for radio silence, we had no means of knowing what carnage and destruction was taking place around us.

It transpired that our convoy, the homeward bound QP 13, sailing on without us had crossed with the Russia-bound convoy PQ 16 off Bear Island and although dogged by enemy aircraft had managed to reach the comparative safety of the waters to the north of Iceland without mishap. However, it was there that tragedy overtook them. The weather suddenly deteriorated. A wicked north-easterly gale sprang up. The blinding rain that followed reduced visibility to a few hundred yards. The commanding officer of the minesweeper, *Niger*, sighting an iceberg in the distance, apparently

378

mistook it for the North Cape of Iceland and altering the course of his section of the convoy led it straight into a British minefield. The *Niger* itself was the first to hit a mine and quickly sank with heavy loss of life, including that of the commander. Within a brief space of time a further four ships struck mines and sank with two more ships sustaining serious damage. One of those lost was the Russian ship *Rodina* carrying the wives and families of Soviet diplomats, who were sailing to join their husbands stationed in London.

Whilst all this was going on, the PQ 16, on having crossed with our convoy safely, and continuing on its final leg to Russia, also met with disaster. They were picked up by enemy aircraft and submarines and seven of its ships were sent to the bottom. The losses here might have been greater still but for two important factors. First, the onset of appalling weather which included dense fog and secondly, the withdrawal of the enemy attacking forces to prepare for an all-out attack on a second outward bound convoy which was on its way from Iceland to Russia and about which the German Intelligence service agency had obtained information.

This was the PQ 17, consisting of thirty-four heavily laden ships that had already left Iceland on 27 June, 1942. The outcome of the attack on this convoy was a massacre. Twenty-three of its ships were sent to the bottom. Scattered and helpless in those icy seas, they had become sitting targets for a merciless enemy.

It was much later when we were back in England that I was to learn the ultimate fate that befell our own ship, a ship that was barely one year old.

Arriving home on 28 July, 1942, she was refitted, loaded and sent off from Hull to join another Russia-bound convoy. This was to be her last voyage — the official communique about her read:

The steamship *Empire Stevenson* on a voyage from Hull to north Russia was torpedoed by a German aircraft, blew up and sank on September 13th, 1942, off the North Cape. All on board were lost, 41 crew and 19 gunners...

The Obituary of S.S. *Empire Stevenson*, sunk with all hands on her return journey to Russia, 13 September 1942. Dictionary of Disasters at Sea by Charles Hocking.

On 13 July, 1942, Nora and I boarded the American SS *Siboney* from Reykjavik. She was a very fast converted lake boat of about 10,000 tons carrying supplies to Britain. We were accompanied by a corvette for the first part of the journey which then turned back. The most astonishing thing was the food we had aboard. Every kind of meat and poultry was served, even roast turkey and cranberry sauce. Fresh fruit including melon, and the most super ice-cream. I had not seen such food for ages, and I was not to see the like of it either for more years than I care to remember. Being a good sailor I was able to enjoy my meals to the full, but Nora, together with many of the crew, was affected by the stormy weather, and hardly ate anything. The ship rolled immensely, and being a converted lake boat with very little draught, the mountainous Icelandic seas made her behave in the most fantastic fashion.

We had only one submarine alarm and everyone was ordered on deck. Nora was so ill at the time that she could not get up, so I stayed below with her in the cabin and we held hands. Luckily nothing happened.

It was on the night of 16 July, 1942, that we slowly steamed into Gourock. We had spent nearly eighty days on those Arctic Seas and now our journey was ended. The dimmed lights on the quayside were a grim reminder that the war was not yet over, yet it mattered not, we were safely home at last. Whether we landed in England, Ireland, Wales or Scotland made little difference, it was still home.

Seventeen eventful years had elapsed since I had sailed from London to seek my fortune, now I was home again, no fortune, but with a bride who had faced a thousand perils for the sake of the love she bore me, and as we stepped ashore we stopped and embraced one another for a few fleeting moments, full of the pent-up emotions that overwhelmed us. The whole world seemed to stand still and as our lips met in one lingering kiss, the muffled blast of a distant ship's siren seemed to echo our unspoken thoughts. We were indeed home at last.

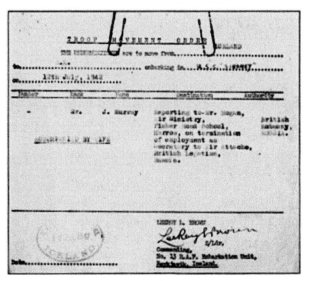

Troop Movement Order transferring Nora and the author to an American troopship for the final leg of the journey home from Iceland

Breathes there the man, with soul so dead,
Who never to himself hath said,
This is my own, my native land!

Lay of the Last Minstrel
Sir Walter Scott

381

EPILOGUE

Nora, after enduring the dangers and traumas of the Arctic convoys for nearly eighty days, finally set foot in a war-torn Britain. Upon arriving in Gourock, on the south bank of the Firth of Clyde in 1942, she was heralded as Britain's first 'Russian War Bride.'

Although faced with an unfamiliar land, language and people, her adjustment was definitely aided by her education. She had grown up with the presence of English books in her father's library and was familiar with the English alphabet through her German language studies. Her ability to make friends and captivate people with her charm and optimism allowed her to embrace her newly-adopted country with gratitude and fervour.

However, life in London would not be easy for her. Soon after their arrival in England, John volunteered for the army. He was enlisted in the Intelligence Corps and would be away from home for much of the time.

Between 1943 and 1945, Nora gave birth to three sons whilst living in a

Nora and John's marriage at St Pancras Town Hall, Camden, London January 1943

small flat in Harrington Square, Camden, London. Their home, next to London's busiest train lines, meant the area was a prime target for the Luftwaffe. Heavily pregnant and with two small children to care for, she endured the blitz huddled inside, physically unable to go to the underground bomb shelters across the road. John's meagre soldier's pay added to their daily hardships. Nevertheless, nothing would stop Nora witnessing the great moment of Britain's victory. Eight months pregnant, she managed to join the happy dancing throngs celebrating VE day in Trafalgar Square in May 1945.

During those early years she succeeded in teaching herself English. Around 1947 Nora was enlisted by the Director Julien Duvivier to be the Russian adviser on his film Anna Karenina. In this role, Nora met Vivien Leigh, the lead male Ralph Richardson and Keiron Moore whom she also befriended.

Nora with Vivian Leigh on film set of
Anna Karenina 1947

Nora was encouraged by many of her friends to write a book about her experiences in Russia. And in 1950, *I Spied for Stalin* was published. It was an immediate success, translated into several languages and published in the United States. This resulted in Nora becoming somewhat of a celebrity, sought by the press and radio. She toured Europe and was received by Pope Pius XII in a personal audience. She also made the acquaintance of many celebrities such as Anthony Steel, Jack Warner and the newly- elected MP Anthony Wedgewood Benn. During this time, she gave talks and lectures to academic and social institutions throughout England. She made many friends and was no longer the quiet, anxious girl overshadowed by the traumas of her past. Instead she was a woman vibrant with determination to set the world to rights. Among her other talents was the ability and aptitude to teach the Russian language, which she did for a select group of fortunate people including her sons John and Peter.

Inspired by her new-found freedom in Britain, she wrote in her 1952 diary the following lines from Philip James Bailey's poem:

'We live in deeds, not years;
In thoughts, not breaths;
In feelings, not figures on a dial.
We should count time by heart-throbs!'

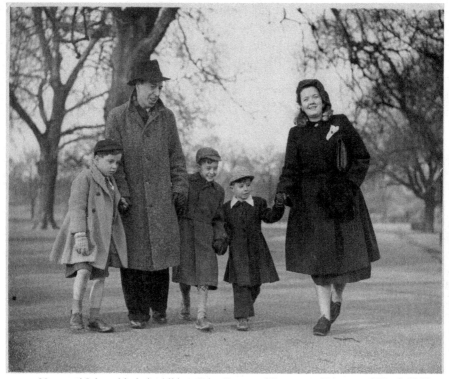

Nora and John with their children John, Peter and Leeroy on Hampstead Heath 1950

But despite her vibrant optimism during those years, Nora remained desperate to know the fate of the family she was forced to leave behind: her father, who was imprisoned in 1939, a destitute stepmother and half-brother shipped to Siberia, and her elderly grandparents.

Understandably it came as a shock to Nora's English family when in 1955, she revealed that she had previously given birth to two sons, and may even have been married before. In her diaries and in letters to the Russian authorities, Nora refers to Yakov Goldin as her husband. Her first son, Arkady, was born in February 1938. His possible father, Goldin, was an officer working in Moscow's Russian Foreign Office alongside her father - Vassily Korzhenko. Both were eliminated during Stalin's purges of 1939.

At just 20 years of age, Nora was fatherless, a widow with a young son, stepmother and half-brother to support. In October 1940, she gave birth to a second son, Azamat. She makes no mention in her diaries of the identity of his father or under what circumstances she gave birth.

How she came to meet John in such dire circumstances is beyond belief and still unknown. Was their acquaintance a mere gossamer of luck, an act of sheer serendipity? Or was it in fact by calculation and design that Nora managed to elude the tentacles of Stalin's merciless reign? Although the exact details of this turbulent period of her life are unclear, it can be presumed that perhaps Nora tried to protect her children by not writing about them until after Stalin's death and Khrushchev's famous 1956 secret speech to the Kremlin.

Once in England, Nora neither forgot those she left behind nor ignored their plight. From her small 'prefab' in Savernake Road, Hampstead, London, she wrote endlessly to the Red Cross, and the British, American and Russian authorities requesting their assistance in finding and contacting her relatives. In 1956 she exclaims in her diary:

'Russia is much in the news. Riots in Georgia. Stalin declared by the Russian Government as a man who held the Russian nation in terror. A mass murderer. Officially!! Hard to believe!!! What a surprise! Hurray!!'

In the same year she received a letter from the Red Cross informing her that her son Arkady was alive, living in Kazakhstan and working along the Chinese border as a railway engineer. A second letter followed informing her of Azamat's death aged two in a Moscow orphanage. From the Russian Embassy in London, another surprise, Nora received a copy of her father General Korzhenko's death certificate. He was posthumously rehabilitated.

Life for Nora in her prefab, which she nicknamed 'the Doll's House,' was constantly busy. During the day she would be out meeting people and in the evening she caught up with her correspondence and her diary. John, on the other hand was struggling to find work in order to provide for his family.

During the mid 1950s, the disparities of temperament and conflicts within their relationship were becoming apparent. No doubt the past traumas they experienced in Russia were now overshadowing their lives. Added to this were the difficulties and deprivations imposed by their poverty. John became increasingly insular and withdrawn, burying himself in the newspapers and playing the Football Pools. Nora was unwilling to accept his complacency but even her sense of hope was now waning.

In the summer of 1956 everything changed. After a week's camping trip to Folkestone, John and the three boys returned to a deserted house. Nora had simply walked out. She knew and understood that things were never going to improve and felt it would be better for her and her family if she left.

Drowning in the depression and despair she so obviously felt at this time, she felt she could do more for her family from afar.

When Nora visited the prefab soon after, her manner was unapologetically honest. She explained that she simply couldn't accept that life had to be 'like this.' She felt that you could always do something to make life better, even if it meant doing things that you didn't like or want to do under normal circumstances. She was not bound by British conventions, but by the notions of survival and of honesty to oneself.

Nora eventually moved back to Harrington Square to set up home with Ismail Petrushevski, a Polish war veteran. He was older than her, walked with a cane and suffered from asthma. She accepted all his limitations but without any income of her own, she was reliant on his small war pension. They lived humbly out of necessity, but were seemingly happy. Soon after, the houses in Harrington Square were condemned and Nora and Ismail were given a small two-bedroom flat in Goldington Crescent, London. They busied themselves, Nora with her writing and Ismail with decorating and building furniture.

Nora did her best to involve herself in the lives of her sons. As a huge advocate of education, she always encouraged them to learn and to advance their intellects. Her constant references to writers and scholars would be inherent in their conversations and it served to inspire their futures and aspirations.

In 1963, while 20-year-old John junior was studying commerce and Russian at Birmingham University, he received a British Council grant to travel to Moscow. For the first time, members of Nora's Russian family met with her English son. In Leningrad he encountered Nora's stepmother Ursula and her son Felix. During this same visit, John also met Nora's Auntie Varaya, her father's youngest sister. On his return to London, he handed his mother a brief note from her along with some photos. She provided a translation of this note in her diary:

'Norochka! Over everything expected in this life, we never knew anything about one another since our last meeting in May 1941, in Leningrad. And, then, suddenly, by accident we met. You have a wonderful son. Be well. But do you know, that I am still alive! Your Auntie Varaya.'

Nora continued to comment:

'My poor, dear kind Auntie Varaya! Who suffered so much and who survived miraculously the most terrible blockade of Leningrad September

386

1941-January 1944. What she went through only in that city during the Blockade!! With her 2 children, 2 daughters: Valentina 16 and Ludmila 4.'

Nora's reaction to the photos of her stepmother is just the opposite. Reminded of the terrible cruelty she underwent in her hands, she proclaimed that Ursula, was the hardest, meanest, and most heartless women she had ever met.

In 1965, John junior and Peter visited Leningrad, staying for one month with Nora's cousin, Ludmila, and her husband, Tolya. Nora had little to say about their visit, but was amazed when a year later her relatives arrived in England and stayed at Welford Court, London as the guests of the Murray's. Nora stated:

'It is a great VICTORY for my relatives to come out of Russia! In times of Stalin, nobody could go anywhere! Except SIBERIA...what change there must be in Russia.'

After three weeks, Ludmila and Tolya returned to Russia. Nora writes in her diary on October 5th, 1966:

'From the moment they came off the boat Baltika to the very last moment...it was a MERRY-GO-ROUND affair! Parties, dinners, dances, receptions, visits, journeys and what-not every single day!'

Because of Ismail's health, Nora's life at this time was fairly sedentary, working occasionally as a translator or teaching Russian. The boys made weekly visits and sometimes brought their friends to see her. All were welcomed with fresh cups of Turkish coffee and biscuits. She rarely talked about herself, or Russia, but focused on her visitors and their efforts to improve themselves. Everyone left inspired, buzzing with caffeine and her contagious sense of positivity.

In March, 1967, Nora received a letter from Stalin's daughter, Svetlana, detailing how she had recently escaped to Western Europe. Nora had met Svetlana's mother in 1932. She was just 12 years old at the time and Svetlana was still a baby. Tragically they shared a common loss, as indicated in Svetlana's letter which read:

'I had no strength to act the way my Mama and your Mama did, dear Nora. I am too fond of the blue skies about my head, I do not like to be imprisoned.'

Both their mothers had committed suicide, Nora's mother Margarita in March 1928, and Svetlana's mother Nadiezhda in November 1932.

387

Ever-optimistic, Nora's long-term efforts to track down her son were finally rewarded. With the help of the Red Cross, the orders of Russia's president - Alexei Kosygin, and the tenacity of a Sunday Mirror reporter, a phone-call was finally arranged. On Wednesday, 29th April 1970, she finally spoke to Arkady in Alma-Ata, Kazakhstan. Nora's first words to her 32 year old son were, 'This is your mama speaking.'

She wrote:

'We had a very interesting conversation over the buzzing lines. First Moscow switched in, then Alma-Ata...you could hear people speaking, mostly women's voices, in English, French, Spanish, Russian, Tartar and Kazakh. The great world suddenly shrunk...and there we were, the two of us, one in Europe the other in Asia!'

Financially these were not easy years for Nora and Ismail. She refused any form of social assistance, feeling this would compromise her dignity and independence. Eventually though, she found temporary work at the local Post Office. Although she never spoke much about her time working there, it seems she made many treasured friends. Even the manager became a regular visitor to her home. She often held small soirees with music, dance, food and vibrant discussion and debate. Nora was not a drinker but was happy for others to do so, most bringing their own bottles of vodka.

In 1974, Ismail died, leaving Nora bereft. She never continued with her diaries after this point. Her three boys provided what support and comfort they could but she was

British Red Cross letter referring to location of Nora's son Arkady, 1970

Nora's son Arkady aged 32

argely on her own for the first time since being in England. Consistent with her indefatigable character, she embraced this time, finding a rejuvenated spirit through travelling, visiting her sons in Bristol and Aberdeen.

Later in the year, with money in short supply, Leeroy accompanied her to Bermondsey Antique Market in south London with the aim of selling antiques left over from Peter's business in Bristol. For the next year or so, every Friday at 5am, they made their way there. For Nora the market was a distraction and an opportunity to meet people from all walks of life. She soon became friends with Peter's colleagues in the antiques business, many from Australia and America.

By 1978, Nora had a new partner, Jan, who moved in with her at her Goldington Crescent flat. He was healthy and more outgoing, though he lacked the sense of humour essential to Nora's outlook on the world. The publication of John's book *A Spy Called Swallow* was a great surprise to her. Her former husband John looked rather dashing on the cover sleeve. And with their story re-told from his point of view, it seemed as if something was re-ignited in her. She began referring to him in softer tones and showed a keener interest in his life.

In 1985, she travelled with Jan to Canada and stayed for a month in Ottawa with her son, Leeroy. The couple also visited her eldest son, John, in Nice, France. She later made regular trips to Nice, meeting up with White Russian emigres. Her life was more settled during this time. It is however photos which document this period of her life rather than writing.

By the age of 68, her health was deteriorating. She complained very little though, suffering in silence, and refusing to accept the realities of her diminishing condition. She would enchant her doctor with her sunny outlook, more interested in knowing about his life, and how he was feeling than detailing her own. In the latter part of the 1980s, she complained of back pain after falling whilst getting off a bus and eventually her partner Jan persuaded her to go to the hospital. Tests revealed she was suffering from terminal bone cancer. Chemotherapy was recommended. She stubbornly refused.

On learning that Nora was admitted to hospital in May 1989, John became concerned. In early June he went with Peter to the hospital, but did not enter the ward. When Peter returned, devastated by the site of his frail mother, John asked if he should go in to see her. Peter just shook his head. Sensing the severity of the situation, John went in regardless.

He wrote:

'I felt a terrible sinking feeling in the pit of my stomach, as I knew there must be something terribly wrong with Nora. The ward seemed very quiet and empty as I entered; there were no visitors at that hour and the nurses were heavily occupied in various corners of the room. I walked down the centre of the ward looking left and right at the beds. The patients seemed old and tired and I wondered if I would recognise Nora. I hadn't seen her in 30 years and it was possible she'd changed a good deal in that time. Seeing one bed with someone lying on their side, their back towards me, I tentatively approached whispering 'Nora' to which she replied, 'Johniks …is that you Johnichka.' As she struggled to get up to face me, I was appalled by her appearance, she looked so ill, all the life seemed to have drained from her. I gently kissed her lips, they were so dry and parched. Hugging her close I buried my face into her outstretched arms. We held each other tightly but gently.'

Crying, Nora asked for forgiveness.

'Ah, Noryshka, there's nothing to forgive,' John replied gently stroking her hand. 'It's you who should forgive me for leaving you alone for so long.

'The tears rolled down our cheeks, 'I love you, I love you! I've always loved you!' was all we could keep saying to one another.'

John would be reunited with Nora from then onwards and understood only too well when she wanted to go home. Over the next few weeks the Murray family was reconciled, including Jan, Nora's partner at the time. John and Jan took it in turns to nurse and comfort Nora. John junior had taken six months leave from his Professorship at Toulouse University, France and, along with Peter, provided much needed support.

In his grief following Nora's death, John wrote the following, bringing closure to one of the century's most remarkable love stories, entitled: Reconciliation and the Last Flight of the Swallow.

'As I sat at her bedside she suddenly became agitated and tried to speak, she waved her arms pointing to the other side of the bed where a small table stood laden with what I thought were very large books. I nodded my head in the direction she pointed and asked if it was one of the books she wanted. 'Da, Da-a,' she whispered.

'I walked round to the other side of the bed and lifted up the top book, it was heavy, it was not a book at all, but a large leather-bound photo album. Returning to my seat with the album she stretched out her hand to open it for me, but she was so weak the effort was too much. Leaning over the bed I opened it. Turning the pages, I saw that each leaf contained an enlarged print of photos taken of ourselves and the children during the early happy years of our marriage.

'I gazed at them with awe and astonishment. I had long since forgotten about them, I did not know even that she had kept them.

'As we silently turned page after page, the tears welled up in my eyes.

'Ah, Norushka!' I said. 'So you did remember after all.' She nodded her head at my remark.

'Then she did something that bought back vividly the old happier days.

'As I leaned over to kiss her, she slowly stroked the side of my face, just like in the old times when I was tired and worried. She never spoke, she always just stroked my cheek gently and slowly.

'This time her grey-green eyes looked steadily at me, they sparkled with a strange light.'

'It was then I understood; this was the moment she had been waiting for throughout all the long years of our separation. She began to say something in Russian, but her voice, so low and feeble was beyond my comprehension, the accompanying wan smile she gave me was, however, one of quiet triumph.

'Slowly I stood up, closing the album. I walked round the bed to replace it on the table. As I did so, I saw she had folded her hands across her breast, I heard a soft drawn-out sigh and as I looked, her eyes momentarily fluttered and then closed - never to open again.

'It was The Swallow's last flight – but she left behind a broken heart.'

Leeroy and Peter Murray, 25 March 2017

RE-PRINTS OF THE ORIGINAL MEMOIRS

www.gbpublishing.co.uk

I Spied For Stalin: Freedom's Sacrifice by **Nora Murray**
(**Companion Title to** *A Spy Called Swallow: An Enduring Love Story*)

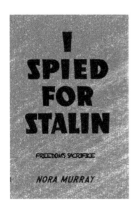

This is Nora's story leading up to and following on from her encounter with John Murray. Republished by GB Publishing.org, in similar fashion to *A Spy Called Swallow: An Enduring Love Story,* a prologue and epilogue is added by her sons Leeroy and Peter Murray.

A Spy Called Swallow: An Enduring Love Story by **John Murray**
(**Companion Title to** *I Spied For Stalin: Freedom's Sacrifice*)

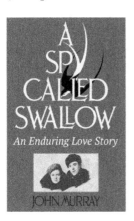

This is John's story leading up to and following on from his encounter with the young spy Nora Korzhenko. Republished by GB Publishing.org, in similar fashion to *I Spied For Stalin: Freedom's Sacrifice,* a prologue and epilogue is added by his sons Leeroy and Peter Murray.

Lightning Source UK Ltd.
Milton Keynes UK
UKOW04f0659031017
310286UK00001B/32/P